The publisher and the University of California Press
Foundation gratefully acknowledge the generous support
of the Richard and Harriett Gold Endowment
Fund in Arts and Humanities.

The Lure of the Beach

The Lure of the Beach

A Global History

Robert C. Ritchie

UNIVERSITY OF CALIFORNIA PRESS

University of California Press
Oakland, California

© 2021 by Robert C. Ritchie

Library of Congress Cataloging-in-Publication Data

Names: Ritchie, Robert C., author.
Title: The lure of the beach : a global history / Robert C.
    Ritchie.
Description: Oakland, California : University of
    California Press, [2021] | Includes bibliographical
    references and index.
Identifiers: LCCN 2020029260 (print) | LCCN 2020029261
    (ebook) | ISBN 9780520215955 (hardback) |
    ISBN 9780520974654 (ebook)
Subjects: LCSH: Beaches—Social aspects—History.
Classification: LCC GB454.B3 R57 2021 (print) |
    LCC GB454.B3 (ebook) | DDC 306.4/81909146—dc23
LC record available at https://lccn.loc.gov/2020029260
LC ebook record available at https://lccn.loc.gov
    /2020029261

Manufactured in the United States of America

25   24   23   22   21
10 9 8 7 6 5 4 3 2 1

For Louise

Contents

Illustrations

Acknowledgments

With a project that has gone on as long as this one, I have acquired a number of obligations. There is no way I can sufficiently thank my friends and colleagues who have listened to my stories patiently even when, on occasion, they were repeated. So rather than having a long list of names, let me just note, you know who you are and I thank you very much.

Anyone writing about the history of the beach benefits from the scholarship of John K. Walton, Alain Corbin, Lena Lencek, and Jim Walvin. I know I have.

There are also individuals who have been important to the shaping of the final text. Lynne Withey (who was also there at the creation), Amanda Herbert, Jim Walvin, and Lena Lencek all read various versions and gave sound advice.

Because of my incompetence around computers, the Huntington IT department, especially Robert Studer, Jon Sims, Nathan Branson, and David Vorobyov, have saved me from my own blunders more often than I care to remember. Andie Reid was also my unfailing guide to various programs. Lindsey Hansen saved me from my initial folly of thinking that I could do it, by taking over the task of acquiring permissions. She also knew how to locate images that I had given up on ever finding. As my assistant when I was an administrator, Carolyn Powell made sure I had the time to work on this project. In the middle of a pandemic, Mona Shulman rescued my notes. There are many others on the Huntington Library staff who have assisted me in finding obscure references and old images. I thank them all.

Besides the Huntington Library, there are a number of other institutions that have helped me over the years by making their collections available—the Library of Congress, the New York Public Library, the New York Historical Society, the British Library, and the Massachusetts Historical Society. Their staffs have also listened to my queries and offered sound advice, saving me no end of time.

Again, a long digestion means that many people have heard me go on about beaches in various settings. Most important, because of the commentary involved from the audience, were the Huntington Early Modern Britain Seminar, the Bay Area Early Americanists, the History Department Seminar at the University of California, San Diego, the McNeil Center at the University of Pennsylvania, the History Department Seminar at the University of California, Davis, the Program for British Studies at the University of Texas, and the Ohmohundro Institute at William and Mary.

I came to my editor Niels Hooper as a legacy, but he has been a sure guide in finishing the manuscript. Ben Alexander made certain the manuscript was readable.

Finally, this project could never have succeeded without the constant support of my wife Louise. As she has a more refined sense of the importance of the comma than I do, she has saved me from a host of infelicities.

Introduction

Come summer, the beach was the center of the world. For a typical Southern California teenager, the attractions were body surfing, lazing around, and girls. Summers went by in a blur of sun, sand, and surf before the water got cold and school beckoned. It was an idyll. Much later, having become an historian but fortunate to live in a beach town, I came to recognize there was a history of going to the beach. It was one of those moments when one realizes that something very familiar—I still loved the beach—also had an intriguing past. Once aroused, this curiosity did not vanish but lingered. Did people in the past go to the beach for the same reasons I did, or did they seek other pleasures? This book, then, is my search of discovery. Why did people go to the beach and what did they do there? It started a long time ago.

The beach was the original end and beginning. The land was home for humanity, the sea the great unknown. The beach was the boundary and last place of safety for our distant ancestors before the restless sea crashed into the sand. The land nurtured them, while the sea promised little and remained a great mystery. Yet the shore attracted them. Perhaps it was the daily drama of sunsets and sunrises and the moods of the sea, but more likely it was access to food. During the summer, mussels, oysters, crabs, and fish were available and certainly varied their diets. Footprints in the sand, left thousands of years ago, mark their passage. Homo sapiens appear to have originated in the Okavango wetlands in present-day Botswana and moved under changing climate conditions toward southern Africa.[1] At two sites in South Africa, Lange-baan and Nahoon, preserved footprints record their visits to the beach over one hundred thousand years ago.[2] Recently archaeologists have found that a group of Neanderthal children cavorted at a beach in Normandy eighty thousand years ago.[3] One can imagine them splashing around in the surf before retreating inland away from the storms of winter on the exposed beach. So we know that, however they perceived the ocean, the beach was a place of relative safety.

Our most ancient ancestors, then, walked upon the beaches and contemplated the sea until they finally took to the sea. With rafts and canoes, they could begin to fish and finally use the sea as a convenient way to explore other lands. The more time they spent at sea, the more they learned to read the moods of the ocean and placate the god who controlled those moods. Over time, more and more people came to accept the sea and build their habitations close to the beach. Some would even become "sea people" in that they lived on, and adapted to, the perils of the sea. Polynesians created the catamaran and with it ventured over hundreds of miles of open water in their Pacific Ocean migrations.[4] As the oceans of the world slowly came to be the scene of more and more human endeavor, they also came to be regarded as a place of religious significance. Various cultures assumed there were gods or spirits who influenced the winds and the waves and appealed to them for a safe voyage or relief from storms.

Ocean water was also imagined to have special powers. Jews had an ancient ceremony, Tashlikh, where the community, at the new year, cast bread on the water in order to erase the sins of the last year. Many communities in France and England went to the sea every year to spend a few days splashing around in a rite of renewal. These are traditional practices that are tied not to medicinal theory, but to time-honored practice and superstition. The comfort brought to the practitioners was real and appreciated. The Romans, however, went further and created a haven at Biaie on the Bay of Naples where they found very many comforts of a more immediate sort, among them licentiousness, a reputation that would always be associated with resorts, where the restraints of one's community were loosened and bathing costumes exposed the body.

However, it was medical theory, accepting the efficacy of seawater, that would create a new phenomenon—the beach resort. Healing waters were nothing new to many people. The medicinal qualities of mineral springs were highly regarded in many cultures. A dip in the water or just a glass of it was enough to derive a benefit. However, a rival arrived in the early eighteenth century when English medical practitioners published books asserting that seawater was therapeutic and curative. In a world with few cures, the rush to the seaside was on, and England created the first beach resorts. Resorts emerged right at the beginning of this movement because they provided needed services such as housing, meals, and entertainment to anyone who sought the comfort of seawater. They would be, from now on, the new site for leisure and recreation in a world of constant change that they would reflect. The existing mineral-spring spas, such as Bath, provided models for the early entrepreneurs who were creating the resorts. The recommended therapy at the sea consisted of no more than a brief dip or in some cases a drink of seawater. Whatever the benefits of the water, beaches also had the drama of the sea. In this they had an advantage over beaches on lakes or rivers, which, however nice the setting, did not have the therapeutic power or the beauty of the ocean. In the long run they would also eclipse spas in popularity, as again they had the ocean versus a building containing the spring where one could take a dip or drink the mineral water. There was no comparison—the ocean won.

In time, a resort might be a single hotel on a small beach or a number of large hotels serving an extensive shoreline. Vacation homes accompanied the hotels, as did boarding houses and other accommodations, all making up part of the resort. The hotels, however, were central, for besides being a place to stay and eat, they also provided entertainment. This latter was important, for the therapeutic dip was a matter of moments, leaving the remainder of the day to be filled with diversions.

At first, only the English upper class—aristocrats, gentry, bankers, and merchants—could afford time for leisure and to meet the expenses of vacations. They also had the means to get to the sea in that they had horses and coaches, among the most expensive attributes of elite status. The early resorts were designed to meet their demands for appropriate housing and services, and when it came to entertainment, they expected the familiar world of assembly rooms where ladies and gentlemen danced, played cards, and had supper. Soon the hotels would absorb the role of the assembly rooms. This Jane Austen world would continue for some time.

Beach resorts, however, did not remain an English monopoly. There was a slow and steady geographic expansion. They developed on the Continent, first in France, and finally, all the way across northern Europe to the Baltic, where Germans turned to the sea. In France, the early resorts were on the English Channel, but soon enough bathers could be seen in the Mediterranean in places such as Nice. The expenses of travel and upkeep meant that here, too, the visitors were members of the upper classes. The emphasis on the therapeutic benefits of salt water pervaded these resorts as well. Americans joined the rush to the beach in the 1820s. Long averse to the sandy shore that attracted only hunters and fishermen, they finally accepted it as a therapeutic site because they read the same medical books as did the English. Soon enough, rustic resorts, in comparison to the English, sprang up from Cape May, New Jersey, to Nahant, Massachusetts. While not as aristocratic as the British and European beach resorts, nonetheless the American resorts were dominated by local elites. Here too, it took a degree of prosperity to get to the seaside and then stay there.

While the early resorts served elites, during the nineteenth century their exclusive reign came to an end with the coming of the railroads. As long as horse-driven carriages were the only way to reach the seaside, elites had a monopoly, but the railroads changed the social composition of the resorts. They attracted customers by dropping fares and running excursion specials, permitting middle- and even some working-class visitors the chance to go to the seaside, even if it was just for the day. Their demands for services and entertainment differed from those of the elites. The hotels were usually beyond their reach, so boarding houses flourished. Resorts had to adapt and decide which group they were going to entertain. If not just aristocrats, their offerings had to be in tune with popular culture. Dance halls and music halls, which blossomed everywhere in the middle of the century, popped up at the resorts. They would bring an end to the assembly rooms. Local entrepreneurs financed these additions plus piers, aquaria, towers, and winter gardens, all to entertain the visitors. The constant demand for something novel for the repeat visitor drove these entrepreneurs to explore every new innovation. As a result, while all resorts seized upon electricity for lighting and power, some used it to turn night into day and to create new and thrilling rides, such as the roller coaster. They evolved into amusement parks of a new and daring kind prepared to entertain the masses. Yet they never forgot that they were, in fact, beach resorts and had to have the facilities that catered to the guests who came to enjoy the water.

The coming of the railway in the nineteenth century affected resorts everywhere, although there were always differences in national outcomes. Americans quickly accepted the steam engine on land and water, while the French were cautious, as railroads had security implications in case of invasion. Yet, in the end, even they could not deny the benefits of steam power. This new mode of transportation caused a significant expansion in the number of resorts. The bigger resorts tried to please nearly all classes, while those operating on a smaller scale sought to build facilities for an appropriate social group. By the end of the century, visitors were counted in the millions. With this expansion, new problems, such as a growing volume of untreated sewage, presented a challenge to the resort towns. The diseases that accompanied sewage directly challenged the claims for cures available at the sea, so it had to be dealt with. As always, growth brought new problems.

Nineteenth-century expansion, no matter how impressive in creating many new sites, was nothing compared to the explosion in the twentieth century. Powerful generators of the increasing number of vacationers were the widespread prosperity and paid holidays, which became a common practice first in the West and then elsewhere. Nations such as South Korea and China emerged as economic powerhouses, and their people joined millions of others in spending their leisure time at the seaside. Exotic resorts on the Maldive islands, the Andaman Sea, the Philippines, and in Thailand suddenly became go-to places for international tourists. Nearly anyplace with a stretch of sand now became a potential resort as hotel chains and entrepreneurs sought places to be developed. Local communities sometimes found themselves overwhelmed by tourists who had scant regard for their societies and cultures. It was a new form of colonialism. Nonetheless, beach resorts had become a worldwide phenomenon, so millions of holiday makers would find the beach of their dreams.

Other drivers of change were national governments and new modes of transportation. Governments decided that developing tourism was a way to boost regional development and national prosperity. Countries such as Mexico and Spain, each with wonderful beaches, aided the development of their coastal resorts and, while local entrepreneurs still played a role, now the big international hotel chains became involved. Besides the governments, transportation innovation played a role as the automobile and the airplane, especially jets, carried people near and far. In the countries that already had resorts, getting to the beach became a quicker journey as new highways whisked families there. The airlines, meanwhile, were able to transport elite travelers to tropical resorts no matter how remote. Like the railways, the airlines also developed excursions, or charter flights, and the low-cost airlines that emerged later made it possible for working-class tourists to leave behind local beaches and experience exotic locales. Suddenly vacations could be had in any number of new resorts such as those in Torremolinos, Spain, or in old favorite locales such as Miami Beach, Florida.

As beach resorts have now been with us for over two centuries, it is easy to record how they have evolved in other ways. Therapeutic dipping started things off in eighteenth-century England and remained important, but recreation in the form of swimming and a plethora of other activities later came to dominate the seaside. Now rather than a quick dip to meet medical needs, adults and children cavorted on the beach and plunged into the water to challenge the waves. As activity changed, so did the costumes of the bathers. To get the full effect of salt water in seeking a cure, it was best to be naked, but that was not possible for aristocratic women in these societies. In the eighteenth century, shapeless gowns from neck to ankle covered women who only expected a quick dunking and then a return to the beach. Men believed they had a natural right to bathe nude. How to maintain modesty? In England the sexes were separated by space, with men at one end of the beach and women at the other. If the beach was not big enough, then they were separated by time—men in the morning and women to follow. While for men bathing naked was nearly universal, still each country dealt with male nudity differently. In France and America, mixed bathing was accepted while clothed. However, men could bathe nude very early in the morning so long as they were out of sight. Afterwards, it was expected that they would be dressed in appropriate bathing attire for the rest of the day and accompany women to the beach. Issues of gender and the body remained. Decade by decade, shorter and shorter costumes for men and women were the trend as they engaged in more and more physical activities. Then in the early twentieth century, sunbathing became fashionable and a tan came to be considered a sign of good health, so bathing suits had to expose more and more flesh. Cartoonists never missed the chance to focus on sex, and romance novels soon followed. The ultimate in exposure was realized in the bikini in the 1940s. The acceptance of skimpier suits was never universal. For instance, in traditional religious communities, protecting female bodies from inappropriate male viewing led to the burkini for Muslim women. In secular countries, the bikini and toplessness, not to mention nudity, have flourished on the beach. These and many other aspects of beach life evolved, always with an eye to national culture and style. The French, for instance, always led the way in beach fashion.

By the twenty-first century, beach resorts have become a mature industry. Some resorts are on a grand scale, encompassing as much as sixty miles of shore lined with hotel and condominium towers. With such huge facilities and millions of visitors, they are a long way from the small resorts of the eighteenth century. They are also embedded in contemporary popular culture through movies and television, mostly through the popularity of surfing and the glamour of lifeguards. Some beaches have even become iconic, such as those in Southern California and the Riviera. With greater and greater numbers involved, new issues have arisen, none more important than that of access. This is especially so on the public beaches, which have flourished in the twentieth century. While the right to access below the mean high tide line is nearly universal, the problem is getting to the high tide line. If a recalcitrant property owner does not want to provide access across his or her land to the beach, disputes are sure to follow. Private property rights versus public access is, and will remain, a volatile issue. Access has also been a problem for those who are regarded as minorities by the dominant culture. Black folks in America struggled to find a place on segregated beaches, as did Jews and Latinos.

There is one looming threat to beaches that may put an end to these disputes, and that is sea level rise. Signs of the rise now come with every king tide as seawater sloshes across the beach, envelops the sea wall, and rolls right over the coastal roads. Predictions of what is to come are dire. Depending on the date chosen—2050, 2100, or later—the rise will be anywhere from three feet to fifteen feet. The latter will be catastrophic to resorts everywhere. Beaches will be erased and hotels moved inland, hopefully to new beaches, or in some instances having to become hotels with nice swimming pools. Some governments, mostly local, are beginning to accept the inevitability of the rise and are elaborating policies to try and meet the threat, but in many places the costs can only be met by national governments. It is one thing to deal with the effects of a hurricane or cyclone, quite another to turn back the sea on a permanent basis. No government can face that with equanimity. So, beach resorts are about to face their ultimate challenge.

Eighteenth-century Brighton and modern Waikiki are very different communities. A long stretch of time lies between them. In that time beach resorts have evolved to absorb many technological innovations and social changes. This book attempts to explain how they came about and how people have experienced those changes.

The Lure of the Sea

Baiae was the first beach resort. Located on a peninsula on the northwest corner of the Gulf of Naples, the resort was built around a small bay. Nearby were the naval base at Miseno and the port of Pozzuoli. The latter was a vital port in the Roman economy, where trade from the East and the grain ships of Egypt stopped on their way to Ostia, the port of Rome. These important shipping facilities were not the main reason Baiae came into existence. Instead, the attractions were the Gulf of Naples and the Phlegraean Fields. The Greeks first settled there in the ninth century BCE and by the sixth century BCE had founded Neapolis, the future city of Naples. As the Romans swept south, they conquered this region and settled there. Neapolis, however, remained very much under the influence of the Greeks and was an important cultural center. Given its prominence, the emperor Nero launched his public career as a singer in Neapolis. Besides Neapolis, around the bay were clustered towns such as Pompei and Herculaneum, suburban villas taking advantage of the superb vistas, and, of course, Vesuvius, the dominant feature.

While Vesuvius was the most famous volcanic site of the region's thin crust, the Phlegraean Fields was less spectacular, with craters, hot springs, and bubbling mud pools all well known to the Romans. Such locations were prized for their curative powers, just as much as cold mineral springs. For instance, the asclepion at Pergamon, one of many sites dedicated to Asclepious, the god of cures, had three cold springs to treat different diseases. The Phlegraean Fields could offer far more choices of curative springs. There was also Lago d'Averno, the entry into the Roman Netherworld, and Monte Nuovo, a volcano far inferior to Vesuvius but dangerous nonetheless. Long renowned for its curative powers, it was not until the second century BCE that this area was sought out as a locale for pleasure.

At that time, Rome's empire was expanding, so loot and tribute poured into the hands of generals, politicians, bankers, and other members of the elite, providing them with the means to indulge in luxurious living. They sought out places to relax away from the bustle and distractions of Rome. Villas started to appear along the coast south of Rome. Unfortunately, they, in turn, attracted pirates, making life uncomfortable for the inhabitants, so in the end they would turn to Baiae. Not only was it adjacent to the Phlegraean Fields, but it was also safely tucked away in a bay, close to a naval base. Few pirates would be so foolish as to attack it. Many of the beneficiaries of empire settled there, such as Lucullus, Caesar, and Pompey, along with emperors—Nero, Hadrian, Germanicus, Titus, and Tacitus among them. They built lavish villas with views of the bay. These buildings were different from the normal configuration of the Roman villa in that they faced out to take in the view, unlike the usual structures built around a peristyle to protect the families' privacy. A sense of the splendor of these buildings can still be appreciated at Oplontis, across the bay near Pompeii, where an imperial villa was built for Nero's wife, Poppea.[1] This more typical suburban villa is grand in size and has elaborate paintings throughout the main living areas. It also has a splendid swimming pool. The opulence of these villas can further be seen in the artwork recovered from the Villa Pappiri at Herculaneum, where an extensive statuary collection enhanced the gardens, and the interior contained a large library.[2] The villas built around Baiae are now mostly lost due to volcanic activity. Monte Nuovo came to life in 1538 with an eight-day eruption, and the earth was warped by tectonics, putting much of the town under water. There are two archeological sites remaining. One is a complex of temples, baths, and administrative and commercial buildings, including the second largest dome (after the Pantheon) in the Roman world, an indication of the wealth that made Baiae famous.[3] The other site is under water and can only be visited with the proper equipment.

The season at Baiae commenced in April when the Senate recessed. Dignitaries and their retainers traveled down the Appian Way and then turned toward the coast when they reached the Via Campana. At Baiae they would find the resources that made resorts essential for leisure—housing, food, drink, shopping, and all manner of services, all in an appropriate setting for a well-off clientele. Once ensconced in their lodgings, the elite could take off their togas and treat themselves to restful and curative trips to the baths before setting out on a round of dinners, beach parties, feasts, theater, concerts, and boating parties. These are the activities associated with resort life, but Baiae had an edge as it quickly gained a reputation for licentiousness and debauchery—orgies and hot sulphur baths could be indulged in equally. Seneca, a well-known stoic, was appalled: "I left it the day after I reached it, for Baiae is a place to be avoided. . . . Luxury has claimed it. . . . Persons wandering drunk upon the beach, the riotous reveling of sailing parties, I need not witness it." Rushing out of town, he condemned Baiae as "dangerous," "a home of vice" that a wise man would find contrary to "purity of behavior."[4] Those enjoying themselves probably did not miss him. Seneca stood for the virtue of true Roman republicans whose simple life and military virtues had made Rome great. Baiae's decadence was regarded as the worst aspect of luxury that the new wealth from the empire introduced to Rome, thereby weakening Roman character and posing a future in which leisure would wreak havoc on manly virtue, dooming Romans to failure.

Almost all the ancient commentary on Baiae noted the reputation for vice that made the resort famous and synonymous with the new luxury economy. Having sated themselves at Baiae in the spring, the notables returned to Rome, then spent the summer in their country villas to rest up in an agrarian setting and restore their Roman virtue. The memory of its decadence lingered on among those who read Seneca and Cicero, absorbing their denunciations. While Baiae might not outstrip the reputation of South Beach in Miami or the most riotous Club Mediterranee for wild behavior, it does prefigure the general reputation of future beach resorts as places where normal behavior could be set aside and fun and games indulged in. However, for a very long time, few resorts would equal the spending power of the Roman aristocracy when it came to leisure and profligacy.

For centuries Baiae remained a part of the Roman social calendar, and as Rome declined, so would it. Locals might continue to use the pools for therapeutic reasons, but the town lost its cachet. As various peoples swept across Italy disrupting the empire, the accumulation of fortunes declined, meaning luxury became more and more limited. The Arabs sacked what remained at Baiae in the eighth century, and when Monte Nuovo blew up in 1538, the site was severely damaged.[5] As Baiae faded, it would be a very long time before another beach resort emerged.

Much of the wealth in the Middle Ages poured into the building of cathedrals, religious decoration, and castles. As for outdoor leisure, it was mostly hunting and hawking. Display and spectacle were present in the Church and with kings and princes, but not the open celebration of hedonism associated with Baiae. Bathing for therapeutic purposes, cleanliness, and for ritual practice did, however, continue in the medieval era. Charlemagne built a large bath in his palace at Aachen, where he bathed and swam.[6] Hot bubbling mineral water and cold mineral springs, present all over Europe, attracted the sick, who flocked to them in search of a cure, or at least a degree of relief. In some sites a saint came to be associated with the cures, adding the aspect of a religious pilgrimage to a medicinal plunge. Elites flocked to the more urban sites, as all major cities had baths for public use. Once there, men and women bathed together in scanty costumes, perhaps seeking more than relief. Poggio Bracciolini, a papal secretary, while on a trip hunting manuscripts in early 1416, visited Baden, the famous spa, where he was surprised at the nudity: "It was comical to see women going naked into the water before the eyes of men and displaying their private parts and their buttocks." Men wore leather aprons and the women short skirts, but both left a lot of naked flesh on display.[7] Vice once more reared its ugly head. Prostitution followed, lowering the tone even more. But now, rather than a howl of indignation from the likes of Seneca, the Church and civil authorities stepped in to police such activities. Nonetheless, the curative powers associated with springs attracted the sick, because a medical practice that had severe limits on diagnosis and cure left lots of room for folk medicine and belief, and those who felt the lure of the springs kept them going. Public baths would only lose their attraction when plague and syphilis made them dangerous in the eyes of many.[8]

In general, the sea was a place to be avoided during the long medieval era. Classical texts and the Bible testify to the presence of monsters in the seas. As one text noted, there was "a vast sea where there is nothing but the abode of monsters."[9] One medieval chronicle notes that on reaching northern waters "certain foul and very dangerous creatures, which indeed up to that time had not been seen, swarmed around covering the sea; and with horrible violence struck the bottom and sides, stern and prow with such heavy blows that it was thought they might go through the ship's covering of hides."[10] Such fears would last for a long time. Henry David Thoreau wrote in 1865, "The ocean is a wilderness reaching around the globe, wilder than a Bengal jungle, and fuller of monsters, washing the very wharves of our cities and the gardens of our sea-side residences.

Serpents, bears, hyenas, tigers, rapidly vanish as civilization advances, but the most populous and civilized city cannot scare a shark far from its wharves."[11] Those who lived on or near the sea and traded, fished, and fought in coastal waters regarded the sea with respect, both for the creatures it held and the great storms that smashed human structures with casual ferocity. However, until about the year 1000, most fishing was conducted in fresh water where conditions were safer. Two factors then turned fishermen toward the sea. First, the inland fisheries were depleted by overfishing, and secondly, habitats were destroyed by dams and polluted by city industries. The adoption of Viking fish drying technology (air drying on wooden frames) also meant that ocean fishing was now viable as ships and men could voyage out into the Atlantic to hunt cod, herring, and other deep-water fishes; thus, the fisheries expanded.[12]

The ocean still retained its reputation as a fearsome place, yet with the expansion of the fisheries and the rise of more and more ports and fishing villages on the shore, there were simply more and more people living near the sea. Those who worked on it or lived near it granted it respect. When a positive reference occurs in literature from the time, it is almost always a therapeutic reference. In France, some curative powers attributed to salt water brought kings to the sea. For example, in 1578 Henri III was ordered to Dieppe by his physician to gain relief from a tormenting skin itch. Also, for some time there was a belief in France that salt water cured rabies. Henri IV took his dog Fanor to Dieppe seeking a cure. In the late seventeenth century three ladies of the court rushed to Dieppe to throw themselves, while nude, into the sea three times after being bitten by a rabid dog.[13] This tradition carried on into the eighteenth century as doctors in Bordeaux sent their patients with rabies to the beach at Arcachon for the cure.[14]

The rabies cure at the beach seems not to have traveled beyond France. Instead, there was a general folk tradition of an annual trip to the beach that cleansed the soul as much as the body. In Jewish communities there is a very old tradition, still carried on today, of casting bread into the sea as a symbolic way of casting off sin.[15] Another folk tradition existed in the midlands in England and northern Wales, where whole communities made long journeys to the sea seeking relief by drinking salt water and dipping in the sea near Blackpool and Liverpool. A reporter for the *Preston Chronicle* counted seventeen hundred people returning from the seashore on one Sunday.[16] When upper-class commentators started touring these places in the eighteenth century, they noted that "country people" or the "lower class of people," whom they called "padjammers," would travel to the beach in wagons or by walking as much as forty miles to "wash away all the collected stains and impurities of the year."[17] What also caught their attention was that those seeking relief went into the water naked and in mixed company. Bathing costumes lay in the future, and these traditional immersions were performed in innocence as they always had been.[18] After an intense few days of bathing, the sojourners packed up and went home. Folk traditions such as these in France and England were repeated elsewhere, so that going to the beach seeking therapeutic relief for many communities was nothing new.

. . .

It was not until the eighteenth century that beach resorts reemerged, and they would first appear in England. During the eighteenth century, England experienced a rapidly expanding economy built on the profits of empire, landholding, early manufacturing, and finance. Sugar, tobacco, indigo, silk, spices, drugs, and all the other products of England's growing empire boosted trade. Driving a lot of these commodities was slavery, another trade from which English merchants profited. On the home front, new techniques in farming brought prosperity to the agricultural sector. And then, during the last third of the century, the manufacture of a variety of domestic goods through the use of improved technology, especially steam power, created another area of prosperity. Finally, growing wealth enhanced London's reputation as a financial center where bankers, goldsmiths, and stockjobbers all pushed forward the boundaries of finance capitalism. Rising prosperity meant that more and more people benefited from economic growth, leading to an explosion of consumerism and of leisure.[19]

As with Rome, the upper classes benefited the most from these developments. The English aristocracy was long used to all sorts of outdoor and indoor amusements. Private spaces in urban and rural palaces and public venues such as assembly rooms, clubs, pleasure gardens, museums, galleries, horse races, concert halls, and theaters all flourished, creating varied settings for leisure. At the other end of the spectrum were the bearbaiting, cockfights, prize fights, and other rough events that played to mixed upper- and lower-class audiences. There was much to excite the attention of the rich in the new world of commercialized leisure, for all of these new activities had to be paid for by investments and subscriptions. The latter had the dual benefit of admitting those who belonged and keeping out those who did not. As the political, financial, and social capital, London had all of this and more, creating the world of the "ton," the most fashionable elements of the aristocracy, combining high fashion with pleasure-seeking in every possible way. Overindulgence in worldly pleasures would lead people to seek relief at one of the spas.[20] Alexander Buchan cynically observed, "In that state of society, when the general diffusion of wealth has removed from a considerable part of the community all apprehensions respecting the immediate means of subsistence, the mind, not being engaged in providing for real wants, is obliged to find employment in the creation of such as are imaginary. Among the most generally predominant of these is the fancied want of health," which led to the need for "a frequent change of place."[21] For aristocrats and gentry, Bath and Tunbridge Wells were the spas to visit and recover from dissipation. Lesser folk were left to the nearly 150 spas in England.[22] There, mineral waters promised cures for many ailments. Familiarity with this sort of treatment would lead the leisure class to be open toward other forms of water treatment.

While the eighteenth century saw advances made in medicine, it was also the case that little was done to improve patient care. As a leading expert has written, "hardly any eighteenth-century scientific advance helped heal the sick directly" and "the net contribution of physicians to the relief and cure of the sick remained marginal."[23] As one contemporary put it, he "preferred the practice of old women, because they do not sport with edged tools."[24] This is a reference to one of the prevailing treatments—blood-letting, an all-too-common practice as physicians tried to "balance the humors" of the body's system by extracting blood. The old women preferred by this individual still practiced the traditional medicine of herbs and spells, which was what most people could afford. For elites, clinicians tailored therapies to the individual, urging temperance, hygiene, good air, careful diet, sleep, exercise, and balancing of the humors through bloodletting and purging.[25] So when learned physicians, during the first half of the eighteenth century, started to recommend cold bathing in the sea and drinking seawater, this did not seem that unusual, especially as many were already familiar with mineral spring spas, which featured a regime of drinking and bathing in cold and hot mineral water.[26]

What attracted physicians and their patients was a new "scientific" literature that actually began in the late seventeenth century, recommending treatment in cold water and introducing salt water as a sovereign remedy. In 1653, Hermannius van der Heyden published *Speedy Help for the Rich and Poor*, recommending cold water for a number of diseases.[27] John Locke, in *Some Thoughts on Education* (1693), recommended it for children as a way of toughening their bodies and as a remedy for weak constitutions.[28] The work that was to have the greatest impact was published in 1697 by Sir John Floyer, *An Inquiry into the Right Use and Abuses of the Hot, Cold and Temperate Baths in England,* a work that went through six editions.[29] He also coauthored, with Edward Batnard, *Psychrolousia: or the History of Cold Bathing: Both Ancient and Modern . . . ,* a long description of cold-water bathing from the classical period forward, giving the practice the validation of time.[30] As a physician, Floyer believed that cold water hardened the body, its organs and glands, and closed pores, keeping in important fluids and compressing "animal spirits." He only mentions sea bathing as something he knows was practiced in the past. But seawater also had a long history for its curative powers. Dioscorides's herbal, written in the first century, was well known in medical circles as it continuously circulated in manuscript and then in print. It recommended seawater as a treatment for disorders of the nerves and as a wash for skin diseases.[31]

Not everyone jumped on the bandwagon for cold-water treatments. Thomas Guidott, the author of *An Apology for the Bath,* maintained that "as to the Cures are said to have been done by the use of the Cold Bath, 'tis too well known to be the common Artifice of Quacks and Empiricks," and, as for the supposed good derived from sea bathing, "Bathing in Salt water is somewhat allow'd by *Avicen* to cure the Itch and Scabs; but Hippocrates in many places protesteth against it."[32] There was much to be said for Guidott's skepticism, but the tenor of the times was against him, and the advocates for cold bathing in the sea would soon monopolize the discourse, as can be seen in the work of Thomas Short. His *Natural, Experimental, and Medicinal History of the Mineral Waters of Derbyshire, Lincolnshire and Yorkshire, Particularly those of Scarborough* was typical.[33] Short praised the value of cold water as a medicine that pressed upon the body, helping to "straighten" blood vessels, thus increasing the flow of bodily fluids. Beginning a long tradition, he enumerated the effects of the water: it dissolves humors, scours glands, frees fluids, increases the flow of blood to the brain, produces a greater flow of urine, removes secretions in the veins and, as a result, cures a prodigious number of diseases—itch, scurvy, leprosy, elephantiasis, palsy, melancholy, asthma, rickets, and on and on—a true wonder drug in an age with few such cure-alls.[34] Short's book was an addition to the "scientific" literature, as it was framed in terms of chemical analysis, giving validity to the cold water cure.

The increasing number of these studies helped convince the public that there was virtue in such "cures" and that they should be sought out. What was needed was a commitment by physicians to cure by cold salt water. All too soon they appeared. The most famous of these individuals was Dr. Richard Russell. After his formal education, he settled in the town of Lewes, close to the south coast. In his practice he noted that people who lived on the nearby coast seemed to be healthier than those further inland and that they used seawater as a tonic for disorders of the abdomen. Out of these observations and others he published, in 1750, *De Tabe Glandulari.*[35] Having proved his learning with the Latin tome, he had it translated into *A Dissertation on the Use of Sea Water in Diseases of the Glands, particularly the Scurvy, Jaundice . . . and Glandular Consumption.*[36] This treatise praised the efficacy of seawater in vanquishing diseases of the glands. Case after case is detailed, along with Russell's interventions with seawater treatments, either by drinking or by immersion. The list of diseases cured is quite long, including leprosy, gonorrhea, ulcers, tumors, and jaundice. There were six editions of this work, and in the 1760 fourth edition there was an additional essay by a Dr. Speed, "A Commentary on Sea Water," where the claims were even more extravagant: "Sea water . . . is not simply a cold bath but a cold medicated bath."[37] Russell would follow his research and move to Brighthelmstone, soon to be shortened to Brighton, for the summer, where he built a large house, the better to lodge his patients and oversee their treatment.

Russell and Speed laid the foundations for many more works praising the therapeutic value of seawater, such as John Awsiter's *Thoughts on Brighthelmstone Concerning Sea-Bathing and Drinking Sea Water, with Some Direction for Their Use.*[38] Awsiter had replaced Russell at Brighton, and his text repeated much of Russell's advice, but went on to stress the additional benefit of cleanliness that sea bathing brings, something of growing concern among elites.[39] Sometimes the advice from this new generation of physicians could be quite specific. Robert White published a long list of dos and don'ts, stating that he had witnessed abuses in bathing and drinking seawater. Among his principles were: no more than one minute in the water, as two dips were enough; no more than three times per week; only a dry costume should be worn, as a damp one could give the wearer a sudden chill; too much bathing could "shatter" a person's constitution; and no more than one pint when drinking seawater, and not every morning, as too much can have a drastic effect on the bowels.[40] Other physicians recommended drinking multiple pints, with who-knows-what effect on the bowels. As these books became more and more common, they would set no limits on the virtues of the sea: as John Crane stated, "the sea washes away all the diseases of mankind."[41]

As more and more of these texts were published by practicing physicians, they stressed the need to have expert advice prior to beginning treatment. These resort physicians were always adamant regarding treatment, for no one should attempt a saltwater cure without a consultation with a physician. Self-treatment was dangerous, and a physician was needed to ensure that the correct amount of salt water was consumed and that the time spent bathing was appropriate. Even their city brethren would follow treatments carefully and scold patients who had done too much or too little, as Mrs. Betsy Francis would find on her return home when her physician admonished her for improper treatment.[42] Often, when one caught a cold or a cough, family members were quick to assert that it came from faulty dipping in the sea. Mrs. Hester Thrale reproached a relative who had improperly taken a girl to the beach, "that to bathe a lean growing girl of large expectations, whom [sic] you say is unhealthy—in the Sea, without more or near Medical Advice than the Isle of Wight would afford—seems somewhat a rash step."[43] So in the second half of the eighteenth century, when trained physicians were making strides in taking over the practice of medicine on a number of fronts, they also tried to ensure that a trip to the beach came under their control.[44]

One additional benefit to trips to the seaside, and one not shared with the mineral spring spas, was the curative power of the sea air.[45] Two reports to the Royal Society, in 1773 and 1780, claimed, with relevant evidence, that sea air was cleansed as it swept across the face of the ocean. Thus, ocean voyages and visits to the beach provided relief from the mephitic city air which caused disease.[46] Given the increasingly crowded conditions of many cities, with garbage and sewage causing fetid air, it did not take much to convince the public that sea air could have a positive effect—besides which, one did not have to go into the water to get the benefits.

Having made up his or her mind to take the plunge with the new therapy, the patient's first decision was where to go. For those who chose to go in the 1730s, there were no guides available to help them.[47] The situation for mineral spas at Bath and Tunbridge Wells was far different, as there were a variety of guides for them that would later provide something of a template for the seaside guides. It was not until the 1770s that guides started to appear for the new beach resorts. After that, guides to all of the resorts became common. At first they tended not to give a great deal of practical advice. Some were more intent on giving visitors a history of the community that they were hoping to visit. Slowly but surely, the guides printed information regarding conditions and costs and the available services at each of the resorts, with a certain amount of local color. Often they would recommend local walks and rides that took visitors to scenic or historic spots that would help fill their days. They were far removed from the glossy brochures that would come to characterize resort propaganda in the future. During the early period, bathers were real pioneers.[48]

While there are few records about early beachgoing, by the 1730s it was clear that seawater therapy had come into its own. Scarborough, Brighton, Margate, and Blackpool all had visitors who came for therapy in the early 1730s. With the exception of Blackpool, which was not much more than a wonderful stretch of sand, these were all fishing communities that had beaches. Scarborough, for instance, was a small port with an active fishing community, a merchant fleet, and a small spa. South of the harbor there was a fine stretch of flat sandy beach. Margate was a small regional port with declining fishing interests. Brighton was a small fishing village. These communities would soon be transformed.[49] They were invaded in the summer months by elite tourists who upset local community life and the economy. It would not always be a happy relationship.

If one wanted to approach any of these villages from the land side, one ran into the problems of transportation. England was laced by many roads, but often these were dusty tracks which turned into muddy trails in the all-too-frequent rains. The main roads between major cities and towns were better kept and easier to navigate. Toward the end of the eighteenth century, turnpikes with better road technology made roads safer and quicker. These were the main roads, but when it came time to head toward a local fishing village, the roads became narrower and rutted.[50] Margate did have one advantage over its rivals, for a small group of local boats, called hoys, were available to bring travelers from London. With good winds the trip down the Thames and into the port could take only ten hours. When the winds turned unfavorable the boat headed out into the North Sea; then the trip could end up taking thirty-six hours and be a stomach-churning voyage for the passengers. Until the roads were modernized, a trip from London to Brighton, just fifty-two miles away, took two full days through the Weald, an area of hills and marshes much loved by smugglers and highwaymen. In 1779, when the young Fanny Burney and her party made their way to Brighton, they were accompanied by two armed men on horseback to ensure their safety.[51] More often it was potholes and broken wheels that endangered the coaches as they rolled along. Such accidents almost had to be expected. Local repair facilities might not be available, and they were sure to be expensive. Then there were the inadequate inns at the end of the day, testing one's stomach with bad food and one's ability to sleep with fleas and bugs of various kinds in an uncomfortable bed.

Obviously, those who could afford to take the time to make such a journey and who had the carriage necessary, or the fare for a coach, were members of the elite. Carriages, from the smallest to the grandest four-wheel coaches, were among the most expensive items in a family's annual budget. The larger the carriage and the greater the number of horses, coachmen, and outriders, the higher the status. Nothing could flaunt wealth and power more than a fancy carriage with the family crest on the door. These vehicles were reserved for the very wealthy. Most people rode in smaller coaches, which proliferated in types and styles in the late eighteenth century. Still the upkeep of the carriage, feed for the horses, and lodgings and maintenance for the grooms were expensive.[52] Those who could not afford the upkeep of a coach had to take to the roads in various public conveyances that went from city to city, and the further from cities you traveled, the more dependent you became on irregular service and crowded conditions. Often, passengers found themselves trudging alongside an overfilled coach with the struggling horses as they labored to get up a hill. The mail coaches were the most reliable, but they were limited to four seats. No matter the means, sooner or later you arrived in a fishing village.

Having survived the trip, the pioneers of beachgoing confronted the second difficulty: where to stay. During the early decades, accommodations could be primitive and difficult to find. After all, fishermen were hardly wealthy, and their homes tended to be back from the beach, dug into the ground and with few windows.[53] They had no love for the winter storms that could destroy everything in their path. Unlike modern beach homes that seek out the best views, houses in these communities eschewed scenery for safety. In 1735, when the Reverend William Clarke visited Brighton, he managed to rent a bedroom and a parlor in a two-story building all of twelve feet high that was built partially underground.[54] Occasionally there were taverns and inns that might have a room or two, which was more common on the highway, but those in villages tended to cater to local drinking habits and did not expect many visitors. For this reason Scarborough emerged quickly as a beach resort, as it already had an infrastructure built around the port and a mineral spring, and thus lodgings were available. This was also true at Margate, another small port. Elsewhere, investors were needed to provide lodgings. In some cases it meant the local inn adding rooms above the stairs, or a home owner building an addition, or even a new house to accommodate visitors.[55] Some of the visitors had wealth enough to build their own lodging. For example, the Dukes of Devonshire and Cumberland built houses at Brighton and the Duke of York built one at Weymouth, but this was a rarity. Local landowners and investors were left to develop facilities as quickly as they could. They were dealing with a clientele that expected a degree of comfort and the best in nearly everything. Aristocrats might rough it for a short time, but only for a short time.

The problem for investors was that they needed to build first-rate facilities with the usual comforts for an audience that only visited during the summer. Rental agreements, therefore, tended to be expensive, allowing the landlord to turn a profit, so much so that the word *extortion* was often used by those who were new to resort accommodation. A visitor to Margate expressed the feelings of many: "The lower order of the natives are cunning, avaricious, disrespectful and sometimes malevolent. No gratitude or civility."[56] The experienced beach visitor simply grumbled and paid up. For women, financial arrangements could be difficult. Often as not they were there with friends, family, and servants. Most of them were on a budget set by their husbands, and they had to make it work. A distant husband might not provide the money in time, forcing the woman to plead with the landlord for more time. One lady regarded her tough landlord as a "Jacobin." Another had to borrow funds from a banker she knew in order to pay off the landlord and leave.[57] For all summer visitors, then and in the future, budgets were constantly challenged by the need for local entrepreneurs to make a living in the limited summer season. Yet without them, the resorts would not exist.

When settled in their quarters, the visitors entered a different social setting from their normal urban or rural homes. Spas and resorts raised issues that were muted on country estates and in the society of upper-class cities. People were thrown together in new settings where individuals of varying status were brought together in ways that created issues of precedence and decorum. On arrival at a resort, it was proper to register one's presence at the local library. These libraries were book shops where one had to subscribe to enjoy the books. They would also sell books, and if the shop was large enough it would also be open at night for concerts and raffles. On first visiting, one could look at the list and see who was present and get a sense of the "quality" of the visitors.

FIGURE 1.1 Thomas Rowlandson, 1756–1827, British, *A Ball at Scarborough*, ca. 1820. Watercolor, with pen, in red ink, brown ink, black ink, gray ink, and graphite on moderately thick, slightly textured, blued white, wove paper. Yale Center for British Art, New Haven, CT, Paul Mellon Collection. A ball typically found on an evening in any assembly room.

Later, as regional newspapers flourished, they were happy to keep a running account of who was in town. Those who lacked status never bothered to register, as that would be foolish. For those who had status, they were close observers of those around them. One 1733 account from Scarborough noted two dukes, seven earls, one marquis, and assorted lords, along with the famous actor Colley Cibber. Even the Duchess of Marlborough and Lord Chesterfield listed the notables in their letters when at Scarborough.[58]

The individual who most closely observed the register was the local master of ceremonies. He was responsible for the social life of the community. Ideally he was, as one guidebook explained, a "guardian over the public intercourse of refined or mixed society."[59] He made introductions between visitors when called on to do so and managed the various balls and other social events in the assembly room. He took especial care of the ladies who were present without their husbands or fathers. Should one of them want to dance, he was the one called upon to find a suitable partner. If a woman did not want to dance, then gentlemen had to be warned off from trying.[60] Mr. Vipont of Scarborough, Mr. Ward of Brighton, and Mr. LeBon at Margate all kept social life moving. For this they were paid by the visitors who, when they registered, paid a subscription to enter local society.[61]

The role of the master of ceremonies was created due to the increasing number of situations where people now came together who might not move in the same social circles in different parts of the country or have quite the same status. Spas and resorts were new public spaces where people of different elite states met. For instance, someone like Colley Cibber had no title, yet he was well known and traveled in elite circles just as some bankers, lawyers, physicians, and other new men did. Yet, they could never imagine that they had the social status to be treated as true equals. When Giacomo Rossini, the famous opera composer, visited Brighton, he was the guest of the king, who treated him with familiarity because he loved music. But members of the king's entourage bridled at the king's allowing a mere musician to be familiar with him.[62] When at home, noble households could easily take care of matters of precedence, as one had to be invited in and rules of decorum were observed. The same was true in church, where the families of high status sat in ordered pews in front while the lesser folk occupied benches in the back, or stood. Similar rules were observed in places such as the Almanack Club in London, where seven ladies of impeccable status controlled admission to the Wednesday evening balls.[63] One critic thought that the ladies created a system of "tyranny."[64] At the center of all of this was the royal court, which kept the strictest rules and insisted on the highest decorum in dress and behavior. Anything less brought banishment from the font of favor and office. So the resorts and spas were new arenas, far from the palace and its rules, thus throwing people together in new configurations that created the need for the master of ceremonies. However, certainty could never be guaranteed; a resort could not be the same as one's home parish. In this sense they were transitional zones from rigidly controlled elite spaces to more modern and fluid social settings where there would be no need for a master of ceremonies.

Elites preferred to be assured about the company they were keeping. That was especially true for mothers who had eligible daughters and the ability to provide a dowry. As one fictional character put it, "Young ladies that have no money are to be pitied."[65] Jane Austen made the marriage market an important part of her fiction and set one story about a bad marriage and a runaway bride in a resort. The regular marriage market was mostly conducted during the season in London, but the summer resorts created a new venue for mothers. As one of Austen's characters notes of Brighton, "That is the place to get husbands. What a pity it is, mamma, we did not all go." Austen wrote about the seaside as a place of flirtation, elopements, love, and sex. Her one book set at a resort, *Sanditon*, remains unfinished but has most of these elements in the manuscript that survives.[66] Diaries and journals kept by women during visits to resorts often make quite calculated assessments of the financial worth of male visitors. Raffish or unsuitable company might bring a degree of titillation while out walking, but not at tea.

Having obtained lodging, the intrepid visitor now confronted the sea, the very cold sea. None of these new resorts had anything like the balmy waters of the Bay of Naples. This was the era of the Little Ice Age, meaning that the water around England, never warm, was even colder. The benefits of seawater came from total immersion, preferably from dipping three times. Fanny Burney, the celebrated young novelist, wrote that her first experience of dipping frightened her terribly as "the shock was beyond expectation great." She could not breathe or speak for a minute or two, but when she returned she was in a "glow that was delightful—it is the finest feeling in the world."[67] Bathers had to deal with the reactions of their systems to the very cold water, as there was no escape from it. One representative doctor advised bathing in cold water, for "the lower the temperature we can accustom ourselves to bear with impunity the more secure is our health."[68] Yet some patients cowered from this. Harriet Cavendish wrote to a friend, "We go on bathing though it requires some courage, as the sea feels like ice, especially this morning . . . it was so bitter cold."[69] In time there would be a set of expectations from the experience. As one expert put it, "Plunging into the sea, occasions a tumult of confused sensations, not easily detailed, but certainly of the unpleasant than the agreeable kind. The aggregate of these constitutes what is usually termed the Shock," followed when dressing by a "glow."[70] The reactions of "shock" followed by the "glow" were described often and came to be expected. For the truly ill, such reactions were the same as a medicine that had a dire taste, where each swallow was a challenge. To slip into the water with no sensation could be interpreted as poor medicine indeed. Thus, dipping in the ocean or drinking seawater, which was often prescribed, was not a pleasant experience, so it had to do some good, or so thought the poor patients.

In time, another reason for dipping would appear for those who were in better general health. Fanny Burney went into the water for twenty days in November. "I bathe, in spite of the Cold Weather," she explained, "to harden me for the winter."[71] This became a common assumption, that constant contact with cold water would help toughen one's constitution and so make it easier to bear winter weather and avoid winter diseases. Burney was serious about this. Her last dip for the season was on November 20. As she described to a friend, accompanied by Hester Thrale and Mrs. Thrale's three daughters, she "arose at 6 in the morning and by the pale blink of the moon we went to the sea side, where we had bespoke the Bathing women to be ready for us and into the Ocean we plunged! It was cold but pleasant. I have bathed so often as to lose my dread of the operation which now gives me nothing but animation and vigor."[72] Animation indeed! Many might choose not to risk their health with such a cure. If you did press on with these treatments, you still had to confront your regular physician when you returned home. One bather returned to be told that bathing twenty-five times was bad and that she had done herself an injury, as fifteen times would have been enough. She consoled herself that she "must now hope for the best."[73]

Burney's example of going bathing by the "blink" of the moon was a good deal earlier than most people would put up with—she had to return to London by dinnertime—but there was general agreement that bathing in the morning was best. Later in the day was acceptable, but towards evening only the healthy young should go in. If everyone went in the morning, how were modesty issues to be dealt with? For men, striding off into the water naked settled the issue. By very long tradition nude dipping or swimming was the male way. At Scarborough, men went out beyond the surf line in small boats and tipped over into the water. Sufficiently wet, they clambered back into the boat and set off for the beach. For women, matters were not so simple, and women made up the greatest numbers of visitors. While there can be no statistical proof of this, visitor after visitor commented on the number of women who were going to the resorts, even in the early days when facilities were primitive.[74] Obviously, many were going for therapeutic reasons, but some were also simply escaping from dull domestic regimes or from the need to entertain local visitors at the country seat. The Duchess of Devonshire, when she had to give a ball for the locals, regarded them as a bunch of "Derbyshire savages."[75]

Once at the beach and ready to proceed with the treatment, one encountered problems. In a society where female costume was complicated among elite women and public nudity was not allowed, how to be dipped? Outside the rather "gamier" parts of London, even partial exposure of the female body was frowned upon. Fanny Burney was disgusted when she witnessed fisherwomen pulling in a seine with their skirts tied up to their knees in order to gain some freedom of movement. It was all very "barbarous."[76] Another ladies' groom expressed his distaste for the way one woman mounted her horse as she displayed her lower leg, which affronted him.[77] Abigail Adams was shocked when she first went to the ballet and saw the dancers in short skirts that showed their garters and drawers.[78] Naked limbs were not to be seen at anytime.[79] So, how to get into the water and out again without gross indecency? First, a long bathing costume that covered the whole body was required, along with a cap to try and keep the hair dry. As one poet put it, "The Ladies dressed in flannel cases, show nothing but their handsome faces."[80] Then how best to get into the water? Should one walk into the water until a sufficient depth was reached and then take a couple of dips over one's head before returning to the beach? Not really, as you would have to walk up the beach with a wet costume wrapped around your body. The solution was the bathing machine, a structure made of wood or canvas mounted on cart wheels. The bather entered the damp, dark box with only a narrow bench to sit on and would take off her costume and change into the bathing outfit while the machine was maneuvered into the water by a horse and a "dipper." When it was far enough out, she stepped down into the water with the help of the dipper. Then, once she had received the benefits of the sea, it was back into the machine as it trundled back up the beach while she managed to dry off with a small rough towel (the better to get the blood flowing) and change into dry clothes.

Local governments controlled access to the beach. They wanted to supervise the process, so they licensed the bathing machines to a person who would manage the experience whether there were two machines or twenty. Each machine would then need a "dipper," such as the famous widow Duker at Scarborough or Martha Gunn at Brighton. The dipper accompanied the machine and determined the appropriate depth at which point the bather entered the water and was dipped three times before clambering back into the machine. In rough surf this could be awkward, with bathers battered by the waves and tossed about. Since women might become exposed at this point, the Quaker Benjamin Beale of Margate developed a canvas hood that came down over the back of the machine, allowing women to enter and leave the water more or less out of sight. The hood became nearly universal. This innovation had special meaning for women leaving the water with a wet costume sticking to their bodies. There was no getting around the way in which a wet dress, no matter how long, would wrap itself around the body; as one female beach observer commented, "How humiliating! More like corpses in shrouds . . . as they kick and sprawl and flounder about in

FIGURE 1.2 Benjamin West, 1738–1820, American, active in Britain (from 1763), *The Bathing Place at Ramsgate,* ca. 1788. Oil on canvas. Yale Center for British Art, New Haven, CT, Paul Mellon Collection. Benjamin West has captured all of the elements of the beach experience: bathing machines, dippers, women bathers in their gowns, even a nude old man being ushered into the water.

their flannel smocks."[81] Since there was also the possibility of waves upsetting the footing of the bather and having her tossed around in an unseemly fashion, this raised the possibility of greater exposure. Telescopes were kept at hand, better to watch the passing parade of ships out at sea, but they could also be used to watch the sea closer to the beach. And so, therapeutics became eroticism, and cartoonists could not pass that up as a subject.[82] Men, of course, did not face all these issues, and if they used a machine they simply changed in the machine and jumped in nude. The swimmers might paddle around longer, but they sooner or later returned to the machine and dressed. They might also be viewed with telescopes, but the cartoonists left them alone as a subject. A group of ladies at Brighton did gather where the men usually bathed and goggled at them.

Since getting in and out of the machine required help so as not to expose oneself too much, the job of the dipper was gender segregated, with men accompanying men and women shepherding female bathers. The dippers made sure that their time was booked and, in general, policed the beach. It was to their benefit to ensure that no one went in without renting a machine, and it suited the municipality to have them watching over the bathers and preventing accidents. Dippers or no, protecting women from rough water and viewers was a problem. In England there was a strong desire to preserve decorum and to keep men and women apart on the beach. The strong desire among men to swim or dip nude, even when they were accompanied by a dipper, meant that for decency's sake they had to be kept apart. One solution was to create specific times for men to bathe, followed by another time for women, keeping them from being on the beach at the same time. At Blackpool a bell was rung that indicated that it was time for the men to leave the beach so that the ladies could enter the water. Here there were fewer machines, and some women wore their bathing outfits under another costume as they walked to the beach. Others used "boxes" on the beach to change. The men were banished some distance away, and should they hang around, they forfeited a bottle of wine. The bell rang out again when it was time for the men to take their turn.

An alternative was gender-specific beaches, where men and women were kept physically apart and propriety was maintained. Such was the case at Brighton, where a long waterfront allowed physical separation. Where possible, physical separation became the rule. Some beaches had to adapt to local conditions. Dover beach was too steep for bathing machines, so women, as one observer explained, "in the morning put on long flannel gowns under their clothes and walk to the beach, undress selves, walk in as deep as they please, hold onto the guide, 3 or 4 at a time sometimes, and dip over their head . . . then come ashore where women attend them with towels, cloaks, chairs. The flannel is stripped off and they dry, while women hold cloaks around them, then they dress selves and go home."[83] Another alternative was to arrange for men to go into the water very early and for women and children to go in around 11 a.m. Every beach resort had to find a method to preserve propriety. No matter the care taken, there were still occasions when more flesh was on display than society normally tolerated. And, as we will see, as Victorian morality settled in, even occasional displays were too much for some. So, between male nude bathing and the possibility of female exposure, the beach was considered an erotic site. Such issues simply did not arise in normal society, so it behooved resorts to create rules that would keep eroticism within bounds. Without this it would be hard to attract those seeking therapy, not sensation.

For those who wanted more privacy and perhaps warm water, most of the resorts developed baths. Piped-in seawater allowed the finicky to avoid public display and yet get the benefits from immersion. Hot baths were also built, but they were more controversial. If cold water was really the chief therapeutic benefit of the sea, warm water could only be used with caution. Dr. Russell, of Brighton fame, did approve of warm water as he built the first warm water bath at Brighton. He and his colleagues would all agree that warm water should be approached with care and then only the most debilitated, elderly patients or sickly child should resort to its use—and only with the advice of a physician. That eminent practitioner Erasmus Darwin advised, "To those who are past the meridian of life the warm bath for 1/2 hour twice a week I believe to be eminently serviceable in retarding the advance of old age."[84] Younger adults should confine themselves to the icy sea or cold bath.

Having enjoyed the benefits of the sea, the bathers were then left with the remainder of the day. What to do? There was an easy answer to this question, and that was to import the existing culture of the spas, as they had a common set of institutions with which to entertain the aristocratic visitor. The social center was always the assembly room. This was a large building that could be used for concerts or balls. It also had rooms for card playing, meals, and meetings. It could be a stand-alone building or attached to an inn or other major structure. Many events during anyone's stay would be held in the "rooms." So on arrival, it was important to register your presence and pay a subscription fee to be a member of the rooms. At the library you paid a fee for use during your stay. The theater usually operated on a pay-per-performance fee schedule. The shops that were present in the spas were soon replicated at the beach resorts, as were the coffee shops, taverns, inns, and country pubs. Some of the resorts also had features such as horse racing, a major annual summer event at Brighton. Bognor attracted an exclusive clientele such as the Duchess of Devonshire, in part because of its proximity to the Goodwood race meet. For the emerging resorts it was necessary to add as many of these diversions as possible as quickly as possible or Bath and Tunbridge Wells, with all their conveniences, would remain the favorite gathering places of the very people they were trying to attract. Here again, entrepreneurship and capital were essential if the resorts were to prosper.

A typical day for those who did bathe was something like this for a visitor to Brighton: "Rise at 7, Bathe or walk from 8–9, breakfast, 10–12 drive [in a horse carriage] on ye downs, sit in our own Bow Windows to ye sea till 1/2 past 3, then Dine, drink Tea at six, drive again

FIGURE 1.3 William Heath, *Mermaids at Brighton,* early nineteenth century. Colored etching. Royal Pavilion & Museums, Brighton & Hove. A scene familiar to all women seeking a therapeutic dip.

until 8 and then Lounge upon ye Beach or Steyne till 9 when we Sup and go to Bed at 1/2 past ten."[85] For the more dissipated, rising at nine seemed more appropriate, although their day would also have some of the characteristic of this more chaste schedule. Breakfasting or bathing started the day, although if you chose to eat first, medical advice was not to go into the water until an hour passed. Once dipped, ladies would need to set time aside for drying their hair. Allowing hair to grow very long was much in fashion, and displaying it in public in an unsightly, wet mess was highly distasteful, as most women took their hair down at the end of the day prior to going to bed, so the only persons who might see them this way were their maids, husbands, or lovers.

After breakfast, men and women set out to walk, ride, or move about in their carriages. Strolling around town was by far the most popular, and this was done at almost any time of the day. In Brighton, walking on the Steyne, a central green where the fishermen still dried their nets, was popular as it was also close to the library and the shops. The beach at low tide provided a nice surface to ride or walk on. The creation of a promenade above the beach had a high priority. Often it served a dual purpose in protecting the town from winter storms while providing a place to walk or ride. It stretched for some distance along the cliffs at places such as Brighton, providing views of the ocean, and at the same time creating a venue for display. Horses and carriages flaunted wealth and privilege, and that had a place even for those on holiday. Riding was much more of a male than a female way of relaxing, and riding away from the resort to nearby towns or out into the countryside was a favorite recreation. For both sexes, traveling about in a carriage was favored, specially in one of the new carriages. There had been many innovations in carriage design in the late eighteenth century, resulting in lighter, faster carriages that moved along quickly behind one or two horses, as opposed to the larger carriages that needed four or six horses. Some women drove their own carriages and so could wander about with friends.[86]

When it came to eating, much of this was done in private. All of the resorts featured places to eat, but visitors often managed this at their lodgings. Most of them had brought their own servants to prepare and serve meals. The main meal of the day often meant having visitors, although women who had only brought female servants fussed at inviting men when there was no male servant present. Tea was another occasion for guests. The long summer evenings lent themselves to more walks and outings, but evenings were mostly spent quietly.

For the more adventurous, there were other entertainments. The libraries remained open at night. To bring in the customers, they provided music and raffles of small token items that people enjoyed taking a chance on. The theaters played regularly all summer, bringing actors in from London at the bigger resorts. The assembly rooms offered a variety of diversions such as concerts, but balls organized several times a week at all the resorts were the real attractions. These were opportunities to see and be seen by the more fashionable people, for the subscription kept out the lower orders. The latest dances and "country dances" were featured. The master of ceremonies presided, earning his fees as he found partners for those who wanted to dance and managed introductions for those who needed them. It could be the occasion for meeting other single people, although the young women were always kept under the scrutiny of their mothers.[87] All in all, most balls were fairly staid affairs that might descend into boredom. If you wanted excitement, it could always be found in the card games, where gamblers passed the time. Given that there were always more women than men, especially toward the end of the season, women would appear in riding costume to play the male role, in order that the dancing might go on.[88] Then there were the occasions when large crowds of highly fashionable men and women combined with groups of inebriated young men.

Affairs could spin out of control, at which time mothers would start looking for their daughters and the exit, seeing no need to imperil chaste reputations. These wild occasions could go well beyond eleven o'clock, the usual closing time, and wander into the early hours of the morning.

Most of these resort activities were enjoyed by men and women. Men, however, had many more options and could go hunting or fishing, play billiards, ride out with friends, drink in taverns, or have coffee in the local coffee shop. Women were not usually allowed in coffee shops, and thus the taking of tea was a female affair. Swimming was a male recreation, not that many knew how to swim. Learning how to swim was uncommon and, more often than not, took place in rivers or lakes where the water was calmer. By the end of the eighteenth century, bathing places were created on rivers in the major cities. These were generally roped-off areas with a small shack where the men or boys changed prior to jumping in. Floating and swimming like a frog were the preferred ways to have fun, and few learned more elaborate strokes. If you were interested, books about swimming techniques had first appeared in the sixteenth century and were often identified with learning a skill that would be of use to your prince. Armies could always use men to swim rivers to spy out the enemy or prepare the ground for bridges, but increasingly men became interested in simply swimming for enjoyment.[89] When they went to a beach resort, they had to deal with the dippers who wanted everyone to use their machines. Anyone not using their facilities was a free rider and robbing them of income. The fact was that they limited the number of machines in order to increase business, as an empty machine earned no fees or tips for the dipper, and local ordinances backed them up by forbidding free swimming.[90] One frustrated swimmer complained that the dippers would get angry when they went out to swim and went out further and took up a lot more time than it did to give someone three dips.[91] Angry dippers could only shout in frustration and accept that a swimmer did not need them. Robust young men were usually the swimmers, so that left the older and less fit men to seek therapeutic dipping and to go in accompanied by dippers. Compared with the young and vital, these men came off poorly, as John Constable put it after viewing men dipping at Brighton: "Old Neptune gets all the ladies with child—for we can hardly lay it to the men we see pulled and led about the beach here."[92] Swimmers could also be made fun of, as the writer Tobias Smollett, an avid swimmer, has happen when his protagonist Humphry Clinker enters the water at 6 a.m. The water is so cold that he "bawl[s]" when he gets his head above water. He then starts his dipping, only to discover that his servant, frightened by his cry, has jumped in after him with his clothes on. The servant pushes aside his dipper, grabs Clinker by the ear, and hauls him crying in pain onto the sand, where a large crowd has gathered in response to all the noise. Clinker can only strike his servant and stride back into the water, dress in the bathing machine, and clamber back out again. So mortifying is the episode that he has to leave Scarborough rather than remain and be the butt of stories.[93] While this is fiction, it might not be unreal.

For women, swimming was something quite rare. On one occasion, when a lady realized her dipper at Buxton Spa knew how to swim, she insisted on learning. Unfortunately, even with the aid of cork wings, she kept sinking to the bottom.[94] Then there was one Miss Talbot, who swam at Broadstairs where a crowd assembled to watch. One observer, characterizing her as the "oddest of human beings," further wrote, "I saw her swim this morning with all of Ramsgate assembled in crowds on the sands to see her. She does not mind tossing her little round body about in the least but floats and swims and kicks about like a fish." One can only wonder at the costume she wore, as the normal flannel shroud worn by women covered everything and, unless it was modified, would likely slip up over her bottom. That would really bring out the crowds. Regrettably, our witness does not mention anything about the costume. [95] There were a few intrepid swimmers such as Hester Thrale, who swam all her life and did so with friends such as Samuel Johnson, whom she invited once to Brighton because there was "fine bathing with rough breakers." Thrale was regarded as something of a "water spaniel" who would swim into old age.[96] She was a rarity; for the majority of women, a trip to a resort was just an occasion for dipping in the sea. Physical recreation was quite limited for upper-class ladies. Beyond walking, riding, and driving their own carriage—not normally done for anything other than a short drive—they had few physical outlets. The rare individuals such as Miss Talbot and Mrs. Thrale stood out and called attention to themselves.

Tanning was similarly very rare. There is an early reference to sunning at Brighton by a Rev. William Clarke, but whether that just meant being out of doors or sitting taking in the sun is hard to tell. Upper classes the world over strove not to look like bronzed peasants, so staying out of the sun had a high premium. Hats, parasols, and even masks kept the sun at bay. There were also conventions of beauty in Europe that made white, the color of purity, the standard for women. Preserving one's whiteness had multiple social and aesthetic parameters that are true in many societies today. One of the few references, other than Clarke's, to "sunning" is

FIGURE 1.4 Thomas Rowlandson, *Salt Water: The Terror of the Sea,* ca. 1800. Pen and watercolor. No. MRGMM217, Margate Museum, Kent, UK. Rowlandson never missed an opportunity to point out the prurient aspects of a scene.

from the feckless Lady Bessborough, who wrote to a relative from Brighton that she and her daughters "are all tann'd like Gipsies . . . they looked comical as they sat with ladies with their Lennox complexions, fair as driven snow, by us women of color."[97] Few among the ladies would want to look like "Gipsies" and would much prefer 'Lennox complexions." In a society that made deep distinctions based on race and color, by far the preferred skin color was white. Seawater and sea air, not the sun, were the attractions that brought people to the beach.[98]

From 1730 to 1800 the beach resort evolved and established a place in the social world of English elites. The growing prosperity of this group allowed them to spend their leisure time in this new activity. It provided them with another public outlet in a growing secular culture. As a result, fishing village after fishing village found its economy drastically changed. What had started with a literature by authors such as Floyer that saw virtue in the use of cold water had evolved into the certainties of Dr. Russell focusing on cold saltwater bathing. Every "scientific" study that followed, adducing greater and greater efficacy to seawater and air, only made for greater certainty among the public about the therapeutic value of a trip to the beach. There were many positive experiences. Mary Anstley wrote to her friend Elizabeth Montague, "I am beyond description healthy and strong, how long I may continue when I go out of my watery element again I know not, for in the sea I live at present and it agrees with me wonderfully."[99] Or as Lady Mary Coke told the king, "I have two or three little comical diseases that carry me there [Brighton] every year."[100] On a more serious note, a report from the resort at Teignmouth gave a particularly strong account: "Cripples frequently recover the use of their limbs, histerical ladies their spirits and even lepers are cleansed."[101] This would seem to be the beginning of a tradition of resort advertising. No doubt there were many poor experiences, but compared to other remedies, such as bleeding, this one was relatively pleasant even if it did not deliver the hoped-for nostrum. As for the physicians, this only increased their meager supply of medicines.

The eager searchers for therapeutic relief in the early days confronted all sorts of challenges from bad roads to miserable living conditions in unprepared villages, the exception being Scarborough. Investments ploughed in decade by decade built better inns, new hotels, and boarding houses to shelter the newcomers. Soon assembly rooms, libraries, coffee shops, shops of all kinds, and all the other pleasures of the leisured life followed to provide the activities already present at the major spas. The facilities would also make it more comfortable to bring children to the sea, and more and more mothers, or their servants, played with them on the beach. The other venues attracted another group, those seeking pleasure rather than therapy, visitors who would never go near a bathing machine but would walk, ride, sail, dance, play cards, and rarely come into contact with the sea. "These well dressed and leading people," one writer remarked, "never look at the sea. . . . Their pursuits are purely social and neither ladies nor gentlemen ever go on the beach. . . . The beach is ignored, it is almost perhaps quite vulgar."[102] The seekers after health and the "gay" crowd that sought entertainment had by 1800 created a new place of leisure that would continue to evolve.

But not everyone was pleased with the creation of these new spaces of entertainment and therapy. One who was not was John Styles, D.D., who preached in Brighton at the Union St. Chapel, a nonconformist church.[103] Styles recognized that the sea had virtues. "The medicinal powers and salutary virtues with which the Almighty hath endowed the waters of the sea," he wrote, "have converted it into a magnificent mineral bath, in which, as formerly in a Pool of Bethesda, the weak become strong and the sick whole." It was the society that gathered to appreciate it that was evil.

"The temptations of a Watering Place . . . are to be found armed with unusual power, and possessing a mysterious and almost uncontrollable agency in places which are devoted to relaxation and amusement. Fashionable watering places are not only filled with the thoughtless, the gay, and the dissipated, but in addition, to many persons of a graver character." In this atmosphere Christians were in trouble. "Few even among consistent Christians, know how to spend a month from home. A state of idleness, is, perhaps more than any other, incompatible, with a state of salvation." Fathers lost control over their families in this atmosphere. What happened then was the decline of order: "Domestic discipline is unavoidably relaxed—pleasure is the order of the day." Servants, for instance, mingled with other servants, "many of whom are deeply versed in the science of iniquity, and soon become insubordinate and vicious." The young were similarly at risk, no more so than from their reading material. "By far the greater part of novels are decisively marked with characters of evil, containing nothing but factious and erroneous views of life . . . Those that display the greatest powers of intellect, are generally the most dangerous vehicles of licentious and depraved sentiment," and reading them "may lay the foundations for an utter depravation of character." And what was the cure for this? "Permit me to recommend to you, the fear of God as supplying the best means of counteracting their influence." Unhappily, he observed, religion "languishes, seldom rising to a character of vigor and intensity, and is too much confined to those of middle age and the poor." Many of his auditors may have nodded in agreement, but the Reverend Styles was preaching a losing game in Brighton and any of the other fashionable resorts. Like Seneca at Baiae, he probably left Brighton to protect his virtue as soon as he could.

The Rise of the Resorts

Year by year through the middle decades of the eighteenth century, visitors to the resorts grew in number, and the resorts responded by adding all the expected amenities. Inns evolved into hotels, boarding houses boomed, villas by the sea dotted the coast, and entertainment facilities flourished. While all resorts shared these characteristics, they did develop distinctive reputations. This was mostly caused by their physical location and the visitors they attracted. Discussing a few of them will reveal their disparate personalities. At the same time as English resorts evolved and matured, they attracted attention elsewhere, so that soon enough resorts dotted the coast of northern Europe. What would become the worldwide expansion of the beach resort was underway.

Scarborough sits in the far north of England facing out into the North Sea. It was one of the first places to develop as a sea bathing resort, as it was already a spa or "spaw" with a well-known mineral spring. Discovered in the early seventeenth century by a Mrs. Farrow, the spring had two flows, one cathartic and the other diuretic. In 1660, when Robert Wittie published *Scarborough Spaw*, he claimed that minerals in the spring water opened up the secret passages of the body and cleared obstructions which caused disease.[1] His pamphlet might have gone with little notice, but instead it ignited a controversy as his opponents claimed that he was "no great chemist." This fierce little pamphlet controversy attracted attention to the spring.[2] Squabbling over the virtues of the spa water illustrates just how seriously mineral baths were taken and point out just how easy it was for salt water to get away with all the claims made for it. With an increasingly famous medicinal spring, the city fathers licensed it and farmed it out. Soon enough there were two buildings just back from the beach as the springs bubbled up at the edge of the cliff. The water was bottled and sent as far as London; such was its fame as a therapeutic wonder.

By the early 1730s, a new element had been added to the therapeutic regime as people started going into the sea, for if cold water was good for you, there was an abundance of it in the North Sea. Sarah, the Duchess of Marlborough, visited in 1732 after reading Wittie's account of the spring water. She hoped to affect a cure or at least get relief from gout and scurvy. She hated the "dirty" spa facilities, especially the public toilet for ladies, and so spent a great deal of time in her rooms, where she drank bottled water. While she did not go into the sea, she reported that the Duchess of Manchester did.[3] Lord Chesterfield, visiting a year later, reported that the ladies seeking a cure were "innumerable" and that "bathing in the sea is become a general practice of both sexes."[4]

Perhaps because of its northern location, Scarborough was more conservative in social matters, and so for women there were issues of decorum that might not be found in London. William Hutton describes how he and his daughter took up residence in a boarding house where four ladies from Sheffield and two from Halifax arrived at the same time, and how he suddenly found himself "squire" of seven women, for they had to "accept me or have no attendance" at social events and in some public places.[5] Resorts might have looser rules, but not enough to permit women to escape proper decorum. A woman could do nothing of importance without a male escort. An anonymous reporter who visited in 1733 faithfully visited the spa, where he liked the effect of the water as it was good for his stomach. He also reported that both men and women went into the sea. Gentlemen were rowed out into the bay a little way in a small boat and then jumped in naked. The ladies repaired to two small houses that sat on the beach, where they changed into loose gowns and went into the water with a guide.[6] Scarborough did have a splendid beach at low tide, when it was a wide, flat, two-mile-long, hard-packed sand surface. During low tide a cavalcade of horses and coaches paraded up and down the beach. This scene of bathing and parading was recorded in a remarkable print by John Stettering-ton, who depicted the whole long seaside of Scarborough. At the southern end of the scene the spa, coaches, riders, and bathers are all recorded, representing the earliest depiction of a beach resort.

FIGURE 2.1 Detail, J. Harris, *Perspective Drawing of Scarborough by John Setterington*, 1735. Engraving on paper. Historic England Archive, Swindon, UK. This is the earliest image capturing casual visitors on horseback and in carriages, while women use bathing machines and men go into the water nude from small boats away from the beach.

Scarborough had the usual assembly room for tea, meals, dancing, gambling, billiards, and a theater for as many types of entertaining events as the proprietor could manage to attract. In addition, there was a library/bookstore, shops of various kinds, and a coffeehouse for coffee and newspapers. The resort attracted the nobility and the gentry of the north of England and Scotland, with the occasional traveler from the South such as the Duchess of Marlborough, plus the top tier of businessmen from the north along with their families. From the beginning, the attention was always on the elite who chose to visit, as they set the tone of the resort. It was common to write in one's letter home, or in a travel diary, a list of the "Quality."[7] So as elsewhere, Scarborough needed a master of ceremonies to manage social events. In the 1730s it was Mr. Vipont, from Hampstead, who ran the assembly room and adjacent restaurant, where he proudly noted that the cooks were from London.[8]

By 1803 a visitor noted there were forty bathing machines and that bathing was more popular than taking spa water. He had come to Scarborough seeking a cure for his ailing daughter. After a stay of eleven weeks, during which his daughter bathed every other day in the sea, drank spa water, and rode a horse daily, she was much improved. No wonder, after her indulgent father gave her such a prolonged holiday.[9] Scarborough remained the resort of choice for the gentry of the North. In the South, the warmer South, rival centers for sea bathing were arriving on the scene.

Margate, Ramsgate, and Broadstairs were a group of small towns on the eastern coast of Kent. Margate was at the far end of the Thames estuary, and the two other towns faced out into the North Sea or, as it was known then, the German Sea. All three were close to one another, and there was frequent traffic between them. Margate and Ramsgate had established fishing fleets and harbors for trade, but their fishing fleets were in decline. As ports, they had piers that not only protected shipping at anchor but became favorite places to stroll out into the harbor, something not every resort could boast. In time the acquisition of a pier, however nonfunctional, came to be a priority for the resorts. Just off shore, the constant panoply of ships heading for London paraded before the towns; the Royal Navy often anchored at the nearby Downs, ready to raise sail and go down the Channel. Sailing out to visit the warships was a favorite entertainment for a day. While geographically close, the three towns developed different personalities. Broadstairs, the most tranquil, was regarded as a place for families and in time would be identified as the resort for upper classes. But as one visitor put it, "The English Reserve is fully expressed." Those seeking livelier times moved on quickly.[10]

For a really good time, Margate was best. You could get there from London by coach by way of Canterbury, in a thirteen- to fourteen-hour trip at the cost of twenty-one shillings. Of course, if you had your own coach, the cost was not a worry. The alternatives were in the Thames River hoys, available to those making the trip down the river from London. These vessels were sixty- to one-hundred-ton freighters that plied the Thames carrying grain to London and returning with a variety of commodities, including coal and timber. As Margate developed, they were turned into passenger ships. The trip to Margate took about ten hours and cost about five shillings, but the return could take a nightmarish thirty-six hours with contrary winds.[11] Many a passenger was introduced to the rigors of seasickness coming and going, although some physicians thought that a good purgation brought on by rough seas could be beneficial. Those who lived through the experience seriously considered going by coach the next time. On arrival, they were subject to the crowds who came out onto the pier to see the bedraggled survivors of the journey. But until the coming of the railway, the hoy was much frequented as the least expensive way to get to Margate, and it was often used as a cheap way to send the servants back to London rather than by coach.[12] Once there, it was easy to transfer to Ramsgate or Broadstairs by road.

As early as the 1730s, it appears that Margate was attracting visitors who put up with the old houses of a declining fishing community. The few inns expanded to add more rooms and please more people. In 1769 a consortium created Cecil Square, a sure sign of Georgian urban expansion, and shortly thereafter Sir Henry Hawley created Hawley Square.[13] As these facilities attracted elites, a Mr. Le Page was brought in as master of ceremonies. He played the same role at Broadstairs and Ramsgate when they needed help in organizing balls.[14] At the same time, boarding houses were built in the older part of town for those of lesser means. So for the visitor the town had two parts, the older, shabbier original town attracting those with a budget and the new squares with fancy quarters for elites. With the new buildings came shops, libraries, a large theater, an assembly room with space for cards and tea, coffeehouses—in other words, all the facilities that marked a first-rate spa and certainly made it more fashionable than Ramsgate and Broadstairs, whose visitors traveled to Margate to partake of the delights. One such delight was the famous *Dandelion*, a former manor house about one-and-a-half miles from Margate that offered meals in private booths or at long tables. A raised dais created a place for dancing, accompanied by a band that played for the crowds, which could number as many as seven hundred. It did not operate every day, but on the days it did it was a significant attraction that mixed different social groups.[15] During July and August, the height of the season, country walks and drives, boating expeditions, visits to the library for books and in the evenings to participate in the nightly raffles, entertainment at the theater and musical events, plus formal social events such as balls all provided a round of activities for those who came to the beach for the social life and the therapy of salt water.

As for the bathing, Margate had a splendid beach that was long, flat, and good for bathing. One difference from nearly all the other resorts was a set of bathing rooms that sat above the beach in the old town. In the morning the visitor arrived and arranged his or her place on the schedule on a first-come, first-served basis. In relative comfort you could visit with your fellow bathers, read the newspapers, drink sea water or coffee, and when your turn came you could change and then descend the steep stairs to get to the beach and enter the bathing machine. For women there was the additional comfort of having a bathing machine with a hood, originally invented in Margate. One of the problems with a broad flat beach was that when the tide was out the trip to the edge of the sea could take time, and so the wait for a machine could be quite long and required patience and dedication to good health. On returning you had to go back up the stairs. One service they could offer for ladies was taking in their bathing costume and having it dry by their next visit.[16]

The combination of inexpensive lodging with cheap transportation also meant that people of lesser means could get to Margate, which caused it to develop the reputation of mixing different social groups, something that was attractive to some but not to all. This was one of the features of Margate much commented on. It had a more diverse population during the season, from June to October, enabling social mixing. As one visitor put it, there was much "fashionable company," and it was "agreeable to see different ranks partaking of the amusement."[17] To another, it seemed that "the very rich and very poor are equally indecent and vulgar and are only differently dressed."[18] Some snobs could not abide the social mixing. As one of them reported, "Yet after all I doubt whether there be a more detestable spot on any part of the inhabited globe."[19] Early on, Margate became known as "Margate the Merry." It was certainly larger, with more facilities than the other nearby resorts, but as it attracted a diverse group from London, among them prostitutes, there was always a sexual edge to the resort. Cartoons of the era stress this aspect of local culture, although it may have existed more around the old town than around the newer squares that had fancy facilities for the well-off and the "votaries of pleasure."[20] After it had built up its facilities, paved its streets, and installed better lighting, another group was noted: young mothers and their children playing on the beach became a prominent group.[21]

Ramsgate had some of the attributes of Margate in that it had a pier that was good for strolling and a fine beach for bathing. As it developed, it sported paved streets and good lighting, a library, and a fine assembly room looking out into the bay.[22] One commentator noted that "many genteel families come to this town for bathing," and it was not as "gay and fashionable" as Margate.[23] Thus Ramsgate, while not as quiet as Broadstairs, acted as something of a suburb of Margate.

Nothing recommended a beach resort more than royal patronage. Indeed, it was also a recommendation for the practice of seawater bathing, and more so when it was the king himself who was the patient. George III's delicate health was well known and, like many others, he sought the benefits of the sea. While his family colonized Brighton, he could not go there because he did not approve of their conduct, especially that of his son George, Prince of Wales. The prince did not approve of his father either, so the king sought relief at Weymouth. Weymouth was yet another fishing village and trading port with a small harbor carved out by the river Wey. The headland known as the Isle of Portland looms over the west end of the harbor, and beyond it lies the eleven-mile-long Chesil Beach. Stretching out on either side of the bay is the Jurassic Coast famous for the fossils exposed along the cliffs. In front of the town is a very pleasant low-lying beach. A Dr. Crane, resident at the resort, noted, "The sea water of this fine Bay is quite pure, of a beautiful color and perfectly clear and transparent . . . the sands soft yet firm."[24] The Duke of Gloucester, the king's brother, tried it out first in 1780, and then returned to build Gloucester House.[25] The king made his first visit in 1789 and visited a total of fourteen times. Getting to Weymouth was a five-day trip from London, and for the royal family this was an opportunity to see and be seen by the people. Fanny Burney, who accompanied the royal party on the king's first visit, recorded crowds in every town and village, dressed in local costumes, singing the national anthem. The king even had to dine in front of an open window to show himself to his people. Burney recorded the first royal dip when the king, accompanied by dippers wearing "God Save the King" on their bonnets, was treated to the anthem "God Save the King" by a group of fiddlers in an accompanying bathing machine. Burney reported that "the king bathes with great success."[26] As with all good patients, the king was accompanied by his doctor, who monitored his progress.

The royal family, like other visitors, had the problem of filling the remainder of their days. Just back from the beach was an esplanade that was thirty feet wide and a mile long when it was completed, and the royal family strolled there in good weather to the delight of the other visitors. They attended the theater, where Mrs. Sarah Siddons, the most celebrated actress of the day, who was also on holiday, performed for the royal family. At balls they played matchmaker, finding appropriate dance partners for the daughters of friends. On Sunday they went to the assembly room to hold a rustic levy, where the people attending created a circle and the king and queen went around separately greeting those in attendance.[27] Needless to say, these were carefully orchestrated, and while the king was often to be seen it was also true that two naval frigates were anchored offshore and a contingent of troops camped nearby providing protection.[28] The royal presence always enhanced a resort, even when the family was not there. Simply that the monarch was a

FIGURE 2.2 John Nixon, *Royal Dipping*, 1789. Etching. Published by: William Holland. © The Trustees of the British Museum, London. Obviously not a life drawing but a satirical image capturing all the awkwardness of King George's dip.

visitor brought other tourists, and Weymouth grew accordingly. The town developed a long line of Georgian-style buildings, including a hotel. Weymouth remained discreet and solid as the number of visitors grew, all the while retaining a harbor for fishing and trade, but in the end tourism would dominate the economy.

Weymouth might have the king, but Brighton had the prince regent, and it became the most famous of the early resorts. Directly south of London, it had proximity to a larger population of the upper classes than did any other resort. In the early days there were obstacles to be overcome. Road conditions were frequently terrible, and there were problems of armed and dangerous men. It was a two-day journey in good weather and near impossible in winter.[29] When finally Brighton was reached, it was not much more than a fishing village suffering from hard times. The town faced out into the English Channel, but without a flanking headland to break the winds, any storm coming up the channel roared into Brighton. The South Downs, just to the north, guarded the town from the cold northern winds, and from the top of the Downs there was a view of the English Channel. The beach was not the greatest, in that it had lots of cobbles mixed up with sand. At its height, the fishing fleet had about one hundred boats, and the fishermen dragged their boats up onto the beach and sold their catch right there. Some of it went to local inland towns, with the better fish going to London, and as the roads improved this became more common. The town green, the Steyne, a large open space, was where the fishermen dried their nets, and, because of its place in the center of things, it would soon be put to other uses.

From this small fishing village, Brighton would grow. By 1780 there were roughly six hundred houses ready to receive visitors. There were also two inns, the Castle and the Old Ship. Both were owned by men who had a flair for development, and each of them was transformed from an old-fashioned inn into a facility with an assembly room, dining rooms, coffee and tea rooms, and card rooms. In other words, the inns absorbed all the roles of the assembly room. Each featured meals, balls, and gambling to attract the growing number of visitors. This is a good example of how local entrepreneurship created the facilities at resorts.[30]

Brighton developed at just about the same time as Scarborough. As noted before, in July 1736 the Reverend William Clarke wrote an enthusiastic letter to a friend: "We are now sunning ourselves upon the beach at Brighthelmstone. . . . My morning business is bathing in the sea, and then buying fish; the evening is for riding out for air . . . and counting ships in the road, and the boats that are trawling."[31] Clark was an early pioneer. His schedule of activities, with the exception of sunning, would be familiar to the many visitors who crowded into the resort in the future. As previously noted, the individual credited with transforming Brighthelmstone, the sleepy little fishing village, into Brighton the resort is Dr. Richard Russell. To gain an advantage for his new cures, Russell moved to Brighton in 1753 and built an imposing house that he occupied during the summer months with his family and some of his patients. Many other physicians would follow his example.

Besides the good Dr. Russell, Brighton had many other advantages over other resorts. Early on Brighton attracted royals and other distinguished guests, no doubt because of its proximity to London and the court. The Duke of Gloucester, the king's brother, first visited in 1765. His other brother the Duke of Cumberland visited in 1771, the same year that the Duke of Marlborough (no relation) bought a house and set up a lavish household. From the literary world Samuel Johnson, Edward Gibbon, Hester Thrale, and Fanny Burney visited regularly, but the most famous visitor was George, the Prince of Wales. If Russell created the sea bathing resort, the prince made it a place to have fun. He first visited in 1783 in the company of his uncle, the Duke of Cumberland. The prince was a mixed character. Given a first-rate education by the best tutors, he spoke multiple languages, knew his music and art, and was a good conversationalist. While his parents sought to give him the attributes of a prince, he worked hard at developing the attributes of a playboy who lived a fast life. His associates were some of the great characters of his time—his uncles Gloucester and Cumberland, Georgianna, Duchess of Devonshire, and Charles James Fox were all well known for hard living. Since the prince was never given a job, he had lots of time on his hands with which to indulge himself in ways that drove his parents to distraction. He had an eye for the ladies that led him into many a relationship, he spent money in a way that drunken sailors would envy, and he lavished a fortune in creating a splendid palace at Carlton House, all of this detested by his father. His circle of friends and hangers-on were a combination of the most fashionable of the "ton" of London and the most raffish characters. His life was a blur of hard living inside a cocoon of elegance.[32]

The prince may have come to Brighton for health reasons, but he soon made it into a home away from home. Its attraction was obvious: close to London, especially as he loved to drive the new lightweight carriages, it had a horse racing season, and it could be transformed into another elegant center, different from the many country houses he had access to. Out of this would grow—slowly—the oriental fantasy that was the Brighton Pavilion. Notable, from then to now, as an outstanding architectural creation, the pavilion was a unique example of beach architecture and an inspiration to those who wanted to build a fantasy by the sea.[33] This was the setting for his many entertainments that brought the ton to Brighton in hopes of getting an invitation. Dinners, balls, and concerts followed one another and, while some thought them "boring," nonetheless an invitation from the prince could make your trip to Brighton. One concession in Brighton was that the ladies did not always need elaborate court dress, but still, if you were being entertained by the prince, you needed to dress up. One lady complained that another had brought nine new dresses as opposed to everyone else's six.[34]

The prince brought with him his penchant for the ladies, and it was in Brighton that he pursued Mrs. Fitzherbert. They were both frequent visitors, and Brighton gave them the latitude they did not have in London, though the prince also courted her there. She had a house on the Steyne across from the pavilion, and the two of them strolled on the Steyne, the grassy center of town, as did many visitors, as a morning stroll on the Steyne and a visit to the libraries and stores nearby could fill a morning. His infatuation with her led him to insist that they get married even

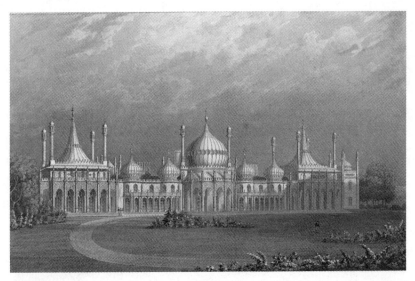

FIGURE 2.3 John Nash, *Views of the Royal Pavilion, Brighton, 1826.* The Huntington Library, San Marino, CA. The Prince Regent's fabulous palace away from home. Still a remarkable building today.

though the law denied him the right, as the future king, to marry a lady who was twice widowed and, more importantly, was a good Catholic. Ignoring all this, the two of them were married in a ceremony that flouted law and social practice. None of the usual actions accompanying a proper wedding, such as posting the bans and holding the service in an Anglican church, were followed. It was held in Mrs. Fitzherbert's house. While not exactly a secret to his friends, it was never publicized. Needless to say, when his father found out about it he was outraged. Legislation passed as recently as 1772 had stated that no descendant of George II could marry without the monarch's consent; however George III's brothers, the Dukes of Cumberland and Gloucester, and his son the Duke of Sussex, had violated the law, and their marriages were tolerated.[35] The difference with the prince was that he was the future monarch and, as such, the future head of the Anglican Church. The fact remained that the prince needed to marry properly and produce heirs, a necessity that was finally forced upon him. The whole episode with Mrs. Fitzherbert was simply overlooked, and the prince finally married Princess Caroline of Brunswick. Mrs. Fitzherbert went through life believing that she was married to George, who in any event continued to see her, among a number of other

FIGURE 2.4 George Cruikshank, *Beauties of Brighton,* March 1, 1826. Etching with hand coloring, plate: $9\frac{13}{16} \times 13\frac{13}{16}$ in., sheet: $11\frac{7}{8} \times 17\frac{1}{2}$ in. Courtesy of UCLA Grunwald Center of the Graphic Arts, Hammer Museum, Los Angeles, Richard Vogler Cruikshank Collection. An early example of the satirical possibilities in depicting beach society.

ladies, once he was married. With the prince as its chief citizen, Brighton acquired a bawdy reputation.

Adding to this reputation were not just the ton but the 10th Hussars, the prince's regiment, which was stationed with the militia who were guarding the coast during the long wars with France. The Hussars' officers were mostly young aristocrats who could afford the uniforms, horses, gambling, and mistresses that came with being an officer. Lord Worcester, for instance, took Harriette Wilson, the famous courtesan, with him to Brighton, and she, in turn, had eyes for a "beautiful" young Hussar much sought after by great ladies.[36] Even Beau Brummel spent time in the regiment, but gaudy uniforms were not for him, and he would serve briefly before returning to civilian life and the world of fashion.[37] While they were in town, the military added to Brighton's reputation for aristocratic hell-raising. When they were absent, the ladies had to make do as best they could. Fanny Burney attended the last ball of the season, and the many ladies needed partners, so some of the women came in riding habits. As Burney put it "They made admirable men." "'Tis tonnish to be so much undressed at the last ball."[38]

For all of its glamour, Brighton was not to all tastes. The very nature of high living with the ton was enough to turn some visitors away; one well-born lady remarked that it was just "great staring, bustling, unsocial Brighton . . . where Judas must have survived."[39] Lord Torington described it as a "fashionable, unhappy bustle, with such a harpy set of painted harlots as bad as Bond Street at 3pm." One estimate has it that there were 325 prostitutes during the season, so Torington had a point.[40] Lady Hilton went with the intent to bathe all of October, but did not look forward to being with the "fine folks" and wanted to see no one, as "dissipation out of London has something particularly disagreeable about it." So she settled in to live the quiet life away from the center of town.[41] John Constable, the artist, a frequent visitor who hoped to cure his ailing wife, wrote, "Brighton is the receptacle of the fashion and offscouring of London. . . . The beach is only Picadilly by the sea side. Ladies dressed and undressed— gentlemen in morning gowns and slippers . . . footmen—children— nursery maids, dogs, boys, fishermen, and those hideous amphibious animals the old bathing women—all mixed together in endless and indecent confusion."[42] Often like-minded visitors would move on to Weymouth or Broadstairs, places known to be staid and quiet.

If Brighton and Weymouth enjoyed royal patronage and became famous as a result of attracting high society, Blackpool emerged as much more of a people's beach. The Lancashire coast had for a long time been the site of popular bathing. It had a tradition of bringing groups of workers and artisans from the towns of the midlands to take the plunge in the sea, which they regarded as having a special "physic."[43] Folk wisdom, not scientific treatises, brought them to enjoy a few days of drinking salt water, splashing in the sea, and enjoying the sea air. Men and women gathered in groups to walk or ride in wagons to get to the beach, where they slept five or six to a bed so that they could enjoy a few days of frolicking in the sea. As one decorous reporter noted, among clusters of visitors there was "a suspension of every feeling of dignity or decorum." He urged them to wear "breeches or petticoats" as they were absolutely necessary.[44] Another reported that it was the "custom of lower class people, of both sexes," from the manufacturing district to make an annual visit "to wash away the collected stains and impurities of the year . . . covering the beach with their promiscuous numbers and not much embarrassing themselves about appearances . . . It is not to be wished that the rigid notions of delicacy should interfere with this only mode which the poor have of enjoying it."[45] Samuel Taylor Coleridge witnessed similar scenes in 1794 at Abergeley in northern

Wales. He wrote to a friend, "Walking on the sea sands, I was surprised to see a number of fine women bathing promiscuously with men and boys—perfectly naked! Doubtless the citadels of their chastity are so impregnably strong, that they need not the ornamental outworks of modesty . . . Concealment sets the imagination a working, and, as it were, cantharidizes our desires."[46] He and the others were observing the beach habits of ancient custom. These traditions lingered in the Northwest without comment until middle-class observers started to wander along the coast to capture the landscape that formerly was more often than not neglected in favor of the vales and valleys of familiar England. Here they confronted the rugged coast and moody sea and the obviously unfamiliar sight of naked bodies. The latter shocked them the most. As upper-class and middle-class visitors became common, their ideas regarding decorum became dominant, but until the early nineteenth century local people practiced their old beach habits of bathing in mixed groups.

Blackpool became the resort of the Lancashire coast. It boasted a long, flat, sandy beach. Few people lived there, as the extensive beach discouraged fishermen whose boats had to be hauled considerable distances. It was much easier to use the rivers Wye to the north and the Ribble to the south as a means of entering or leaving the sea. Fifty cottages dotted the beachfront when the first visitors started to pay notice. Visitors also had to find their way along poor roads from Preston and Manchester. By about 1790, only four hundred visitors were counted at the height of the season.[47] Inevitably, the attractions of the extensive beach brought higher status groups. They traveled by coach and horseback and found accommodations in four boarding houses that were not of the highest standard, but then there were few if any aristocrats among them. Nonetheless, the long, flat beach allowed them to parade on their horses when the tide was out. There was also a two-hundred-yard-long parade or esplanade for walking by the beach.[48] In time, bathing machines made their appearance, but in a change from practice elsewhere, there were male guides for the women as the sea was considered too rough when at high tide.[49]

Until about 1800, Blackpool remained undeveloped. Entertainment was limited, there was not even a church or wandering Methodist minister, but by 1788 there was a coffeehouse and a place to read newspapers. In the meantime, each boarding house organized its own singing and country dancing under a "president" chosen by the visitors. Otherwise it was cards, sailing, walking, and amateur theater in a local barn.[50]

Out of this developed the Blackpool that became a world-famous resort that outrivaled all but Brighton among the resorts created in this era.

. . .

By 1800 bathing resorts were well established in England, and knowledge of the new therapeutic regime had percolated to the Continent. As the literature on the new "science" of ocean bathing spread out, visitors to England went out of their way to experience resort life and to carry the news home. Georg-Christoph Lichtenberg, a noted anglophile and scientist, visited Margate and Deal and took this experience back home, where he was involved in the creation of a resort at Cuxhaven on the North Sea.[51] There were also the peripatetic English who, in their travels, went into the sea when the urge arose, often to the amazement of the locals. Tobias Smollett, an asthmatic convinced of the efficacy of sea bathing, swam in 1763 in Boulogne and in 1764 at Nice, seeking and finding relief. So, through a variety of means knowledge of beach resorts and the new medical phenomenon traveled far and wide. Some time passed, however, before resorts came into being. Not every area was as prosperous as England with its large elite ready to enjoy leisure. Also, there were the upheavals caused by the French Revolution and the Napoleonic wars, which spread devastation and disrupted economies. Elites, the chief advocates for resorts, had many other calls on their resources, so few initiatives were undertaken. Nonetheless, slowly but surely, new resorts appeared along with the new therapeutic regime in a variety of places.

Spas were familiar throughout Europe. There was a long tradition of seeking therapeutic relief or the promise of a cure by going to a local or distant spa. In Belgium it was the eponymous Spa, and in the German states, it was Baden Baden and Wiesbaden, both known to the Romans who had developed extensive facilities at these warm springs.[52] In France there were the spas at Evian les Bains, Dax, and Aix les Bains, and in Hungary, Budapest. And while spas declined somewhat in the seventeenth century, they had been brought back by aristocratic patronage during the eighteenth prior to a boom in other creations such as Bad Homburg and Marienbad in the nineteenth century.

Growing acceptance of the baths may have, as it did in England, made it easy to accept the new therapy of cold salt water. By the 1750s it was being discussed in medical circles.[53] Among the first treatises to appear was that of Hughes Maret, in 1769.[54] Noted physicians such as Samuel Gottlieb Vogel and scientists such as Georg-Christoph Lichtenberg wrote and spoke

FIGURE 2.5 *Heiligendamm um 1841 Salon und Badehaus.* The History Collection / Alamy Stock Photo. One of the earliest German beach resorts.

about the new therapies, as did a number of other scholars who published in the late eighteenth century.[55] More often than not, the development of beaches in the German principalities was pushed by physicians operating much as Russell had done at Brighton, but with a significant difference in that a local magnate was the chief sponsor.[56] In almost every instance the noble granted permission or actually invested in the new resort.

The North German principalities faced out onto the Baltic and the North Sea, and these were the obvious sites for beach resorts. That was just as well, as the spas were located mostly in the Southwest and middle of Germany. A new therapeutic regime focused on salt water was one that could find new patients in the northern states. Strung along the southern edge of the North Sea in the Wadden Sea is a group of islands stretching from the Netherlands to the Danish coast. These are the West and East Frisian islands. Over millennia, currents have pushed sand from west to east and built up a string of sand banks that slowly became islands. Not suited to agriculture, except some animal grazing, the human population remained small and survived by exploiting the abundant fisheries. Similarly, at the western end of the Baltic Sea, as the currents turned and moved north along the east coast of Denmark, beaches and islands formed. It was here, on the Baltic, that the first German resorts appeared. All that was needed was an aristocratic patron and an ambitious physician ready to take his patient to experience the saltwater cure.

Finally, in 1793, Samuel Gottlieb Vogel convinced Friedrich Frances I, Grand Duke of Mechlenburg, to go to the beach at Heilegendamm near Rostock on Mecklenburg Bay.[57] A revived, and ambitious, grand duke immediately saw the benefits of a resort on this lovely wooded section of coast and set about creating a resort to cater to aristocratic tastes. One visitor noted that, in season, the resort was crowded with crowned heads and that during his visit he sat with a reigning sovereign for the first time.[58] Buildings in a neoclassical style soon graced the site, and Vogel was there ready to offer advice to the health seekers, but as in England the resort also reached out to those who only sought a pleasurable break from routine. By 1823 a race track, the first in Europe, with a casino to follow, signaled the commitment to pleasure besides therapy. Heilegendamm flourished and become better known in the future as Doberan and would still be elegant enough to serve as the site of a Group of Eight meeting in 2007.[59] By 1802 Travemunde, uniquely a fishing village, offered patients an alternative site on the Baltic. The glistening beaches of East Frisian Islands beckoned, and in 1797 Dr. Friedrich van Halem opened the first bathing establishment in the North Sea on the island of Nordernay, which was quickly followed by Wangerooge in the Duchy of Oldenburg.[60] However, as quickly as the new resorts emerged, development was brought to a halt.

First came the war that dominated the 1790s as the forces of the French Revolution moved against royal governments on the eastern borders of France. Then came Napoleon, who waged aggressive and successful campaigns against the other European powers, leading to massive disruptions of borders and economies. He also displaced royal and noble families as he gave his family members and generals kingdoms and ducal estates, replacing the old elites. These families thus found themselves in exile without the resources of their estates until Napoleon's final defeat in 1815. The Congress of Vienna, tasked with bringing about peace, mixed diplomacy and leisure activities in equal measure, while establishing a new European order. With the peace, nobles and royalty could return to their estates and reestablish their finances and indulge themselves in all the leisure activities that war had deprived them of. As the war approached its end, Nordeney reopened and by 1819 had a Royal Institute of Seabathing, one assumes to advance the new science of thalassotherapy (treatment of disease by sea bathing), which it still practices today. Almost immediately new resorts were developed: on the Baltic, Rugenvald (1815), Putbus (1816), Sopot (1821), Graal-Muritz (1819), and Swinemunde (1819); and on the North Sea, Cuxhaven (1816), Wyk (1819), and Helgoland (1826). Many of these resorts had royal sponsorship. For instance, Prince Malte of Putbus was responsible for Putbus on the island of Rugen, and the King of Prussia sponsored Swinemunde. A combination of noble and nonnoble investment slowly built the facilities that would change the new resorts from rather primitive camps for the determined patient to resorts with hotels and villas that catered to patients and to frivolous visitors. Early on, almost every one of them had a casino or Kurhaus which featured gambling and also provided many of the same facilities as the assembly rooms in England.[61]

A slightly different development came to Scheveningen, the most famous beach in the Netherlands. It was only two miles away from the Hague, home of the royal court and the government. The beach had a large fishing community, which added a colorful note, with women in costumes and the fishermen spending a great deal of time pulling their boats up onto the shore and then returning them to the sea before hauling up their red sails and proceeding out to fish. On return they sold their catch on the beach. The long and broad sandy beach lured horseback riders and coaches out at low tide to take the air.[62] A final aspect of the spectacle were the naval ships that rushed in to deliver messages and diplomats to the government. Visitors could enjoy the colorful scene and purchase fish. Only a few came to bathe. They were considered quite a scene by the fisherfolk, so they tended to wander up the beach to get privacy. Thus, while Scheveningen was well known, it was not developed for bathing until 1818, when Jacob Pronk built a wooden building in which people could change. A hotel followed in 1828, as the beach was slowly changed into a resort.[63] Further along the coast at Zandvoort, another long flat beach attracted bathers, so that by 1828 a Groot Badhuis (great bathhouse) was constructed for their convenience. The West Frisian islands off the Dutch coast were every bit as attractive as those to the east, but it would be some time before the Dutch developed them for bathing.

The North Sea coast of Belgium is short, only forty-two miles long compared to its neighbors, but nice and sandy nonetheless. An English bather, William Hesketh, part of the bathing diaspora from England, went to the coast near Ostende in 1783 and brought with him a bathing machine. Bathers started to use the beach during the '80s, but as elsewhere in Europe the wars stopped development. Belgium, as part of the Netherlands, suffered a great deal during the conflicts, and under Napoleon it was dismembered, so Hesketh's enterprise came to little. It was not until Belgium was created as a monarchy and Leopold I in 1831 came to the throne that things changed. He and his family rather liked Ostende beach and so, after 1834, he furthered the building of the resort, as did his successor Leopold II.[64] While Ostende was the first, now thirteen resorts dot the coast.

France developed in a different fashion. France had three coasts with beaches, each of which had different characteristics. The English Channel beaches, sharing the same water as the English south coast beaches, were attractive to English tourists. The beaches of Brittany were smaller and, as they faced the Atlantic, were battered by the stormy North Atlantic and so developed late. Brittany was also difficult to get to, and so the Channel beaches were always more popular. South of the Garonne, on the Atlantic coast, the beaches were longer and would be attractive in time. Before they were developed, the Mediterranean beaches beckoned to many with good terrain and a much warmer climate. Most of these beaches were in the territory of the Kingdom of Savoy, and not France, and when they became attractive it was to people from the North who were seeking out a relief from winter weather. The beaches were not the best, but then there was the warm winter climate.

It was in the Channel that French resorts would first originate. As noted earlier, in 1578 Henry III was sent to Dieppe to bathe in hopes of curing a skin disease. Facilities were at a minimum, so sufferers such as Henry were attached to a rope and then tossed into the sea. A cure, hopefully, was affected. Seawater in France had the reputation, in traditional medicine, of curing rabies, so people and dogs were tossed into the sea in hopes of a cure. As one female sufferer recounted, "How strange to be thrown totally nude into the ocean."[65] There must have been sufficient cures of all kinds, as Dieppe continued to get visitors until finally, in 1778, a "House of Health" was built to help bathers. As elsewhere, revolution and war slowed development, although in 1806 the Comtess de Boigne, who had experience in England, tested the waters at home. She had to acquire a horse-drawn covered carriage with a driver and two attendants to get her into the sea. As this was still a novelty, a large crowd gathered, curious to know if the nice lady had been bitten by a dog, so the old tales regarding disease lingered on. She remarked, "One did not know the inhabitants of the seaside had such a fear."[66] One of the other visitors to Dieppe's rough facilities was Queen Hortense of the Netherlands. In 1813, she exited a tent in a chocolate-colored outfit, whereupon two sailors with white gloves dipped her in the ocean. The large crowd gave a cheer when she was finished.[67]

The facilities to this date had been barely adequate, so the Prefect of Dieppe, Comte de Brancas, built a pavilion for bathers, but the person who really put Dieppe on the map for bathing was Caroline, Duchesse de Berry. A committed bather, she inaugurated the season every year, beginning in 1824, with an official dipping. The mayor and a physician

FIGURE 2.6 Eugene Isabey, *Beach in Granville*, 1863. Oil on canvas. Isabey captures a small resort on a very windy day.

accompanied her to the water's edge, where a crowd was gathered, and as she stepped forward a cannon signaled the beginning of the season. Her *baigneur*, Louis Courseaux, took over to dip her in the incoming waves. An elegant, aristocratic lady, she wore a long, dark wool shift, wool trousers, a waxed taffeta cap, and boots. While she was regarded as a beauty, one of her ladies had to admit that on coming out of the water a fashionable woman was turned into a "monstrosity as she emerged from the water enveloped in clinging, sagging wool."[68] Such a sight kept many women on the beach fully clothed. Identified with a noble family, and within the orbit of Paris, Dieppe had a cachet that it would keep for some time as the bathing spot of choice on the Channel.

In the Mediterranean it was not France, but Savoy, that was invaded by the English in search of a new therapeutic center. Savoy was part of the Kingdom of Sardinia and was often allied with Britain during the many wars of the eighteenth century. Army officers and Grand Tourists passing through the kingdom, such as Lord and Lady Cavendish and Joshua Reynolds, the artist, made the side trip to Nice.[69] Nice was never easy to get to as it was at the foot of the Maritime Alps, which plunge into the sea leaving little room for roads and farming. When intrepid travelers did arrive, they found a small town built on the Paillon River.

While the beach was steep and not very pleasant, the real attraction in Nice was the balmy winter weather, as the town was protected from north winds and was, as a result, sunny and pleasant. Tobias Smollett reached Nice during his travels in 1764 and stayed to enjoy the climate. As he did nearly everywhere he went, Smollett went swimming from a tent on the beach, a sight that always brought out the locals who packed fishing boats to get a good view.[70] After Smollett published his experiences in France and Italy, other tourists slowly invaded Nice, including the Dukes of Gloucester and York and the Duchess of Devonshire.[71] Most of them stayed in local villas as there were no hotels as yet, and they were there in the winter. When Lord and Lady Spencer visited in 1769, they stayed in the home of the Count of Ventimigho, which they enjoyed as it was quite warm. Lady Spencer did not much like the local people, finding them "the awkwardest stiffest figures you ever saw and strangely dresst and talking a language that is neither French or Italian but a harsh unnatural mixture of both that is difficult to comprehend."[72] As a result, she had little to do with the locals, as was true of most of the English, and enjoyed the company of the Duke of Beaufort and his ill daughter and Lord and Lady Holland.[73] The other scene that distressed her and the others who witnessed it was the parading of galley slaves through town, a "melancholy sight."[74]

By 1800 the English traveled to Nice as tourists, some with an eye to developing it as a resort. At that time there was a hotel owned by an Englishman who served roast beef. One visitor commented that "the whole neighborhood has the air of an English watering-place."[75] The French Revolution and the wars brought this to an end. The French invaded in 1792 and occupied Nice until after the peace. The English then returned and seriously moved in by building villas and sponsoring the famous Promenade des Anglais. At the same time they started to colonize other parts of the Riviera. Lord Brougham, fleeing a cholera epidemic in Nice in 1834, went off to Cannes and settled there. And Mentone, at the far eastern end of the Riviera, was discovered by the truly ill and made into a health resort. It was famous not for seawater but for beneficent air.[76] However, Nice developed as the winter resort favored by the English. They built much of the new town to the west of the river and the famous Promenade des Anglais, where the best hotels and shops were. While the steep beach remained a problem, wooden shacks replaced Smollett's tent, and it was recommended that a bathing attendant or stout rope be utilized to bathe safely. It was never attractive to women.[77] Most visitors settled for the benign climate and fresh air.

Finally, Italy also joined the lengthening list of resorts. Viareggio was a small town in the Duchy of Lucca, an estate put together at the Congress of Vienna to give Queen Maria Luisa of Spain a home where she could still act as a queen, having had to surrender her title as queen of the short-lived Kingdom of Erturia. She spent little time there, as was true of her son Charles Louis, Duke of Lucca. His patronage, however, created the first two beaches at Viareggio along with a casino. He soon lost control of Lucca, which was turned over to Florence. In the midst of this shuffling of mini states Viareggio was established as the first beach resort in the emerging Kingdom of Italy.

After two decades of the chaos of war and the creation and destruction of states in the Napoleonic era, there followed an era of peace that allowed the recovery of economies and the reestablishment of princely and aristocratic finances. Out of this came the creation of resorts and the expansion of those already established. For peripatetic Continental nobles there were options not only on different coasts, but on summer and winter places of escape. The next few decades witnessed the expansion and elaboration in the number and facilities of places at the beach. As the Continental resorts multiplied, they looked much like those in England. The facilities catered to an elite audience with villas, hotels, and boarding houses and the expected facilities for bathing and entertainment. Therapeutic bathing was provided for the sick, and for the frivolous there was enough to keep them all occupied. Walking, riding on the beach, dancing, gambling of various kinds, and just people-watching and reading filled the days.

The bathing scene on the beach was different from England and from place to place. At first there were no local ordinances setting out proper conduct. Along the German coast there was little mixed bathing. Few resorts took up the bathing machine, so tents or cabins or even sand dunes became places to change. In Belgium and the Netherlands the bathing machine arrived early and stayed. They mostly allowed mixed bathing. The long, plain shift was standard wear for ladies and the oil cap, to keep hair dry, was soon added. For men, if there was mixed bathing, they had to wear drawers and a top of some kind to cover their bare chests, as even partial nudity was not allowed when women were present. As in England, many men insisted on swimming nude, so the resorts had to provide a place or a time for them to do so. As time went by, more and more of the resorts tended to have local ordinances that brought order to the beach. At Swinemunde the regulations mandated five zones. At one end, lower-class men with bathing costumes were permitted to swim, but with few facilities. Next to them were elite males who had changing cabins, chairs, and a boardwalk. Then there was a five-hundred-yard neutral zone before the area where elite women could bathe with the same facilities as the elite men, and then another boundary before lower-class women could bathe, again without facilities. So not only was there gender separation; people were also divided by class.[78] French resorts had greater variation than the other Continental resorts. At Granville in France there were three areas—one for women, another for men clothed, and then farthest away nude men.[79] For elite women at Dieppe there were always places to change, and when they went into the water their baigneurs, nearly always men, took over and dipped them. A baigneur was recognizable for wearing a blue costume and a hat. Dieppe also developed the most advanced facilities early in having a pavilion for changing and resting. Along the coast at Le Havre there was no establishment for bathers, so huts and shelters built of canvas permitted changing. The bathing machine never caught on in France as it did in Belgium. Huts and tents prevailed before permanent facilities were built, and mixed bathing was common. Male nudity was permitted early in the day or on distant parts of the beach. By the 1840s regulations about beach wear and behavior on the beach were common.

The English and the French would stare across the channel and wonder what was happening on the other side. Each was bemused by the beach practices of the other and prone to render opinion about the other's national character or lack of it, based on the differences. The French were decadent, the English cold and puritanical. In the end, the English surrendered to the French, for they were far more often visitors to French beaches than the French were to English beaches.[80]

Leisure Comes to America

The advent of beach culture in America followed a different path from both England and the Continent. There were, of course, hundreds of miles of magnificent beaches stretching from Florida to Maine. Along some coasts there were strings of barrier islands where one could walk for miles on the narrow strip of sand and sand dunes protecting the coast. On the more rugged coast of the North, there were rocky headlands sheltering lovely small beaches. However splendid, they were mostly uninhabited. Timothy Dwight, who traveled extensively, complained, "The American coast, as you know, is chiefly barren, and of course, thinly inhabited."[1] The farmers who dominated the inland landscape had little need for the beach. Many felt as did Fanny Kemble, the famous English actress, who reported, "The coast was a fearful stretch of dismal trackless sand, the ocean lay boundless and awful beyond the wild and desolate beach."[2] In an economy based on farming there was not much interest in barren sand. And unlike the new resorts in Europe, where often noble patrons stood ready to enhance their lands with a resort, America lacked such wealth and patronage.

Hunters were the one group who sought out the beach, but more particularly the marshes, where during the annual migrations vast flocks of birds streamed north and south. Hunting camps were set up on the beaches, all the better to avoid the mosquitoes, but also to permit access to the sea if one wanted a dip. These were rough establishments that served a male population for short times each year. Tuckerton, on a

FIGURE 3.1 *Nahant Island Outer Banks*, 2014. www.carolinadesigns.com. This image clearly shows the narrow strip of sand that makes the Outer Banks so vulnerable in hurricanes.

New Jersey island that no longer exists, was one such hunting camp that also took in boarders who wanted to be beside the sea.[3]

In fact, it is difficult to imagine a more forbidding place for the growth of beach resorts. Founded in the seventeenth century by mostly Protestant farmers, the colonists accepted the Protestant precepts regarding spiritual discipline, hard work, and avoidance of sin and looked on leisure as something that would permit the devil to find a way to subvert good character. Many colonists did not even celebrate Easter or Christmas, let alone all the many other days that were still observed in Protestant England. The society they created by 1700 was overwhelmingly rural and dominated by smallholding families. The exceptions were the port cities—Boston, Newport, New York, Philadelphia, and Charles Town—and, while these cities created alternative societies, they contained only a small minority of the population. Most of the wealth was accrued there by merchants, who shared the same Protestant beliefs as did the farmers.

In the South, the emergence of slavery and tobacco made it possible for the few to build plantations and fortunes, but the great planters were few in number compared to the family farmers who dominated. But it was the planters who created the first resort in the North, as they sought to escape the sweltering summers. Families from as far away as the West Indies traveled to Newport, Rhode Island, seeking cool breezes. On arrival, they lodged in houses and inns at the prosperous seaport, built largely on the profits of slavery. The town provided cool, sparkling weather not available at home. The visitors indulged in all of the pleasures of a lively port city until returning home in the fall.[4] During the American War for Independence, the British occupied the city and left it in disarray, physically trashed, with its trade networks in ruins. It would never recover its prosperity, as the larger ports of Providence, Boston, and New York thrived during and after the war. Newport would not be discovered again as a place to enjoy a summer of leisure until the nineteenth century.

The eighteenth century witnessed a slow and steady growth in the economy that brought prosperity to many and growing wealth to the few. Elites emerged, although none would compare them to European aristocracies, as they lacked the legal protections granted to nobility and their great wealth. Nonetheless, their prosperity allowed them to enjoy the fruits of success. Fashionable dress and refinement in manners and deportment all were indicators of a new status. There was still a sense that leisure had to be used for self-improvement, but the trend of the times was against this. Still, most leisure activities were within the family or community and rarely beyond the locality, unless it was for a special occasion such as a wedding.[5] Growing consumption of all sorts of material goods was also an indicator of social change.[6] An anecdote illustrates this trend. One morning Ben Franklin came down to breakfast to discover that his old bowl, "a two penny earthen porringer," and wooden spoon had been replaced by a new porcelain bowl and a silver spoon. When he queried his wife about this sudden and unexpected change, she informed him that she was sure he would want to have the same things as his neighbors.[7] In this way consumerism and fashionability spread, and with it came balls, teas, and other polite entertainments which required a new world of manners and gentility. Leisure made this possible, and while there were no beach resorts, slowly but surely they too would become a part of this world.

A few colonists had the experience of going to the beach in England. One of them was Abigail Adams, who went to Southampton and Weymouth when her husband John was the American ambassador to the Court of St. James. She wrote a friend that it was unfashionable to remain in London in the summer, so much so that the town was a "desert." For those who visited the seaside, she thought they went both for their health and for pleasure. When at the beach, she went into the water fully clothed in a bathing outfit, accompanied by a female guide. One can well imagine her covered from her toes to the tip of her head. She had been to the opera, where she was "shocked" by the costumes of the dancers as their short skirts showed their garters and drawers, but as she came to appreciate their skills she got over her "disgust."[8] Given these attitudes, there would be no revealing costume for her. She also came to have a very low opinion of resorts, for watering places were "a national evil as they promote and encourage dissipation, mix all characters promiscuously, and are the resort of the most unprincipled female characters."[9] Her puritan values never deserted her, even though Weymouth was far different than Baiae. As for bathing, she thought, "It would be delightful in our warm weather." There is no evidence that she turned to the beaches at home, as her duties as the wife of the vice-president and president kept her away from home, so that any time she could, she fled back to Massachusetts to her own hearth, family, and friends.[10]

Of the factors that led to the rise of the beach resort in England, many of them appeared in the colonies. The colonists brought with them the same attitudes toward medicine that existed in their home countries. Educated physicians were few, as it required a stay in Britain to obtain the necessary education. Not until 1765 was there a medical school in Philadelphia, and Harvard did not follow until 1782. Folk medicine was widely practiced, and it was enriched by the additional knowledge that native peoples had of local medicinal plants. Books such as John Wesley's *Primitive Physick* and John Tennet's *Everyman His Own Doctor* circulated in the colonies to proffer simple advice, among which was the efficacy of cold-water immersion.[11] William Buchan's *Domestic Medicine*, published in Philadelphia in 1772, advocated seawater bathing as a cure.[12] The common belief in the efficacy of mineral waters was widely shared by medical practitioners, patients, and Native Americans, who knew the site of many mineral springs and shared them with the colonists. For example, John Winthrop, one of the founders of Massachusetts Bay, sought a cure at a local spring recommended by a Native American. Later, in 1748, George Washington visited the already-famous Warm Springs (later to be known as the Berkeley Springs). Washington's home state of Virginia boasted a number of springs, especially around Winchester, where invalids could seek relief from Sulphur Springs, Yellow Springs, and Sweet Springs. In the middle colonies there were springs at Bristol in Pennsylvania and Saratoga, Ballston, and Lebanon in New York. New England had springs at Stafford, Connecticut, and at Newton, Massachusetts. The lodging at all of these springs was crude at best. Often they were no more than a clearing in the woods with a few rustic buildings. Most visitors just drank the water. Finding a place to sleep could be difficult, and even Washington had to send for a tent to get a roof over his head at Warm Springs when he visited again in 1761. Bath had no fear of a rival American resort.[13]

The colonists who sought out the springs sometimes had strange reactions to them that reveal much about their attitudes toward their bodies and the therapeutic effects of the springs and, for that matter, salt water. In a fascinating diary, Elizabeth Drinker, from the noted Philadelphia family, recorded her health and that of her family in considerable detail. In 1771 an indisposition drove her to Bristol Springs. Taking the cure was new to her, and immersion in a bath a unique experience. She records, "Afternoon in the bath, I found the shock much greater than expected." The next day, however, she "had not the courage to go in." She then confronted the bath with "fear and trembling," but she did get in and, over the next few weeks, bathed and drank the spring water regularly and felt better.[14] Her "shock" can be explained by the fact that being totally immersed in water was an unusual experience. At that time most people, even elites, washed their hands and faces, but rarely took a bath.[15] For instance, in 1794, Mrs. Drinker recorded her feelings about the shower bath her husband had just installed. Showers were coming into fashion in elite households, and while they were put in place for cleanliness, the cold rainwater used was thought to have some curative properties. She and her family approached the shower with trepidation. Her daughter Nancy's courage "fail'd" her, even after she had used the shower, and so she could not go on. When her grandchildren were introduced to it they bore it "wonderfully," but they could not be convinced to go in again. In the end her daughters and maids enjoyed it and used it regularly in the summer. A year after it was installed, Mrs. Drinker braved the shower and recorded, "I bore it better than expected not having been wet all over in 28 years."[16] Such an attitude expressed by an elite Philadelphia lady explains much about attitudes toward the body and cleanliness. A similar sentiment was expressed by Anna Cabot Lowell when she confided in her journal that "I went into the shower bath on Monday for the first time and again today. I mean to persevere with it. I hope it will do me good."[17] But then there were the few like George Templeton Strong, who confided to his diary that he was "constantly making new discoveries in the art and mystery of ablution. Taking a shower bath upside down is the latest novelty."[18] One can only imagine! Hopefully he had soaped up first.

Besides visiting the springs, colonists did start to explore the beach. Early in Mrs. Drinker's diary (1760) she mentions that a relative is going to Cape May. She does not say why, but it could be for the beach there.[19] There is an advertisement in 1766 in the *Pennsylvania Gazette,* for the sale of 254 acres that are half a mile from the sea at Cape May "where a number resort for health and bathing in the water."[20] Then in 1772 in the *New York Journal or General Advertiser,* there is an advertisement for a "BATH" at the end of a wharf in Perth-Amboy, in which is a room. "to undress and dress in," and then the "Bathing-Room where persons of either Sex may bathe in Salt-Water in the greatest privacy and for those that choose to swim off into deeper Water a door is so placed that they can conveniently go out and return."[21] In 1773 Sir William Johnson, the famed Indian agent who lived near Albany, traveled to the east end of Long Island following the advice of his physician to seek a cure in the sea.[22] Again, he found a complete lack of facilities for visitors. In 1784 Mrs. Drinker was advised to go to Shrewsbury near the Jersey shore and bathe in salt water for her health. She bathed in a tub filled with salt water and only went to the beach for a walk. Her daughter, who suffered from a facial cancer, was sent to the beach for a cure, but to no avail. She died soon after.[23] Jacob Hiltzheimer, another Philadelphian, sought to escape the city's ninety-degree temperature by going to Long Branch on the shore where he could "take a bath in the ocean."[24] Henry Toler, a Baptist preacher, had a nagging disease for which he could not find a cure, so he thought "to try another method, the Brethren going fishing I went also; and waded in the salt water very much; at last went in all over. And felt much revived and ate a hearty dinner."[25] The Reverend William Bentley of Massachusetts noted the increase in visitors to the Nahant peninsula for the wholesome air and that some were going in the water.[26] These stories all indicate that salt water and the beach were being sought out for therapeutic reasons and that there were limited facilities. There were, however, other uses of the beach.

Young people were also resorting to the beach, just for fun, in ways that are reminiscent of popular practices in Europe. John Peebles, a British army officer and a swimmer, noted that in early June when he went for his first swim of the season at Rockaway, Long Island, a large number of young people were there wading in the sea wearing their old clothes until they were drenched before returning to shore to put on dry clothes. Getting soaked wearing old clothes was modesty indeed. Given the large

Dutch population in New York, this may have been a continuation of an old Dutch tradition of sea bathing fully clothed.[27] Charles Wilson Peale, the artist and a swimmer, joined a different young people's frolic when on Plum Island, Massachusetts, in 1765. He went out to the dunes with a group who paired off and then went rolling down the dunes together. Peale was quite attracted to the flashing, bare legs of the girls. Having watched the activity for a while, Peale ventured down the beach, stripped, and plunged into the ocean to refresh himself. As he turned to go back to the beach, he discovered that a group of young girls had followed him and were now sitting by his clothes. What to do? "Whether the sight of a naked man was frequent to people who inhabited the coast [so that he was] not so liable to produce a blush, the writer does not know, but from his short acquaintance with the inhabitants here, he is inclined to believe the female sex have as much modesty as in other places in America." Modesty caused him to remain in the sea until the girls moved off and he could scamper out, frozen, and get dressed.[28] Rolling down the dunes seemingly was a popular diversion as it was also practiced on Abescom Island, New Jersey, where young men sent girls down the dune alone, but with their legs tied together.[29] All of these episodes of recreation and therapeutics indicate a growth in leisure and a rising use of the beach as a site which was no longer viewed with trepidation, but as a familiar place to seek relief from the unrelenting heat of the summer. Resorts with organized activities were just around the corner.

By 1800 some identifiable beach haunts started to emerge, although with minimal facilities. By this time the disruption created by the War for Independence and the emergence of new governments had passed. Cape May, Tuckerton, and Long Branch, in New Jersey; Bath and Rockaway, on Long Island; Nahant, Massachusetts, and Point Comfort, Virginia— these were not all towns at this time; however, all were within reach of a city. The proximity of the cities was important, as they were the sites of growing wealth in the economy of the young republic, ushering in the arrival of an upper class with a penchant for leisure. As the cities also became more and more unpleasant in the summers and positively dangerous with the arrival of yellow fever and cholera, the leisure class escaped in growing numbers. By the 1820s there were resorts. The delay was the result of the distortions of the War of 1812 and the financial panic of 1819, the former disrupting travel along the coast and the latter making capital scarce and expensive.[30] The recovery of the economy brought investment. As usual, the investors were local entrepreneurs willing to take a risk on the newly fashionable leisure activity and the fact of the short season. At Cape May, for example, the Hughes family built the first two "hotels," although neither would pass muster as such in England. They were rustic buildings of unpainted wood board with no plaster and not much finish—nothing like the Georgian Squares of Margate or the grand buildings in Brighton. But, as many of the resorts were not fishing villages as in Britain, few buildings of any kind were present at the beginning. And as the roads were more often primitive, making getting there all the more adventurous, the whole experience was more often pioneering in the rough and ready.

Cape May brags that it is the oldest seaside resort in America. It may well be, if one accepts that Newport was just a place where people appreciated the local weather but stayed away from the beach. As Mrs. Drinker noted in her diary, one of her relatives went to Cape May in 1760. Her relative would have had a difficult journey of two days across the sandy Pine Barrens in a Jersey wagon, which was a large wagon with wide wheels, the better to navigate the sand. As one traveler noted, "You travel silently, softly through the warm gushing sand and still pines."[31] Somewhat easier was the trip by water down Delaware Bay, but as there was no regular service until much later, this could also be complicated. Once passengers were dropped off, they still needed to clamber into a Jersey wagon to get to the abandoned whaling station that was now a small village where there was lodging. By 1801, Ellis Hughes advertised that he was open for business and was ready to entertain sea bathers for seven cents a night. Food was extra, featuring fish, oysters, and crab.[32] Hughes's establishment would evolve into the grandly named Atlantic Hall, which was not much more than a 50-foot square barn, without paint or plaster. At night the management just hung sheets across the middle of the room and women slept on one side, the men on the other.[33] Yet it appears that "gay girls and festive gentlemen" were not put off by these conditions and could be found enjoying the Cape.[34] William Brobson, a Delaware attorney and politician, visited in 1825. By this time Thomas Hughes, son of Ellis, had created a new hotel, 108 by 40 feet with three stories, soon to be named the Congress Hall. Bedrooms were on the top two floors while the first floor was for meals and entertainment. In his diary, Brobson noted that within the last ten years "the fashionable propensity for tours of pleasure and visiting watering places and sea shore during the summer when relaxation from the labors of business is desirable, has I think very much increased."[35] The "fashionable" were by now, it seems, committed to a regime of leisure, whiling away the summer relaxing. Brobson went to Cape May for ten days, where he and eleven friends went sea bathing in old clothes that they had brought for the occasion. There is a slightly later magazine image that clearly shows bathers in street clothes.[36] Brobson's comment and the image show that the Americans were committed to wearing convenient clothing and not some bathing costume. While the accommodations might not be first class, they still changed costumes three or four times a day to maintain fashion, something Brobson disliked. He also got no benefit from the bathing and still preferred swimming in fresh water. Edmund Canby, a Quaker miller who visited that same summer, enjoyed the surf and sailing. The crowds were thin at this point with only thirty visitors, mostly from Philadelphia.[37] But the development of two "hotels" by local entrepreneurs was very typical of these early resorts. They were not much on style, but they served the purpose for the summer months.

While Philadelphians enjoyed the rough pleasures of Cape May, they did have other alternatives, although they were equally undeveloped. Tuckerton was no more than an old hunting camp and difficult to reach. After having struggled across the Pine Barrens, visitors found twenty-five miles of splendid beaches and very few visitors.[38] Any of the small places on the coast that attracted the adventurous were difficult to get to and would remain so until the railway or better roads reached them. Long Branch was easier to reach as it sat at the northern end of New Jersey where the sandy coastal plain was narrower and less daunting than the broad plain to the south. Even so, the ubiquitous Jersey wagons were required for the final part of the trip. Long Branch was first discovered by a British Army officer, a Colonel White, who built a house there which was confiscated during the Revolution and sold to Elliston Perot in 1788. Perot converted it into a boarding house and was bought out, in turn, by Lewis McKnight, who then invested $2,000 in the building and turned it into more of a tavern with rooms. Mrs. Drinker was a patron, as was Benjamin Rush, Philadelphia's most famous physician.[39] As McKnight's, it became the place to stay and was the beginning of what would become a very fashionable resort sought out by Philadelphians and New Yorkers.

New Yorkers had other options. Long Island was mostly made up of the remnants of the age of glaciers. The last glacier had paused on its way north and dumped rocks, boulders, sand, and clay, creating the island. While the north side was rockier, the south side of the island consisted of a long chain of beaches, many of them barrier islands. Farmers stayed to the north side of the island and left the south side alone. Closest to the city was Bath Beach, which sat inside the New York Harbor and, while not the Atlantic, did attract visitors who looked for relief from the heat and for their health conditions.[40] Rockaway, on the Atlantic, which was easily reached from Manhattan by land and sea, emerged as the preferred beach spot. As elsewhere there was a long sandy beach. There were other attractions. John Pintard, a New York merchant, records that while his sister benefited from the air and water, his mother's health seemed the same, but on the other hand the latter enjoyed the "genteel company" and "promiscuous parties." A Mrs. Fairlie reigned as queen at Rockaway over a "dissipated, drinking, gambling circle of . . . bon vivants." So, even if Pintard did not much care for the "genteel" company, his mother got her way and continued to visit.[41]

Another frequent visitor was Philip Hone, a New York merchant and investor who was also a noted philanthropist and supporter of the theater and arts in the city. While he visited other resorts, he found the situation at Rockaway to be a good one for his family, and he sent them there for the summer in 1831. He himself enjoyed the sea bathing, which he constantly described as "delicious."[42] While he might go back and forth to the beach, he was always careful to get his family out of the city when cholera struck; then, he only ventured into town when he had to.[43] Enamored of Rockaway, he decided to build the first hotel there, the Marine Pavilion. He and his partners spent about $35,000 for construction, a handsome sum at the time. By 1834 it was up and running, and initial reports were positive, with about thirty-six hundred guests in the first season.[44] Typically, the Marine Pavilion was a large wooden building, of which Hone was proud. Foreign visitors had a less positive view. Frances "Fanny" Kemble, the English actress and writer who married an American, would write to a friend, "You cannot conceive of anything more strange and to me more distasteful than the life one leads here . . . one enormous hotel, a huge wooden building in which we are at present among the inmates." Further, "the bed rooms are small and furnished barely as well as a common servant's room in England. They are certainly not calculated for comfortable occupation or sitting alone in; but sitting alone any part of the day is a proceeding contemplated by no one here."[45] Kemble had put her finger on the plan of most of these hotels: to keep the rooms small and serviceable, pushing the residents out into the public areas where they could walk or bathe, sit on the verandas, eat in the dining hall, and shop in the stores. At night there were balls, hops, concerts, and theater—all to keep the visitor entertained in the public areas of the hotel where the owner spent money on decorations and comfort. By design, it was replacing the functions of the assembly rooms. It would be some time before bedrooms became

luxurious and worth spending time in. To keep the entertainment flowing, Hone mimicked English practice by having a Count Streleski as the
social manager of the hotel.[46] In this he was unique, for American beach
resorts expected guests to make their own social life, which usually
meant organizing the balls and hops.

But while the first season was a success, things turned against Hone.
Saratoga Springs and Ballston Springs near Albany, New York, expanded
rapidly just before Hone started building. There were four large hotels in
Saratoga alone that copied the standard pattern of small bedrooms with
opulent public areas.[47] Hone had to admit that the United States Hotel
was the finest he had ever seen although it was filled with "awkward
women and stupid men," unlike the fine people who came to Rockaway.[48] In fact, Saratoga was attracting the "ton" from New York City
and the South and remained the premier mineral springs resort for many
years.[49] Hone was also fighting the downturn in the economy that became
a panic by 1837. He and his partners decided to cut their losses and sold
the hotel at auction in 1836 for $30,000, after investing about $40–
45,000.[50] While licking his financial wounds, he kept his faith in Rockaway by continuing to visit. By 1840 things had recovered, and he noted
that the hotel was full of New Yorkers, who he ruefully noted were now
"flocking to it."[51] Hone's misfortunes were symptomatic of the difficult
finances of early hotel owners.

Further north there was a similar development, but with a different
outcome. Nahant is a peninsula that juts out into Massachusetts Bay, just
north of Boston. There is a long, sandy beach that is the entry to the rocky
island, and crossing the beach to get to the island was one of the attractions of Nahant. By the 1780s it had started to attract visitors. The Reverend William Bentley visited in 1790 with friends who drove out to the
island, where they would "sport in the surf' and dine alfresco before
returning home. In 1806, he recorded that there were fifty carriages, and
shortly thereafter, he noted, "The increasing number which visit here will
oblige more building."[52] The breakthrough came in 1817 with the arrival
of *Scoliophis atlanticus*. This is an early and distinguished chapter in the
sleazy history of property development in America. The famed sea serpent *Scoliophis atlanticus* appeared just off Nahant that year and was a
boon to local boat owners who rented out their vessels to those who
wanted to see the marvel more closely—and many swore that they did.
The sea serpent kept appearing just off Nahant, for some strange reason,
much to the benefit of those who sought to develop the island.[53] In 1819
a small hotel was built, but it proved to be inadequate and finally burned

down. Seizing on the continued sightings of the serpent, Colonel Thomas Perkins and his syndicate raised $60,000 to build a proper, modern hotel to meet what they hoped would be a growing numbers of visitors. The dining room alone could hold 125 for meals. The doors opened on June 26, 1823, and fortuitously, the serpent made one of its last appearances two weeks later.[54] The hotel's advertisement touted its hot and cold sea-water baths, showers, bowling alleys, billiards, and a marine hippodrome cleansed by the tide twice a day. There was great stress on sea bathing and sea air for their healthful qualities. Both aided in the treatment of "summer and autumnal diseases of children, indigestion, nervous complaints, some chronic rheumatism and many of the scrofula." While country air might help some of these diseases, the advertisement continued, it did not compare to sea air, and a cure of a month in the country could be accomplished in a week at Nahant. An appeal was made to "men of property" who might feel debilitated by the rigors of business, or who just wanted to ensure their family's health, to enjoy a week at Nahant. If the man of property was wealthy enough, the syndicate was willing to sell him a home lot.[55]

Should you have any doubts regarding the benefits of sea air and water at Nahant, you only had to turn to the *New England Journal of Medicine and Surgery*. There, Dr. Walter Channing provided a map of Nahant and meteorological tables for the months of July, August, and September. He states that the air is "perfectly pure and has a coolness and elasticity to it" as it comes directly across the ocean and is so exhilarating that it is an inducement of exercise. As for sea bathing, it is simply superb. All of this hyperbole is followed by a pitch for real estate on the island. Was the good doctor a member of the syndicate? After touting the healthfulness of the island, he admits that the success of the hotel depends on the "healthy, gay, and fashionable," without whom the hotel will fail. He closes by pulling his punches. What diseases might be helped by this experience can't be fully proved, as there is insufficient evidence, but he is sure there will be in time. Nonetheless, his arguments for the new hotel would be familiar to any number of English resort physicians who made similar claims.[56]

Channing was correct in one of his assumptions, and that was that Nahant would not succeed unless the fashionable decided to visit the island. Soon after it was built, the hotel attracted Boston's finest, who came not for their health but for fun. In 1823 the daughters of Josiah Quincy, president of Harvard, visited for an event-filled weekend. They went by carriage, stopping in Charleston to change into more appropriate costumes for their arrival. They appear not to have gone into the water, but made the second bell for every meal, changed clothing frequently, and visited with friends such as the Cabots and Tuders, who had already built cottages. The highlight of their weekend was the ball, the big attraction that packed the hotel, forcing many men to sleep on couches as women shared rooms. Exhausted after an entertaining weekend, it was home to Boston.[57] Charles Frances Adams vacationed during the same year, and then in July, 1824, he drove out with friends to fish and play billiards and eat a disappointing dinner.[58] Anna Cabot Lowell first went to Nahant in 1820 to dance and visit friends in their villas. She returned in 1828 to enjoy the society and active social life. Soon she was a regular visitor during the summer and enjoyed walking, riding on the beach, the sea air, and her first warm salt bath. By 1836 her family had a cottage, and she now walked to the hotel, the better to get warm baths and ice cream.[59] For these two young visitors, therapeutic bathing was not on their agenda— only having fun.

By the 1830s Nahant was an established part of life for the Cod Fish Aristocracy of Boston. To be really fashionable, one had to own a villa or spend at least a week in the hotel. Foreign visitors were also attracted there. Harriett Martineau, the English writer and social commentator, visited in 1836 and enjoyed the "stupendous" hotel, the fashionable balls, carriage rides on the beach, and swimming at the women's beach. She describes the latter as secluded by rocks and a fence along the cliff that provided complete "retirement."[60] The British Consul, Thomas Grattan, visited in 1839 during a terrible heat wave. He was less enamored of the hotel than Martineau, as he described it as a grand pigeon house on account of the small rooms. He loathed the food, especially the chowder, and the need to eat at the hotel's appointed times. He was angered to discover no bathing machines, so much a part of English beach life, yet entirely missing at Nahant. There were only a few changing huts at the hotel that were reserved for the ladies. He had to clamber over rocks to undress and swim. He did rather like the fashionable women; he stayed for a month, until September 1 when the season came to an end.[61] As a final certification of Nahant's status, a novel, *Nahant or the Flower of Souverance,* was published in 1827.[62] The novel dwells on the "brilliant" society at the Nahant Hotel, where an overwrought young man commits suicide because of his unrequited love, and his fair maiden dies shortly thereafter by pining away. Unrequited love or no, Nahant remained the summer residence of choice for many Bostonians.

One cynic wrote, "The Nahantese cling to their acres with a grip that cash in hand has no power to unloose."[63]

While Nahant was well established by 1840, Newport was struggling back to life. Badly damaged during the American War for Independence, it subsequently lost much of its cachet. A visitor strolled through town in 1820 and found it "desolate," with the houses going to ruin, streets dirty, and no trace of "what made this the favorite resort of Southern Planters."[64] But the locals and outsiders were not willing to give up on its superb location. Slowly but surely, it returned to life with a good hotel and boarding houses, yet the future of Newport was not to reside in hotels, but in the mansions for family living that very quickly became the "cottages" of the future. By 1840, Philip Hone, that connoisseur of resorts, made his first visit and was quite taken with the town; he wrote in his diary that he "no longer wonders that so many persons prefer it to every other watering place."[65] The Philadelphia esthete Sidney George Fisher, in his first visit in 1843, found much of the town "detestable," as the people there were frivolous, indolent and wanting in culture, and the Ocean House Hotel "dirty."[66] He mostly loathed the many New Yorkers who were visiting, as they were "ultra-fashionable people who live for dissipation" and were of the "upstart school." But as more mansions were built and as entertaining moved out into the mansions that were "owned by very rich people who know how to entertain," he reported that the elite of Boston, and even New York City, were there, and "no place could exhibit a crowd [more] distinguished of refinement, wealth and fashion."[67] Finally, it was his kind of town. As *Harper's Weekly* reported, "It is only at Newport that you find people who really do nothing well."[68] Newport had returned and was on the verge of transforming the nature of resorts.

While the North was developing a number of beach resorts, the South lagged behind. The only seaside resort that developed in the South was at Point Comfort. In 1820 the Hygeia Hotel was constructed near Fort Monroe. The hotel attracted visitors from Washington, DC, and the surrounding area. While it may not have been fashionable, it did attract politicians such as Andrew Jackson, who built a cottage near the hotel.[69] The truly fashionable in the South went to the mineral springs. Berkeley Springs, White Sulphur Springs, and Yellow Sulphur Springs, while known in the eighteenth century, developed rapidly in the nineteenth as the transportation network reached into the mountains. These were elegant resorts with Greek Revival hotel buildings and cottages where those who could afford them came for health reasons. However, as in the

North, elites came for the cooler weather of the mountains and the balls, horse races, and the other attractions offered by the resorts.[70] Northern mineral springs also attracted southern visitors, who traveled north to New York City to shop and then moved on to Saratoga Springs, where they appeared in large numbers. However, as the North turned against slavery and became more abolitionist, it became unpleasant for southern elites, who were mostly slaveholders, to visit resorts. In 1848 Rhode Island passed a law stating that it would no longer participate in the Fugitive Slave Law and so would not hold enslaved persons in its jails, so no more slaves could be brought to the state. As one report expressed it, "At Newport . . . a slave owner must wait upon himself, or, contrary to his usual custom, pay for being served."[71] As one young southern belle put it, "I cannot bear to be washed and dressed and waited upon by white folks," as she had to leave her "indispensable" slave behind.[72]

While polite disorder may have reigned in the resorts, all was not secular pleasure. This was, after all, a United States in the middle of the Second Great Awakening, a period of intense religiosity where the moral effects of leisure were still feared.[73] Nonetheless, in 1835 the Methodists created the first Christian beach resort, Wesleyan Grove on Martha's Vineyard. This occurred in the middle of a wave of revivals in New England Methodist churches.[74] One revival attracted twelve thousand worshippers.[75] At the Wesleyan Grove the godly could seek the healing powers of salt water and sea air and spiritual renewal. There were issues in the godly taking leisure, for any time taken away from one's occupation was viewed as dangerous. American culture still had strong Protestant beliefs that looked askance at leisure. Holidays and resorts were not likely to be places where the righteous felt comfortable. Yet, prosperity allowed middle-class churchgoers to have vacations and leisure. The way around this seeming conflict was by claiming that religious retreats were spiritual refuges that permitted rest and relaxation from the pressures of busy lives. At these retreats there were frequent sermons by renowned preachers to assuage spiritual concerns.

Wesleyan Grove was similar to the tent revivals popular all over the country. These revivals were part of the Second Great Awakening, which created a heightened spirituality among evangelical churches. Thousands were lured out of the towns and cities and away from farms to rural camps, where preachers made the audience aware of their depravity and the promise of God's grace. Renewed in their piety, the audience members returned to their normal lives.[76] Such was also true of Wesleyan Grove, which proved enormously popular, attracting

FIGURE 3.2 Carpenter Gothic Cottages with Victorian-style gingerbread trim on Lake Avenue, Oak Bluffs on Martha's Vineyard, Massachusetts. iStock by Getty Images, courtesy of Travelview. These charming small Victorian cottages at Oak Bluffs are now a heritage site.

twelve thousand people in a summer and in the meantime becoming the Martha's Vineyard Camp-Meeting Association. Cottages started to appear, as those who enjoyed the camp meeting experience as part of their summer built more permanent lodgings to escape the tents. These structures, as small Victorian houses, became famous in their own right, making the Grove a modern tourist attraction. As it became more popular and travel to the island was made easier with steamboats, unwholesome elements started to move in, forcing the church's leaders to urge their members to buy property to protect the site. In the end, they created the new resort of Oak Bluffs, which would prove something of a model for other religious groups.[77] Asbury Park, New Jersey, was another Methodist camp that depended on the faithful buying property to keep out secular folk and maintain a religious community.[78]

The flourishing American economy, even with occasional panics, brought prosperity to many and, for a few, great wealth. The wealth, in turn, would permit more consumption and opportunities for leisure. An important site for the new world of leisure was the hotel, an important aspect of the resorts. The old inns and taverns were replaced by the new buildings, as during the 1820s the whole country started on something of a hotel boom.[79] Urban palaces such as the Tremont in Boston (opening in 1829) were to be found in more and more cities until the panic of 1837, when capital and customers curtailed the boom. The success of the hotel signaled the evolution that was occurring on both sides of the Atlantic in the emergence of the hotel as more than just a place to sleep. In England, elite social life had circulated around the assembly room. While never as popular in America as in Britain, elite "assemblies" started in America as like-minded groups sought proper and genteel company for balls, card playing, and all the other activities associated with the assembly room. More often than not, they met in varied settings, as few actual assembly rooms were built in America.[80] At this time, the new hotels started to take on many of the functions associated with the rooms. With their large public areas featuring dining halls, bars, parlors, and ballrooms, the hotel monopolized the space formerly occupied by the assembly rooms. Soon they would add gaslight and elevators and other amenities that made them luxurious, totally eclipsing the rooms. While public spaces in a democratic nation, they kept an elite audience simply through the furnishings and high prices. The ordinary person could probably buy a drink but would not get a room, especially if one was not white. While rarely as grand as the urban hotels, the resort hotels still managed to provide the exclusive space sought by the gentry. From rather primitive beginnings, the beach hotels increased in sophistication and in facilities to meet the demands of the American elites. Soon enough they would be grand indeed.

One factor that always made the beach hotels different was that they operated in a different market. As noted before, they had a three-month high season, no matter how much they tried to lure the out-of-season visitor. June, July, and August—with a heavy emphasis on August, when the cities were miserably hot, fetid, and unhealthy—was their season. Resort investors, therefore, had to build buildings that made economic sense. Wood, not stone, was the most frequently used material, and it was never even painted or covered with plaster. The logic of their situation was to build as many bedrooms as cheaply as possible. Consul Graton's sneer about the Nahant Hotel resembling a pigeon coop is not far off the mark. Even though the rooms were small, visitors, even in exclusive Nahant, were asked to double up, one hopes with people they knew, during the big weekends such as the Fourth of July. Women scrunched together while their menfolk slept in chairs on the piazza or in the billiard room.[81] To make up for the small rooms, the public spaces were as commodious and as luxurious as the owners could afford. Dining halls were large, and meals were regimented by the dinner bell, as the guests were fed on the American plan in multiple sittings, something else Consul Gratton hated.[82] The verandas or piazzas were also large, and the hotels often boasted of their length. Deep verandas with chairs and tables for people to sit, read, and watch the passing spectacle appeared everywhere. Bands played to entertain the guests and to help in passing the time. Billiards, bowling, baths, beach bathing, fishing, lectures, hunting, boating, and any sort of entertainment that could be laid on with little expense were featured, all to keep the paying customers out of their rooms and in the public areas.

Evenings were taken over by an endless series of balls and the new "hop." Balls were formal affairs requiring managers, usually prominent men, who arranged the evening's entertainment. At the hops women could preside, at least in Newport, and one English visitor thought that "an accomplished master of ceremonies from Margate could not do it" as well as the women did.[83] So even though one was at the beach, and on holiday, formal wear had to be brought along, which for women meant a supply of gowns. Hops were less formal and more likely to feature newer dances such as waltzes, polkas, and predowas, which society still viewed askance. Needless to say, the young preferred the hops.[84] Nearly every night was filled with something to keep people occupied, so the managers of the hotels had to provide suitable public areas and entertainment to keep the holiday-makers happy. All of this cost money, yet investors kept coming forward to build the resort hotels no matter the constraints of season and cost. Depressions and panics, or changes in fashion, haunted them and would often force an investment group to sell. This had been the fate of Philip Hone's Rockaway syndicate.

Another problem for investors was the fact that these large wooden buildings, standing empty for much of the year, burned down with great regularity. The first hotel at Nahant burned down, as did the second, and Cape May had multiple fires. In one of these, the Mount Vernon Hotel, advertised as the world's largest hotel with rooms for twenty-one hundred people, burned to the ground in 1856, prior to its opening. Then in 1869, a fire that had its origins in a small shop spread to the United States Hotel and really took off, burning two square blocks before subsiding.[85] Only a special kind of entrepreneur could stand the anxiety.

While therapeutic bathing was an important consideration for many, relaxation and entertainment were essential at the resorts. Without the fashionable, who sought experience rather than therapy, the resorts could not have made a go of it financially. Given the situation in East Coast cities during the summer with heat, humidity, and disease, fashionable

Americans needed to flee, and a resort was the perfect place. Resorts soon became an arena for performance and display, as society had a set of fixed rules for proper behavior.[86] Balls, hops, gambling, billiards, bowling, and other means of excitement were attractions for the fashionable and arenas for showing off. Even when out walking or riding or managing a carriage, your dress and deportment were assessed. It was not unusual for women to change their costumes three times or more each day to ensure that they were appropriately dressed for each occasion. One young woman changed costumes nine times in a day while at Newport.[87] Men were conscious that they, too, had to cut a figure, and formal wear was used at a rate that many today would find excessive, even though society at the beach was never as formal as it was in the city. Typically, there were many strangers present, so performance at dances, conversation, riding, and other activities meant pressure to excel. Not doing well meant being marginalized in this competitive setting. Sidney George Fisher used his diary to assess his performance. After a lecture he had delivered, he thought his performance as manly, simple, and unassuming.[88] Such an environment also created opportunities for various elites from around the country to socialize with and assess one another. While more often than not they found compatible company, certain groups started to stand out, mostly New Yorkers. Fisher, the ever-tasteful Philadelphian, found New Yorkers "vulgar, fashionable pleasure seekers, lovers of show, sporting men, fast men, gamblers, adventurers, demimond, thieves and whores."[89] They were very different from the Philadelphians with whom he felt comfortable—people of sophistication and good taste. But it was not just the New Yorkers who invited comment. John Pintard, one of the New Yorkers, found southerners "dissipated Company."[90] Going on holiday was not always fun and relaxation, because social challenges came with resort society.

That was particularly true for women, whose dress could be censured, as was their dancing. Miss Cabot of Boston, while at Newport, found the scene there "very objectionable." "By what argument or means, mammas, who faint at the very idea of their daughters polkaing [dancing the new rage, the polka], overcome their scruples here, I cannot imagine." She also saw "several dames or damoiselles enter their open carriages, without stockings, collars, or muslin sleeves, a degree of negligence that was not becoming," and remarked that "sweet young ladies in dainty dresses, too languishing and delicate to live, do not hesitate here to appear as ugly, undressed . . . coarse women." She normally summered at the far more sedate Walpole.[91] And then Miss Lowell was "completely disgusted" by waltzing couples who had their arms around one another.[92] George William Curtis, a displaced New Englander living in New York, still reflected old values, for when he visited Newport he did not like the fashionable ladies who "dress too well, dance too well and were too elegant," amounting to "gilded vulgarity."[93] Young, unmarried women had to be particularly careful. As Miss Cabot noted, mothers were not much on having their daughters do the new dances, such as the polka. Ever mindful that their unmarried daughters were on display, mothers were loath to have them appear too forward. They were also disapproving even of the waltz, which was banned in England until 1813 and in Boston until the 1830s before it became common. As late as 1858, one father in Newport kept his daughter from dancing the waltz and only relented when a male cousin appeared.[94] But Sidney G. Fisher noted that at Newport the polka and the predowa, another part of the new rage in fast dancing, were danced with the "handling being very free," and where such dancing would have driven half the women to leave the room just ten years before, it was now acceptable to the "ultra-fashionable." While he might find this behavior "vulgar," he kept going back to Newport, and one tends to think he rather liked the "free handling," especially when he vacationed without his family. One cannot imagine such things at Nahant, which Fisher found to be a "barren rock."[95] So, the stakes were high for women, especially those of marriageable age, for the marriage market for elite young women flourished in America, as much as in England. Creating the proper image, while appearing to be fashionable, meant a lot of pressure on young women.

The resorts were also risky environments in another way, for they were places where the body was put on display in ways that simply would not occur in normal society. While the "ultra-fashionable" obviously pushed the limit on display, this was still a time when women were more than a bit prudish, which their menfolk approved of. However, this was an era on both sides of the Atlantic when costume for men and women was changing. For the men, it was the great change from knee breeches and silk stockings to trousers. While not tending to the dandyism of Beau Brummell, it did accept his dark colors in dress, and men turned toward what is close to a modern suit and left behind the gaudy colors and textiles of eighteenth-century dress. For women, fashion was more complicated.[96] They too left behind the costumes of the eighteenth century, by first accepting the high bust line and long drapery of the Empire style, before moving on to a silhouette dominated by a pinched waist, making the corset essential. And while more casual clothes could be worn at home, going out meant long full dresses and

FIGURE 3.3 Cham (Amédée Charles de Noé), *Ostende*. Lithograph, 1850–69. Musée Carnavalet, Histoire de Paris. © Musée Carnavalet / Roger-Viollet Agency—All rights reserved. The cartoon makes fun of the potential for embarrassment waiting in the changing cabin.

dark colors. As the decades went by this became more complicated with bustles and hoops, so that Victorian dress was ever more restrictive and, for many, unhealthy. Dress codes and physical decorum were conservative, so appearing at the beach was a problem for many proper ladies.[97]

American behavior at the beach was quite different from that in England. The bathing machines, so significant a part of the English bathing scene, did not cross the Atlantic. Instead the Americans, like the French, changed their clothes in huts close to the beach and then walked into the water. For upper-class women, this meant having the appropriate attire, as the early use of old clothing faded while the bathing costume became fashionable. Some wore wrappers around their costume, which was the usual all-covering shroud, or went without and tried to move quickly back and forward. For safety reasons but also for decorousness, it was not seen fitting that a woman should go alone into the water. There were many places where a proper lady could not venture alone—bars, hotels, bowling alleys, stagecoaches or railway coaches—without calling into question her status, so a man was needed. But the dippers of England, or the baigneurs of France, did not appear in America. Their function was filled by male relatives or friends. The English, touring in America, took note of this. When a woman was at a resort and not accompanied by a male relative who swam, she might meet a gentleman at dinner and, if he seemed appropriate, would ask him to accompany her into the water.[98] We will explore this at length later. One foreign observer thought that American women did not lack in courage in having to walk to and fro. "That so many Americans are to be found who are willing to put suits on and walk unflinchingly across the stretch of sand between the disrobing hut and the surf under the fire of hundreds of glances is proof that the bravery of the nation should not be impugned."[99] So, the beach was a place that challenged ideas about propriety. Yet for many, a trip to the beach was still therapeutic, so going into the water was part of the reason one was there, and it was hard to avoid doing the appropriate thing and still keep all the social mores of society as they were defined in the cities.

The building of villas at Nahant, cottages at the Wesleyan Grove, and homes elsewhere signaled a change in the American resorts. Villas had already appeared in the major English resorts. Members of the royal family had built grand homes in Brighton and Weymouth. Nothing in North America could stand in comparison. As a result of growing prosperity among urban elites in the colonies, the building of second homes flourished during the eighteenth century. Country retreats were built around cities such as Philadelphia, New York, and Boston. Bourgeois gentry sought ways to flaunt their prosperity while escaping from the worst of the city in summer. By the very end of the century and into the nineteenth, yellow fever epidemics haunted the increasingly crowded, and during the summer fetid, cities, providing another reason to escape.[100] At Nahant there was a concentration of villas that marked a fashionable community where like-minded people gathered—Longfellow, Emerson, Prescott, Cabot, Lowell, Whittier, Lodge, and Agassiz. This truly was a gathering of Boston's finest. Soon Newport, Long Branch, and Cape May, to name a few resorts, witnessed a building boom of new villas. Families could spend the summer away from the heat and corruption of the city, and the husband could come down on the weekend and, if business allowed, visit for a week or two. So, the investment in a villa signaled prosperity and membership in elite company. Entertainment could be as private as the new owners wanted, or public in the hotel. The local beach could be adopted by the family and used as needed, rather than relying on the facilities of the hotel. And so a new community was created that was the beginning of what would become, in time, familiar to millions of Americans.

By 1840 beach resorts had crossed the Atlantic and been embraced by Americans. The substantial number of popular beach resorts was testimony to that. American prosperity had created a leisure class, and changing attitudes toward leisure permitted them indulgences. Still, for many of the visitors, the therapeutic possibilities were the prime reason for their existence. Given the uncertain nature of diagnosis and treatment at the time, the appeals of salt water and sea air were hard to beat. Other visitors went for the entertainment and the possibility of feeling better, just by being at the shore. The rough, unpainted wooden hotels could not rival the Georgian Squares at Margate or the splendid esplanade at Brighton. Nonetheless, the Americans did not know of the splendor of these resorts and were happy with the available accommodations. English visitors could sniff at these approximations of English resorts, yet they continued to visit the American beaches. An American beach culture had come to stay, however different from that of England and the Continent.

4

The Industrial Revolution
Finds the Beach

Sea bathing and the resorts that made it possible continued to flourish in the early nineteenth century. Entrepreneurs braved the seasonal market to build wholly new resorts or to add hotels and summer homes to the established places. New modes of transportation powered by steam, on ships and trains, created a transportation revolution that expanded the number of resorts and the number of people who could access the resorts. For not only did they shrink travel time, but their cheap fares also allowed working-class people to plan a trip to the beach. How would this affect the resorts? Would people of different status mingle? Were new forms and formats for entertainment needed for the growing diversity? Did people react to the experience of sea bathing the same way? In the countries that now had resorts, how varied were the answers? Broad trends appeared, but they were not universal. National traditions and cultural practices would militate against singular answers. This was the first great challenge to what had been a fairly stable world at the resorts since their emergence in the 1730s. How would they meet the challenge and survive?

By 1800 there were nearly forty resorts in England.[1] Steadily, through the last third of the eighteenth century, new resorts appeared as the lure of sea bathing and sea air plus new possibilities for entertainment attracted more and more people. Resorts close to London emerged as the leaders, in terms of the numbers of visitors and the resulting demand for facilities. Brighton remained the choice of the "beau monde," who flocked there in the summer and started to visit at other less salubrious times of the year, attracted by royal patronage and a busy season of activity. Many other resorts served mostly local audiences and were modest in their growth. Such was the case of Scarborough, which continued to attract the aristocracy and gentry of the North. The new Devon resorts are another case in point. Located in the far southwest, they benefited from a better climate than many of the existing resorts and also had fine beaches. One drawback to their growth was the fact that only the town of Exeter was nearby, and the larger seaport of Bristol was eighty miles distant over poor roads. They, like many of the other resorts away from cities, served a local clientele and thus never rivaled Margate and Brighton in the numbers of visitors. Nonetheless, by 1750 bathers were present at Exmouth and then, in time, at Teignmouth, Sidmouth, Dawlish, and Torquay. Like so many other sites, these were old fishing villages or small ports now starting a new economy with limited facilities and few visitors. By 1770, Exmouth had an enlarged inn with an assembly room. Teignmouth followed in 1781.

Those communities on the north side of Devon facing the Bristol Channel got an even later start. Ilfracombe, which would emerge as an important resort, did not really get underway until 1788. As opposed to the south coast resorts and their fine beaches, Ilfracombe had a small beach surrounded by a gorgeous, wild, and rocky setting. On a small scale, these resorts duplicated life at the seashore elsewhere. They would never have as extensive entertainment facilities, but they did have warm weather in the summer—some even claimed they were too hot—and, in addition, a mild winter.[2] With this attribute, they touted their winter season, none more so than Torquay, and claimed to be the best health resorts in England. The elderly, the infirm, and the tubercular, all from the upper classes, now wanted to spend the winter safely ensconced in the comforts of Torquay, which had a "brilliant" winter season of theater, concerts, and balls. During the summer life lagged in Torquay, as the winter season residents all traveled elsewhere, a circumstance unique to the town.[3] The number and types of resorts slowly grew along more of the coast. However, change was about to sweep over the resorts as the transportation revolution engulfed them.

As long as transportation depended upon expensive private carriages or public stagecoaches, the resorts would remain the domain of the upper class, and an increase in numbers or broadening of the class base seemed unlikely. But technological innovation would change all this. The heralds of this change were in coal mines, where the Newcomen steam pumps thumped and hissed away, pumping water out of the mines. Thomas Newcomen had invented a primitive steam engine that went into service after 1715, solving the miner's problem of removing water from the coal face, allowing the exploitation of deeper seams.[4] Once on the surface, crude wooden rail systems utilizing horses and natural inclines moved the coal off to the ports. While an improvement over buckets and baskets carried by horses, the prevailing method in the seventeenth century, this system was inefficient, as only relatively small amounts could be carried. As the demand for coal increased year by year, it called out for further improvement. Mine owners sought better pumps for the mines and a more efficient means to transport coal.

The promise of steam power attracted inventors in hopes of break-throughs that would create more powerful and efficient steam engines that would meet both needs. James Watt and Matthew Boulton produced an innovative steam pump in 1776 that was much smaller and more powerful than the crude Newcomen. While it was a significant improvement, welcomed by the miners, it quickly found its greatest use powering the Industrial Revolution in England, as it was adapted to replace water power at many factories. Watt would continue to tinker with his engines and defend his patents, but would leave it to others to evolve steam power into new technologies.[5]

Transportation was the focus of a great deal of innovation.[6] In the late eighteenth century, inventors tinkered with steam-driven boats and land vehicles. But it was during the first decade of the nineteenth century that experimental engines reached commercial success. On land, Oliver Evans, Richard Trevithick, and George and Robert Stephenson made the most significant improvements. Their engines started to impress entrepreneurs looking to use the technology for land transportation.[7] They did not want individual trucks, but sought engines that could pull many carriages across rails as the most efficient way to proceed. Before much progress could be made, the opposition of aristocratic landowners, canal operators, and turnpike trusts had to be overcome. Aristocrats did not want to have their land appropriated, even when they were paid for it, and the other two interests had significant investments that were being put at risk. However, the logic of a system of power, capable of carrying larger loads at higher speeds than any system then in existence, won out, and Parliament passed laws that gave rights to investors to operate across designated lands.

While there were earlier railways such as the Stockton to Darlington, which focused on moving coal, the Liverpool and Manchester Company, created in 1823, united the great port of Liverpool, where the raw

FIGURE 4.1 F. Nicolson (after A.B. Clayton), *View of the Liverpool and Manchester Railway Crossing the Bridgewater Canal at Patricroft,* 1831. Lithograph. © NRM / Pictorial Collection / Science & Society Picture Library—All rights reserved. It was a thrilling new technology at the time, but it certainly looks primitive now. For the resorts it would bring a revolution.

cotton poured in, with the textile factories of the Manchester area, becoming the first railway to attract national attention.[8] In 1826 its charter was approved by king and Parliament, and the task of raising the money and building the railway got under way. To push forward the technology of the locomotive engine, the company sponsored a race at Rainhill in 1829, which was won by the famous engine the *Rocket.* It had a top speed of twenty-eight miles per hour, much better than the ten miles per hour of the stagecoaches.[9] Now with a better, if not quite reliable, engine and new innovations coming at a fast pace, the railway could enter regular service.

In 1830 the Liverpool and Manchester opened to great acclaim, with even the prime minister in attendance. The day before the event, the chief engineer had invited a small party of notables and friends to experience the new technology. One of the guests was the actress Fanny Kemble, on tour after her first highly acclaimed season in London. She wrote, "You cannot conceive what that sensation of cutting the air was;

the motion was as smooth as possible too. I stood up and drank the air before me. . . . When I closed my eyes this sensation of flying was quite delightful and strange beyond description."[10] Far beyond the expectations of the entrepreneurs who built the railways, people flocked to experience the new sensation, and on many of the early lines ticket sales exceeded freight charges. The speed and power of the "snorting little animal" made it immediately popular.[11] Not that it was terribly comfortable, but it was cheap in comparison to other modes of travel. The railways quickly developed a class system for their carriages. The cabins would evolve, but initially first class was a cabin much like that of a horse-drawn carriage, with no bathrooms and no food. Second class was similar but not so nice, with more people per carriage, and third class was not much more than an open carriage with benches where the traveler was exposed to wind, rain, and cinders.[12] Such was the experience of modernity. When the engine stopped for water and coal at the new stations, passengers had to quickly get to the bathrooms and to the restaurant before the whistle indicated the train was ready to go again.

Besides the scheduled trains, the managers started to run special excursion trains. These trains did not travel from city to city on a schedule. Instead, they were trains that could have many more carriages than the city runs required and were one-time, special trains that ventured to events such as horse races, prize fights, public executions, and temperance meetings. Special one-day fares attracted hundreds to the trains and, as many carriages would arrive at a station near the event, the crowds swelled into the thousands. Varied groups of people would arrive, some singing psalms for temperance meetings, others well on their way to drunkenness. At the fights and horse races, drinking and gambling combined to create unruly crowds, much to the horror of the local authorities, who had few resources to contain the crowds. Here, the old world of the village constable met the latest form of transportation. However, having discovered this profitable sideline, the railway companies were loath to give it up.[13] They continued to permit, indeed encourage, excursions financed by companies large and small. John Heathcoat, for instance, hired an excursion train to take all of the workers at his lace factory to Teignmouth for the day. On a far more significant scale, Bass Breweries took tens of thousands of its employees and their families to resorts from 1860 to 1914.[14] Other entrepreneurs realized that trains offered opportunities, and they emerged as packagers. The most famous was Thomas Cook, who built an empire from organizing excursions. His first one was to a temperance meeting, and this was followed this with excursions to the beach and beyond, right down to the present day.[15]

As the race for steam-powered transportation on land flourished, so did the competition for steamships. In the late eighteenth century, inventors worked tirelessly to marry steam engines to ship hulls, and, after the usual fits and starts and a few disasters from exploding engines, they had, by the second decade of the nineteenth century, succeeded in producing reliable steam-powered ships.[16] These vessels were the first to provide transportation to the resorts. Margate witnessed the first steamer visit in 1814, and by 1818 there were nine steamboats in service on the Thames.[17] Innovations appeared year after year, the boats got bigger and faster, and their ability to handle rivers and the sea increased. The public responded to the new speed and convenience. The Thames hoys had managed to carry most of the seventeen thousand visitors to Margate each year, but now with steamboats forty-four thousand visited in 1820.[18] Power and speed meant larger ships that could carry more passengers and provide new parlors, private rooms, and greater comforts in the cabins, a joy for the seasick. As they did not rely on wind, they established regular schedules, another attraction for the public. Long before all the resorts could be serviced by trains, steamboats brought visitors to resorts along the coasts. Even after the trains arrived, steamboats could still take vacationers on excursions to view the scenery and experience the sea. As with the railways, steam conquered time and space and ushered in a new world of transport.[19]

By 1843, Britain had the makings of a railway network, as eighteen hundred miles of track had been laid.[20] A lull then occurred, as the business cycle and entrepreneurial vigor declined, but by the end of the decade the boom was on again, and bill after bill landed in Parliament to acquire rights to new destinations. A web of tracks spread across the landscape, knitting cities, towns, mines, and industry together, remaking the transportation system, and turning stagecoaches into carriers that brought people to the railway station. Trains now carried larger numbers of people and heavier cargoes at a higher speed—approaching a steady twenty-five miles per hour and bursts up to fifty miles per hour—a miracle of the modern age. Even with frequent changes of horses, stagecoaches were limited to about ten miles per hour, and while the trains also had to stop to take on water and coal, they outpaced the fastest coaches.[21]

The resorts soon attracted the attention of the rail entrepreneurs, and by 1849, fourteen had railway service.[22] As always, Brighton led the way. In 1837 the London-to-Brighton railway line was organized. After the usual difficulties of finance, acquiring the land, and building the

FIGURE 4.2 *At the Sea-Side Landing—Waiting for the Evening Boat from the City.*
Harper's Weekly, September 2, 1871, 485. Scan courtesy of The Huntington Library,
San Marino, CA. Husbands arriving for the weekend.

tracks, service was finally begun in September of 1841, and the trains
quickly established a time of two hours for the journey. To maintain
Brighton's reputation as an upper-class resort, fares were kept high for
a while, until the managers realized this would not help their bottom
line. To make it easier for ordinary Londoners to enjoy the delights of
Brighton, the railway line added excursions. The first one was so popular that it took fifty-one carriages and six engines to make the trip there
and back in a day.[23] Another innovation that affected the resorts was
the introduction of the weekend fare, where your ticket was for a round
trip, but you departed on Saturday and returned on Monday. In a
quaint way to the modern traveler, many of the companies observed the
Sabbath, true for all railways in Scotland, and they would not move a
train on Sunday.[24] So the man of business, whether or not he was a Sab-
batarian, could get away on a Saturday and be back at work on Monday. The "husband's" boat or train was the result, as men crowded on
board to visit the family while the latter remained on holiday. Children
and wives waited at dockside or the train station for the "pater familias"
to arrive and share a part of a weekend.[25] The entrepreneurs in the new
rail lines experimented in a variety of ways to build an audience of
travelers that supplemented the daily, scheduled intercity trains.

In Devon, the resorts had mixed results from the railways. In 1844 the South Devon Line reached Exeter, the local town. From there it proceeded west across the Axe River. The Axe was not quite a mighty river, but more than a stream, so the railway only wanted to cross it once while heading west along the coast. Those resorts south of the river, such as Exmouth, Seaton, Sidmouth, and Budleigh, were left to use old roads, and the townspeople could only stare jealously at their more fortunate neighbors north and west of the river who could reap the bounty of more tourists. For the South Devon, not one of the great railways of the time, did connect the south coast with London, and travel times decreased accordingly, from sixteen-and-a-half hours from London to Exeter by coach to four-and-a-half hours by rail. The network that reached out from the main lines meant that the pool of travelers increased significantly. But, as the clientele of Devon resorts was more aristocratic than most, the rail company was able to keep fares high. By 1861, branch lines were built to the towns south of the river so they could also begin to enjoy growth in the numbers of visitors. But their predicament of nearly fifteen years points out the significance of having a railway connection.

The transportation revolution roared ahead. By 1848, 2,893 miles of trackage had been laid, increasingly powerful engines crisscrossed the landscape, and steamboats were to be seen on every large river and increasingly out at sea.[26] This enabled elites to journey to any place they chose at reduced costs. As a result, they continued to dominate the resorts. However, change was on the way. Cheaper fares, mandated by the government in 1844, also meant that other social groups could now begin to imagine traveling outside of their home territory.[27] By the middle of the century, economic development had created a growing middle class of shop keepers, clerks (in large companies such as the East India Company), artisans, bank clerks, and other similar white-collar workers, who all expanded their ability to enjoy leisure.[28]

However, before the social composition of the resorts could evolve, those who had to work for a living, whether white-collar or miner, had to get time off from a work schedule that was uniformly six days a week with a ten-hour work day. During the first half of the nineteenth century, little changed, except that some workers, such as at the Bank of England, lost holidays because managers believed that to get the best out of their employees it was necessary to keep them working.[29] The holidays that were celebrated consisted of the traditional Christian holidays of Christmas, Easter, Whitsuntide, and Shrove Tuesdays, with the more political Guy Fawkes Day and the secular New Years. Other holidays were regional—fairs and wakes—where communities celebrated traditions mostly related to the local parish church. For these the community took time off and local industries could only go along with them, as there was not much they could do, because these holidays were taken without pay and with little regard for managerial desires. Booths were put up on a village green or local field where goods, alcohol, food, and traditional handwork were for sale. There were contests to see who was best on a greasy pole, in wrestling, cudgeling, and other sports. Fairs also featured parades and fetes that could turn rough, as there was competition as to which group had the best float or display. One contest came from the tradition in many parishes of renewing their floor rushes once a year, so various groups competed to have the cart with the highest pile of rushes.[30] Those competitions could be rowdy. John Constable reported that the fair at a local town was "a tumult of drums and trumpets and buffoonery of all sorts."[31] For most of a week, musicians played, dances were held, and young men tested their strength in various competitions. Then it was back to work, drunk or sober.[32]

Changes in work schedules mostly developed regionally and haltingly over time. There were still a significant number of believers who resisted leisure, as it surely weakened character and led to sin. Indolence was a sin, work a virtue, thus holidays were suspect. Yet new voices were advocating rational recreation as a virtue, in that it led to personal improvement. Vigorous outdoor activity developed good health and self-discipline and other manly virtues; most of this literature was aimed at men.[33] Appeals to women came later. In 1843, the Saturday half-day off came to bank clerks, solicitors' offices, and government bureaus. Annual national bank holidays were declared in 1871 and more added in 1875. While bank holidays were, in their origin, for this narrow group of workers, they were soon understood to encompass most middle-class workers.[34] These holidays usually came with paid time off, and that concept slowly gained acceptance. Industrial workers, miners, and many artisans preferred to be paid more rather than given holidays, but growing prosperity and increased wages slowly turned workers toward time off, especially if it came with pay.[35] In 1867 postal letter carriers received two weeks off with pay and a few factories started to close for a week, allowing the workers time to enjoy the growing number of events such as race meetings and soccer games.[36] When holidays coincided with the summer months, a trip to the seaside became an option.

Those who could afford the new first-class carriages—aristocrats, upper bourgeois, prosperous artisans, and shopkeepers—enjoyed the speed and comfort of the new trains. No longer was it necessary to own a carriage and horses with the attendant expenses just to get to a resort. Many other travelers settled for second- or third-class travel, and the result was steady growth in the number of visitors at the beach resorts. Resorts, with all their attractions, also pulled in those seeking a home away from the increasingly noisome big cities. Some resorts became among the fastest-growing municipalities in Britain.[37] There was also a growth in the sheer number of resorts as local demand caused townships and entrepreneurs to look to tourism as a way to build local economies. By 1851 there were 71 resorts and, by 1881, 106.[38] Along all the coasts, new resorts appeared until they outnumbered the old spas, which were in decline because of the new competition. The spas, no matter how nice, did not have the many moods of the sea and all the drama of the beach. And as the new resorts, especially, had superior new accommodations and facilities, the spas could not compete in the new health market.

Summer holidays had become something of a necessity to show the neighbors that you could afford to take the time away and bear the expenses. Middle-class folk might save up just for the occasion, while the working class developed all sorts of saving societies that allowed them to save during the year to enjoy a summer holiday.[39] As more and more people were able to take holidays, the railway companies had a real incentive to build ever-growing networks. Scarborough acquired train service in 1845, and the following year Margate, Ramsgate, Blackpool, and Redcar (one of the newer resorts) were all added, followed by Weymouth, the favored royal resort, in 1857. The North Devon resorts were some of the last, with Ilfracombe in 1874 and Lynton in 1898. The railways also helped create some of the resorts. Rhyl, in North Wales, suddenly found itself with a rail station in 1848 and went from being a hamlet with two buildings to a resort with 212 lodging houses.[40] Steam also transformed Whitby from a fishing, alum manufacturing, and shipbuilding town into a resort that served Yorkshire.[41] Decade by decade during the nineteenth century, railway networks transformed the landscape in many ways, making leisure available to ever-greater populations.

There was an inevitability about the growth of the networks that led in turn to a flow of population to the shore. Some went seeking cures, as always, some to have an enjoyable time, some to work, some for a day of fresh air, and some to settle, but no matter the reason, the resorts were faced with population inflows on a scale that would give them problems and opportunities. Brighton, always the trend setter, had 117,000 visitors in all of 1835, but with the rail service opening in

1841, there were by 1850 73,000 passengers deposited in one week, and then, on Easter Monday 1862, 132,000 arrived in one day.[42] Blackpool, which had grown slowly, started to really take off as the railways tied it to a booming hinterland filled with industrial cities and towns. By 1873 it managed to entertain 850,000 for the season.[43]

The majority of these travelers were one- and two-day trippers who might go into the sea but also came to enjoy the entertainment. The railway companies had learned that there was money to be made at the lower end of the social scale, and after the passage of William Gladstone's Railway Act in 1844, the companies had to provide reasonable fares for the working class.[44] This was not greeted with universal glee, as one disgruntled gentleman from Scarborough had "no wish for a greater influx of vagrants and those who have no money to spend . . . Not having a railroad will be its [Scarborough's] great asset."[45] And as the *Preston Pilot* thundered, "Unless immediate steps are taken Blackpool as a resort for respectable visitors will be ruined. . . . Unless the cheap trains are discontinued or some effective regulation made for the management of the thousands who visit the place, Blackpool property will be depreciated past recovery."[46]

While most working-class and even some middle-class people could stay no more than a day or two, they nonetheless came to enjoy a holiday by the shore. The ones most often complained about were those who came only for a day and who would be known in the future as "trippers." They arrived at the beach with their own food and were happy to sit on the beach not purchasing anything except alcohol and enjoying the entertainment. They often came on the weekend and could be rowdy, but at the end of the day they returned home. Vacationers who could stay longer simply conceded the beach and other facilities on the weekend and waited for peace and quiet to be restored before they ventured out again. Some were not willing to concede, "The hordes who may come will desecrate this beautiful place and spend absolutely nothing. . . . Pandering to cheap trippers has been the ruin of most south-coast watering places."[47] Issues of class are obvious in these comments. Hitherto upper-class enclaves, the resorts were being invaded by the lower class, and that was not easy to deal with for those so used to the resorts before the coming of the railway. The problem of trippers would continue for some time, and resorts everywhere would have to deal with this class issue. Should they keep the trippers away or should they allow them in, and if so, how would that affect their regular visitors? It was even on the minds of the lower-class visitors. John Betjeman was hardly lower-class, yet he stayed at a boarding house and wrote poems complaining about the house rules. He also wrote a poem about experiences at the beach:

> A single topic occupies our minds
> 'Tis hinted at and boldly blazoned in
> Our accents, clothes and ways of eating fish
> And being introduced and taking leave
> "Farewell, 'So long,' 'Bunghosky,' Cheeribye"
> That topic all absorbing, as it was,
> Is now and ever shall be, to us—CLASS.[48]

This poem was published in 1959, so class remained an important aspect of resort living. Only the arrival of the public beach would ameliorate the situation.

While the trippers did not need many services, many other visitors did, and this would start a building boom at many resorts. Easy transport, rising prosperity, and more time off combined to create new markets for development. As Anthony Trollope would put it, "That men and women should leave their homes at the end of summer and go somewhere—though it only be Margate, has become a thing so fixed that incomes the most limited are made to stretch themselves to fit the rule."[49] As a result, choices needed to be made regarding what sorts of facilities to build. Landowners, builders, local authorities, and entrepreneurs all made decisions that shaped resorts. At Torquay, the Palk and Cary families controlled most of the land, and it was they who made the big decisions. They wanted an upper-class resort, and they created the roads and buildings to appeal to such a clientele. As a result, Torquay attracted families that wanted to stay in a villa with a view, invalids, and health seekers, who often came for the winter season. Torquay played to this by touting its healthy conditions and mild winters.[50] It also actively discouraged day-trippers. At Eastbourne the considerable resources of the Cavendish family, Dukes of Devonshire, came to play an important role in a resort that was not doing terribly well. Beginning in the 1860s when Eastbourne was a second-class resort, the Seventh Duke essentially turned the town around and made it into an aristocratic venue. Wide roads well planted with trees were a hallmark of Eastbourne, and on the streets large villas offered views of the coast. Hardly any aspect of improvement escaped the duke, as he took an interest in promenades, parades, sewers, fresh water, a pier, sea defenses, grand hotels, and even his own symphony orchestra.[51] As with Torquay, Eastbourne eschewed the casual visitor in favor of the fashionable resident. Those who built the buildings and serviced the inhabitants were taken care of at the east end of town in their own district.

At the other end of the scale were towns such as Blackpool and Margate. Blackpool had no dominant aristocratic family. Most of the land was held in freehold, and decisions were made by local landowners, builders, entrepreneurs, and speculators. While the north end of the beach was kept apart as a place for well-off visitors, the rest of the beach was dedicated to the millions who lived in the industrial towns of the interior. They had been coming to the beach for decades and staying as long as they could, sometimes under rough conditions such as sleeping out. Now excursion trains brought trippers by the tens of thousands for a quick trip. But like the old "wakes," holiday weeks diminished in importance in the towns and villages of the midlands, and the extra days became available to the workers who could now contemplate tourism. They had to be catered to in very different ways. No villas, certainly not grand hotels for them, as they crammed into homes managed by landladies who would become infamous for their regulations and very tight way with money—the guests' money.[52] These were homes controlled by a single family, with the wife managing the boarding house and the husband usually employed elsewhere. They created facilities that appealed to different groups in the working class, from more prosperous artisans to those barely hanging on to working-class status but who still wanted to get away for a few days and escape the grinding working conditions of the new factories. To serve them, bathhouses were built that provided a place to store clothes and to acquire bathing costumes. General prosperity and rising wages slowly enlarged this group through the last quarter of the nineteenth century. In 1873 there were 850,000 visitors, and, in 1893, there was the astounding number of 2 million.[53] Blackpool by this time could offer grand hotels and thousands of boarding houses as it emerged as the largest of all the resorts.

Margate never could rival Blackpool in the sheer number of visitors, but among the southern resorts it played an important role. With steamboat and rail connection to London, it shared that vast market with Brighton until other resorts developed on the Thames estuary. Cheap transport meant that working-class Londoners could afford the trip, and many did so. Yet it continued to attract better-off visitors. By 1800 it had developed proper Georgian squares and the amenities to please upper-class guests. The old town near the harbor was where the inns and boarding houses served a different clientele. As one observer noted, it was for "the intermediate rather than the opulent classes."[54] By 1830 the steamships landed

109,000 persons in a season, and by the end of the 1870s the railway brought approximately 700,000 visitors.[55] Accommodating this horde was left mostly to local finance and not London speculators, so there was no grand hotel, but the boarding houses flourished. Margate kept its reputation as "Margate the Merry" by providing for all ends of the social spectrum. As one cynic commented, "The Company here is divided as usual, into people of fashion; people of fortune and of genteel professions; and a rabble, consisting as it may happen of rich and poor."[56] As the decades passed, however, and cheap fares lured ever more people, elites started to look elsewhere as Margate lost some of its charm for them. For some, Margate was "unfashionable and should be abandoned to the cheap and ignorant."[57] Its notoriety for social mixing waned. One aspect of its reputation did remain and that was for overcharging. "The genius of this place is extortion," one visitor observed, "which actually could be said of many resorts."[58] So for a time Margate maintained its distinction, but inevitably the inundation brought about change.

Brighton was, as always, an exception. As a Georgian resort it had been built out with crescents and squares to the east and west of the Steyne, the old central village green. But investors built to suit the various segments of the Brighton audience. On the one hand were the elegant villas of Kemp Town and Brunswick Square that catered to the fashionable crowd and to royalty.[59] Along with them were created a series of hotels that also joined them on the cliffs and served those who did not want to rent a villa. Among these hotels was the Grand Hotel, opened in 1864, which sought to fulfill the promise of its name in being large, imposing, and filled with every comfort, including an elevator. The Grand Hotel in Scarborough followed three years later in 1867.[60] Catering to every elite need, these new hotels set a standard for luxury. The Grand would be an important part of the Brighton scene, where it helped create a wall of buildings that took up prime land facing the sea. In front of them were a road and a promenade that ran along the top of the cliff. Every resort had to have a promenade, all the better to fulfill the need of providing a stage upon which people could present themselves and their carriages and horses. Here was proof of the saying "if you've got it, flaunt it" as, either walking or riding, one could look upon the finery of the fashionables. Hardly anyone missed this daily parade except the truly cynical or those unwilling or unable to keep up.[61] Behind the wall of buildings rose the boarding houses for the middle classes and, further back, the homes of the families who made their living in Brighton. As for the wall of buildings along the sea front, this

EVIDENCE OLFACTORY

Angelina (scientific). " Do you smell the iodine from the sea, Edwin? Isn't it refreshing?"
Old Salt (overhearing). "What you smell ain't the sea, miss. It's the town drains as flows out just 'ere!"

FIGURE 4.3 Charles Keene, 1823–1891, "Evidence Olfactory," in *Mr. Punch at the Seaside* (London: The Amalgamated Press, 1898). Mechanical reproduction, cartoon illustration. Mark J. Cohen and Rose Marie McDaniel Collection, The Ohio State University Billy Ireland Cartoon Library & Museum. *Punch* could always find humor in even the direst problem. In this case, the issue was sewage.

would presage a pattern that would become all too common, with sea frontage displaying the villas and hotels that catered to the upper class. Later, it would be the hotels, apartment buildings, and condominiums that front the modern beach and create great walls of prosperity while enjoying the best views and access to the beach, one difference being that the old buildings were never much more than five stories high, while in many modern resorts, large, multi-story buildings dominate.

With the growth in the number of buildings and people, another problem quickly became apparent, as it was throughout the burgeoning cities of Britain, and that was sewage. Some homes dumped their waste into the sewer drain, most homes still had outhouses, others were hooked into a cesspit, some had pigsties, and some families kept cows in the basement for their milk. The modern flush toilet had been invented, but it would be many decades before sewage treatment and underground sewers became the norm.[62] In the meantime, sewers ran through town, across the beach, and into the sea.[63] The drains, mostly open, relied on the English climate to provide a regular source of water to flush the material into the sea. In the summer, when rain was irregular and the temperatures higher, fetid air, indeed really foul air, even to the less refined noses of those days, was offensive. In the summertime people fled the putrid cities for the clean air of the sea, only to discover rotting sewage. It was a revolting development. Strolling on the promenade with "meandering streams of pollution" and the effluvia poisoning the air was hardly a holiday.[64] It is ironic that the resorts were advertising their health benefits at the same time sewage was flowing across the beach. Going into the water could be even more of a challenge. *Lancet,* the medical journal, reported that the Thames River was stinking in the summer and that mortality rates were higher at seaside resorts. It also noted that diarrhea, diphtheria, and other diseases were prevalent due to "defective sanitary arrangements" and that the disease rate at Scarborough was twenty-three per thousand although it should be seventeen per thousand.[65] Blackpool had forty-five drains crossing the beach.[66] More serious diseases, such as cholera and typhoid, were also emerging in the cities. Solving the sewage problem would be expensive, and local government was hardly up to the task.

Governance was a problem as many resorts were still part of townships or parishes that were embedded in county governments that were ill prepared to deal with urban problems. What would catalyze the situation was the deathly shadow of disease. While the drains were inadequate and the cesspools obnoxious, they leached bacteria into the ground and contaminated the water supply, for almost all the resorts took their water from wells. The water off the beach was also awash in raw sewage. The combination was an invitation to disaster.

Cholera first struck England in 1825, but the epidemic outbreaks in 1849 and 1853 were deadly affairs. The Devon resorts were soon afflicted. Torquay, which had long prided itself on being the healthy resort, faced the menace of cholera during the great epidemic of 1849. A few deaths could be ignored, but once the disease was established, it could no longer be taken lightly as it caused an exodus of visitors. Exmouth and Ilfracombe were similarly afflicted. Nothing could be more painful to the Devon resorts than seeing the visitors vanish.[67] When it finally dawned on people that the problem was related to the filth on the streets, the bad drains, and the contaminated water, the towns took action. In 1848 Parliament passed the Public Health Act as a response to the growing public health crisis. The act permitted towns to apply to the General Board of Health for the powers allowed in the act. An application to the Board, favored by at least one-tenth of the rate payers, elicited an investigation by an inspector who would then report back on conditions to the General Board, which then granted permission for a local board, which had to be elected. The reports of the inspectors are quite alarming—Exmouth, "the dirtiest place in the whole county," and Ilfracombe were said to harbor "a large open cesspit." Such reports as these were quite common as resort after resort applied for the new status. It was not always easy to pass plans for a cleanup, as the boards often had local farmers and rate payers who were more interested in their taxes than in improving the resorts.[68] These individuals also felt maltreated, as any system that had to be built had to be big enough for the summer crowds and not just be capable of handling the town's normal population. For them, "the minimum of rates (taxes) was the maximum of happiness."[69] Nonetheless, those involved in the resort economy prevailed, and year by year open drains on the beach, cesspits, pigsties, and wells disappeared, replaced by closed drains emptying out in the bay away from the beach. Doctors were appointed as medical officers to advise local governments, and inspectors patrolled the streets on the lookout for malefactors who were dumping slops or garbage. Yet even when Margate had a pipe of nearly twelve thousand feet, there were still problems with untreated sewage floating near the beach.[70] Most outfall pipes would prove to be too short, and strong tides and storm surges could still make waters off the beach polluted.[71] One significant improvement was the building of fresh-water reservoirs away from town to clean up the water supply for drinking. Unfortunately, not all problems were solved, as the prevailing belief for some time was that the ocean was so vast that it had an infinite capacity to absorb everything poured into it, an attitude that still lingers as we fill the oceans with our garbage. To convince skittish tourists that they had cleaned up their act, the resorts started to print guides that spent considerable time describing the lengths they had gone to making the beach safe. Then they could get down to extolling their healthful climates.[72]

With the railway boom and the expansion of the number of visitors leading to increased housing and sewage problems, resort leadership moved slowly to define their audience. Some resorts, such as those in Brighton or Margate, could have broad attraction to all social groups, but most made decisions as to what group they would appeal to. For instance, Torquay attracted invalids, retired army officers, and civil servants. It did nothing to encourage lower-class excursionists or trippers; in fact, it got the railway company not to run on Sunday so that people could not even get to town.[73] At the other end of the spectrum, Blackpool accepted its destiny as the beach resort closest to the great industrial towns of the English midlands and the workers who lived there. The town fathers did reserve the north beach for the wealthy, who benefited the most from the booming industrialization, while cultivating the middle-class and working-class as an audience further to the south of town.

The resorts had to create new opportunities for leisure based upon the customers they now hoped to attract. This also meant staying in touch with changes in popular culture that could be imported to beach communities and then developing ways to present it to various groups. It was always easy to design things for the aristocracy, as leisure was almost a lifestyle with them and beach resorts had come to be very much a part of their world. As the *London Times* commented, "Among those who are well to do the annual trip to the seaside has become a necessity of which their fathers, or at least their grandfathers never dreamt."[74] Politics and estate management took time for upper-class males should they do either, and not all did, leaving them with days on end to fill with hunting, racing, gambling, travel, hobbies, and attending the "seasons" in London and Brighton. For women the many genteel exercises of managing a household, taking tea, caring for children, playing cards, reading, collecting, etc. meant that they and their menfolk were used to filling much of their day with what would be considered leisure activity.

During the early decades of the nineteenth century, most of these needs were met by the established entertainment provided at spas and resorts with assembly rooms for dancing, dining, and gambling, with time to display horses and carriages and themselves on the promenades or to go on walks or carriage rides into the countryside, with time still left for dining and socializing with friends. Mothers still looked out for their daughters while examining the young men for potential partners, because the summer "season" was one of the ways of disposing of daughters. One cynical lady, in casting her glance over the presentation of a relative, noted, "Then she will be fairly out, a bill [notice]) upon the door to say she is to be had."[75] While the world of the assembly room might seem endless, it was in fact changing. A measure of this was the gradual elimination of the position of master of ceremonies. Captain Wade, the first master at Brighton, remained in place until his death in 1808. A Mr. Forth replaced him but was gone by 1828, succeeded by John Eld. He was the last, as when he died in 1855 he was never replaced. Wade could be autocratic, but each of his successors had

A LAMENT

Dowager. "It's been the worst season I can remember, Sir James! All the men
seem to have got married, and none of the girls!"

FIGURE 4.4 Charles Keene, 1823–1891, "A Lament," in *Mr. Punch at the Seaside*
(London: The Amalgamated Press, 1898). Mechanical reproduction, cartoon
illustration. Mark J. Cohen and Rose Marie McDaniel Collection, The Ohio State
University Billy Ireland Cartoon Library & Museum. This mother has her work cut out
for her in finding appropriate husbands for her daughters.

diminished authority. Upper-class sociability was changing as private
entertaining became dominant. And as more and more "grand" hotels
were built, each with splendid facilities, the assembly room lost its
cachet and faltered before finally fading away.[76] Balls and banquets
were still showcase events, but they were either in the best hotels or finest private homes. Besides the glittering social life, there was a decidedly
seamy side to Brighton and probably other resorts. An 1859 official
estimate of the number of prostitutes in Brighton put the figure at 325,
but it was believed to be close to double that, and there were at least 97
brothels. As the "ton" left London for the holidays, so did the prostitutes.[77] Needless to say, they were not on holiday.

For the new middle class, entertainment choices were more difficult.
Members of this emerging group, growing in numbers and with an
expanding standard of living, confronted leisure with a certain amount
of ambivalence. Decade by decade during the nineteenth century, their
prosperity and numbers grew, with occasional economic downturns to

cause a temporary halt. Leisure time expanded as a result. Their homes grew, as did their material goods, and the home came to be the center of social life and domesticity for the Victorian male.[78] On the domestic front, the growing number of books, newspapers, and magazines filled many an hour, as did music, games, and genteel occupations, especially for women, as prosperity brought the ability to hire servants and avoid hard chores at home. Beyond the home and work, leisure choices were more difficult. Experience and religion turned them toward hard work and discipline.

This was the age of Victoria, and the emerging bourgeoisie reflected that era with ambivalence toward leisure. For some, the old religious verities held true that idle hands did the devil's work and that indolence was sin. For others, rational entertainment was sought after. Travel was approved if it was for educational purposes. If sports encouraged manliness and muscular Christianity, then it was good for building character and accepted. Thus rugby, cricket, athletics, lawn tennis, and vigorous walking were favored. For women, a new set of outdoor activities joined walking, such as archery, then later croquet, tennis, and golf.[79] When at the beach this new agenda including, by the middle of the century, swimming, not just dipping for health. Riding, walking, visiting friends, and reading good books (not trashy novels) were supposed to fill the day when at the seaside, although one dyspeptic observer would comment, "Not only do they read more novels than at home, but they are content to read novels no one reads at home."[80] Evenings were devoted to supper, concerts, theater, visiting the library to indulge in a lottery run by the proprietor, and conversation with friends. The assembly room might be something that they aspired to, but as it waned in popularity, even they abandoned it.

For the working class, this was an era of some change in leisure activities. One aspect of change was the growing discipline and longer hours of the workplace in the early nineteenth century.[81] One reaction was to join the Chartist movement and seek a political solution.[82] Some workers responded by seeking solace in the Methodist or Evangelical churches, which taught them to live a good life, stay away from alcohol, and follow a strict observance of the Sabbath. A day spent in religious observance was leisure enough. The alternative decision for many men was drinking on a significant scale.[83] Saturday night through Sunday was a time to indulge. The resulting Blue Monday was a fact of life that managers hated, but with which they had to put up. In popular culture there was also a cruel streak that was manifested in bullbaiting, cockfighting, and dogfighting, not to mention the brutal prize fights that attracted large crowds. Repelled by these blood sports, middle-class reformers condemned them and sought to open new venues for themselves and for workers in museums, libraries, and public parks.[84]

Whether in villages or in urban neighborhoods, the working class had a strong sense of community that made them suspect outsiders, keep their own traditions, and travel in groups rather than as individuals. Neighborhoods were tied together with saving clubs, choirs, brass bands, and ritual feasts and parades. The saving clubs provided the means of putting aside small sums through the year. Retail banking did not penetrate working-class communities, so it was the clubs that allowed families to not just dream of holidays but actually plan and go away. Holiday trips became more common and were still occasions for the community to travel together. Railway excursion trains took advantage of this. Community wakes edged into memory as holidays took over. A major beneficiary were the beach resorts, which had the travel facilities and lodging to make tourism available to all.

As for rational recreation and personal improvement, eminent Victorian goals, nothing fit the bill so well as collecting the natural world. During the late eighteenth century, nature worship had blossomed, and the rise of the Romantics had only increased the love of outdoors.[85] Poetry and painting about the countryside flourished. When they turned to the beach, collectors of all kinds sought out shells, seaweed, and tidal animals, which held a natural fascination for beachgoers. Strolling along the beach, turning over shells, and wading in tide pools to poke the animals is an old entertainment. Collecting them became a hobby during the eighteenth century.[86] There were fabulous collectors such as the Duchess of Portland, who acquired shells from around the world to create the most magnificent collection of her time.[87] Most people had much more modest intentions. In the nineteenth century, collecting came to appeal to a broad middle-class audience who could afford holidays at the beach. As scientific endeavor became a major aspect of Victorian life, it percolated down to amateurs, who scoured the beach in more systematic ways and built collections at home aquaria to show to friends. It carried a social cachet: as one writer put it. "You are hardly fit to live unless you know something of anemones."[88] The Devon coast became a center for collecting—particularly Ilfracombe, which had an abundance of rocky pools.[89]

Ardent observers of nature could sometimes get in trouble, as did Fanny Burney, who found herself caught on a cliff with a rising tide. Luckily friends and family missed her, as she had been away for some time, and mounted a rescue that brought her safely off the cliff.[90] Writing about collecting also became something of a phenomenon. Philip Gosse published a number of books, such as *Tenby: A Sea-Side Holiday, A Naturalist's Rambles on the Devonshire Coast,* and *The Aquarium: An Unveiling of the Wonders of the Deep Sea.*[91] Then there was Isabella Giffords's *Marine Botanist,* as well as Charles Kingsley, *Glaucas; or, the Wonders of the Shore.*[92] This dash into print caused a rush to the seashore, where the beach and tide pools were scoured for the growing number of home aquaria and dry collections. The inevitable result was that all too soon the favorite resorts were ransacked of everything collectable. Amateur scientists were driven to search out new horizons and new resorts to keep their hobbies going. Meanwhile, serious collectors such as Gosse could only regret touting the wonders of the Devonshire shoreline, which was soon bereft of everything he treasured. The same thing would happen to fern collecting, publicized by Charlotte Charter, who wanted to share her passion regarding ferns and did so in *Ferny Combes.*[93] She too would come to regret publicizing the best places for ferns, as collectors followed in her footsteps leaving little behind. Luckily for the creatures of the shore, the collecting hobby faded in the 1870s, and they were left to the tender mercies of young children who found examining beach creatures irresistible.

If entertainment was needed, one new site for it was the pier. The new piers had two functions. The pier at Ryde, on the isle of Wight, illustrates one function. Ryde was the port of arrival for the island, and it had such poor landing facilities that passengers had to be carried ashore. This became very awkward when the new steamships came into service and increased the numbers of passengers. The town fathers responded by funding and building a pier that would service the new ships, which was completed in 1814.[94] The second function of the pier was a place to promenade. What better way to breath the fresh air of the sea than by walking along above the waves, and what more exciting way to view the sea than to stride along above it? It was a thrilling new experience that quickly caught on. In Brighton, the Chain Pier, completed in 1823, was destined to be one of the most famous of all piers and was painted by the likes of Constable and Turner. The pier was the product of the industrial age in that it copied none of the old styles, such as Gothic; instead, it had a functional suspension design. The Chain Pier serviced steamships going to and from France, but it quickly became a place to take a walk. To control entry and keep the experience exclusive, two pennies were charged, which in those times kept out a lot of people. Thus promenaders along the seafront at Brighton could leave

FIGURE 4.5 John Constable, *Chain Pier, Brighton*, 1826–27. Oil on canvas, 161.3 × 214.3 cm. © Tate, London, 2020. Constable went to Brighton often because of his wife's ill health. Here he captures the new wonder—the Chain Pier.

the land and walk out into the Channel to view the shipping traffic, the fishermen setting out and coming home, and the moods of the sea, and turn around, the better to admire the built environment of Brighton. They also had the extra cachet of being seen in a rather exclusive place that confirmed their social status, at least to their own comfort.[95] Such an experience was quickly copied elsewhere.

During the 1830s, piers were built at Southend, Walton on Naze, Herne Bay, and Deal. The explosion in pier construction came in the 1860s when twenty-one piers were completed.[96] Besides the function of promenading, the piers quickly became centers of entertainment as bandstands, restaurants, and shops were built onto their decks. The strength of the piers benefited from railway bridge technology and the extensive use of iron. No matter the technology, piers were not made to withstand the raging sea in the middle of a winter storm, when the gigantic waves or a ship in distress could smash a pier in no time. The Chain Pier at Brighton was damaged in 1833 and 1836 before being destroyed in a storm in 1896. The other enemy of piers was fire, as some of the piers were built of wood, as were all of the decks and the adjoining buildings. So if the sea did not destroy the pier, fire certainly would.[97]

FIGURE 4.6 Samuel S. Carr, *Punch & Judy on the Beach, Coney Island,* 1880. Oil on canvas, 25.5 × 41 cm. Private collection / Bridgeman Images. For some time, much of the entertainment was right on the beach, as Carr depicts the crowd around the Punch and Judy show.

Entertainment slowly evolved at the resorts. In a sense the world would split in two, and these two worlds would exist side by side for some time. On the one hand there was the world of formal entertainment, which was focused on the assembly hall, with balls, concerts, card games, and other activities managed by masters of ceremonies. This Jane Austen world continued into the early nineteenth century, but would be forced to evolve as society and culture did; nonetheless, it had considerable momentum. On the other hand, a new world of entertainment emerged at the resorts that kept up with changes in popular culture. All resorts had promenades besides the beach to encourage walking, and now, especially as families spent more time with children playing in the sand, they became an audience. Into this space moved a number of entertainments. The Punch and Judy show, familiar to adult audiences since the seventeenth century, was transformed into a hand puppet show for children at the seaside. It soon became a staple feature of beach life.[98] For the children, another established aspect of beach life was the donkey. It was hardly a trip to the beach for young children unless they had a donkey ride. Musicians were also attracted to the new audience. The German brass bands were the first to invade this new

FIGURE 4.7 William Powell Frith (1819–1909), *Ramsgate Sands (Life at the Seaside)*, 1851–54. Oil on canvas, 77.0 × 155.1 cm. RCIN 405068, Royal Collection Trust / © Her Majesty Queen Elizabeth II, 2020. Frith depicts a Victorian beach in all of its lanquor and bustle.

space, followed by Italian and British performers. At times the rival groups drove the audience away as they competed with one another. Finally, the blackface performers who had sprung from the success of the Christy Minstrels on both sides of the Atlantic invaded the shore to entertain there.[99] These and other performers all had to hustle to make money. There was a long list of different entertainers and peddlers strolling the beach such as acrobats, performing canaries, monkeys, and dogs, as well as sellers of fruit, cakes, flowers, pincushions, lace, and shell vases.[100] They were unpaid and lived off what they could solicit from their audience, so while some would enjoy the free entertainment, others got sick of being approached for a donation. "Remember the performers" was an oft-heard solicitation.

The beach was transformed from a place with the sound of the sea meeting the shore into a bustling scene of noisy entertainment. As one auditor described it, one heard "squealing, squalling, screaming, shouting, singing, bawling, howling, whistling, tin-trumpeting, and every luxury of noise."[101] Needless to say, many did not like this transformation. They hated the cacophony and left for quieter, more distant, less populated beaches. Jane Carlyle went from resort to resort, finding them all too noisy, but thought Ramsgate the "horridest, noisiest place."[102] Some of the resorts, such as Torquay, simply banned all forms of entertainment from the beach, the better to serve their upper-class visitors.

As the seaside became more of an area of social mingling, this did not pass the notice of social commentators. Opportunities for misunderstanding between groups that met rarely in their normal routines suddenly became possible, if not routine, at the seaside. Even Dickens could not resist the opportunity to write a short book, *The Tuggs's at Ramsgate,* about the adventures of an artisanal family who come into a legacy and think that they must go to the seaside to celebrate their good luck and display their new status. Disaster follows as misunderstandings accumulate and the family has to retreat, sadder and poorer for the experience.[103] A similar tale in cartoon form is recounted in *London out of Town,* by John Leighton which relates the adventures of the Brown family in Margate.[104] Cartoonists took full advantage of the opportunity to poke fun at the many awkward moments. Cheap production techniques, fewer taxes, and inexpensive wood pulp paper meant that books and magazines proliferated into middle-class homes. None was more popular across classes than *Punch,* which started in 1841. While nearly every aspect of life in Britain was grist for *Punch*'s pages, the seaside had a special place every summer as people flocked to the shore.[105] The fact that these cartoons flourished was testimony to the way in which resorts brought forth comic situations. There had been comic images from the eighteenth century when elites dominated, but now there was a much greater audience and cartoonists flourished, afflicting all classes.

There is one fascinating painting from the mid-century. William P. Frith specialized in large canvases that captured life in railway stations, at race tracks, and one at the seaside, *Ramsgate Sands* (originally titled *Life at the Seaside*).[106] Frith spent a couple of seasons at Ramsgate before painting a scene between 1851 and 1854. It is easy to note that not a single person is actually in the water. One little girl is being dipped by her mother while another buries her head in her mother's dress, not yet ready to confront the sea. Frith has positioned himself at sea, looking onto the beach, where nearly every character to be found on the beach is depicted. Those in the largely female crowd are all dressed, as are the children, in full street costumes with sun bonnets and parasols. The men are mostly working at the beach or, if they are visitors, reading the papers, looking through a telescope, most likely at female bathers, or else trying to catch the attention of young ladies. Of those working at the beach, there is a blackface group entertaining in the left corner. Other hustlers try to get beachgoers to pay attention to their pet animals or employ other ways of extracting money from the loungers. In the background, a family walking to the beach is solicited to arrange donkey rides for the children—all in all, a day at a Victorian beach.

. . .

England led the way into the steam era and to the possibility of expanded leisure opportunities for larger numbers of people. Other nations were slower to follow. It was not that the other nations lacked experimenters in steam power. For instance, in America steamboats on the rivers were well advanced by 1800. However, the English in the midst of the Industrial Revolution were quicker to exploit the new technology. With successful beach resorts in operation, it was only a matter of time before steamships and railways connected them to the cities and towns where their customers lived. As they rapidly exploited the new steam technologies, the English would lead the way into the future elsewhere as English engineers, construction workers, and engines were exported to Europe and America. It is also true that other nations lagged behind England in that they went through the creation of an industrialized manufacturing sector and other modern economic changes at a later date. Their societies remained more rural and agrarian than the English until the second half of the nineteenth century, by which time most European countries were experiencing the full effects of industrialization. So the development of an expanded new middle class and a new working class was also delayed.

Each nation absorbed the railway as it met its needs. In Belgium the government was involved in the planning and building of a rail system.[107] After years of wars and disruption and the creation of a new monarchy, the government was intent on providing for the defense of the kingdom and aiding economic growth. With the help of George Stephenson, an Antwerp-to-Brussels line was completed in 1836, and in the following years the main cities were tied together. Resorts came later. In the German States, Saxony took the lead. After hiring British engineers, a line from Leipzig to Dresden was finished in 1839. Prussia started with private ownership of lines that served cities, but as Prussia rose to be a dominant power, state ownership came to be the norm. France initially looked askance at railways, as it had a good canal and road system. Why did they need rail? Besides, it would ruin the tranquility of the countryside. But the new technology could not be denied. Once the government decided that railways were the wave of the future, it played a significant role in the creation of a network. The government choose the route, built the track, and then turned it over to an operator.

Due weight was given to defense, as there was a serious concern for railroads in the northeastern part of the country, where lay the typical invasion routes. While the system would not really take off until after 1860, a few lines started earlier. One, to the future resort of Arcachon from the city of Bordeaux, was built by local entrepreneurs in 1841. It was barely eighteen miles long.[108] The channel resorts came later. Spain started late in obtaining railways and, as a protective measure, avoided the standard gauge of trackage for a larger gauge. In Italy railways started as early as 1839, but there was no real takeoff until the Pope approved the new technology for the Papal States in 1846; the real boom came later, in the 1860s. In contrast with England and America, European governments tended to be more concerned about national needs and put them ahead of entrepreneurial demand. This tended to support defense and industrial needs and less so those of leisure.

In America, it was the steamboats that got an early start. With great rivers such as the Hudson and Delaware, which had major cities on their shores, steam power easily found markets and audiences. In the 1790s steam experiments flourished, but it was Robert Fulton's *Clermont* that established regular service on the Hudson in 1807. Fulton's technology was directly copied from the English boats he saw when he visited England, and when he returned to America he brought with him one of Watt and Boulton's engines. Soon enough, steamboats found their way to every river and lake in America. By 1815 they started to go out to sea, as the first steamship went up Long Island Sound and made for New Haven, and by 1822 they were sailing for Providence and Newport. The state governments had not played much of a role in the expansion of steamships except to issue licenses to proceed, sometimes to more than one company at the same time. Entrepreneurs battled for dominance on various routes. One result of this was that American steamships became larger and more luxurious in order to attract customers. City-to-city travel was where the customers were, and it took time for ships to reach out to resorts.[109]

When it came to the railways, the first change was that in the United States they were called railroads. The word did exist in England, but it came to be used exclusively in America. Experimentation and imports of English engineering began in the 1820s, and by the 1830s railroads were functioning in a number of states. More often than not, the state governments chartered railroad schemes and then let them rise or fall. Some states, to encourage growth, undertook to provide credit for the entrepreneurs, sometimes to ill effect. After the panic of 1837, a number of states defaulted on their debt, much of it derived from railroad credit.[110] At the national level, visionaries looked west in order to knit the country together and to exploit the resources they hoped would be there. The federal government took the lead in transcontinental routes, leading to a new level of chicanery and rapacity on the part of the developers.[111] Local, more mundane routes took time to develop and often were the inspiration of an individual or small group who thought it worthwhile to extend the system to the sea.

New Jersey, with mile after mile of beaches, was among the first states to consider tracks to the shore. The real visionary in this case was a physician, Dr. Jonathan Pitney, who was convinced that the sea and air of Abescon Island had serious therapeutic properties that needed to be developed. But Abescon was in the middle of nowhere, and railroad entrepreneurs thought the whole scheme ridiculous and did nothing to help the amateurs who chartered the railroad in 1852. Any such scheme had to be tied to a large city, and in this case it was Philadelphia, which would be served through Camden on the Jersey side of the Delaware River. The Camden and Atlantic was underway and opened by 1854, offering the public a trip through the pine barrens to the marshy shore of Abescon Bay, where they were transported over by boat to the island. Once there, one found the partially completed United States Hotel, owned by the railroad, a few farm houses, and a horde of ravenous greenflies and mosquitoes. Thus started the fabulous history of Atlantic City. The company quickly laid on excursion trains to attract the weekend visitor, and by 1870 forty-two hotels and fifty boarding houses greeted over three hundred fifty thousand visitors in a season, all seeking relief in the cool air and the sea.[112]

If a railroad could create a new resort, what was an old resort such as Cape May to do? It had steamboats in service, but nothing so fast as the new trains. The West Jersey line, pushing through southern New Jersey to the sea, was supposed to be the answer. But it took its time doing so. Originally chartered in 1830, the plan collapsed in 1850, was revived in a fit of optimism in 1852, and finally reached Cape May in 1863, at the end of the tourist season. When it functioned, it could get Philadelphians to Cape May in three hours, a remarkable improvement over the trip down the river or the even longer trip across the pine barrens.[113] Cape May now faced a new future.

The railroads did not stop with the creation of Atlantic City and the inclusion of Cape May. Those hundred miles of beaches quickly attracted many entrepreneurs who faced the obstacles of getting rail lines out to barrier islands. Creeks and bays had to be overcome before resorts could be brought to life. Then the sea was always ready to smash the lines that probed along the coast too close to the sea. Long Branch was reached in 1860, bringing new life to another old resort, so much so that by 1875 another railroad reached the town.[114] One by one, new resorts benefited from the entrepreneurship of the rail companies and hoteliers. Ocean Grove, Sea Isle City, Avalon, Ocean City, and some fifty resorts emerged in the '70s and '80s, as the Jersey shore became a premier playground for the booming areas around Philadelphia and New York.[115] By 1890, 127 miles of rail running north and south knit together the shoreline, making tourism New Jersey's number one industry.[116]

Up and down the coast, steam reached out. Nahant was served by steamboats from Boston by 1818, and the railroad came close in 1838. Cape Cod, the "wilderness of sand," was slow to develop. There were fishing and hunting lodges on the Cape, a large inn by 1823, and by 1860 a hotel at Cotuit.[117] All of the towns are accessible by sea, but the railroad made it to Sandwich at the land end of the Cape in 1848, then to Orleans by 1865, and finally to Provincetown at the northern tip by 1873.[118] As in New Jersey, from the train station you needed to get a ride in what here was called a "Cape Cod buggie" to cross the sand to your final destination. In fits and starts, trains also made their way out onto Long Island as various lines stitched New York City into the countryside. Far Rockaway was brought into the network by 1869, after the consolidation of the Long Island Railroad. It was not until 1895, when the railroad pushed all the way to Montauk Point at the eastern tip of the island, that East Hampton acquired rail service.[119] Before that, intrepid tourists made it out to East Hampton over rough roads or by sailing. There they could find lodgings with farmers like Thomas Parsons, who started taking boarders in 1849.[120] Soon there were tents and brush arbors on the beach for a very casual setting. Only later, with the coming of the railroad, would the large mansions to serve elites willing to make the journey out to the end of the island become the hallmark of the Hamptons. So the railroads built this way and that, spanning out across the eastern United States as investors and corporations drove the railroads out to existing small enclaves or likely spots for resorts, as the seaside prepared for a new era.

There came to be a theory about the creation of summer resorts. Edward L. Godkin wrote that resorts were discovered by families of small means or artists, who sought out-of-the-way places where farmers were willing to board them for what the farmers considered lots of money but what was within the budget of artists. Boarders would soon move on to acquire modest cottages and make it their summer place. Inevitably, the first hotel would be built, and the great "tragedy" would begin for the cottagers who now found themselves in the middle of a fast crowd. So, the original vacationers had to decide to move on or learn to ignore the big money that was increasing land values. This theory works for places such as East Hampton, where the early visitors were boarders, among them were artists such as Thomas Moran, and it also works at Prout's Neck in Maine, where Winslow Homer pioneered a summer beach community.[121] There are other theories that involve brooding, cunning entrepreneurs; this one, however, has a certain charm.

England led the way into the transportation and industrial revolutions and was also more progressive in terms of workers' paid holidays. Other nations were slow to follow. In Germany, it was only after 1871 that industrialization really got underway. While Chancellor Otto von Bismarck enacted advanced social policies, he did little for holidays. They were few and tied to religious celebration, whether at the local or national level. France similarly industrialized late and did not have as many advanced social programs as did Germany. In America, it was the impact of the Civil War and the years afterward that drove industrialization. As for holidays in America, states or companies might grant them, but the federal government lagged behind. Even today, when paid vacations are universal in advanced nations, the United States is the only national government that does not mandate them. Still, Sunday remained the day of rest and thus was inviolate to the vast majority of Christians. Even in America many railroads did not run on Sunday, thus leaving few alternatives to those seeking something other than rest. In Vermont the railroad functioned on Sunday, but the passengers had to listen to the conductors reading the Bible.[122] At religious resorts such as Asbury Park, Ocean Park, and Oak Bluff, the Sabbath was strictly observed. In fact, Ocean Park did not permit Sunday bathing until 1979.[123] The rigid Sabbath yielded slowly to rest and relaxation as acceptable, and later still, recreation. Leisure was still something that elites took for granted and other social groups learned to accept as normal in the second half of the nineteenth century.

As a result, elites continued to dominate many resorts long after English resorts had started to deal with a broader cast of visitors. At Heillendamn, on the Baltic, an English visitor noted that three kings had been at the resort the year before and that assorted princes, princesses, grand dukes, and dukes were there during his visit.[124] At Biarritz, the emperor and empress of France made it their summer place, alongside assorted Spanish royals and aristocrats. Ostend was favored by the Belgian monarchy. Long Branch lacked true aristocrats, but it did have presidents, politicians, and fashionable society from New York City and Philadelphia. These were typical of the resorts that kept their usual customers. Most others adapted as the railroad and holidays made vacations available to different visitors. Atlantic City always provided space for upper-class visitors, while accommodating more and more middle- and working-class holiday-makers. As other resorts snagged more elite visitors, Cape May adapted. Our effete Philadelphian, Sidney George Fisher, only went to Cape May once, and while he liked the beach and the fresh air, he was bored and disgusted by the "shopkeeping class, who though respectable are intensely vulgar." They lacked education or refinement, and he would rather be back in the city than put up with them.[125] Fisher's tart response to the visitors at the Cape signals that "shopkeepers" were now a prominent part of the audience enjoying the facilities.

The dreaded trippers showed up everywhere with the coming of the railroad. For instance, in Germany, Thomas Mann had his hero in *Buddenbrooks* sneer at the "good middle-class trippers" who crowded the beach and were "kill joys in Sunday clothes" at the Travemunde resort.[126] Even in America they started to show up, but they were known as "shoobies," from their carrying their lunch in a shoebox. They appeared long after Fisher's visit to the Cape, when the railroad reached Cape May in 1863. The hotels hated them, as they took over public areas, but the town did have to allow a bathhouse to be built in order to let them rent bathing costumes, for the town had legislated against nudity.[127] At Nahant the trippers caused a problem for a group of male friends who swam every summer Sunday in the nude. Trippers came for the show, and finally forced the men to give up their ritual bath.[128] As in England, wherever they appeared the trippers raised the issue of class, and those beaches with a high-class clientele sought ways to keep them out.

The trippers were one group represented in the rising number of visitors at all the resorts; by 1874 Atlantic City had five hundred thousand visitors in one season.[129] Such numbers brought the need for more hotels, boarding houses, and facilities for entertainment. When it came to entertainment, one difference in America was the creation of the boardwalk. Unlike the grand promenades in England, America built boardwalks. The most famous was in Atlantic City, which was underway in 1870. This was a response to the heavy sand typical of many New Jersey beaches. At origin they were simple walkways of boards to help strollers get above the sand. In time they would get larger and larger, as they accommodated more and more visitors and also many of the entertainments that could be found on the beach in England. So one could stroll along and find places to eat, drink, buy souvenirs, dance, or be entertained in a myriad of ways. The boardwalk provided all of this above the beach, which was left empty except for swimmers and those who chose to walk along the hard sand at the water's edge. As elsewhere, piers also appeared to provide docking facilities for the steamboats and then expanded to include places to eat, theaters, and dance halls. While storms afflicted all beach resorts, two major afflictions in America were the summer hurricanes and winter nor'easters that slammed into the coast with great regularity, destroying piers, boardwalks, beaches, and, on the occasion of a monster storm, even hotels. So, entrepreneurs still had to be especially strong or foolhardy to invest in them. They did find relief when towns started to take responsibility for the boardwalk, piers, roads, and defense against the sea. Local governments also confronted that other accompaniment of expansion, the threat of disease. There was no national response until much later, unlike in England, where Parliament mandated solutions. Cape May had to close beaches in the 1880s because of sewage pollution. It was Asbury Park, however, that created the first resort sewage system in America in 1881, and it was 1888 before Atlantic City created a sewage company.[130] They were the leaders in a belated attack on pollution. It would be pleasant to announce that the measures taken at that time solved this lingering health and aesthetic problem, but it is with us still.

The transportation revolution affected all the resorts. By the middle of the nineteenth century, resorts nearly everywhere absorbed the impact of the transportation revolution. They would have to continue to meet the very real challenges of growth in the number of visitors, yet certain dynamics that arrived in the second half of the nineteenth century brought about dramatic changes to some of the resorts and created a wholly new type of resort by the beginning of the new century.

Can a Proper Victorian Be Nude?

As the numbers of visitors increased at the resorts and as they became more varied in terms of class and background, the problems relating to the body and dress became common. Early in the nineteenth century, the rise of evangelical belief and practice inside the Anglican Church raised objections about the male habit of nudity at the beach. By the middle of the century, questions regarding appropriateness of bathing costumes had become a matter of public comment, and by the second half of the century—the heyday of high Victorian morality—the debates were even more pointed. How to ensure that modesty was observed on beaches where men bathed nude and women and children were present as the family summer holiday became more common? Each country developed a beach culture that satisfied local morality and good taste. They differed significantly at first before coming to a general consensus at the end of the century.

Issues regarding beach behavior in England were contested against a background of evolving gender definition and social change. Victorian upper-class men were raised to be hard-working, independent, courageous, selfless, and hardy. Gone were the gaudy eighteenth-century male costumes, to be replaced by sober, dark suits. As family men, they were to assume the role of patriarch at home. More and more men worked somewhere other than home and aspired to acquire a suburban house, where their families were removed from the chaos of the city and where they could return every evening to a domestic scene administered by wife and servants. If a man stayed out, it was often to go to his club and associate with other men engaged in the enjoyment of food, drink, and conversation.[1] For working-class men, their lives were filled with hard physical labor, little rest, and often lots of drinking in public houses. But as wages increased toward the end of the century, working-class men could indulge in commercial leisure at the music halls and soccer matches. Young men of the working class, and of the higher classes, also engaged in all sorts of rowdy, disruptive behavior.[2]

At the beginning of the century, and through most of it, women were relegated to managing the household and family. For working-class women, that remained true throughout the century. For higher-class women, their roles became more varied as they managed larger households with servants and multiple social responsibilities. It was not until the latter part of the century that more of them, especially the young, found work and a measure of independence in such roles as teachers, nurses, and secretaries. Some even entered the professions. These "New Women" were less likely to accept the role of helpmate to the patriarch and thus became something of a threat to masculinity. They were also more likely to indulge in recreation, which meant swimming, tennis, golf, bicycling, bowling, and croquet.[3] They had to carve out new roles while men still dominated society.

There was a darker side for women and men as the pressures of social and economic change created a new condition—neurasthenia. This came to be a common diagnosis for what one writer called the "the stress of nineteenth-century civilization . . . on the brain and nerves."[4] Patients with this condition showed signs of fatigue, anxiety, headache, palpitations, high blood pressure, and depression. Men were subject to the stresses of business competition, rapid urbanization, and societal change. So the sturdy Victorian male weakened in the face of modern life. The cure frequently recommended was more leisure and travel, and where better to shed anxiety than at the beach? Women were far more often diagnosed with the new disease than men. It was caused by the pressures of "overcivilization," which came about from their involvement in the rapidly evolving modern world bedeviled by industrialization and urbanization, in the women's rights movement, higher education, and activities in the public sphere. These multiple engagements that modern women lived with brought new dimensions to their lives in ways never experienced by their mothers. One of the most serious problems was their declining fertility.[5] This was seen as especially prevalent among upper- and middle-class white women. The medical profession wrestled with diagnosing "hysterical" women and finding suitable treatment, but obviously rest was recommended.

Much of European society was characterized by similar attitudes—dominant males, women thought to be weak and in need of protection, and traditional ideas of family. Conservative Catholic areas tended to keep old-fashioned values longer, while other regions were more accepting of change. Industrialization and economic change evolved later in Europe than in England and varied around the continent. Almost everywhere there was a growing bourgeoisie that created its own social rituals, one of which was the annual vacation, which became a family necessity as the century wore on.[6] Given the national differences in economic development and social change, how each country decided what was appropriate on the beach was determined by the evolution of style and accepted cultural norms.

Everywhere, female nude bathing was a rarity in the middle and upper classes. As noted before, there was a long tradition of nude bathing by female peasants and workers. This informal bathing occurred along many coasts at some point during the summer, as individuals or communities sought to escape the heat or to ritually wash away sin or the cares of a year. One typical eyewitness was Samuel Curwen, who visited Exeter, went to a local beach, and noted "shoals of Exeter damsels, whose insufferable undress and ill breeding" offended him.[7] However, it was one thing to have ordinary folk cavorting in the sea, but a gathering of elite women at a resort was not the site where naked bodies should be on display. The standard means of getting into the water in England remained the bathing machine.[8] Generations of women climbed into the dank contraption to change into the shapeless gown that came to be universal. As they clambered out into the water, the dipper took over, and here things could go amiss. If the sea was rough, the women could be upended and their costumes gathered up around their bodies. Then there were the more adventurous women who moved away from the dipper and went out further to lie on their backs and float, but if a wave caught them and they were dumped, they were likely to be exposed.[9] Waiting for these mishaps were the idlers on the beach. Thomas Spencer reported that onlookers had telescopes, the better to witness the accidents. He thought these reprobates had "no more sense of decency than so many South Sea Islanders."[10] Telescopes were universally used to spy inshore. How to protect female modesty? For sure, no mixed bathing. Men had to be kept at a distance either by physical separation, which was the most common, or, if that was not possible, by time. If the latter, that always meant men

FIGURE 5.1 Thomas Rowlandson, *Venus's Bathing (Margate), A Fashionable Dip.* Colored etching, ca. 1800. Wellcome Collection. As usual, Rowlandson captures the male fantasy.

had to go out early in the morning to swim. These patterns were in place by the end of the eighteenth century, and it was hoped that they would "operate as an effective check to this offensive breach of decorum."[11] Unfortunately, decorum was often neglected, and as resorts evolved in the nineteenth century it would be even more so.

For most men, nudity while swimming was taken for granted.[12] It had been commented on in the first account of bathing at Scarborough in 1733 and continued over the years.[13] The *Brighton Morning Herald* in August of 1807 reported, "The beach this morning was thronged with ladies . . . the machines, of course, were in very great request . . . The greatest novelty, however, that this part of the coast exhibited this morning was in a gentleman's undressing himself on the beach for the purpose of ducking in front of the town, attended by his lady, who, sans diffidence, supplied him with napkins and even assisted him in wiping the humid effects of his exercise from his brawny limbs as he returned from the water to dress."[14] So over the seventy-four years between these reports not much had changed. Commenting on behalf of many men, Anthony Trollope, the novelist, wrote, "My idea of sea bathing for my own gratification is not compatible with a full suit of clothing. I own my tastes are vulgar and perhaps indecent, but I love to jump into the deep clear sea from off a rock and I love to be hampered by no outward impediments as I do so."[15] Then there was the Reverend Francis Kilvert: "I was out early before breakfast this morning bathing from the sands. There was a delicious feeling of freedom in stripping in the open air and running down naked to the sea where the waves were curling white with foam and the red morning sunshine glowing upon the naked limbs of the bathers."[16] He was rather taken with "naked limbs," for on another occasion he waxed ecstatic as he noted "the gentle dawn and tender swell of the bosom and the budding breasts, the graceful rounding of the delicately beautiful limbs and above all the soft and exquisite curves of the rosy dimpled bottom and broad white thigh" of a young girl.[17] Some years later, when he was at a resort that made men use drawers, he obeyed reluctantly, and, as it happened, the drawers fell down around his legs when he was leaving the water, causing him to fall. "After this I took the wretched and dangerous rag off." He assumed he had to wear them because of female opinion, but for him, "If ladies don't like to see men naked why don't they keep away from the sights."[18] As this was increasingly the age of science, one man provided a sort of scientific reason for nudity: "the saline solution of the ocean, so invigorating to the human exterior, will attach itself in larger proportions to the apparel than the person, so that the clothes will absorb more than the wearer and in that case will derive most benefit from the operation."[19] It is clear that many men were committed to swimming and dipping in the nude and that they were not about to give it up. Their unwillingness would continue through the century, causing considerable controversy. There was also some bad poetry:

> I would lodge in that row near the town's magazine,
> Were there not at all hours, such nudities seen,
> Fellows running about like Di's nymphs without smocks;
> Where the devil's the constable? —where are the stocks?
> Bite their toes, famish'd crabs, as they lave in the deep;
> Scorch their buttocks, high Sol, till they fry and they weep.[20]

Much of the commentary on male nudity was negative and would get more so, until by the mid-nineteenth century it became more and more

FIGURE 5.2 Thomas Rowlandson, *Summer Amusement at Margate, or a Peep at the Mermaids,* 1813. Hand-colored etching. The Elisha Whittelsey Collection, The Elisha Whittelsey Fund. 1959, Metropolitan Museum of Art, New York. This cartoon shows just what telescopes were used for at the beach.

hostile. As one viewer put it, did society want to continue to have "shameless men going stark naked in and out of the water close to the ladies' bathing places when a number of girls are waiting for machines?"[21] A visiting Frenchman was also surprised as "bathing takes place in full view of the [beach] front, swarming with idlers of both sexes. Men go into the water stark naked, which surprised me knowing how easily shocked English people are." He concluded that "when English people are not icicles, they are apt to become shameless."[22] He discovered, however, that there was a puritanical side to the English. He went swimming dressed, as the locals did, in his birthday suit and stayed out for some time. On his return his bathing machine was now well out of the water, as the tide had gone out and he would need, as there was no seaweed about, to walk out nude. Confronting him and seated right by his bathing machine were three women waiting for him. In the end he had no option but to walk out and clamber red- faced into the machine. His crime was to go bathing on a Sunday, and these ladies were strict Sabbatarians who tried everything they could to enforce their own rules.[23] Adding to the upper-class male right to bathe as he chose was the problem of the trippers. Beaches where working-class visitors were common had the same problem as fancy resorts. Unable, and perhaps unwilling, to pay the price of renting a bathing machine, men and women simply stripped and went into the water, "not much embarrassing themselves about appearances."[24] This brought objections "touching the indecent exposure which too frequently occurs in sight of the parade [promenade]. A proper feeling of delicacy, one would think, should operate as an effectual check to this offensive breach of decorum."[25] Proper feelings did not seem to penetrate too far. Gilly Williams wrote a friend, "It would astonish you to see the mixture of sexes at the place [Brighton] and with what a coolness and indifference half a dozen Irishmen will bathe close to whom we call prudes elsewhere. . . . Can you imagine Lady Catherine will ever appear on the beach, when there are such indelicacies staring her in the face?"[26] Across the classes, men were outraging those of a sensitive disposition.

By mid-century, opinion had become even more hostile to open nudity in public places. Much of this was the result of growing religious fervor among Methodists, Baptists, and other reformed churches, plus the evangelical wing of the Anglican Church. Their feelings were reflected in the *Observer* as early as 1800: "The indecency of numerous naked men bathing in the sea close to the ladies' bathing machines, and under the windows of the principal houses at most watering places has long been complained of, but in general has not been redressed."[27] It was time to stop this "heathen indecency" among men. By the middle of the century, as Victorian decorum and respectability dominated social opinion, the attacks became ever more intense. In 1856 there was this complaint in the *Illustrated London News*: "Before the bathing season is over I entreat you . . . to use your powerful influence against the utter indecency of our summer Tritons and Nereids . . . who, without a stitch of clothing ,stalk coolly about knee deep within a few yards of a crowded promenade. [They are] but the fattest and baldest and most inelegant of their species." As for women, "Have English women of the nineteenth century less modesty than either Spartans or Parisians?"[28] And this was all happening at Margate! The *Observer,* reporting on Ramsgate, joined in: "There is not even the slightest pretension to common decency. The men gambol about in a complete state of nature and the ladies frolic in very questionable bathing garments within a few yards of them, while the sands are crowded with spectators of the scene of all ages and both sexes."[29] The bathers seemed to be taking their therapeutic dip seriously while those on the beach enjoyed the sight. If you really wanted the maximum titillation, it was reported that between five and six hundred naked men and boys could be seen at Brighton.[30] It is hard to believe that

English beaches were becoming more like the wildest contemporary spring break crowd, yet that apparently was the case. The *Observer* conducted a campaign against Margate and Ramsgate for allowing this scene of "depravity" to go on. The editors urged the authorities to compel men to wear calecons (trunks or drawers), as the French did, to restore decency. A man could then bring his wife and children to the beach without fear of their witnessing a scene. The magazine kept hammering away on this theme and mentioned to boot that Margate was doing a terrible job managing its sewage.[31]

Resorts, or at least some of them, responded. They began to order that men wear calecons.[32] In 1862 Margate passed an ordinance mandating them, and Scarborough and Brighton followed in 1866. Brighton also hired six special constables to enforce the rules, and Margate put boats in the water with "severe looking policemen" to hover off the beach to make sure there were no improprieties as "dreadful scenes had been reported."[33] The *Observer* was not ready to surrender. While the mayor of Margate claimed to have stopped the "indecencies of the past," the reporter noted that he saw a naked man with a woman in a bathing dress in the presence of other naked men and spectators. This was all "not quite proper."[34] It was a case of cultural change versus commerce. If the customers wanted to bathe naked, resorts were reluctant to stop them. One commentator in Scarborough noted, "We know from experience that first-class (male) visitors object to wearing drawers when bathing, so we will lose them."[35] So, however much rules were put in place, the complaints continued, for the resorts were not able to enforce their rules, and some of the smaller resorts did not even try.[36] One official testified that they had difficulty when men went out in a boat and jumped in nude, and they could do nothing about it as they could not identify the men later when they had their clothes on.[37] One can only think this was said tongue in cheek.

There were always the recalcitrant few. As late as 1880 William Ulyat advised, "Where persons go to the shore alone, or with only their families or intimate friends, and they find none others there, they may use their own everyday and commonest clothes with which to go into the water. If practicable, as to weather and those present, they may go in naked. This latter may be the better way."[38] Yet the tenor of the times was against such sentiment. A compelling reason for men to wear something was that more and more families visited the seaside for their holidays. As the century wore on, the patriarch was being challenged by a new role as masculine domesticity came to be accepted. It was expected that the man of the house would accompany his wife and children in and around the water, and so men found themselves forced into more and more appropriate dress. They, like their wives, now had to have a costume. For men it was from neck to knee, and for the women, neck to ankle. In 1895 Lland-udno, Wales, became the first resort to officially introduce mixed bathing, which was not unknown, but during the '90s other resorts soon followed, and this quickly became the norm.[39] If a man really wanted to swim nude, it had better be early in the morning and in an out-of-the-way spot. In front of the grand hotel would not do. The irony in this trend is that, as mixed bathing became the norm and male nudity diminished, the natur-ism movement was just over the horizon.

As the English wrestled with what was proper at the beach, other nations were doing the same. As noted, there were a variety of solutions to the possible exposure of the female body and the overexposure of the male body. Each country had to discover the balance with its own culture and sensibilities. And as international travel was becoming easier, with steamboats and railroads, there was a regular commentary about differ-ences. The English led the way and were always ready to criticize. One English traveler, on witnessing the beach at Biarritz, thought that the scene would strike an English observer "as an infringement of the laws of propriety and decorum," but after a second look it was "infinitely more decorous and decent than that which is pursued on our own shores." He was complaining of the French practice of mixed bathing, not yet a fix-ture of English beaches.[40] Yet if the English visitor was initially offended in France, an American could characterize European bathing as tied to an "old idea of exclusiveness [that] still prevails; at home the ocean bath is the essence of democracy."[41] As railways and industrialization came later to the Continent, the problem of trippers was not as pronounced until much later in the century. The railway system in France, for instance, did not expand until the reign of Louis Napoleon, who pushed the expansion of the system in the 1850s. As was appropriate given the clientele, trains to the northern resorts were first class only.[42] But across the many resorts that were created in Europe, there was a diversity of practice.

The nation that remained closest to England was Belgium, with most of northern Europe following the same pattern. As noted earlier, the Bel-gians were committed to the bathing machine and imported it onto their beaches. Ostend, the major resort, used bathing machines exclusively, and they fitted well onto a broad sandy beach. Belgian bathing costumes were unrevealing for women, even to the need for stockings and a cap to make sure every part was covered up. In a departure from the English pattern, men were covered up with a suit, and mixed bathing was allowed, but if women wanted privacy there was a beach set aside for them. For men who wanted to swim nude, there were always the dunes further along the coast where "obscene nudity" appeared.[43] It is hard to imagine how private it would be, as Ostend had a magnificent promenade that went along most of the beach. On the landward side of the beach, hotels and private homes made a wall along the promenade.[44] Further north, on the German beaches, the sexes were separated, and there were rules against nudity. At Swinemunde there were five separate zones: upper-class men and women had separate areas with cabins for changing, chairs, and a boardwalk, lesser folk had two areas with no facilities. The men were all on one side, and between them and the two women's sections there was a five-hundred-yard break.[45] This type of segregation remained the pattern on the northern beaches until later in the nineteenth century.

French beaches were different. Dieppe remained a popular beach and benefited from a remarkable building created in 1822 by the Count de Brancas. It was part casino, part baths, and part changing facility. At the edge of the beach there were changing tents where you left your clothes prior to taking a dip with a baigneur. Mixed-gender bathing was the rule, as men and women went in together without the clumsy bathing machines. If men wanted to swim nude, they had to do it far away from the casino facilities. The beach at Dieppe was often the first time Britons came into contact with the French practices, as steamship service from Brighton and a four-hour train ride to Paris meant that more and more Britons were passing through Dieppe. Along the channel coast, as railway service was extended, resort after resort was created. Among them were Boulogne, Deauville, and Trouville, mostly funded by Parisian money to serve elite Parisians. At this stage the channel coast was still the scene of upper-class bathing.

Besides the channel resorts, the railways reached out to the Atlantic coast. Biarritz, for instance, emerged as one of France's leading beach resorts by the middle of the century. Never easy to get to, it sat in the far south on the Atlantic coast near the Spanish border. Terrible roads limited access for local people. The few who made the trip changed in the dunes, the women well draped, then walked to the surf, and the men waded in nude. Even as the roads improved, not much changed. Then came the railway to nearby Bayonne, making it possible for the empress Eugenie to reach Biarritz with relative ease. She had first visited with her mother in 1835, prior to the railway, and it obviously made an impression. She was Spanish, and so Biarritz had an appeal as a place close to home that could

FIGURE 5.3 Jean Jacques Alban de Lesgallery, *The Beginning of Sea Swimming in The Old Port of Biarritz*, 1858. Oil on canvas. Private collection, Archives Charmet / Bridgeman Images. Biarritz at the height of its fame was a rather small enclosed cove.

attract her Spanish aristocratic friends and Spanish royalty. When she returned by rail in 1855, after her marriage to Louis Napoleon III, it was to build a large villa and begin the history of the resort.[46]

There were three beaches at Biarritz, with Port Vieux the most fashionable. Changing cabins sat at the back of the beach, divided by gender, where women changed into a pair of pantaloons that went to the ankle, and over that they wore a tunic that went to the knees. Over this went a cape and a broad-brimmed hat. Men wore a costume that covered most of the body, although it left the ankles and feet bare, as an English observer snidely commented.[47] Women wore canvas shoes. The women trooped down to the water's edge, divested themselves of the cape, and then either their male relatives or a baigneur helped them into the water.[48] The male baigneur was a French institution even this far south. The baigneurs stood at the water's edge in dark costumes and dark hats and aided those who needed help. As opposed to an English beach, couples and single people mixed together—children and their nannies went to the beach in the morning—and it was this fact of mixed-couple bathing that caused the Englishman to write that the scene was an "infringement of the laws of propriety and decorum." But, as he recognized, it was in fact very proper, as decorum was observed at all times as strangers kept "at a respectful distance as they would on dry land."[49] At Biarritz people stayed in the water longer than was true in England, as the water was warmer (seventy-plus degrees), encouraging play in the water. People clustered around rafts, went canoeing, and chattered away to one another. An American commentator also reported on the "perfect decorum, a telling lesson to Britons who bathe."[50]

The empress was one of the attractions at the beach. Liveried servants carried costumes down to two tents, one occupied by the empress while she changed, the other by four of her companions. When all five emerged, they were in matching outfits of black silk consisting of a coat, vest, trousers, boots, and a black straw hat, which in the case of the empress was decorated with a red ribbon. They marched the few yards to the beach through two lines of spectators and were greeted at the water's edge by five baigneurs in red flannel who tied gourds around their waists for flotation and then carried them into the water. There they floated on the water and let the waves roll by. Close by, men in a boat beat the water to keep away the sharks. Once entertained enough, they went back up the beach for another change of clothing and a return to the empress's villa.[51] The empress was ahead of her time in wearing a revealing silk outfit, as universally the costumes were made of wool or flannel and, as one young woman complained, weighed a ton.[52] Meanwhile, as most eyes were on the empress, the Emperor made his way through the spectators to the beach.[53] Around the turn of the century, one young female English visitor at Trouville remarked how the Marquise de Vermandois, "a goddess," had a bathing dress of red silk and one could see "how beautifully she is made."[54]

No matter the fabric, the new costume of pants with a dress that came to the knee provided women with much better mobility in the water. This was the costume of the future, and it would be one that ultimately evolved into the modern bathing suit. Similarly, the practices of mixed bathing, of men in costumes, of changing huts on the beach, all became common practice at the fashionable beaches in most of France. Biarritz was made fashionable by imperial patronage and the infrastructure that such patronage brought. Completion of the railway, the addition of paved streets, gas lighting, new paths to the beach, and a number of grand hotels besides the empress's villa (which itself was ultimately made into a grand hotel) created the infrastructure so necessary for elites. It attracted kings and queens from all over Europe. Queen Victoria and King Edward VII visited, the latter on a regular basis. Even Chancellor Otto von Bismarck, no friend of France, was among the many politicians who flocked to the coast.

New resort towns such as Biarritz did not have to deal with the traditional sensibilities of an old community that could be offended by behavior on the beach. So while Biarritz represented the future when it came to beach behavior, there were other communities that were not so enthused. Arcachon, squeezed between the Atlantic and a large pine forest, sat on the edge of a large bay. It was a small community of fishermen and peasants who made a living from the bay and the forest. The local roads were bad, and so only the locals occasionally went into the sea. Then in 1841, one of the earliest railways in France connected the coast to the nearby city of Bordeaux. Soon enough, merchants from Bordeaux started to push tourism on Arcachon, but the local community was not about to put up with the costumes, or lack of them, appearing on the beach. In 1847 the town council passed by-laws governing bathers. They had to be decent on shore and in the water. Men had to wear "wide trousers" and remain away from female bathers. Bathers had to dress and undress in cabins, and if they dressed in their rooms they must cover their bodies while walking to the beach. Women had to wear a large gown reaching to the heels when walking to and from the water and wear a conservative bathing costume. Bathers must not speak to one another or make gestures while bathing.[55] The fast life of resorts such as Biarritz had to stay there. Traditional communities did not permit such things to infect an old town's ways. Unfortunately, they would later have to confront the changes that came with trippers and others invading the dunes and beaches and with the onset of modern beach behavior.

Not far away to the south was San Sebastian on the Basque coast, one of the earliest Spanish beach resorts. It was patronized by Spanish royalty, who had a bathing machine on rails from the top of a small cliff down to the water so that they could get in and out of the water without walking across the sand and exposing themselves to the public. When the railway arrived in the 1860s, it made it easier for elites from Madrid and elsewhere to join the summer holiday, the *veraneo*, which was soon a part of the social year. San Sebastian was never international, but very Spanish. Given the conservative nature of Spanish society and the influence of the Catholic Church, bathing costumes covered the body and remained that way until the twentieth century. When modern bathing suits finally started to catch on, one Spanish clergyman thundered that they were changing Spanish women into "carnal goddesses." But as elite members of society traveled in European circles and witnessed the changes happening elsewhere, they slowly accepted the new fashions. The Church may not have liked it, but in the end fashion prevailed.[56]

American behavior at beaches was far closer to France than it was to England. There are fascinating accounts by foreigners that describe American beach conduct and reveal the writers' own ingrained attitudes about their familiar home resorts. We can sense the difference from English practice in two letters by Fanny Kemble, the English actress, written in 1838 from Far Rockaway. On leaving the hotel for a dip, she confronted

> two small stationary dressing huts on the beach, and here one is compelled to disrobe and attire oneself in the closest proximity to any other woman who may wish to come out of the water or go into it at the same time as one's self. Moreover, the beach at bathing time is daily thronged with spectators before whose admiring gaze one has to emerge all dripping, like Venus, from the waves, and nearly as naked; for one's bathing dress clings to one's figure, and makes a perfect wet drapery study of one's various members, and so one has to wade slowly . . . under the public gaze, through heavy sand, about a quarter of a mile, to the above convenient dressing-rooms, where if one finds only 3 or 4 persons, stript or stripping, nude or semi-nude, one may consider one's self fortunate. This admitting absolute strangers to the intimacy of one's most private toilet operations is quite intolerable, no benefit from bathing worth it.[57]

These things in "civilized parts of the world human beings perform in strictest seclusion." She also hated the hotel, where she was an "inmate" with a crowd of strangers.[58] She did like to get out and about in a modern way, for she described herself as a "coffee color" or a "Red Indian Squaw," as she would not wear sun bonnets or sit indoors all day until the sun was down, as did other women who were "careful above all things, of their appearance," and who "marvel extremely at my exposing myself to the horrors of tanning."[59] Kemble obviously favored bathing machines and gender-segregated beaches to the rough-hewn American practice she experienced. Her vehement reaction speaks volumes about the difference between the two societies.

A very different appreciation of American resorts comes from Fredrika Bremer, a Swedish author and feminist who visited Cape May in 1850. By that time there were more hotels and better conditions at the Cape, where she thoroughly enjoyed her stay. She, like many Europeans, commented in an early letter to a friend about a unique American custom: "'Miss——, may I have the pleasure of taking a bath with you or of bathing with you?' is an invitation one often hears at this place from a gentleman to a lady, just as at a ball the invitation is to a quadrille or a waltz, and I have never heard the invitation refused, neither do I see anything particularly unbecoming in these bathing-dances, although they look neither beautiful or charming."[60] This was the product of American mixed bathing and not having bathing machines. It was one thing to jump out of the back of a bathing machine and be dipped three times and return. It was another to walk across the beach and go into the water alone, especially into the surf. Atlantic surf was quite boisterous and could be dangerous. It was best to go in with company, preferably male, and if no relative was handy then a suitable candidate had to be found. That this was a commonplace can be seen in a dialogue composed by the young Sarah Putnam, who wrote in her diary, "Miss Pimkin, may I have the pleasure of a bath with you today? Mr. Smith I'll be delighted, any hour you say," and then later for Miss Pimkin, "That wave was a perfect crusher, to bathe alone is forlorn."[61]

It was not acceptable for women to bathe alone because of the danger, yet as women were still very much the most numerous sex during the week, the system of requesting, by men or women, that they accompany one another was a socially acceptable way of dealing with this. But to foreigners it was strange indeed. It was not always practiced, as Bremer wrote: "There is a group of wild young women holding each other by the hand, dancing around and screaming aloud every time a wave dashes over their heads; and there in front of them, is a yet wilder swarm of young men, who dive and plunge about like fishes." [62] For Bremer, the whole scene was wonderful:

> More than a thousand people, men, women, and children, in red, blue, and yellow dresses of all colors and shapes—but the blouse-shape being the basis of every costume, however varied—pantaloons, and yellow straw hats with broad brims, and adorned with bright red ribbon, go out into the sea in crowds, and leap up and down in the heaving waves, or let them dash over their heads, amid great laughter and merriment. Carriages and horses drive out into the waves, gentlemen ride into them, dogs swim about; white and black people . . . all are there. . . . It is . . . a republic among the billows, more equal and more fraternized than any upon dry land; because the sea . . . treats all alike . . . purifies them all, unites them all.[63]

In another letter she goes on about the scene again: "The presence of that great and august Ocean, makes you make light of the crowd of men, women, children, black and white, dogs, horses, carriages in whose company you must take the baths here. It is a shockingly democratic scene which at first almost [makes you] start back."[64] Indeed, she is put off by this "at the unlovely, apparent rudeness of this kind of republic," but will come to accept it.[65]

It is obvious that Bremer's experience to date was with quiet, elite beaches in Sweden and in America, where she visited Nahant. The diverse crowds she mentions are an indication that by the 1850s Cape May was attracting a broader community. The part that does not ring

FIGURE 5.4 *Scene at Cape May, Godey's Ladies' Magazine,* v. 39, August 1849. Digital scan courtesy of The Huntington Library, San Marino, CA. The bathers in this image clearly show that they are wearing old clothes and not bathing costumes.

quite true within Bremer's account is her comment about Black people. The only Blacks at Cape May were the serving staff in the hotel dining halls and the slaves of southern visitors. If Black folk went swimming, it was early in the morning, away from the hotel district, and before the crowds arrived, and they were unlikely to be accepted as equal participants in the "republic." There were indeed incidents between Blacks and slaveholders that caused bloody heads before growing abolitionist pressure made the situation uncomfortable enough that slaveholders preferred to go elsewhere.[66] These two different accounts are a good introduction to the mid-nineteenth-century American beach, which had created similar but different behavior.

One significant difference in America was the way in which men stayed with the women while bathing. The American way provided women with a certain amount of protection while they were in the water. In England, men "go outside the line of the breakers, or they swim still further out and ride at ease where the wave, however large, merely lifts them pleasantly as it rolls under. But the smashing force of the wave is where it curls and breaks, and it is there the ladies wait for it."[67] This late-nineteenth-century English account also describes the trials of one group of women:

> Along the yellow line where sand and pebbles meet there stood a gallant band, in gay uniforms, facing the water. . . . Perhaps forty or fifty, perhaps more, ladies: a splendid display of womanhood in the bright sunlight. Blue dresses, pink dresses, purple dresses, trimmings of every colour; a gallant show. The eye had but just time to receive these impressions . . . when, boom! the groundswell was on them and, heavens, what a change! They disappeared. An arm projected here perhaps a foot yonder, tresses floated on the surface like seaweed, but bodily they were gone. The whole rank from end to end was overthrown—more than that, overwhelmed, buried, interred in the water like Pharaoh's army in the Red Sea. Crush! It had come on them like a mountain. Crestless and smooth to look at, in reality that treacherous roller weighed at least a ton to a yard.

As the observer describes, the water recedes, but the women do not retreat from harm's way:

> I looked up for a moment out to sea and saw the smack [ship] roll heavily, the big wave was coming. By now the bathers had gathered confidence, and stepped, a little way at a time, closer and closer down to the water. Some even stood where each lesser wave rose to their knees. Suddenly a few leant forwards . . . and others turned sideways; they were the more experienced or observant. Boom! The big roller broke near the pier and then ran along the shore. . . . Group after group went down as the roller reached them, and the sea was dyed for a minute with blue dresses, purple dresses, pink dresses; they coloured the wave which submerged them. From end to end the whole rank was again overwhelmed, nor did any position prove of advantage; those who sprang up as the wave came were simply turned over and carried on their backs, those who tried to dive under were swept back by the tremendous under-rush. Sitting on the beach, lying on this side or that, doubled up—there they were, as the roller receded, in every disconsolate attitude imaginable. . . . Was there ever such courage?[68]

FIGURE 5.5 Winslow Homer, *Long Branch, New Jersey,* 1869. Oil on canvas. The Hayden Collection—Charles Henry Hayden Fund, Photograph © 2020 Museum of Fine Arts, Boston. The white flag indicates that the beach is clear of nude males so the ladies can go bathing.

While it is nice that he admired their courage, it would have been a whole lot better if he had been in the water to help, as did the baigneurs in France or men in America. But preserving gender separation was more important than helping the ladies.

While mixed bathing was common, there were still men who wanted to swim nude. Many American Victorian males at mid-century were much like their English counterparts. Swimming nude was important for men such as Walt Whitman. He also wrote about it:

> I see a beautiful gigantic swimmer swimming naked through the eddies of the sea,
>   His brown hair lies close to and even to his head, he strikes out with courageous arms, he urges himself with his legs,
>   I see his white body, I see his undaunted eyes.[69]

For men who wanted to, they could always swim nude very early in the day or in an isolated spot, but if they did it at a resort, a red flag flew over the beach to remind everyone that naked men were about.[70] This diminished as the century wore on, as there was a slow evolution in

FIGURE 5.6 Robert L. Bracklow, *Beachgoers on Coney Island Beach in Front of Balmer's Bathing Pavilion, Coney Island, Brooklyn,* August 6, 1898. Glass negative, 5 × 7 inches. Robert L. Bracklow Photograph Collection, New-York Historical Society, Photography © New-York Historical Society. The bathing pavilions gave day visitors a place to rent a swimsuit, change, store their clothes, and if they wanted to, eat and drink.

gender roles. While males were dominant, as usual, there was also a sense that men should be involved in the household, and there was a drift to more companionate marriage. It was expected that males play a role at home and be involved with the children.[71] One aspect of this was the summer holiday. As soon as they could, middle-class men sought to have their families go to the beach for a week or two, and for elite males it could be much longer. Father would try to be there for the whole time, and he certainly tried to have a holiday away from the chaos of the urban life. If he could not, there was always the father's train or boat on the weekend. Most middle-class men might learn to swim nude, but would you want to do so in front of your children? This was unlikely, so bathing costumes became more and more common.

While Fanny Kemble had to change with company, it was quickly settled that changing would be done in private and not in public. At the back of every beach there was a line of small wooden cabins which families either owned or rented for the day or season. The public part was getting out of the cabin and into the water, so all the better to swim at high tide and minimize the walk. As in France and elsewhere, long

capes were adopted that were shed at the water's edge and put on immediately on leaving the water, helping to ease the tension involved in the
walk back. Men had to dress in the usual drawers and blouse—no bared
chests. Thus, early on there were mixed-gendered beaches and everyone
in a costume. These rules were for the upper and middle classes, who
could afford the hotels. Working-class bathers were usually to be found
on beaches close to the cities, not at the fancy resorts. Atlantic City,
which had easy transportation from Philadelphia, attracted workers. By
the middle of the century they could find a place in the three hundred
boarding houses where working-class people could stay. When they
went to the beach, they could use old clothing or patronize the new
bathing houses. These were wooden buildings on the beach where you
could change into a rented costume, leave your street clothes in storage,
and then have immediate access to the water. One always hoped for a
dry suit, but on busy days a damp suit was likely. Without booking into
a hotel or renting a cabin, one could enjoy the beach. There was still no
desire to do more than frolic in the water and then leave and put on
regular clothing. Wandering around in a damp bathing suit was not
practiced. The bathing houses flourished at popular beaches and became
quite significant buildings, with other services such as food and drink
added, until they were an important part of beach life.

During the remainder of the century, change would come to the
beaches in ways that affected behavior and dress in more ways. The
greatest impulse came from recreation. While organized sports such as
baseball and soccer grew and prospered, informal activities such as
bicycle riding, croquet, archery, tennis, badminton, golf, billiards, and
bowling all flourished. This was very much the case at resorts, as most
of these activities were suited to the summer months and added more
activity to the summer scene, which was dominated by bathing, walking, and riding. Women were involved in these sports as the "New
Woman" emerged, who sought out physical activity as never before.
Women's fashions still kept them wrapped from head to toe—you
should never show a leg. Indeed, to show too much flesh could bring
ignominy and social banishment, as Virginie Gautreau discovered when
John Singer Sargent painted her portrait with dress strap undone,
revealing too much bare shoulder. The painting was in the 1884 Paris
salon, where one would have expected a good deal of tolerance.[72]
Instead she was shunned by high society and humiliated. Sargent would
later add a strap to the dress to make it proper. The fashions worn by
elite women still included corsets and bustles emphasizing breasts and

posteriors. For some, the looser dresses that were a part of the Aesthetic movement at the end of the century were far more appealing.[73] Women who did not want to be involved in high fashion could find other, more practical, clothes to wear, but they still had to watch how much flesh was exposed. So even with more recreation options, women still struggled to find a fashion alternative that gave them more freedom.

Another sport, though hardly new, was swimming, which brought a new dimension to bathing resorts. Anyone who went to the sea for therapeutic reasons did the three-dips-and-out routine as recommended by physicians and others. Real swimmers were few and overwhelmingly male. For swimming to become a general recreation at the resorts, there would have to be a series of changes such as schools to teach swimming and costumes that would permit swimming. There was a long history of books recommending swimming, including that of Benjamin Franklin, who published his *Art of Swimming* in 1748. It was then reprinted in New York in 1818, in London in 1820, and in Glasgow in 1840, and it existed alongside other books advocating swimming.[74] In the 1830s a surge of opinion pushed men to learn to swim, and at the same time proprietors of "pools" (which were still usually enclosed parts of rivers) advertised swimming lessons. This was a general phenomenon, and men responded, as it meant another fun activity they could enjoy while at the resorts. Inspired by classical learning and ancient swimmers, the first swimming society was created in 1828 by boys at Eton who swam in the Thames, and a book was published, *The Art of Swimming in the Eton Style,* to spread their methods.[75] As many of the resorts were sprinkled along the English Channel, there was a challenge tempting many swimmers: to be the first to cross the channel. The first male to do so was Captain Mathew Webb, in 1875, when on his second attempt using the breaststroke he completed the swim in twenty-one hours and forty-five minutes.[76] His success was a significant boost to English swimming, leading to the creation of three hundred swimming clubs by 1880. Most of these clubs were not at the beach, but in towns and cities that built pools to further recreation. Their clientele was mostly male. Women generally lacked access to the pools, and if they had access it was limited in time.

As we have seen, women swimmers were few and far between. Yet as recreational opportunities increased for women, swimming was one of them.[77] In 1854 it was reported that at Ramsgate a young man was teaching women to swim, but the reason this was commented on was that he was bare-chested and his arms were similarly bare. This probably helped him in teaching ladies to float, but a bare torso was regarded as

FIGURE 5.7 *Bathing Costumes, Godey's Lady's Book and Magazine,* 1871, v. 83. The Huntington Library, San Marino, CA. Here, *Godey's* is advising its lady readers on the new fashions and how to make them.

indecent. Exposed nipples and belly button would remain forbidden into the twentieth century.[78] Then, in 1860, *Godey's Lady's Book and Magazine,* a popular women's magazine in America, advocated swimming for women and recommended Cape May and Atlantic City as good flat beaches on which to learn.[79] The article noted that while recreation was one thing, swimming should also be done for reasons of health and cleanliness. In this the old therapeutic idea lived on. The article also had practical advice: learning should be done with the help of a teacher, one should learn to tread water early, it was good to start with a wooden board in front as this would aid in floating, it was best to walk out using a rope as a guide and then turn and swim back in using a frog kick, and the newer styles of over-arm swimming, "winging," were good to learn in time. This may have appealed to daring young women, but for most women who spent their lives in corsets and dresses that covered their bodies from shoulder to ankle, this was not attractive. Anyway, it was next to impossible to swim in the baggy costumes that women wore.

They were only good to jump up and down in the waves, but not to move and kick around. Depending on the cloth, most of these outfits weighed as much as twenty to thirty pounds when wet, and they clung to the body in ways that were revealing. Proper beachwear was needed, and that came from the general mood of reform that emerged that made it possible for women to enjoy a recreational life.

Changes in costumes came slowly. By 1866 *Harper's Weekly* featured the new swimwear with pants, and then in 1871 *Godey's* could point out that there had been "great reforms" in bathing dresses in the last few years.[80] The flabby gown was out, and in its place came new French fashions—not that they were particularly good for swimming, but they did feature a pair of "Persian" pants covered by a dress with a skirt that came to the knees. The wearer of the new costume was covered in the same way as the old sack that covered the body, but at least had better mobility. This made it easier to jump up and down in the surf, and there was not the risk of having the sack dress rise up in the water, leaving the wearer half naked. Dress reform was on the way for the fashionable. Many women, especially working-class women who could not afford these new suits, would still dig out an old dress to wear for the annual few dips in the sea or would rent a costume from the bathhouse.

Bathing costumes continued to evolve through the end of the century. The French led the way as their costumes became more and more functional, but still covered most of the body. Elsewhere for men, they became a single garment that reached from the shoulders to above the knee. The trend was to make the suit shorter, but for some time it was not possible for men to bare their chest—that was a step too far and could get you arrested. For women the break had come with the evolution of the "Persian trouser." On top of the "trousers" one wore a dress. The skirt of the dress always had to reach her knees, and the skirt remained a feature as other parts evolved. The pants reached the knees rather than the ankles, so stockings had to be worn because the leg or limb could never be naked. Slowly the arms were revealed, as the dress reached first to the elbow and then just below the shoulder. Every change increased mobility. Also, new fabrics cut the weight of the suit, making water activities more enjoyable. The real breakthroughs would await the twentieth century and changing mores.

Many also would not bother with the new costumes, and they would be among the many standing on the beach, watching the bathers who featured in the many images of beach life. For some, the beach was a holiday, and it was easy to forget the sea, as it should be "ignored, as it

FIGURE 5.8 *Surf Bathing*, 1900–1905. Dry plate negative, 8 × 10 inches. Detroit Publishing Co., Library of Congress, Prints & Photographs Division, Detroit Publishing Company Collection. This photograph clearly shows the use of posts and ropes. While everyone faces the camera, a big wave is on the way.

is, almost, perhaps quite vulgar."[81] While they may have been enjoying the ocean air, they were still within easy sight of the bathers, and, given the numbers of people just standing around, the bathers were among the bravest people when they trudged up the beach soaking wet to a changing cabin. As one reporter put it, "Many sensitive ladies have been prevented from entering the water through dread of the ordeal."[82] But beaches were also places of display where rules could be bent or broken. One young woman at Long Branch believed in flaunting herself. Just before high tide her servant came out and set up a wicker sentry box. He was followed by a "beautiful" young woman in a blue and red flannel outfit, who marched over to a private changing cabin and then emerged in a tight-fitting blue silk bathing dress. By now there was a big crowd. She went over to the sentry box and entertained some "gentlemen" visitors before dashing into the surf. When she exited, she just marched up the beach with her soaking silk outfit to the cabin, and her maids were there to help her change before she returned to the sentry box to receive her male admirers. One supposes it was a case of "when you have it, flaunt it."[83]

As numbers increased, so did the possibility of tragedy. "Every summer what multitudes of these cases we see reported—distressing cases of bathers swallowed up by the sea in the presence of loving friends, powerless to aid them."[84] With more and more bathers and swimmers, it was inevitable that the sea would claim a number of them every year. This meant that the newspapers now reported doleful news on a regular basis during the summer. Something had to be done, as this was bad publicity for the resorts. The solution was lifeguards. As they appeared, rescues were effected. The resorts with bathing machines did not worry that much, as the machine was a safe haven. Those without machines had to do otherwise. In France, the baigneurs provided help to those in trouble. In America, the resorts aided those who were just jumping up and down in the surf by placing stout poles near the water line and then running cables or ropes out that were secured by the poles. It was easy for anyone to grab a rope and stay close in to frolic and play with a sense of safety. The real problem came when swimmers started to leave the surf line behind and venture out farther. If they got in trouble, they needed professional help, or at least the help of a strong swimmer. Recognizing this new danger, resorts started adding lifeguards. Long Branch had a bathing master who determined if the surf was safe; once he did, boats went outside the surf line to be ready to help.[85] By the 1880s Atlantic City had men and boats at the ready to protect the swimmers. As soon as they could, the hotels, which initially provided this service themselves, turned it over to the township as a municipal responsibility.[86]

By 1900, issues relating to the body were evolving toward modernity. Among the last to do so, Britain adopted mixed bathing, so that it finally became the norm at resorts. Female bathing costumes were at last beginning to give women the ability to move and enjoy playing in the surf and even to swim without exposing themselves. Men's bathing costumes were becoming standard wear. On the land side of the beach, more fundamental changes were underway that would transform many resorts.

6

Entertainment Comes
Front and Center

In 1880, John H. Packard published *Sea Air and Sea Bathing*.[1] Much of his general advice about the efficacy of bathing and the benefits of sea air would have been familiar to the readers of eighteenth-century guide-books. A few comments regarding nude sun baths, the common practice of swimming, the circumstances against male "buff baths," and the need for strong men and strong rope to protect against accidental drowning might well have puzzled the same readers. So even as the century was coming to an end, there were still advocates for ocean water and air as cure-alls, and some would still go to the beach seeking good health, but the reality was that far more people now came for entertainment and recreation. The last twenty-five years of the nineteenth century witnessed huge crowds surging to the seaside, bringing about another revolution in beach resorts. If railroads had initiated great change in the early nine-teenth century, it was the need to entertain prodigious crowds that cre-ated a new style of resort at the end of the century.

Making this possible was the march of technology. Nothing was more important than the new source of power—electricity. During the 1880s and '90s, great strides were made in taming electricity and mak-ing it a practical power source. Electrical lighting was especially sought after, and the 1882 London Crystal Palace Electrical Exhibition and the 1893 Chicago Columbian Exposition featured displays of electrical lighting.[2] Such displays came to be mandatory in the new amusement parks, which sought to turn night into day and keep the customers

FIGURE 6.1 *The Promenade, Blackpool, England*, ca. 1890–1900. Photomechanical print. Library of Congress, Prints & Photographs Division, Detroit Publishing Company Collection. Blackpool at the height of its popularity in the Victorian Era. The famous tower dominates the scene.

coming long after sunset. Even most city dwellers might see the occasional gaslight on a street corner, but for rural folk there was no such thing. So the blaze of lighting featured at the resorts was a dazzling portent of modernity.[3] The new power source also transformed the new machines of entertainment. While steam had powered most of the nineteenth century, electricity started to push it aside. Soon a whole industry of entertainment would be built around the new power source.

Western Europe, Britain, and America all experienced an era of economic growth during the last quarter of the nineteenth century. Not all sectors benefited equally. Agriculture, for instance, did not do well in Europe and Britain as produce from the Americas poured into local markets. However, in manufacturing, chemicals, finance, retail, and insurance, there was significant growth that percolated down to the clerks and workers who made up the bulk of the workforce. They could now afford more of the nice things in life, and that increasingly meant a holiday of some kind. People still traveled in groups, but now they were more often work groups rather than community or neighborhood groups. Railways still offered the cheapest and most convenient way to travel, whether in third-class cars or excursions. For workers who were only getting away for a few days or a weekend, third class was their mode of travel. Higher up in the class system, better-off artisans, shopkeepers, clerks, managers, and on up traveled in more spacious surroundings. In fact there were more and more of every class.[4] Just taking Blackpool as an example, it received 850,000 visitors in the summer season of 1873, and, by 1893, two million.[5] In America, Coney Island witnessed a similar increase as it went from being an empty beach that Walt Whitman loved for its isolation to a great national attraction. Between 1875 and 1881 four railway lines, two large piers for steamships, and a highway tied the young resort to New York City and the world beyond. By 1909, 20 million visitors came during the summer from late May through September.[6] Blackpool and Coney Island were exceptional, yet the rising numbers were felt at all the resorts. Evolving attitudes toward leisure combined with a growth in days off created the expansion in vacations. Aiding in this was the constant elaboration of the transportation network with more extensive railway systems, better roads, and urban streetcar lines. Sundays had evolved from Holy Day to a holiday for a great many people. In an increasingly secular world, leisure time was transformed from something potentially sinful to a time for healthy recreation free of sin and beneficial to the body. Recreation was a more robust term and increasingly favored over leisure, which has connotations of languor. The seaside was nothing if not healthy recreation. This combined with a Saturday half-day off plus Sunday opened the way for a quick weekend, or at least one day away and, in combination with holidays such as the August bank holiday in Britain, meant bigger crowds.

This was also the era in which advertising started to push products and services on a national scale.[7] The emergence of national magazines and regional newspapers, of new technologies in printing that created colorful posters, and of national brands all contributed to the emergence of robust advertising campaigns. Competing railroads advertised, and often it was not so much their trains as destinations, such as the resorts, that added glamour to their campaigns. Resorts acquired the ability to boost their images and define themselves to potential vacationers. They often stressed how even a few days at a resort could provide relief from the arduous business world. And if it was not an appeal to the men to relax, it was to mothers that they must get their children out of the ever more polluted atmosphere of the city. This was particularly true for London, as this was the height of the terrible coal smoke pea-soupers that would ruin anyone's health.[8] But the advertising images focused on glamour, as the resorts wanted to stress that they were a special place that you, too, could enjoy and be a part of.[9] These appeals were made to the middle class, who could now finance a week or two away. For elites this was never a problem: it was taken for granted that they would get away during the summer.

Resorts had had to deal with expansion before, but now the numbers were simply overwhelming. Building to deal with the growth required capital on a scale not known previously, and thus outside investors were needed to help with the scale of expansion. It was no longer a single grand hotel, but a number of them, at the main resorts. Similarly, boarding houses proliferated to manage the growing trade at the lower end of the income scale. By the turn of the century at Atlantic City, there were 225 hotels and over 700 boarding houses.[10] Growth on this scale required capital from Philadelphia and New York City, as local entrepreneurs could no longer finance their ambitions, and the risks always remained the same with the problem of the limited season. As we will see, fire and storms also mangled the best-made plans and forced a lot of refinancing. In addition, the building of multiple theaters, music halls, piers, bathing houses, and shops of all kinds also required financial outlays on a new scale.

At the other end of the resort economy were the little entrepreneurs, especially the boarding house owners. These were homes that local couples, mostly, rented out for the season. Different sectors existed in this market, from fairly high-end lodgings that attracted middle-class families who could not quite afford a hotel and wanted to stay for a week to, at the other end, homes that packed in young workers who were just there for a few days and who were on a very tight budget. The landladies who served this broad market would become a familiar character type in cartoons and comedy of all kinds. The Blackpool landladies were especially renowned, or reviled, as the case might be.[11] Often depicted in cartoons as towering over their diminutive guests, they were regarded as tough operators who were out to fleece all who came their way. For these ladies, cheating on everything from meals to fees for all sorts of "extras," such as towels and sheets, was commonplace. As one sour observer stated, "That the lodging-house has become a torment has become notorious. A workhouse or a gaol is bad enough; but their inmates are scarcely in more melancholy quarters than those gloomy rooms, at once bare and frowzy," with "a slatternly landlady downstairs, and a select party of parasitical insects in the bedrooms, in which the English paterfamilias consumes uneatable food."[12] Doubtless there were penny-pinching landladies, but they also had the problem of a season and had to make their profits from that season last through the rest of the year. If they had a working husband, chances are that he too worked in the tourist industry and faced the same problem. So landladies had to cut every corner to make a go of it, packing in as many lodgers as they could and skimping on food or services. John Betjeman composed a poem of house rules in his boarding house:

Don't waste the water. It is pumped by hand.
Don't throw old blades into the W.C.
Don't keep the bathroom long and don't be late
For meals and don't hang swim-suits out on the sills
(A line has been provided in the back).
Don't empty the children's sand shoes in the hall
Don't this, Don't that. Ah, still the same, the same
As it was last year and the year before—
But rather more expensive now, of course.[13]

However true that there were hard-hearted ladies in the business, it was also true that most tried to make a living and give people a fair deal. To survive, they needed customers to return, or at the very least not to spread stories about them, for it was true that people who came from the same community usually stayed in the same vicinity. There were also stories about landladies to whom the same families returned year after year as they felt they got a good deal on food and clean and comfortable lodgings. It has to be said, moreover, that the guests kept a tight grip on every penny, especially if they were working class. When they were at the beach, they wanted to indulge in as many of the experiences and entertainments as possible. It was no fun to return home without being able to tell stories about the only vacation they would have that year, so every step on to the beach or into a dance or music hall was a treasured moment that needed retelling.[14]

One group that also grew in numbers and continued to be looked down upon were the trippers or shoobies in America. There were many workers for whom a trip to the seaside held special allure, even though they had few opportunities to go. Whether they came as a group of singles or as a family, the trippers found their way to the resorts mostly from a nearby city or town where there was easy rail transport. They showed up carrying their own food and sometimes their own beer and drinks, and so used few services.[15] They did like to listen to the beach performers and were quite happy to join them in song. The upscale visitors greeted all of this good cheer with dour looks and open complaint. Some resorts such as Bournemouth simply told the rail companies to cease having trains stop on Sundays, the better to keep the trippers away. Many tourists just decided to stay home on any day that promised a crowd of them.[16] A. B. Granville regarded them with contempt: "The upper and wealthier classes of society, who ought to be encouraged and enticed to remain at home . . . have been driven away from every point on the coast by the facilities afforded to the 'everybody' and the 'anybody' of congregating in shoals . . . creating bustle, noise, confusion and vulgarity."[17] Thomas Mann, in *Buddenbrooks*, writes about the beach at Travemunde on Sundays as crowded by "good middle class trippers" who packed the beach and were "kill joys in Sunday clothes."[18] But boisterous young men drinking and having a good time were only the harbingers of a long tradition. Given the numbers that now flooded onto the beaches at holidays, they would be difficult to segregate, so some resorts had to put up with them. In the eyes of some, "The hordes who may come will desecrate this beautiful place and spend absolutely nothing. . . . Pandering to cheap trippers has been the ruin of most south coast [England] watering places."[19] However much they were disliked, the trippers were here to stay.

The wealthy, of course, did have options. There was always Newport or Biarritz or Nice, and even Brighton, where one could avoid the masses by going in the winter. This happened more and more. They also had the ability to seclude themselves. In America one way to seek privacy was to buy an island and open a club, as was done in Georgia in 1886 for the Jekyll Island Club, whose members included Morgans, Rockefellers, and Vanderbilts. It was limited to one hundred members, where each could have a cottage or an apartment in the main building. A member could stroll the eleven miles of beaches and never fear confronting the hoi polloi.[20] Or one could buy into the Cumberland Island Club, the creation of Thomas Carnegie, with similar facilities and with an equally impressive member list.[21] Another alternative in the United States for those seeking relief in the winter was to seek out distant places made available through the constant expansion of the railroad system. Henry D. Flagler took his immense fortune from Standard Oil to Florida, where he had great ambitions.[22] Florida as a winter tourist center was the creation of Flagler, who had a belief in the state and in his resorts. Starting in the north at Saint Augustine, he built the luxurious Ponce de Leon Hotel to lure tourists and, if they could not quite manage the prices at the Ponce, he built the Alcazar across the road.[23] Visitors had access to all the facilities of a grand hotel plus the beach and the warm waters of the Gulf Stream. Realizing he could create his own

Riviera, Flagler built the Florida East Coast Railway and continued down the coast, building or buying hotels along the beaches of Daytona and Miami and not stopping until the railway reached Key West in 1912.[24] Modern Florida developed from Flagler's ambitions.

If going south was not adventurous enough for jaded northerners seeking relief from the winter, there was California. The southernmost grand hotel in California, the Hotel del Coronado, was completed in 1888 in San Diego. Three entrepreneurs dreamed of having a grand hotel in San Diego, which could be a year-round resort. They created the "Del," an architectural icon and gem that attracted the wealthy and celebrities.[25] So by 1890 American elites could choose between private clubs and grand hotels on both coasts to seek privacy and quiet in both summer and winter.

While elites could find a preferred setting, those larger and more diverse audiences strained the resorts' abilities to provide entertainment, as not everyone came with the idea of bathing. How to entertain them? The old assembly room lived on only in novels. As urban areas burgeoned in the nineteenth century, modes of entertainment evolved to entertain the masses. For many generations, taverns had provided drinks and singing for mostly male audiences. But the music hall tradition overtook the taverns, evolving in the 1840s as bigger halls were built for as many as two thousand auditors. Amateur talent was displaced as the new halls had a commitment to professional entertainment, whether singers or dancers or acrobats. Some of the halls attracted the traditional working-class audience with their boisterous behavior, rewarding the talent they liked while being tough on those they disliked. Other managements moved toward catering to a broader audience that included women and families.[26]

The mainstay of all the halls was a commitment to popular music. Certain characters became standard acts, such as the shy maiden, the naughty girl, the man in the street, ethnics such as the Irish, and the ever-popular male dandy. As they tried to attract a broader audience and appeal to family groups, the big halls also produced spectacular dramas, often based on recent events. Some of the halls were committed to the scandalous and featured burlesque. On both sides of the Atlantic the music hall came to dominate entertainment in the second half of the nineteenth century.[27] It created the opportunity for professionals to lead very peripatetic lives. The dancer Lydia Thompson spent three years touring Europe and Russia before returning home to England and then traveling to America.[28] Her travel reveals how music hall culture was spreading throughout the great cities of Europe. Elite response to this boom was to retreat into the concert hall and opera house, where the great tradition of classical music dominated.

Dance halls or ballrooms also flourished as another aspect of popular culture in the latter half of the nineteenth century. The descendants of the assembly rooms of the eighteenth century, they were much bigger and the dances very different. Gone were the sedate minuets and country dances favored by aristocratic society as new dances came in. The waltz, often banned because of the close dancing by couples, gradually won acceptance and became the rage with its lilting tunes and graceful motions. It was followed in the 1840s by very different styles such as the polka and mazurkas, all faster and more dynamic and, toward the end of the century, the arrival of even faster dances, which would be associated with jazz music after the turn of the century and that would transform social dancing altogether. Like the music halls, the ballrooms attracted large crowds in the age before radio and television.[29] As dance halls and music halls proliferated, it became necessary for the resorts to follow popular culture. By mid-century the popular resorts built them, especially on the newer and larger piers. Come what may—and the financial outlay was considerable—the resorts kept up with trends in popular culture. By the end of the century yet another boom was underway.

As much as any resort, Coney Island, New York, led the way into the future. For many years Coney Island lay in the shadow of Far Rockaway. The earliest images we have show few buildings and few people.[30] It sat on a barrier island projecting out into New York harbor. Its proximity to the city and to Brooklyn, both of which were booming, meant that there was a ready audience for innovation. New York City was the largest urban area in the United States, with just under one million people in 1870, and Brooklyn was the third largest with 396,099, so within a short boat ride or railway trip was the most significant agglomeration in America. In response, entrepreneurs such as William Engeman created the Manhattan Beach Hotel, which opened in 1877, followed by the lavish Oriental in 1880.[31] These hotels started to define the social geography of Coney Island in that they were built at the east end, which became the elite part of the beach, where there were upscale dance halls and fancy piers. In the middle of the island, the hotels and facilities were for the middle and working classes, while the western end was for the raffish, for here the gamblers, "sporting" men, and prostitutes congregated. This was the notorious Bowery, named after the more famous and notorious neighborhood in the city. Pious folks avoided it while ministers and social reformers denounced its wicked ways. Shady characters were ready to steer the innocent into sin, or at least to gambling away their funds. Three-card monty was a Bowery specialty, played on the beach beside the Punch and Judy shows and the donkey rides. The gamblers lured the innocent into choosing the right card and, when they became overconfident and the stakes were higher, the player always lost and could only mourn his bad luck while the gambler moved on to the next victim.[32] All that was sleazy was to be found in the Bowery. Crime flourished as various bosses presided over the rackets and ensured that profits and good times flowed—at least in their direction. One observer said it was "a byword for all that was vulgar, vicious and deplorable. It was the epitome of human nature at its worst seeking its amusements. Its pleasures were those no self-respecting man or woman could possibly enjoy."[33] Yet the Bowery remained one of the enduring parts of Coney Island.

Access to the beach was through the major streets in Brooklyn and by steamboats that served the island until 1876, when the first railway arrived. In quick order, three other lines and a tramway provided ready access. It was possible for nearly everyone in the city to think of a quick trip to the beach. A young man, for instance, could take in the sea air, stroll along Surf Avenue past the big hotels all the way to the very fancy Manhattan Beach Hotel, and imagine the world within. If he wanted to swim, all he had to do was visit one of the bathhouses where for a few pennies, he could undress and put away his street clothes in security before putting on a slightly damp bathing outfit. He could then wander onto the beach, there to confront the donkeys, hawkers of various kinds, and three-card monty gamblers while others in street clothes admired his outfit. Then it was into the ocean, where wave after wave rolled in. Out beyond the surf, men in "surf boats" waited to rush in and help the unwary or unfortunate. After jumping up and down in the surf and getting tumbled a time or two, it was time to struggle ashore where the crowd could now admire his bravery as his suit was plastered to his body in revealing ways. Back in the bathhouse, a quick toweling dried him off, then into his street clothes and back out onto Surf Avenue. It might be time for a Nathan's Famous Hot Dog and a beer. There was still time to wander around and inspect all the booths where there were shooting galleries, ball throwing for prizes, candy, restaurants of all kinds, weird animals, and for that matter odd humans, all to titillate the visitor. Finally, before the young man headed home, there were shows at the music halls or the chance to dance in one of the ballrooms, so that when he got on the train he could count the good times and reflect on his lighter wallet.[34] If young women wanted to share some of these thrills, they would go in groups, as single females would find it difficult to participate. Families might want to focus on going to the beach and might stop to view the sights on Surf Avenue. They would certainly avoid the Bowery and its sleaze, not that Surf Avenue was a sleaze-free district.[35]

While development until the 1870s was similar to other resorts, Coney Island was about to be transformed. Perhaps it was the building of the Blue Elephant Hotel. There was nothing like the 150-foot-high hotel made of tin that attracted the attention of, if it did not startle, the visitor. It was a sensation.[36] In 1879 one hundred thousand came to enjoy the many pleasures on the Fourth of July Independence Day celebration. How to keep them entertained brought out the innovators. Novelty was in demand, and the entrepreneurs of Coney Island were ready to supply it. In 1876, a three-hundred-foot-high tower came to Coney, from which one could oversee all of the beach and look out into New York Harbor. That same year, one of the enduring features of beach resorts arrived with the first carousel. A steam-powered wonder, with beautifully carved animals, led to an industry as men competed to carve the next most beautiful ride for children and adults.[37] It would be the harbinger of the search for the next mechanical device to entertain the public.

In 1884, the roller coaster arrived. At first it was a novelty, but a tepid one, as the cars went down a gentle slope with bumps to arrive at a terminal where one walked across to transfer to another car to return to the station. New coasters came in 1884 and 1887, and then nearly every year there was a new coaster ride. Each one would be bigger, faster, and more thrilling.[38] Innovation was always in demand, and designers even considered having the cars plunge through the air to land on another track. That idea never went beyond concept. Bigger and faster led ultimately, in 1901, to the Loop the Loop, the last great thrill of this era before the monster rides—the Thunderbolt, the Tornado, and the Cyclone—took over. Meanwhile, engineers and designers pushed newer and bigger versions of old rides as almost all of them had predecessors in a more innocent age. Shoot the Chute was nothing more than a large toboggan that carried passengers to the top of the ride; from there, the carriage was let free and it went gliding down the track into a big pond, where it made a mighty splash before arriving at a dry dock. Another attraction mimicked a horse race, as it was a number of undulating tracks with mechanical horses that had riders (the paying customers) competing and, while each race started at the same time, workers manipulated the horses to produce a different winner in each race.

FIGURE 6.2 *Steeeplechase at Rockaway, Long Island,* ca. 1903. Library of Congress, Prints & Photographs Division, Detroit Publishing Company Collection. Among the most popular rides at Steeplechase Park.

Among the rides that came along in the 1890s was the Ferris wheel. First shown at the Midway in the Columbian Exposition in Chicago, the idea was transferred to Coney Island in 1893 and quickly became a fixture at many resorts.[39]

Besides mechanical rides, Coney Island had one other major innovation, which was the creation of amusement parks. These were enclosed spaces with attractions that you had to pay to enter. It was not a new idea, for Tivoli Gardens (1843–today) in Copenhagen and Vauxhall Gardens (1728–1859) in London featured an enclosed area where one had to pay to enter before enjoying the gardens, concerts, fireworks, and hot-air balloon ascents.[40] On a less grand scale, the beach resort at Eastbourne had Devonshire Park, where for six pence one could enjoy games such as cricket, tennis, roller skating, and concerts.[41] Paul Boyton took this concept and brought it into the modern era for Coney Island. In 1895 he opened Sea Lion Park, which had sea lions plus all sorts of game booths, carnival sideshows, and a number of rides such as the Whirlpool and Shoot the Chute. After two years he sold out to Edward Tilyou, one of Coney's most imaginative showmen. Tilyou changed the Sea Lion

Park's name to Steeplechase Park, featuring the mechanical horse race and many other attractions.[42] An observer noted about Steeplechase, "Steeplechase believes in a few simple truisms. It believes that most people never grow up and that even adolescents like to escape back into childhood. It believes that half the world likes to show off and that the other less daring half is perpetually interested in the performance . . . And because of these truisms the crowds in Steeplechase park are big and noisy and predominantly young and almost frantically amused."[43]

The third amusement park was the extraordinary Luna Park, which opened in 1903, the creation of Frederic Thompson, another fabled showman. It had extravagant architecture combined with a brilliant display of electrical lighting, the modern innovation that boomed in the 1890s. The dazzling effect surpassed the experience of nearly everyone who, at best, had a light on his or her street corner. It was fantastic, and the visitor entered another world. There were fifty-three buildings around a lagoon where the Shoot the Chute plunged into the water from a slide starting over the entrance. The buildings all had oriental flourishes, and one section was based on Venice, with a Grand Canal and gondoliers. The buildings contained wild animals, a monkey circus, a Chinese theater, and villages with aboriginal people. Spectacles were produced, such as the War of the Worlds, which depicted a sea battle between European warships trying to seize New York Harbor from Admiral Dewey and the triumphant American navy. Then there was the 20,000 Leagues Under the Sea ride, which took the audience to the North Pole. There were also stages under a tower, with performing acrobats and jugglers. Everywhere the jaded visitor turned, rides and shows beckoned. It was a sensation. Having created a new concept at a resort, Thompson could not rest; he added sixteen more acres to the park and more shows. Thompson labored for eleven years before selling Luna Park.[44]

Success bred yet another park, called Dreamland, which opened in 1904, funded by former senator William Reynolds and a group of investors who raised $3.5 million for construction. Dreamland was a larger version of Luna Park, with one million lamps to dazzle the visitor at night. There were chariot races, a Shoot the Chute longer than any other and ending in the ocean, a ballroom with space for three thousand dancers, wild beasts, a city based on medieval Nuremberg inhabited by dwarves, a replica of Venice with Gondola rides, and a 370-foot-high tower, stark white and ablaze with one hundred thousand lamps at night. As one reporter put it, "Such splendor [was] never seen before at Coney Island."[45] Dreamland, like Luna, was caught in the great challenge of

FIGURE 6.3 *Night in Luna Park, Coney Island, N.Y.*, 1905. Library of Congress, Prints & Photographs Division, Detroit Publishing Company Collection. Resplendent in its hundred thousand electrical bulbs, Luna was a symbol of the modern era.

these new resorts—what can you do for next year that will wow the audience? They always had to be ready to create a new ride or a new, bigger, faster version than before. Or, with Igorot headhunters from the Philippines having been on display one year, what group of natives would attract attention the next?[46] Spectacles of all kinds needed to be ready for the summer season to ensure that the new visitor was thrilled and the jaded, frequent visitor could be tempted to come again. It was a never-ending challenge, and having created the special resort venue, the owners needed imagination, money, and talent to go forward.

Nowhere was this need for innovation more true than with the spectacles. Over the years, one could see "20,000 Leagues Under the Sea," "The Dance of the Seven Veils," "The Boer War," "The Destruction of Babylon," "The Defeat of the Spanish Armada," "A Trip to the Moon," "The Battle of the Clouds" (with balloons and airships), "The Great Train Robbery," "Mt. Pelee Erupting" (a famous 1902 eruption), and "Buffalo Bill's Wild West Show." Hundreds of entertainers were required

FIGURE 6.4 *Boardwalk, Showing Front of Blenheim Hotel, Atlantic City, N.J.*, 1911. Photographic print. Library of Congress, Prints & Photographs Division, Detroit Publishing Company Collection. The Atlantic City boardwalk on Easter Sunday. The crowds give a real sense of just how popular the resorts were at the turn of the century.

to put on these spectacles, performing them two or three times a day. The payoff came in attendance. In 1899, Steeplechase Park was the first amusement park to entertain one million visitors in a season.

Coney Island was a modern novelty. The lovely beach was there for the many thousands who still came to do nothing but have a dip in the ocean on a warm summer day. It was also a sprawling, gigantic assault on the senses as every booth, every amusement park, and every ride tried to overwhelm you and take you out of your ordinary world. On arrival, visitors passed across a boundary into an extravagant, fantastic world that took them away from the constraints of their normal lives. Young men and women, particularly, were thrown together on rides and could lose their inhibitions in an unconventional setting. Romance was sure to follow, and occasionally lives could be changed. If nothing else, people could go home having escaped the daily grind with memories and the desire to return.[47] Yet for those steeped in Victorian values, it was an abomination. For appealing only to pleasure, having no redeeming social value, and in fact furthering sinful behavior, the new resorts would be denounced from many a pulpit and decried by social reformers. Such voices, however, represented the past and not the new, modern world.

"It is overwhelming in its crudeness, barbaric, hideous and magnificent. There is something colossal about its vulgarity."[48] So the new 1893 Baedaker Guide described Atlantic City. If Coney Island entertained New Yorkers, Atlantic City did the same for Philadelphians and visitors from the towns and cities of New Jersey and Pennsylvania. While it could entertain all classes, it was built mainly to keep the lower and middle classes happy, much as did Coney Island.[49] Still, the Marlborough, Blenheim, and Mansion House hotels attracted the elites who wanted an orderly holiday with a little excitement. There were no amusement parks, but the famed Boardwalk, built and rebuilt over the years because of storm damage, always to make it wider and longer, was the center of activity.[50] Hotels, bathing houses, piers, shooting galleries, beer gardens, carousels, fortune tellers, Fralingers salt water taffy (which had water but no salt), vaudeville shows, and dancing pavilions, plus a universe of shops clustered on or near the Boardwalk, all competed for the visitor's attention and dollars. By the 1890s Ferris wheels, merry-go-rounds, scenic railways, roller coasters, and all of the mechanical entertainments that Victorians loved were in place. But Atlantic City also thrived on booze, sex, and gambling, and bosses such as Louis Kuehnle and Enoch "Nucky" Johnson kept this part of the city thriving, along with the protection rackets on which they also thrived.[51] Big and boisterous Atlantic City left Cape May, Asbury Park, and Long Branch behind as it carved out a new destiny. All it took were local investors happy to take the risk that their resort could create the right mix and take off.

The other challenge to developers was the constant threat of natural disaster. It came in two forms—fire and weather. As we have seen already, the cheap wood construction of so many buildings, without any of the modern fire prevention systems and with volunteer fire departments at best, meant that they were all vulnerable. Cape May's frequent fires testify to the problem.[52] Yet even the best-planned developments were at risk. Dreamland on Coney Island burned to the ground in 1911, wiping out the whole enclosure as well as the pier; as the fire engulfed the great tower, it blazed in the night as a beacon seen far at sea. Such was Dreamland's popularity that 350,000 came to view the ruins.[53] Miraculously, a roller coaster newly installed next door survived. Many of the small shops on Surf Avenue were wiped out, but they were back in business in tents the next day. Dreamland was never rebuilt, as the investors had had enough.

The other threat, the storms great and small, had smashed into the Atlantic coast for centuries. As long as people avoided the coast, the storms might come roaring in and then dissipate in the interior, remarked upon only for the rain or snow they left behind. By the middle of the nineteenth century, long stretches of the coast were filled with resorts, so that storms had much greater impact. Since there were no early warning systems, they came ashore with little forewarning. New Jersey was a well-developed coast by then and was regularly victimized as hurricanes smashed piers, boardwalks, and homes with great regularity during the summer and nor'easters did the same in the winter. Boardwalks were created to help people move across the sand and to keep the sand away from shops and other facilities, thus they were built close to the ocean and suffered as a result. The Atlantic City boardwalk was built for the first time in 1870, but by 1879 a hurricane had smashed it, and this was repeated in 1884 and 1890, so in 1896 it was rebuilt with steel in hopes of keeping the sea at bay. But in major hurricanes of force four and five, not much survives. The Great Atlantic Hurricane of 1944 was such a storm, and it smashed the boardwalks and the piers in Atlantic City and those in Asbury Park and Cape May. This storm also raised another issue that would come to prominence later. Cape May had been suffering from slow and steady beach erosion, but the storm destroyed the beach and left hardly any sand. It was a harbinger of problems to come.[54]

Toward the end of the nineteenth century, ocean liners crossing the Atlantic became larger and faster, and crossings became more and more frequent. Among the passengers were Englishmen coming to America to study the new technology of amusement parks even though there was an existing tradition in Europe for amusement parks. Tivoli in Copenhagen, which dated to 1843, featured different mechanical rides such as a merry-go-round and a primitive scenic railway. England had a variety of pleasure gardens that entertained visitors at night with music and dining.[55] But Blackpool had a special interest in the new technology in American amusement parks. Blackpool always had elements of the parks in various places. Raikes Hall had a variety of attractions, as did the Winter Gardens, with dancing, concerts, and an aquarium, besides a Ferris wheel by 1896, and the Blackpool Tower offered far more than just a ride to the top: it had many attractions, featuring a dance hall and exhibitions on its ground floors. But it was Pleasure Beach that brought a true amusement park to Blackpool. The resort had been growing significantly, still supported by a strong working-class base with an added elite sector at the north end of the beach. The central part of the town was focused on the train station, where most of the facilities were built. These included the Tower, the Alhambra, the Winter Gardens, the Grand Theater, and Victoria Pier. Here were the theaters, dance halls, music halls, and other features, plus nearby was the "Golden Mile" of stalls and booths, with freaks, monsters, fortune tellers, and cheap restaurants. At the south end of town, among the sand dunes, were a gypsy encampment, funky stalls with phrenologists, chiropodists (corn cutters), and other odd services, all sitting outside the control of authorities.

Desirous of tidying up this unsightly addition, the city went along with plans to develop forty acres into a park. This was slightly risky on the part of the entrepreneurs involved, as there was no sea wall to protect against storms and it was far away from the center of town; even the promenade did not reach that far. Yet they persisted, and Rainbow Park came into existence, starting with a bicycle railway and a carousel. The leader of a syndicate of investors was William George Bean, one of the men who visited America and, in his case, actually working in the Philadelphia amusement machinery industry. From 1906 on, he imported and created new mechanical rides—a bicycle railway, flying machine, scenic railway, joy wheel, water chute, a ride that would be the ancestor of dodgem cars, plus roller skating, music venues, and spectacles such as the battle between the American ironclads, the *Monitor* and *Merrimac*. By 1914, Rainbow Park employed six hundred people and entertained one hundred thousand visitors on an ordinary summer's day, and as many as two hundred thousand on a bank holiday. While the upper classes might visit Rainbow Park, it was built to serve the working class, who appeared in their Sunday best, mostly young and older couples with very few children attending, as little was done for them at this time. The park was profitable, and, under the management of Bean, and later Leonard Thompson, it continued to keep a steady flow of innovation along with its traditional rides, as some of the rides went on for sixty years. So electricity and mechanical innovation performed their magic in Blackpool as they had in the American resorts. Rainbow Park, however, maintained a strong link to its steady customers. Long after Coney Island had failed as a place of parks, Rainbow kept on going, so that even today it is one of the most frequented parks in all of Europe.[56]

While Coney Island and Blackpool led the way to a new era of amusement parks, most beach resorts remained much the same. Perhaps a carousel or a Ferris wheel was added here and there, but few resorts decided to implement the expensive new rides.[57] However, roller skating and bicycling were introduced as "modern" entertainments that kept a lot of young people happy. Bicycling was particularly popular among women who could enjoy riding along without a horse and share in speed and thrills. Otherwise, resorts remained focused on the beach and on more traditional ways of entertaining their visitors. This might include a new pier, or the elaboration of an old pier, as piers became bigger, having acquired large theaters, restaurants, and dance halls besides shops. Whether on piers or on land, theaters and dance halls were getting larger to take in the increased number of visitors. The theaters were more likely to feature music hall culture in England and vaudeville in America. These were highly popular art forms that attracted wide audiences among the middle and working classes. The songs sung or played there had wide distribution and gained large audiences, as they were repeated at home around the piano or on the guitar or simply sung a cappella on the street. As the number of theaters grew, the professional musicians and singers who performed in the major cities in the winter now had a choice of many venues during the summer.

There was one final innovation to keep and attract audiences—festivals. Of course, these were nothing new, as religious festivals, especially, were to be found in villages, towns, and cities all over Europe. Nice was among the first resorts to implement a festival, a secular affair to celebrate the coming of spring. It featured flower decorations on houses and on carriages, and, as the flower-decorated carriages filled with people passed by, visitors pelted them with flowers and the folks in the carriages returned the favor. Queen Victoria particularly enjoyed the flower festival and timed her visits to attend it, as did thousands of others, including more and more members of the Russian aristocracy who were fleeing the winters at home.[58] While festivals could be built around any secular event, some were odd. In New Jersey baby parades attracted thousands of visitors. These toddler versions anticipated the bathing beauty pageants. The first one was held at Asbury Park in 1890. They might also have been part of an educational program that sought to inform the public about the special health needs of infants.[59] Atlantic City had a quasi-religious festival in its annual Easter parade on the boardwalk. Photographs of the parade show a boardwalk packed with people, stretching to the horizon, testifying to the popularity of dressing up and showing off at the beach in cold weather. Needless to say, all of the shops and hotels that were open enjoyed the extra trade. Even Coney Island got into the business, as it ended each season with a version of the New Orleans Mardi Gras with illuminated floats and pretty ladies that brought out the crowds for one last flourish before shutting down for the season.[60] For Blackpool, it was the famous Illuminations which ran from August to November, featuring a display of lights made possible by electricity. With static lights along the route and a parade of brightly decorated vehicles of all kinds, large crowds flocked to visit one last time. Festivals helped sustain and lengthen the season, even though there were few people going to the beach.

With the ever-growing crowds flooding into resorts, elites decided that, while an occasional visit to a Coney Island or Blackpool might be entertaining, they were not places one wanted to spend one's holiday. Vacations had to be taken at appropriate places where one could spend time with one's equals. That meant somewhere exclusive. European elites still clustered at favored resorts such as Biarritz or Nice and new resorts such as Deauville and Trouville, which were built for an exclusive crowd, attracting many Parisians.[61] Not much had changed in these resorts. Vladimir Nabokov and his family visited Biarritz in 1909 and stayed in a grand hotel. He went into the sea in much the same way visitors had for some time:

> The process of bathing took place on another part of the beach. Professional bathers, burly Basques in black bathing suits, were there to help ladies and children enjoy the terrors of the surf. Such a *baigneur* would place the *client* with his back to the incoming wave and hold him by the hand as the rising, rotating mass of foamy, green water violently descended from behind, knocking one off one's feet with a mighty wallop. After a dozen or so of these tumbles, the *baigneur*, glistening like a seal, would lead his panting, shivering, moistly snuffling charge landward, to the flat foreshore, where an unforgettable old woman with gray hairs on her chin promptly chose a bathing robe from several hanging on a clothesline. In the security of a little cabin, one would be helped by yet another attendant to peel off one's soggy, sand-heavy bathing suit. It would plop onto the boards, and, still shivering, one would step out of it and trample on its bluish, diffuse stripes. The cabin smelled of pine. The attendant, a hunchback with beaming wrinkles, brought a basin of steaming hot water, in which one immersed one's feet.[62]

Refreshed, Nabokov strolled back to his family's hotel, as many generations had before him. In England, Brighton still had its attractions, but newer resorts such as Frinton on Sea, which was built to attract those who could afford its expensive building lots, quickly established a reputation for exclusivity.[63] And grand hotels everywhere kept their clientele by being imposing and expensive, ensuring that the "wrong" sort did not expect to be served.

America in the last third of the nineteenth century witnessed the decline of one of the favored resorts. Long Branch was the reigning resort for the high society of New York City and Philadelphia, where one could mix with presidents and captains of industry. By the 1880s it had lost its cachet. Partly this was due to a badly eroding beach, as the berm that sat at the back of the beach collapsed, leaving a smaller beach area.[64] As with all of the popular resorts, there was a growing residential community of resort workers and residents in Long Branch who just wanted to live near the beach. As a community, they did not share all the values of the visitors, and they expressed this at Long Branch by closing all the gambling dens, even though the fanciest parlors did not allow locals to gamble. Then the state government decided to ban horse races because of the gambling, and so Monmouth Park was closed.[65] When it came to horse racing, it had already lost out to Coney Island, which had become the center for the sport as it had three tracks.[66] So no gambling and an unsatisfactory beach made elites start to look elsewhere. They found what they wanted soon enough in Rhode Island.

Newport, Rhode Island, finally came out of its torpor after 1850. At first it was very much like other resorts in that hotels such as the Ocean House and the Atlantic House attracted fashionable people. Visitors enjoyed the beach; as Julia Ward Howe would write, Newport "swarmed with straw hats and canes, the Beach with nankeen tights, life preservers, oil cloth caps, bathing dresses—red, blue, green and purple—tutti quanti—a ragged rainbow." Her daughter Maud remembered swimming at Easton's Beach, where their "wet bathing suits of heavy ticking weighed a ton. But the surf was glorious; every seventh wave was a monster. Friends, and even strangers, held your hand as you stood in line to meet each breaker and jumped as it rolled in."[67] The hotels hosted balls and hops, and parties were organized to walk, sail, fish, and ride. It was, in other words, very much like any other resort.

By 1875 a reporter for the *New York Times* wrote that Newport was going down a different path than resorts such as Long Branch. There the visitor wanted to be casual and disheveled. At Newport, "the proprieties must be observed." There were "staunch old millionaires who live in the utmost retirement . . . who despise conventionalities," and "who enjoy their souls in peace in quiet old mansions buried in magnificent shrubberies," but around them were "the whole herd of Proteus" who "dream of nothing save being fashionable." He even derided Bailey's Beach, where there were small waves and no excitement.[68] The growing image of exclusivity was symbolized by the arrival of Ward McAllister. He had modest wealth, but had traveled extensively in Europe, and while enriching his knowledge of wine and food, he came to appreciate the social importance of traditional aristocracies. When he returned to New York City he wormed his way into the confidence of Mrs. Constantine Astor, the queen, or at least chief arbiter of the city's high society. The two of them shared a dislike of the new wealth, of the crude parvenus or robber barons, who were ever more prominent in the social scene of the city; their fortunes, while great, did not provide the birth and breeding needed to be a member of their select four hundred.[69]

In New York City, McAllister became the person who arranged all of the balls and banquets to which the right people were invited. At Newport he provided the same service and came to dominate local society. The acceptable summer visitor should have birth, breeding, ability, and a lot of money. Social recognition could be granted or withheld, and it took three seasons to get a foothold.[70] Hotels and restaurants were closing, as more and more of the entertainment was in private homes. If you did not have the appropriate contacts you needed to stay at Narragansett Beach. Just to the west of Newport, Narragansett had a good beach and hotels, but while being a very nice resort, it had far less social distinction than its neighbor. McAllister managed many of the events as Newport turned into the "very Holy of Holies, the playground of the Great Ones of the earth from which all intruders were ruthlessly excluded by a set of iron rules."[71]

One of the great definers was an ability to buy a prime lot and build on it—not just a villa, but a "cottage" that was more like a palace. These homes did not have an address, but announced themselves by name: Ochre Court, Rosecliff, Belcourt, Marble House, Belmont, Crossways, Malbone Hall, and the famed Breakers. Each mansion also announced the arrival of an important and wealthy family as New York colonized Newport—Astor, Belmont, Lorillard, and Vanderbilt.[72] One very impressed Englishman wrote that Newport consisted of "avenues lined with magnificent summer houses; 'cottages' only in name for many of them cost more than half a million dollars and a number over a million. And in these palaces a right royal life is lived. Hospitality is generous and days fly by as if on golden wings—and truth to tell, gold in full measure alone could buy such 'wings.'"[73] Or as one wag put it, "It is only at Newport that you find people who really do nothing well."[74] But it wasn't all fun and games, for this was a place where all of the proprieties had to be observed, so women and young men had to spend a part of every afternoon wandering from cottage to cottage, leaving their cards as a part of old-fashioned society practice.

And there was also the constant changing of clothes necessary to be fashionable.[75]

Another necessary definer of status was membership at the Newport Casino, which opened in 1880. Besides defining social position, as in the older English resorts, one had to sign the register so that the right people could know you were there. It had shops, lodging for gentlemen, tennis, billiards, and spaces for dances. Just behind the Casino was Bailey's Beach, owned by the Spouting Rock Beach Association, where membership also defined status. While it was not the best beach for swimming—too narrow and clogged with seaweed—it was the only acceptable place to bathe.[76] Yet another definer of status was the carriage one displayed when joining the afternoon parade on Ocean Drive. As established elsewhere in resorts, such as Brighton, it was a necessity for high society to display horses and carriages in the late afternoon. Connoisseurs reckoned that at Newport there was the finest display of horseflesh and carriage equipment to be seen anywhere, dazzling the eye.[77] If beach resorts were platforms upon which the visitor was on display, no audience was more discerning than that at Newport during the ten-week season. The proper costume for the time of day, the ability to dance well, to make small talk, to perform at dinner, and to manage a four-in-hand carriage—these and other small things, if not done well, would cause negative comment and, in the worst case, consignment to Narragansett Beach. For the ultrafashionable, these challenges made Newport the place to spend the summer. Acceptance meant being a part of the crème de la crème and opened doors in the highest of high society.

One final aspect of Newport's dominance was its involvement in sports. Here again, it was not enough to have sports—it had to be the best. In yachting—the America's Cup races were held there; polo—the first international polo championship; tennis—the National Lawn Tennis championships started at the Casino; golf—the local club held the first national golf championship; and, finally, the first automobile race was held on Second Beach, the best beach at Newport, as it was long and flat. And by the by, people also went swimming. The ladies, however, turned away from this because it exposed one to the sun, and then there were the ridiculous costumes.

Newport was rather a hothouse environment that represented the Gilded Age. It was the preserve of a segment of American society that was traditional in many of its attitudes. While it had many old-fashioned ideas regarding proper manners, it had very great wealth. Fortunes could be spent on a single ball, just as they would be in New York City. In the city, however, the very great inequality of that time was never that far out of sight. In Newport, with the beautiful bay and surrounding scenery, it was feasible to keep out all awkward signs of poverty. It was possible to live in a different, if unreal, world that was perfect for the gilded audience.[78] No other resort was like it, even those that attracted elites. Newport defined ultra–high fashionable society, setting it apart from resorts where there were villas and grand hotels but no rows of "cottages" and estates on this scale. It would not last forever, but while it did it was unique.

Not everyone wanted to put up with the constant need to be the best at Newport. They actually wanted to spend their summer holiday taking it easy and doing the usual swimming, walking, bike riding, and generally having fun. They might have the money to stay at Newport, but they decided to go elsewhere. One Newport doyen reported that a number of old wealthy families were now summering at Southampton on the eastern end of Long Island. They had nothing to prove and preferred the quiet life.[79] These were the pioneers of what would become the Newport of our time—the Hamptons.

A young reporter getting the plush assignment of reporting on life at the seaside in 1900 would have a varied experience to write up. Given the number of resorts and the enhanced transportation network for getting around presented few problems. It would be easy to find a nice stretch of sand on which to enjoy a swim and a leisurely morning resting in the sun. He could, in fact, if he had an indulgent editor, find such beaches in many countries. If he did wander around, the variety of bathing costumes would attract his eye as the modern suits could be found here and there. But if his editor wanted a story about recent, notable changes, then he would have to wander further afield. Coney Island or Blackpool immediately commanded attention. Both had good beaches, but the real attractions were the amusement parks, mechanical rides, dance halls, towers, music halls, spectacles, and ever more variety brilliantly lit up at night in the glare of electric lights. It would be hard to leave all of this to explore further. He would surely want to go to the boardwalk at Atlantic City, different from Coney Island, with some of the same new features, yet worth a visit. A cynical reporter might visit the fading glories of Brighton to comment on times past. His toughest task would be trying to penetrate the world of Newport. Without the right kinds of introduction, he could be reduced to admiring the cottages from the outside and goggling at them during the afternoon promenade. He certainly would find it difficult to get a swim at Baileys Beach; for that, he would have to wander to

Second Beach or even Narragansett. Back at his desk staring at the type-writer, he could only wonder at the variety of experiences the beach afi-cionado now had.

By 1900 beach resorts had evolved in ways unimaginable to the pio-neers in eighteenth-century England. Gaudy Coney Island was a far cry from Margate, as was modern Blackpool for that matter. The consider-able variety of resorts from Scarborough and Cape May to the private clubs for American millionaires in the southern United States and the improbable, staggering wealth on display at Newport—all were resorts, but in many ways incomparable. Even ordinary resorts had to deal with the other phenomenon of the time, the very great numbers of people. Rising prosperity and the possibility of holidays meant that the great attractions of the resorts did what they were intended to do, namely attract great numbers.

7

The Modern World Intrudes

The twentieth century started with a general sense of peace and prosperity. As always there were political, social, and diplomatic issues demanding attention and filling the newspapers. In the cultural world, the rise of modernism caused conservatives fits and brought joy to the young and adventurous. Away from all the hustle and bustle, the easy lifestyle at the beach continued to prosper. Dazzling Coney Island was in its heyday and gleamed in the night as it entertained millions. Elsewhere, the height of the surf or the evening dance attracted attention among those fortunate enough to loll at the beach. This world would soon be shattered by war and then depression, and each affected the beach resorts. Yet they continued to grow in numbers and geographic extent as resorts started to dot the coast nearly everywhere.[1] But no matter where they were, all resorts would be challenged by an unprecedented number of social, technological, and fashion changes. Among them was the arrival of sunbathing, which was perceived as a boon to good health. This would force the evolution of the swimsuit, and if the sun was so good, why not just go nude? The latter was not something most resorts wanted to encourage. The same was true when hand-held cameras started to appear—not all resorts encouraged their use, as the casual photo could be too revealing. The automobile made the seashore even more available to many, and as the numbers grew and people went to the beach less for therapy than for recreation, safety loomed as an ever-more-important issue. One aspect of the war would also change who was at the beach. Aristocracies all over Europe were either displaced—as in Russia—or financially weakened nearly everywhere, and so their dominance at many resorts ended. In their place, celebrities—movie stars, novelists, and sports figures, who were now followed closely by the popular press—crowded the resorts. So the postwar era ushered in many challenges.

A "Norwegian Riviera" emerged on the southern coast in Sorlandet. Artists and writers had flocked to the area in the summer; then, with paid holidays and the railway reaching the coast, boarding houses and cottages brought in a more diverse group of bathers. So by the 1930s the region was established as a summer retreat during the all-too-brief summers.[2] Far to the south in Sicily, with its much longer summers, the high bourgeoisie and aristocracy of Palermo decided it needed a beach resort and created one along the coast at Mondello. Beginning in 1912, art nouveau villas (a style still in fashion), clubs, a bathhouse, and hotels created a summer place that is still quite exclusive.[3] In Portugal it was royal patronage that created the first resorts. King Luis I, concerned about his wife's health, started in the 1870s taking the family to Cascais Beach, just west of Lisbon. Cascais and its neighbor Estoril quickly attracted Portuguese nobility. The latter, which promptly built a reputation as the luxury resort, hosted numerous European royals during World War II when they escaped to neutral Portugal.[4] Much farther afield, European empires had expanded across the globe. In those colonies that attracted settlers, they took with them their preferences for leisure, one of which was sea bathing. During the late nineteenth century, resorts started appearing in the new nations, as by then most of them had escaped their imperial ties.

In Argentina, the Atlantic coast was opened up to elites in Buenos Aires when the railway reached Mar del Plata in 1897. They no longer had to contemplate the two-day trip along a bad dirt road to reach the coast. Soon the usual pattern of hotels, a casino, and villas provided the basics of a new resort. Later, planned resorts such as Pinamar and Carilo proved more appealing to elites than Mar del Plata. The latter became more of a people's beach. On the west coast of South America near Santiago, the beaches of Vina del Mar attracted city dwellers early, and they have become the most notable beaches in Chile. One thing they shared with the Atlantic beaches is that they had very cold currents that swept the coast, so that even in high summer the water was bracing at best.[5]

Australia had a different pattern in that close to Sydney there were two beaches that became famous—Bondi and Manly. Both beaches were used mostly by male, nude bathers until the end of the nineteenth century when new regulations were imposed. This was an echo of the arguments over appropriate apparel and mixed bathing that had been fought over in England. In Australia there was to be no daylight bathing, and at Manly costumes had to be worn and no mixed bathing was allowed. Ultimately, one way of taking care of a lot of problems was to ban public bathing.[6] These were all quite draconian solutions to the problem of offending the viewer, but after dark, many felt, who cares? Only after the Great War did the rules let up and daylight bathing and mixed bathing come to be accepted at all the beaches. Conservative opinion was still against it, as Archbishop Kelly of Sydney made clear: "I believe that the promiscuous intermingling of the sexes in surfbathing makes for the deterioration of our standards of morality."[7] By the 1920s, Australian beaches were well on their way to matching contemporary standards. Australians, however, did take very seriously the problem of safety. They invented a new life-saving culture. All-male clubs devoted to life-saving were created for each beach. The members went through rigorous training, military style drills and, as members of a club, had access to changing facilities and bathrooms which were often missing for the public. Their annual competitions and parades came to be an iconic aspect of beach life.[8]

In India there were traditional sites such as Puri, where pilgrims had come to go into the sea close to the temple of Lord Jagannath, making it one of the most important pilgrimage sites in India. When the railway arrived in 1897, it built a hotel that offered a unique experience in that the hotel gave a personal lifeguard to accompany each bather.[9] But as European ideas of leisure enjoyed by the sea penetrated aristocratic society in Asia, they created their own beaches. For instance the Maharini Sethu Bayi, of Travancore in Kerala, built a palace, Halcyon Castle, on Kovalum Beach for her personal use. By the 1930s her relatives were sharing the beach with European visitors. Later Thomas Cook Travel was brought in to develop the area. Now there are three beaches and an international crowd.[10] Similarly, in the 1920s the railway reached Hua Hin beach in Thailand. Prince Purachatra built a hotel, creating the first resort, and his family adopted the beach and started to build palaces there. King Rama VII erected a summer palace near the beach that is still an official royal residence. While open to the public now, the beach has long been the home of royals and aristocrats.[11]

In Japan, the Meiji emperor had started the modernization of Japanese industry and business and pushed Japan forward as an international power. After his death in 1912, the new emperor, Taisho, continued to open up Japan to further waves of social and cultural change. One aspect

FIGURE 7.1 Terasaki Kōgyō, 1866–1919, Japanese, *Bijin no kaisuiyoku* (Sea-bathing beauty), 1903. Woodblock print; ink and color on paper. Gift of Patricia Salmon in honor of Arthur and Tena Salmon, 2000 (26782), Honolulu Museum of Art. A daring young woman wears a fashionable costume as Japan begins a beach culture.

of this was a boom in sea bathing on the coasts near Tokyo. While traditional Japan ruled in the countryside, the modern world intruded into the Tokyo resorts. It was here that young people adopted going to the beach and wearing the new and revealing bathing suits, as opposed to the traditional costumes such as the kimono.[12]

Modernization was also a factor in the evolution of sea bathing in Turkey.[13] There was a long tradition of sea bathing around Istanbul in specially built wooden piers that permitted hidden access to the water. Given the strong religious prohibitions regarding the mixing of men and women, there were separate facilities for each sex. Change started in the late nineteenth century when physicians began publishing books on the benefits of sea water. Bathers moved away from the tightly regulated wooden piers and toward beaches. Bathing places for women were made of wood that permitted no viewing of the bathers, and there were police on shore and in boats to make sure of their privacy. In the early twentieth century, new beach customs were introduced by White Russians who had settled in Istanbul after fleeing the Bolsheviks. During the summer they gathered at Florya Beach, where men and women, many wearing modern bathing costumes, introduced contemporary beach practices to Turkey. Seeing an opportunity, entrepreneurs started new beach resorts along the shore. Much of the impetus for this came from the economic and social reforms put in place by Kemal Atatürk, the leader of the Turkish revolution. He went beyond reforming his country to actually creating a modern resort. He had a small palace built at Florya and opened up the beach to the public. This became his favorite summer place. Modern resorts quickly appeared on both sides of the Bosphorus with beaches, *gazinos* or casinos, which were centers of entertainment. Among the most popular was Suadiye, which had a hotel, a gazino, a restaurant, and a nightclub. As the new government pushed for female equality, women could now appear at the beach in modern costumes, beginning a new era in Turkish beach practices.

What had started as a movement for better health in England in the 1730s had by the 1930s become a worldwide phenomenon involving millions of people who sought out the beach not so much for therapeutic bathing, but for recreation and leisure. One of the reasons for a surge in numbers at beaches was the legislation coming from mostly liberal and left-wing governments in the 1930s. In Britain the Trades Union Congress had taken up the cause of paid holidays in 1911. This was a major policy change for them, as they had previously concentrated on issues of pay and working conditions. The TUC's was a major voice that added weight to the popular push for paid holidays. Some middle-class occupations and upper artisanal positions had already secured this entitlement, but the ordinary worker still went without. It was not until a Parliamentary Commission report in 1938 that the case was made for the need for paid holidays. "It cannot, in our view, be denied that an annual holiday contributes in a considerable measure to workpeople's happiness, health and efficiency, and we feel that the extension of taking consecutive days of holiday annually by working people would be of benefit to the community."[14] Later that year legislation mandating ten paid days passed the Commons.[15] France had already passed a paid holiday act, and many other European countries followed suit. Of all the advanced economies, the United States did not and still does not have such a law. Some American states, however, do legislate paid holidays[16] Paid holidays were a great boon to the resorts. Ordinary workers who had been limited to being trippers on the weekend could now contemplate longer stays at the beach knowing that it was not coming out of their savings. Thus, the years between the world wars brought greater and greater numbers of visitors to the resorts.[17]

By the 1920s, the old health reasons for going to the beach had waned, as for too many people the expected cures from seawater and sea air failed to materialize. There could be no denying, however, the impact of swimming and cavorting in the surf as pleasurable activities that left the bather feeling good. Recreation and leisure were now the measure of a good time. Physical fitness, outdoor sports, and youthful appearance were the hallmarks of an active life. One aspect of a youthful appearance was a tan. In 1929 Vogue magazine editorialized that the Vogue girl must have a tan. This was after advocating in 1917, "The Newport woman avoids a tan as she avoids the plague."[18] Such was the rapid fashionable acceptance of the tan. There was also the fact that tanning had become recognized as therapeutic.

While the sun had been identified as potentially useful for the treatment of tuberculosis in the 1840s, it languished as a cure. Later research claimed that sunlight killed certain bacteria and so was good against rickets and tuberculosis.[19] Against this was the still-strong tendency for women to regard an alabaster complexion as an indicator of status. At the beach the all-covering costume, along with the usual straw hat, protected the bather from the sun. With this attitude there was no hope for sun-bathing unless sunshine could be seen to be curative not just for one disease, but for many. Slowly but surely, that evidence emerged. Arnold Rickli was a pioneer in opening a sanatorium that featured sunbathing as curative for tuberculosis and other lung conditions. Others followed, but a major advance came with Auguste Rollier, who opened his Institute of Heliotherapy in Leysin, Switzerland, in 1903. His institution and numerous publications led the way for the advance of heliotherapy into popular culture.[20] What he and others claimed was that sunshine could cure a number of diseases, in an echo of the medical literature on seawater in the eighteenth century. Evidence piled up that sunlight could kill anthrax and rickets and relieve rheumatism, blood pressure, and other maladies. The ultraviolet component of sunshine was credited with much of this.[21]

All the evidence of the time paved the way for a mass movement. It was easy to become a sun worshipper because more and more urbanites worked in offices or factories and were every bit as white as the most fashionable lady, but a tan on a city dweller indicated that he or she had the leisure time to acquire the tan. These reasons helped the new phenomenon of heliotherapy to become a hot topic. Books, journals, and newspaper articles touting its virtues rushed to press.[22] The resorts were not far behind in pushing tanning. This was a great boon for them, for what better place to enjoy the sun than at a resort? And, as a tan identified the individual as someone who had been to the beach, all the better for the resorts. For the very modern person with a tan in the early years, it was also thought to be a sign of youth and sexual potency.[23] The supposed benefits of tanning would lead to two movements—briefer swimsuits and, once again, nudity.

If tanning was to be part of a modern health regime, bathing costumes would have to change. Costumes had continued to evolve as women exercised more. They now bicycled and played croquet, tennis, golf, and badminton, and, of course, more and more of them swam. Ladies' domestic dress still required corsets, bustles, petticoats, and yards of cloth to create the ideal Junoesque figure popular at the end of the nineteenth century.[24] At the beginning of the twentieth century, beach costumes were similarly conservative, featuring a dress with a skirt that reached the knees in order to cover the groin, with the "Persian pants" underneath the skirt. Variations on this had been around for some time, but the pants now only came to the knee and below that with stockings that covered the legs. Bare legs could still get a woman arrested at many beaches.[25] As noted, this sort of costume made from heavy cloth could weigh as much as twenty pounds when wet and it clung to the body. Only athletic young women could feel secure in these costumes, especially on the walk back to the changing cabin or bathing machine. Yet the path to briefer costumes was set by the "modern woman," who wanted more activity and a tan.

Suits that covered women from neck to ankle and men from neck to knee allowed little room for the sun. For women, change was slow in coming. For a young woman looking to become a "modern" woman with a more active, if not athletic, profile, a costume that allowed for swimming meant a briefer costume. During the first three decades of the twentieth century swimsuits, as opposed to the old bathing costumes, were the subject of a great deal of controversy. Attitudes toward revealing the female body were not easily changed. Victorian propriety continued to rule, especially with male politicians who felt it incumbent to protect women. Even women resisted change. Rose Scott, president of the New South Wales Ladies Amateur Swimming Association, wrote that, "I also object to mixed bathing on the beaches. I was brought up in a school that considered it an insult on the part of a man to stare at a girl . . . It is not a compliment to be stared at by a man. Familiarity breeds contempt."[26] The new swimsuits, as they developed, were no doubt more eroticizing in that they displayed the figure by leaving much of the body bare. So from 1900 to 1930 each advance toward a modern tank suit met hostility.[27] For the mostly young women who led the way, the cost of functionality could be notoriety or worse. Local opinion never moved as quickly as the newest trend and was in favor of laws protecting public decency. The *Ladies Home Journal* warned the reader that there was licentiousness at the beach and asked, would you want your daughter to be exposed to it?[28]

Female athletes such as Annette Kellerman, the famous Australian swimmer, acted as fashion leaders: when she needed a functional suit, she designed one that gave her maximum mobility. When she appeared at Revere Beach, Massachusetts, in 1909 in her tank suit, Kellerman was arrested as a depraved woman.[29] Women encountered new rules at other beaches. Atlantic City had monitors on the beach who measured the length of the skirt and made sure that women wore stockings. If they failed the test they went to jail.[30] In one incident, a woman was mobbed by a crowd for wearing too short a suit.[31] Thus there was a long struggle over the new suits. The swimsuit manufacturers, such as Cole and Catalina in California and Jantzen in Oregon, led the way with new tank suits from the middle of the 1920s (famously represented by the Jantzen logo of a young woman diving in a red tank suit). They advertised nationally and reached out to fashionable young women. In the 1930s, Fred Cole led his company into deals with Hollywood, the most powerful image maker.[32] The forces for good taste at the beach were constantly challenged.

MISS ANNETTE KELLERMANN,
Champion Lady Swimmer and Diver of the World.
Copyright.   SEARS. Melbourne

FIGURE 7.2 Photograph of Annette Kellerman. State Library, New South Wales. In a costume such as this, Kellerman, already a famous swimmer, was arrested on Revere Beach in 1909, as the swimsuit was far too daring, at least in Massachusetts.

For men, the change to new bathing suits was easier. Their costumes became shorter, with one proviso—the upper body must be covered. The bare chest with nipples and navel still had to be hidden.[33] As tanning became more widespread, it became common for men at the beach to pull down their tops and sunbathe. This could not be allowed: "The practice of pulling down [the bathing suit] to the waistline for the purpose of exposing their bodies to the sunrays," one petition declared, "[this] practice is offensive and objectionable to the finer senses of those who visit beaches."[34] The Los Angeles City Council considered this practice and formulated an ordinance but ended up setting it aside. Men who wanted to wear only the trunks of a suit on the beach had powerful allies in Hollywood. It would never do to have Tarzan in a T-shirt, so Johnny Weissmuller, an Olympic Gold Medal swimmer used to practical swimsuits, played Tarzan in a brief costume with no top.[35] Other Hollywood male stars soon had publicity shots with bare chests. Traditionalists found that the tenor of the times was against them and, by the 1940s, topless costumes for men were common.

So, slowly, men and women could take advantage of the freedom of the new suits and also acquire a tan. This revolution in swimwear would play out with different timing in other cultures. For example, Vaslav Nijinsky was painted in 1910 by Leon Bakst in a very brief pair of trunks at the Lido. In France, much of the posturing of traditionalists in fighting the advent of comfortable suits was laughable among the fashionable beach visitors. There was generational conflict: one grandmother thought even getting into a bathtub nude was "deplorable immodesty." Nonetheless, the younger generation thought "smart girls bathe."[36] France would always be more advanced in fashion than the Americans or the English. All too soon, France shocked the world with the bikini.

Opposed to the introduction of the new suits were the preservers of morals. These people saw a need to keep women and men covered up, not just at the beach, but elsewhere, as wearing a swimsuit coming and going to the beach became fashionable. One horrified opponent stated, "It's time we do something about men in skintight, sleeveless and neckless bathing garments, about a yard in length, and bare-armed girls with skirts and bloomers above the knee: lolling together in a sort of abandon."[37] Sex was rearing its ugly head! In Santa Monica, California, an emerging beach community, there was a protracted struggle in the community as the city council banned going to and from the beach without an "outer cloak" and lounging around at the beach in a casual fashion. Beginning in 1912 men and women, boys and girls were arrested for appearing without an "outer cloak" even if one was in a "fetching bathing suit of the latest style and cut" while out buying groceries.[38] Then there was the problem of what to do about people riding in convertibles in only a swimsuit. By 1919, the judge in charge of enforcement was saying that he did not believe in making Santa Monica a laughing stock or in carrying out the "old blue stocking ideas of some rabid church people that are not in vogue."[39]

The struggle over people wandering around in swimsuits also went on in Los Angeles. Beginning in 1904, and then in 1911 and 1917, ordinances were passed forbidding public parading without a bathrobe. Divided opinion about swimsuits can be seen in a 1926 feature in the *Los Angeles Times*. It showed a young woman in a very modern suit in a report about tanning, "Tan Is the Smart Shade This Summer, and Olive Oil Will Cure the Smart."[40] The age of suntan lotion was yet to arrive, and many rostrums existed. When Robert M. Smithers discovered that several young women were going to swim between Los Angeles and Catalina Island "cloathed in Axle grease only," observing that when they arrived "very little if any of the protecting film of grease will remain, and the offense committed would therefore be greater," he demanded that the city authorities deal emphatically to forestall such a flagrant violation of all moral codes. He undoubtedly found the response mealymouthed, as the city clerk pointed out that the race was to start on Catalina Island and that was outside the jurisdiction of the council.[41] The forces of order made something of a last attempt to control the situation in 1932. The prosecutors and chiefs of police of all the cities in Los Angeles County that had beaches met to consider the advisability of a standard bathing suit ordinance. Manhattan Beach and Long Beach shared a law that was recommended to all jurisdictions. This ordinance was necessary to protect "public peace and morals . . . as the Police Department . . . are now unable to compel persons using the beach to dress in a proper bathing suit." As an example of bureaucratic language, the ordinance is perfect: no one should appear upon any beach

unless attired in a bathing suit or other clothing of opaque material, which shall be worn in such a manner as to preclude from, and provide against exposure of the front of the body from above the nipples of the breasts to below the crotch formed by the legs of the body, the lower extremities of the trunk of the body and all parts of the buttocks down to a line, no part of which line shall be more than one inch higher than, and /or above, the crotch formed by the legs of the body. All such bathing suits or clothing shall be provided with double crotches or with a skirt of ample size to cover the buttocks.[42]

FIGURE 7.3 Miles F. Weaver, 1879–1932, *Annual "Bathing Girl Parade," Balboa Beach, Cal.*, June 20, 1920. Photograph photCL_555, Ernest Marquez Collection, The Huntington Library, San Marino, CA. A "bathing girl" parade in 1920 was one predecessor of the Miss America pageants.

Public response ranged from tepid to being very much opposed, with some saying that there should be a public referendum to settle the issue. As one letter pointed out, the "unanimous judgement of the medical profession" was in favor of sun tanning, and "in the ballroom low backed gowns are the mode; on the legitimate stage and in the movies abbreviated costumes appear as of course; in the prize ring and wrestling bouts the men wear only trunks."[43] In the end the city council let the whole matter drop. Public opinion was clearly moving toward acceptance of the new suits, and so it was better to file the whole issue and leave it alone. So it was a year-by-year struggle in many communities as local authorities bent to fashion and the benefits of tanning. In most places, it was between 1920 and 1930 that women were finally able to wear a tank suit that was functional. They now had bare arms and legs and often an exposed back to acquire the tan that made them look good.

In England there was a similar situation, for it appears bathers who wanted to avoid the fees in bathhouses or bathing machines started to come to the beach dressed in a "MacIntosh" (a raincoat). Local authorities were alerted to this by the owners of the bathhouses and bathing machines. This obviously could not be allowed. Town councils certainly did not want people wandering around town in bathing suits, but for the proprietors it also affected their income. Ordinances were passed to keep the MacIntosh bathers off the beach. One had to come clothed and change once there.[44] Yet public opinion was on the side of the new bathing suits, and the local councils could only give in to the changing times.

With swimwear finally exposing a lot of skin, bathing beauty contests were not far behind. On both coasts of America they blossomed. Venice Beach in Los Angeles was an early pioneer. It had started a competition in 1912, but not without vocal opposition from some in the community.[45] In 1929 the Reverend A. J. McCartney was still denouncing these pageants, for "there is no virtue in parading half-naked girls for the salacious scrutiny of a jury of men whose social standards are of the gutter."[46] In most other places contests began in the 1920s when the most famous of all beauty contests, the Miss America pageant, got underway in Atlantic City.[47] In the early contests there were a variety of costumes, mostly of the modest old-fashioned type. By the 1930s the contestants were in tank suits, and, while they might not show much cleavage, they were modern. Given the publicity the contests received, the bathing suit manufacturers could hardly ignore them. Catalina made the pageants a specialty, developing a number of alternatives such as Miss Universe. Venice Beach even tried male pageants with female bathing beauty contest winners as the judges, but this was not well received and went nowhere.[48] As a sign of what different cultures would tolerate, it was 1945 before Morecambe inaugurated the first bathing beauty contest in Britain.[49]

Another innovation that came with sun worshipping was the Lido, or grand swimming pool. For some time, resorts had featured various types of baths. As early as the eighteenth century, baths were built as part of the therapeutic regime, often with heated seawater. At Brighton, Dr. John Awsiter was the first to offer heated baths to some of his patients, but then Sake Dean Mahomed created exotic baths in Brighton with vapors, expensive oils, and massages that were famous for some time, until the building was finally demolished in 1870.[50] In the nineteenth century these therapeutic baths had been joined by pools, many built by municipalities to serve the joint purpose of furthering swimming among mostly male groups and providing a place for working-class men to get a bath, so that they were more for hygiene than therapy.[51]

By the 1930s, a new type of bath emerged. Resorts decided that the new fad for swimming and heliotherapy needed large pools, which also had the benefit of getting people away from the ocean, which could be dangerous and unpleasant when the sea was rough. Better that they were in a controlled environment. Such was the case with the Sutro Baths in San Francisco, where a large complex of pools was built above the ocean and allowed the bathers the choice of different waters to bathe in.[52] Resort after resort felt the need to build these new pools, which were modern in design, quite large, and all had seated viewing areas.[53] For the resorts, pools also had the added benefit that one could charge for the use of the pool, the changing rooms, and the other facilities that were built in. Solaria, where those seeking a tan could rest and have supervised sessions so as to avoid sunburning, were common, a tradition that continues today at tony resorts in California and Florida.[54] The Lidos stressed health and exercise for all classes and ages. In England this conformed to government policy that encouraged physical activity in order to have a "fitter Britain."[55] To this end, swimming and diving lessons were taught, and, with all the facilities of a large pool, competitions and exhibitions were also a feature. Such were the attractions that in 1932 it was noted at Blackpool that twice as many people were at the pool than in the sea.[56] Many of these Lidos went out of style in the 1960s as they became somewhat obsolete and the costs of repair and maintenance were more than town governments wanted to pay. As tropical vacations became affordable, holidaymakers decided that they would rather go south to either a sunny beach or a hotel with a beautiful pool.[57]

Tanning quickly became heliotherapy, for if a smaller suit gave you more exposure to the sun, then the completely naked body could absorb much more of the beneficent rays. This led quickly to the advocacy of nudity. Champions emerged in print and in action making the case that the naked body walking, dancing, and doing athletics in the sun was a sign of good health and needed to be advocated.[58] As always, there were classical examples, and none better than Pliny, who took off all his clothes once a day and walked in the sun. More recently there was Walt Whitman: "Is not nakedness then indecent? No, not inherently. It is your thought, your sophistication, your fears, your respectability, that is indecent. There come moods when these clothes of ours are not only irksome to wear, but are themselves indecent."[59] Whitman not only swam and ran on the beach naked; he also had a secret dell near Coney Island where "nature was naked and I was also."[60] He was before his time, because nudity (or naturism) emerged in the twentieth century. While nudism was the condition sought by those who practiced it, naturism came to be used to describe the movement. In doing so they were adopting a word commonly used before to describe a belief in nature.

Naturism as a movement had its origins in Germany and France.[61] Advocates saw nudism as a means not just to enjoy the warmth of the sun, but also to shed the effects of industrial and urban living that were corrupting the body. Enjoying the beneficent rays of the sun on the body was one aspect of this movement, which was often combined with the good effects of a vegetarian diet. This push for a return to a simpler life became a back-to-nature movement, attracting many of those who felt the stress of the modern world. For them running, walking, gymnastics, and dancing untrammeled by burdensome clothing brought positive effects. In dancing, more and more dancers seeking "modern" dance wanted freedom of movement and sought it in nudity. Books and articles pushed the agenda of the naturist movement from the nineteen-teens on. But all the print in the world could not defeat old-fashioned Victorian values, which pushed back and marginalized this literature. Yet the early leaders persevered in forming naturist groups and trying to practice what they preached. They bought property in the country and fenced it in to provide a setting for nudists who could enter and enjoy. Since there was no public exposure, local officials either approved of these camps or looked the other way.[62]

However convenient these sites were, they could never rival the beach in the summer as a place to practice heliotherapy. Before long the reality of sunshine and the beach took hold. There is, of course, a delicious irony in this, for just as men were finally confined in a bathing costume, nudity became a big issue at the beach. But unlike the argument that men had always swum nude, naturism came with volumes of philosophical writing.[63] By the 1920s nude beaches started to appear. For instance, in 1920 the North Sea island of Sylt became the first official nudist beach in Germany. This long narrow island had many fine beaches, and so it was easy to find a place and undress. By this time there were other informal nude beaches that were out of the way and not easy to get to. This would continue to be a theme in the creation of nude beaches—out of the way and out of sight. In France the naturists turned to an island off the Riviera coast—the Ile du Levant. A rocky island near Hyeres, an established resort, Ile du Levant required a great deal of work to make it acceptable as a naturist retreat, but soon it was attracting elites because it was not cheap to get to. At first it was only private villas; then in 1936 two hotels were built. With hotels it attracted larger numbers of visitors and became a place that created tradition. In the beginning everyone wore a "slip," a brief covering of the genitals, until the acceptance of full nudity. With beaches on three coasts, France established a reputation for nude beaches that remains true today. It is the most visited country by people who go to nude beaches.[64]

In the United States and Britain, naturism found a tougher environment. As in continental Europe, there were individuals who felt the body needed to be freed so that it could enjoy light and air, both so essential to their well-being. Arrayed against such thinking were powerful forces that could still keep men with bare chests off the beach. Full-body exposure anywhere in public was a long way off. In the United States, advocacy of naturism was dangerous.[65] Surreptitiously at first, books and magazines were published advocating the health benefits of nudism out of doors. It was not always advisable to advocate nudity at the beach if the state had already passed laws against violating public decency. In 1915 a Washington State newspaper editor published an article titled "The Nude and the Prudes," assailing the arrest of four citizens who were nude and had gone "into the woods to escape the polluted atmosphere of priest-ridden, conventional society." But because of a "few prudes [who] got into the community and proceeded in the brutal, unneighborly way of the outside world to suppress the people's freedom," they were arrested. He was tried and found guilty of advocating against a law banning public nudity. The editor lost again when he appealed to the Washington State Supreme Court. When he appealed to the Supreme Court of the United States claiming violation of his First Amendment rights, he lost the case again. In an opinion written by Justice Oliver Wendell Holmes, the court sided with the state in enforcing public decency, as that was more important than the editor's rights.[66] The decision reflects the temper of the times, and it was not until the 1960s, when public opinion had changed drastically, that it was possible to create a nude beach such as San Gregorio Beach, which would become California's first public nude beach. Many others would follow.[67]

In Britain the 1920s witnessed the beginning of advocacy of nudity and the creation of private clubs, such as the Sun Ray Club to endorse nudity and provide opportunities to practice it. Over the next decades larger and larger numbers were attracted to the idea of nudism, but it would be 1978 before the first publicly approved beach was created at Fairlight Cove by the Hastings Borough Council. In the following year five other beaches were approved and, in 1980, Brighton followed suit.[68]

Before officialdom finally gave in to changing public attitudes, nudity at the beach went on furtively at out-of-the-way places. Even the official beaches were not easy to get to; at Fairlight one had to hike toward a cliff and then clamber down to reach the beach. Even in California today, one of the largest nude beaches—Black's Beach in La Jolla—requires one to climb down a narrow path on a cliff, or hike along the beach for over a mile, to get to the beach. Sandy Bay, near Cape Town, follows this pattern, as it is a difficult hike to get there along a rocky coast. So while heliotherapy bloomed in Europe, it fell on stony ground elsewhere, and for that matter there are still states that have legislation against public nudity. While controversies over how the body was to be displayed aroused controversy, millions enjoyed the many new and old resorts, but not everyone was equally welcome. Old prejudices reared their ugly heads at the beach. Around the turn of the century, the Jewish

FIGURE 7.4 Cartoon in the *California Eagle,* July 15, 1927. UC Libraries. The dilemma of Black swimmers trying to find a place on the beach, as depicted in Los Angeles's Black newspaper.

population in America swelled as millions of new immigrants poured into the country and settled in many of the cities, especially New York. Regarded as aliens, Jews experienced much anti-Semitism. Austin Corbin, a wealthy railroad man, openly stated he would not allow Jews into his two hotels at Coney Island—the Manhattan Beach Hotel and the Oriental—two of the swankiest hotels at the resort. His ban aroused a furor, but he stuck by his policy. As the secretary to the American Society for the Suppression of Jews, he was a deeply committed anti-Semite.[69] From New York to Florida, even prominent Jewish families found themselves banned from hotels.[70] In time, they would have to build parallel institutions in which to enjoy their leisure time. In Florida, Miami Beach became a notable Jewish colony.

Another group that found problems of access to the beach was African Americans. While elite Blacks might venture to Cape May and even Newport, most Blacks present at resorts were there as workers—cooks, servants, bartenders, and barbers—for wherever personal services were needed, they were often rendered by Blacks. As such, they relied on the summer months to provide enough income to get through the winter. "Lord please don't take me in August" was a plea that made plain that the wages and tips of the summer were needed.[71] At places like Atlantic City, year-round permanent residential colonies of Black folk were created in the growing tourism industry. They by and large kept to themselves and created their own shops and services by way of building their own community. They did use the beach, but kept to places where they were comfortable.[72] They generally swam at different times and in out-of-the-way places so as not to disturb the White guests, especially those from the South. It was in the South that Blacks had more trouble. In the decades after the Civil War they had been accepted in some places. Elite Blacks from the Washington area had gone to nearby Bay Ridge to get relief from the summer heat and humidity in the capital. With the failure of Reconstruction in the South, the increase in segregationist legislation and hostile racialist attitudes everywhere meant that Blacks were commonly excluded from many public areas. In response, Charles Douglass, son of Frederick, bought Highland Beach in 1890 and created a Black resort.[73] Other Black beaches followed, such as Manhattan Beach, Florida, created by the railway workers who were building Flagler's east coast railway, and American Beach, where an African American businessman bought a piece of Amelia Island, Florida, and created space for Black bathers.[74] To escape Jim Crow laws that prevented Blacks from using White facilities, including White beaches, Blacks had to go to out-of-the-way beaches or to one of the few that had Black ownership. Only then could Black communities find relief from the heat and White oppression.

Yet even in distant California, Jim Crow and the Ku Klux Klan bedeviled Black attempts to find space on the beach. The Black community at Huntington Beach, in Orange County, bought land and was building a club house, the Pacific Beach Club, to secure a foothold on the sand. Membership in the club was advertised and, prior to the building opening, a bathing beauty contest was held. However, just as the building was nearly finished, arsonists burned it down, and a White club then moved in to take over the property and exclude Blacks.[75] As another indication of growing segregation, the beach city of Manhattan Beach expropriated property that had been owned by Blacks since 1911 and denied them access to the beach. In 1927 the city police force started to arrest Black bathers on the beach to make the point that they were not welcome. An NAACP suit gained them access to the beach, but the KKK and real estate interests would deny them the right to buy property.[76] In 1922, rumors of a Black bathhouse pushed the city council of

Santa Monica to pass ordinances to prohibit construction, and to make the case clearer they closed a Black dance hall. In the end, the Black community was limited to the ill-named Inkwell, a small tract of sand south of Venice Beach, as the only place they could safely swim.[77] For decades, a single beach provided space for Black people to enjoy a day in the sun without having to worry about growing segregation.

In time, these beaches would fade. With the end of legal segregation in the 1960s and the ability to gain access to nearby beaches rather than traveling to out-of-the-way spots, fewer people, especially from the inner city, went to Black resorts. As these resorts declined, beachfront properties such as Hilton Head, South Carolina, and the Amelia Island Company, Florida, in their quest for expansion, squeezed out black property owners to create exclusive and expensive resorts.[78] The first half of the twentieth century was an era of setback for African Americans. No matter that they had initially achieved a certain amount of autonomy, that was lost in an era dominated by the KKK and rising segregation. While many prejudices fell away as they related to swimsuits and the body, no such developments aided Black folk.

. . .

While the resorts had more than enough to do in dealing with rising numbers and engaging with popular culture, emerging technologies also had an impact. Two, in particular, had a dramatic affect—the automobile and photography. Technology in the form of the steam engine had transformed resorts in the nineteenth century, and the internal combustion engine did the same in the twentieth. Rather than rail lines snaking across the countryside with stations acting as a focus, now it was the autonomy of the automobile on the open road and the inevitable search for a parking place that brought about a revolution. Photography would have a less dramatic effect, but nonetheless, a new form of image creation gave individuals the ability to record their experiences for the first time.

The first automobiles appeared at luxury resorts where stately and beautiful limousines such as the Pierce Arrow, Renault, Mercedes-Benz, and Rolls Royce motored onto promenades, rivaling the horse-drawn carriages that had dominated that scene for decades. By the 1920s, as cars became a mass-produced product in Europe and America, they penetrated into the middle class. The Ford Model T and the Austin 7 were typical of these new cars in that they provided relatively cheap and dependable transportation to customers who could never afford horse carriages and relied on the railway for travel. Now they were liberated to go on their own time and to the place they wanted. There had always been individuals who sought a quiet, private beach away from the throngs at resorts. This had never been easy and took a good deal of initiative in a carriage or on a bicycle, the latter being much cheaper. Now with cars, it was possible to go where the roads would take you and find the beach of your dreams. Towns and villages that had been left out of the resort craze now found that they could attract tourists to their beaches. If that was the case, they had to develop the facilities that would ensure that the newcomers would return. Like it or not, they became resort destinations. At a minimum, it meant that parking spaces close to the beach were needed, and, as these early adventurers were often campers, spaces for tents had to be included.[79] Hotels would come later.

The other aspect of the internal combustion engine is that it allowed cheaper transportation for many, as cars were soon followed by buses. One of the earliest of motor coaches was the charabanc. An open-air bus that originated in France, it was copied at many resorts as a way of moving people around.[80] Uncomfortable in wind and rain and unstable with a high center of gravity, it was quickly replaced by the motor coach, which protected the passenger and allowed for a degree of comfort. The motor coach could operate rather inexpensively over some distance, making it quite competitive with the railways, forcing the latter to reduce fares or even give up some routes. The final motorized innovation was the trailer (or caravan). Mass-produced in the 1930s, it gave tourists even more independence because it was a traveling home that only required parking. While not numerous until the 1950s, trailers still presented problems for the resorts, as they required even more space than cars. This was not always an easy issue to resolve, because the resorts had built the local infrastructure around the railway station so that, after one arrived, most of the facilities were reachable on foot, creating a pedestrian experience. Also, how much did you want to do for people with trailers and tents who were largely self-catering?[81] In general, trailers were condemned to the periphery of town. Realizing that the automobile and bus were the future, resorts finally made the decision to create the needed facilities, although they too might be on the outskirts. They could only hope that their entertainment facilities would attract these new visitors, yielding an income from them.

Holiday photographs at the beach can be found in the photo albums of most families. These have become even more common in the age of the digital camera. This is a very long way from John Stetterington's large print of Scarborough, the very first image of bathers at a resort. In

FIGURE 7.5 Louis-Eugene Boudin, 1824–98, French, *Beach at Trouville*, 1873. Oil on panel. © The Norton Simon Foundation. Boudin captures life at Trouville in 1873. Not many people are in the water.

the decades that followed his pioneering effort in the 1730s, prints, caricatures, paintings, cartoons, and watercolors by artists known and unknown illuminated every aspect of resort culture. Late in the nineteenth century, Impressionist artists took the new techniques of outdoor painting to the oceanside and added another dimension to beach images. Eugene Boudin, for instance, vacationed at Trouville and painted summer scenes to pay for his holiday.[82] By 1900 innovative technologies were creating new and different images. Photographers had been present for some time near the beach, where a studio portrait could be acquired, and as the equipment became less cumbersome they went out on the beach to catch people there.

Another photographic advance came in 1900 with the marketing of the Kodak Brownie camera. There had been handheld Kodak cameras, invented by George Eastman, since 1888, but the Brownie changed everything with its light weight, portability, and low cost at one dollar.[83] Amateurs could now control an easy process of shooting images and leaving it to Kodak to develop the film, thereby permanently recording images of holidays and special occasions. Its portability and ease of concealment meant that candid shots could now be made that were flattering, or otherwise, to the subject. Pablo Picasso liked to take photos of people's bottoms as they leaned over on the beach.[84] It was this sort of playful behavior that angered some resort managers, who banned "camera fiends." As one newspaper put it, "The sedate citizen can't indulge in any hilariousness without the risk of being caught in the act

" Now, mind, if any of those nasty people with cameras come near,
you're to send them away ! "

FIGURE 7.6 Charles Keene, 1823–1891, Cartoon
captioned "Now mind if any of those nasty people with
cameras come near, you're to send them away!" in *Mr.*
Punch at the Seaside (London: The Amalgamated Press,
1898). Mechanical reproduction, 17.5 × 11 cm. Mark J.
Cohen and Rose Marie McDaniel Collection, The Ohio
State University Billy Ireland Cartoon Library & Museum.
This cartoon catches the downside of hand-held cameras
in the era before they became ubiquitous.

and having his photograph passed around among his Sunday school
children."[85] However, the Brownie was just too popular with families to
be banned, as trips to the beach needed to be recorded.

As photography became more ubiquitous, it found a new market in
postcards. The first postcards with images emerged in France in the
1870s, and during the decade that followed postcards became available
all over Europe and America. By the 1890s they were widespread, and
there were more and more photographic images of places and people.
For vacationers, this was the ever-more-common way to write "wish
you were here" to their hoped-for envious friends. The postcard craze
reached its height from 1901 to 1910, with 677 million mailed in the
United States in 1908. Postcards also developed a bawdy side, often
featuring a drawing that played upon the many awkward situations
that could come with people in ever-shorter bathing suits. These cartoons were very popular in Britain, so much so that by the 1950s a
Conservative government tried to ban them as they seemed to be corrupting public morals. The popularity of the postcard declined in the
more liberal 1960s, but its final demise came with the advent of email.[86]

Movies also invaded the beach. These were not moving images created by people on the beach, but the work of technicians and photographers who developed the new medium as they went along. Filmmakers wanted films with plots featuring drama or comedy, and where better than the beach with action and crowds? Since the early film industry in America was clustered in New York City, it was natural that filmmakers would look to Coney Island as a place to film. Here was the quintessential modern place with lots of action. Between 1895 and 1904 there were fifty films made at the resort, as it was a nationally known playground with all sorts of rides that could lead to awkward moments for the film stars of the day. *Shooting the Chutes* of 1896 was typical of the first wave of movies in that it just featured the ride and the participants. More plotting was involved in *Boarding School Girls at Coney Island* in 1905 and *Coney Island at Night* of the same year. They were followed by films featuring stars of the day such as Fatty Arbuckle, Mabel Normand, and Buster Keaton in *Fatty at Coney Island.* As a result of these early films featuring Coney Island rides and illuminations, it became even more of a national playground and a place that must be visited.[87] The development of beauty contests in the 1920s led the director Mack Sennett to create a series of silent films known as *Mack Sennett and his Bathing Beauties* featuring young women in the latest beach costumes.[88] These images encouraged young women to follow the fashion of the new, more revealing swimsuits. While these were mostly comedies, there were also serious dramas such as the English film *Hindle Wakes* of 1927, shot at Blackpool, tracing the consequences of resort romance on a "modern" young woman.[89] In the usual telling of such stories the young woman is abandoned, but in this case the young man actually shows up to offer marriage. The plot twist is that the young woman turns him down and gets on with living her life. Between family snapshots and successful movies, resorts entered popular culture as never before, furthering the boom in visitation.

All of these technological innovations swept over the resorts and confronted them with problems they could not avoid. They had to adapt. For instance, they were unable to avoid the controversy about the new swimsuits and old-fashioned values. Resorts were caught between their customers, who might want to dress in the most fashionable beachwear, and the communities that surrounded them. As we have seen, many resorts tried with mixed results to enforce modesty. Even at Dieppe in the 1920s, a woman walking from the casino to her hotel in a bathing suit, without the appropriate cover, was arrested and

FIGURE 7.7 Irving Underhill, 1872–1960, American, *Coney Island Bathers*, 1913. Gelatin dry glass plate negative, 8 × 10 in. (20.3 × 25.4 cm). Brooklyn Museum / Brooklyn Public Library, Brooklyn Collection. © Estate of Irving Underhill. There are more people standing around on the beach than there are people in the water.

fined one thousand francs.[90] Within a decade that would be laughable. Conservative local governments responding to die-hard public opinion did not adapt to changing public taste as readily as the young bathers who were prepared to push for change. Hotels could only let their guests wear what they wanted on hotel property and warn them about community rules. No matter how hard they tried, conservatives lost out to the desire for fashion, a suntan, and freedom of movement.

The social geography of beach resorts also changed. With bathing suits designed to be practical with sunbathing a goal and with swimming far more common, new patterns emerged. Photographs from the late nineteenth and early twentieth centuries show packed beaches with most people standing around fully clothed and with a few people bobbing around in the water. Yet more and more bathers needed to stake out a place where they could put down a towel or blanket and put up an umbrella, the better to settle in for a few hours and soak up the sun. If you wanted to stand fully clothed, you would look rather strange; those folks were finally banished to the boardwalk or promenade. Hotels moved quickly to take over the sand in front of their buildings and cover it with umbrellas of their colors, the new deck chairs to lounge on, small tables to rest drinks on, and towels, all the better to meet every need of the bather. Beaches soon took on a patterned array of colors as each hotel or beach club set out its own equipment. Visitors to the hotels only had to sashay down in the morning to find a place. Not all beaches looked alike. Along the North Sea and the Baltic, the Strandkorb, a large wicker chair invented by a basket maker, dominated the beaches. It provided a covered place for two to sit facing away from the sea to avoid the constant cool breeze. If you piled up a sand berm in front, you could focus the sun's rays and enjoy some warmth—or you could head south to one of the new resorts.

A day at the beach also changed. The one-hour bathe at 11:00 now became a day, or at least some hours, at the beach, where lounging around in the sun and swimming were combined. Acquiring a tan in order to impress one's fellow workers was a necessity. It was an expression of youthful vitality, no matter one's age. Some resorts responded by providing a concierge to watch over you and ensure that you had an appropriate amount of sunshine to get a light tan. It was also in the 1930s that a deep tan came to be recognized as a problem. All sorts of nostrums and lotions emerged, but a serious sunscreen did not appear until the 1940s when Coppertone brought out the first sun blocker that actually worked.[91] Bragging about how you dealt with the surf with your new swimming skills was equally important, as was dressing appropriately as you shared your Brownie photos. Women still wanted to appear fashionable going to and from the beach, and a simple wrap might not be quite the height of fashion. Coco Chanel provided the appropriate attire, when in 1922 at the Lido in Venice she wore a set of "pajamas" with a wide leg, showing a healthy tan. Soon women aspired to wear the beach pajamas at posher resorts.[92] This was more radical than it sounds, as women did not normally wear slacks.

With the ocean filled with swimmers and frolickers, safety came to the fore. For a while poles with cables running into the water had provided a degree of safety to those cavorting in the near shore. As swimmers went out further, men in boats were employed to watch over them and rescue those in need. Paying for these men was an issue. Lifeguards were hired at Atlantic City in 1872, paid for by the Camden and Atlantic Railroad, before the town decided in 1884 that it needed to bear the expense.[93] Soon beach resorts everywhere had lifeguards who became iconic figures, perhaps not as much as those in Australia, but celebrated in the media, notably in the television show *Baywatch* (1989–2001) and the movie based on the series.

FIGURE 7.8 Winslow Homer, *Undertow*, 1924. Oil on canvas. Image courtesy of Clark Art Institute, clarkart.edu. Homer's painting catches the tragedy of a drowning.

In 1916 a new dimension would be added to the role of the lifeguards. Walt Whitman had warned that sharks would ignore civilization and haunt the piers of modern cities. For a long time this did not matter much, as sharks were regarded as being very docile and thus no threat to humans. Then in July of 1916, a hungry great white shark launched a reign of terror on the New Jersey coast. Over a period of two weeks the shark struck five times, killing four victims. Day after day, headlines fanned the horror of the attacks. The man-eater traveled north along the coast before it was killed by two fishermen. Swimming near the shore all but stopped for the rest of the summer.[94] Such was the impact of the attacks that even in 2016 the people of Matawan, New Jersey, observed the one hundredth anniversary of the attacks.[95] But in 1974 the whole country was introduced to the great white and the terror it could induce in the novel *Jaws*, followed soon after by the movie, causing many to stay out of the water. As recently as the summer of 2017 in Southern California there was an abundance of sightings of great whites. No matter the statistics regarding the frequency of shark attacks that try to reassure the public of the unlikelihood of being victimized, evening news images of big sharks meandering offshore cause some to rethink their trips to the beach. Such fears have added a new dimension to the work of lifeguards, who have to look out for foolish

FIGURE 7.9 Reginald Marsh, *Coney Island Beach,* 1935. Etching, 13 1/16 × 17 15/16 in.(33.1 × 45.5 cm), Gift of Miss Bartlett Cowdrey, 1940, Metropolitan Museum of Art, © 2020 Estate of Reginald Marsh / Art Students League, New York / Artists Rights Society (ARS), New York; Image copyright © The Metropolitan Museum of Art; image source: Art Resource, NY. Marsh always captures an abundance of writhing, fleshy bodies.

swimmers, rip currents, wandering children, and now that frightening fin tracing lazy arcs in the water.

With more and more people packing onto the beaches with skimpier and skimpier bathing suits, the inevitable result was to enhance the beach as a site for sexual adventure. It might not be Baiae, but there was certainly more exposure of the female body than was true in the nineteenth century. In the past, when at home people were surrounded by family and friends and were part of a community that enforced rules of conduct. At the beach this framework diminished. Instead, visitors confronted novel situations and a relaxation of norms that the resorts encouraged with entertainment, rides, and dress that were far from what was normal at home. The images created by Reginal Marsh and Paul Cadmus at Coney Island in the 1930s, for instance, depict a landscape of bare flesh being appraised openly by both sexes.[96] In every direction people cavort, play games, fend off unwanted advances, and fondle a loved one. Advertising images for many of the resorts also featured young, healthy bodies to indicate that the site was very up-to-date. For youngsters coming of age in the dawn of the automobile and the modern beach scene, there was little left to the imagination. Adventures and misadventures followed, whether in the car or under the boardwalk. It was not yet the age of sexual liberation, but it certainly flowed in that direction.

. . .

By the middle of the twentieth century there were subtle, but obvious, changes in the social composition of the resorts. The European aristocracy, long the lead element at posh resorts, proved unable to hold its place in the new century. Undermined by a long agricultural depression and then by the taxes imposed by World War I, it was grievously damaged financially by these two blows.[97] There were still landowners, such as the Duke of Westminster, who had a fortune, but then the land he owned was most of West London. Few were so lucky. Then there were the ravages of the war which destroyed empires—German, Austrian, and Russian—and the social order they supported. Also, a generation of young aristocratic men suffered significant losses in the war. Even if one survived the war, the following years were a grim struggle to maintain what was left. The glory days of resorts such as Brijuni Island, a favored resort of the Hapsburgs and the central European High Society, were over.[98] Not that the aristocrats would vanish, just that they were diminished in numbers, influence, and finance. Perhaps this was not as much so in Britain, where John Betjeman could write a poem about his summer holiday at the beach and his reaction to beach topics and society and close it with:

> That topic was all absorbing, as it was,
> Is now and ever shall be to us—CLASS.[99]

Elsewhere the titans of commerce, manufacturing, and finance, whose fortunes had survived the war or even increased because of it, could fill the gap left by the aristocracy. In American, high society played as before. Old families and new fortunes, which were socially acceptable, could enjoy Newport, the new resorts in Florida, and their private clubs. Yet they now had to compete with a new group for the limelight—the celebrities.

The comings and goings of kings, queens, and aristocrats had long dominated social news in the newspapers. Now movie stars, actors, sports stars, writers, and other artists became the preoccupation of reporters and gossip columnists. Newspapers, magazines, and radio, at a time when they had huge audiences, all devoted resources to covering the life and times of the new stars. Specialty magazines such as *Photoplay*, devoted to the movies, developed new audiences for their gossip coverage. Their readers cared far more about Fatty Arbuckle and Mabel Norman than some duke or other. Celebrities at resorts were nothing new. There is a long list of notables in various fields who delighted in visits to the beach—for example, Sarah Siddons, Fanny Burney, Charles Dickens, J.M.W. Turner, Victor Hugo, Karl Marx, Friedrich Engels, Claude Monet, and on and on. They all loved the beach and carried their fame with them. Added to them in the twentieth century were the movie stars and sports stars who brought their own glamour.

The Lido in Venice is an example of how things changed over time. In the early days, Lord Byron galloped on miles of flat sand. By the 1850s bathhouses started to organize the beach and make it more commercial. Then private villas appeared to claim chunks of the beach. Shortly after the turn of the century the grand hotels, the Excelsior and the Des Bains, brought in a cosmopolitan crowd. The new hotels and villas appropriated much of the beach for private use, pushing ordinary folk to the sidelines. Should one persist in going swimming, the beach was blocked with buildings, and all that was left was a narrow passageway with a turnstile where one had to pay for admission.[100] On the other side of the barrier, long the province of the Central European aristocracy, now appeared the growing number of celebrities such as Serghei Diaghalev, Igor Stravinsky, Coco Chanel, Isadora Duncan, Thomas Mann, Henry James, Elsa Maxwell, and Cole Porter, who all brought the glamour of their arts to the Lido. It was now a place to be seen and recognized as somebody of importance for accomplishments, not just for ancestry.[101]

At the same time, the Riviera was being refashioned as a haunt of celebrity. While settlement along the French coast had been led by the British for some time, the area around Cap d'Antibes started to attract a different crowd.[102] Wealthy Americans such as Gerald and Sara Murphy (the original Dick and Nicole of F. Scott Fitzgerald's *Tender Is the Night*) brought an avant-garde group from Paris. Rather than in the winter, they left the city behind in the summer and went to Antibes and Juan des Pins to escape, thereby creating the summer season on the Riviera. The beaches and hotels might have been small, but not the surrounding villas, as Picasso, the Fitzgeralds, Gertrude Stein, Alice B. Toklas, Dorothy Parker, Archibald MacLeish, Ernest Hemingway, Rudolph Valentino,

Ferdinand Leger, and John Dos Passos all joined an international crowd of the new celebrities at the beach.[103] Novels such as Cyril Connolly's *The Rock Pool* skewered the new social groupings on the Riviera.[104] But as the notoriety of these new settlements grew, the French train service created *Le Train Bleu,* an overnight express from Paris to Cannes that was mandatory for those who had any pretensions of being fashionable. Such was the notoriety of the train that a ballet was named after it and Agatha Christie published a mystery titled *The Blue Train.*[105] The ballet was the creation of a group of artists: Jean Cocteau wrote the story, Darius Milhaud composed the music, Chanel the costumes, Picasso the backdrop, and it was danced by the Ballet Russe.[106] The summer visitors brought with them their celebrity and frequent notorious escapades. All of this fed the gossip magazines and the fame of the Riviera. In this world dukes and counts, no matter how noble, were passé.

Celebrities, who were performers, did not just hide themselves away at exclusive resorts. They appeared before their fans at places such as Coney Island, Blackpool, Atlantic City, and Scarborough. The price they paid for celebrity was keeping their name before the public. It was also true that the ever-more-splendid auditoria, dance halls, movie palaces, huge new piers, and theaters were all in need of talent to entertain the millions. Stars of all kinds were willing to appear once the regular season was over. This was a chance to take a rest on the beach and perform. Or, if you were just beginning your career, summer bookings could only boost your reputation. Just about anybody who was anybody in America showed up in Atlantic City.[107] Being close enough to New York City that new shows could try out before going to Broadway meant that actors, singers, and dancers had to be there. Movie stars went there for the opening of their films. The Steel Pier Dance Hall was one of the centers of the dance craze that flourished on both sides of the Atlantic as never before during the 1920s.[108] The ballrooms had to be made bigger and bigger during the twenties to contain the number of dancers who were moving well beyond the waltz to enjoy the faster, livelier, and jazzier dances of that era. Leading the way were the big bands that drove and benefited from the craze. American popular culture was on full display. Should one not want to indulge in this raucous world, one just had to go up the road to Ocean Grove and Asbury Park where preachers still filled the days with sermons.

If high society and celebrities found resorts that catered to them in the new century, so did the middle and working classes. As stated before, resorts had to discover their niches and, once discovered, they had to build the facilities that would best serve that group. Many families returned year after year to the same boarding house or hotel where they felt comfortable and enjoyed the familiar beach and entertainments. There would seem to be little room for innovation, yet it did occur as entrepreneurs were always willing to try new approaches to the holiday business.

A very different type of resort emerged in the early twentieth century. Holiday camps that featured all-inclusive services and entertainment had started in Britain in 1908 with working-class camps, but in the 1930s they really took off. Fred Pantin, Harry Warner, and Billy Butlin led the way in England, but the movement was particularly identified with Butlin.[109] He started in stalls in fairs that traveled the countryside and progressed until he opened an amusement park at Skegness, a beach resort on the North Sea. It was there in 1936 that he created his first camp. This camp featured individual small cottages, or chalets, that were rented by the week, and full board was part of the deal. Butlin always remembered a bad feature of boarding house life, when, come rain or shine, the landlady pushed everyone out so that she could clean. In his camp guests could stay in their chalet, but that might be boring, so Butlin realized that there would also have to be entertainment and activity provided. Out of this came the "Redcoats" who organized activities, including games, all sorts of amateur entertainment with guest participation, talent contests with prizes, and everything to keep people happy and busy. Guests could, if they wanted to, even go to the beach. Special events were organized for the children to keep them occupied while their parents enjoyed themselves as guests. Butlin also used his own celebrity to attract professional entertainers to the camps during the summer, which gave an even higher profile to his camps. This was an all-inclusive holiday that appealed to the middle class. It was not for everyone, especially with the stress on amateur entertainment and guest competitions.[110] Butlin rode the holiday camp idea to a knighthood, fame, and fortune, as it was an idea whose time had come and for which there was a demand.

Governments elsewhere were inspired to create their own holiday camps. The National Socialist government in Germany tried to emulate Butlin on a grand scale. At Prora, near Rugen, Nazi leaders planned a resort building for workers that was designed to be 2.8 miles long and would house twenty thousand workers at a time. It was part of the "Strength through Joy" movement, which had the goal of giving workers holidays, but also to teach them National Socialism. Started in 1936, it was stopped before completion in 1939 by the needs of the war. Various military units used it over the decades as it slowly decayed. At the

time when this book went to press, negotiations were underway to reno-
vate it and create a modern facility from part of the gigantic structure.[111]

Another holiday camp was the far more cheerful Club Med (Club
Mediterranee). Started after the war in 1954 in France, it was originally
a rather primitive camp intended for young singles and couples at the
beach, but over time it evolved into upscale holiday camps with ski
resorts and ships. Some of the resorts have kept an emphasis on families
while others are still for the young adult seeking adventure. True to the
old Butlin model, it does have "genteel organizers" who lead games and
entertainment with audience participation. It still has all-inclusive vacations in exotic spots and advertises them in upscale travel magazines.[112]
It has evolved a long way from its original intentions.

The answer to holiday camps in America was the public beach.
Access to such beaches was free, or at most there was a parking fee.
There might be kiosks with food and drink, but most people would
bring their own. The first one was at Revere Beach in Massachusetts
where the state, in 1895, bought three miles of beach property. Later
purchases stretched it out to six miles. The township created all the
rules and controlled access and there was no intermediary land owner.[113]
Back from the beach, where they could exercise no control over access,
were the hotels and other facilities, including rides of all kinds and other
entertainments.[114] The idea of the public beach would flourish in the
twentieth century. Some were the work of powerful individuals such as
Robert Moses, who created Jones Beach on Long Island in the face of
considerable opposition from property owners and municipalities.
Moses could not be denied: whether it was in building Jones Beach or
diminishing Coney Island as an entertainment center, he always got his
way. For example, at Jones Beach he discovered that he had imported
sand that was far too fine and was prone to blow away, so he resolved
the problem by planting prodigious amounts of grass to stabilize the
dunes.[115] Jones Beach is now the most popular beach in the region. Not
every city had a Robert Moses. In Los Angeles it was sustained public
pressure to ensure public access to what was fast becoming a wall of
private holdings keeping visitors out that worked. In the end, the state
and county governments provided the funding to secure public beaches
as they were the way of the future. Resorts would always survive, but
public beaches were the visible sign of democratization of the seafront.

By the middle of the twentieth century, the beach resort industry
would be described as "mature" in the world of business. It offered a
wide spectrum of styles that appealed to many varied groups. It had also

become an international phenomenon, with resorts spread all over the world and adapted to local cultural needs. As a leisure activity, there was nothing like it, and the modern tourist industry could only adapt to it and begin to explore further opportunities. In the end, it did not adapt to every circumstance, for, however "mature" it was, the future demanded even more change.

Beach Resorts Become a Cultural Phenomenon

The advent of World War II brought violence to many beaches, making them dangerous places. For countless young men they were scenes of terrible carnage best crossed as quickly as possible. Whatever happy memories they might have of beach vacations, they had to hold on to them through bitter times. Outside the zone of conflict, from Kent, England, to California, beaches were off limits as barbed wire, pillboxes, and troops made beaches the first line of defense. In England, trips to the southern and eastern beaches, vulnerable to German air and sea attack prior to a possible invasion, remained prohibited for much of the war. Blackpool, safely out of reach on the northwest coast, entertained hundreds of thousands of troops. Its hotels and boarding houses were obvious places to keep men while training to go into action and then to have them recuperate from the experience. This was true of many resorts, where the facilities spared the armed forces the expense of having to build barracks. In America the coasts were guarded, and in some areas defended, as in Southern California where Japanese submarine activity caused a scare that covered the beaches in barbed wire and brought about nightly blackouts. Coastal blackouts were the most common experience for civilians, while the rest of the nation felt few of these immediate effects of the war. On the continent, the Nazi regime and its collaborators kept their enemies busy and vacations were few. Good Germans, mainly party members and military personnel, could vacation at the spas, but most of the beaches along the coasts were off limits during the war. Only locals could furtively use out-of-the-way beaches to escape the summer heat or local authorities. Among the allies, leaders were always concerned with the need to permit holidays as a way of keeping up morale and a rested workforce. However, the extended summer holiday at the beach was for almost everyone just a fond memory.

The war's end brought an immediate and massive surge of holiday lust where the public sought out beaches. They were anxious to reacquaint themselves with the delights of sun, sand, and surf. In some areas such as Normandy, the destruction of the beach and local communities was such that years would pass before they could be deemed ready for holidaymakers. Even in areas that never witnessed fighting, the resorts looked tawdry after four years of neglect and lack of investment. In some cases it was not simply neglect so much as hard use, as training brought service personnel in and out of hotels and boarding houses. Wounded combatants were sent there to recover, while others, more fortunate, spent precious leave time at the resorts before going back to the front.[1] This meant a great amount of wear and tear on facilities that survived the war. The war over in 1945, a surge of happy vacationers returned to the resorts, which meant happy days for the owners, but left them to ponder the need for repair and rehabilitation of their facilities. Investment on a significant scale meant lots of pressure on local resources and a call for regional and national funding at a time when postwar recovery was in full swing and resorts were far down the list of national priorities. It would be the 1950s before investment was reliably available and rebuilding could begin.

As the number of people flooding onto the beaches increased, it is obvious that attitudes toward leisure continued to evolve. Traditionalists might still regard leisure with disdain and keep to a straight path and a life dominated by righteous thinking, but the reality was that organized religion waned and lost its hold on people's lives. Those otherwise minded, in an increasingly secularizing society, regarded leisure as a necessity. Threats of idle hands and the devil might be used against errant children, yet as adults these same youngsters were happy to sit watching football on television, play golf, or spend the day at the beach on Sunday. The weekend was not a time for reflection and Bible study, but a time to do those things that made life good. As tourism captured more and more people around the world, religious ideas regarding discipline withered except among the most ardent disciples. Secularism and middle-class lifestyles constantly enriched by technology created vast audiences for leisure activities. For those with the means, they

FIGURE 8.1 *Seaside Beach Crowd Watching Pierrots Entertainers in North Yorkshire in 1899.* Dave Bagnall Collection / Alamy Stock Photo. Here were the last of the on-the-beach entertainers just as they were passing from the scene.

could define their lives by work if they wanted, but even 24/7 types knew to break away in order to thrive. Leisure, even if it was in the form of adventure travel, became a necessity.

After the tensions and sacrifices of the war years, visitors crammed into the old and familiar resorts to relax and connect to happier times. Swimming, sunbathing, creating sand castles, going dancing in the evening, eating fish and chips, guzzling oysters, and watching some of the entertainment on the beach and in the theaters were all part of established regimes. They were comforting activities and sought out by vacationers. However, the spirit that animated these visits would not last forever, as inevitably change would sweep away the old and familiar. The '60s brought rock and roll, improved cinemascope movies, an ever-deeper penetration of the market by television, and a number of other cultural changes. Pierrots, popular since Edwardian times on English beaches, when they had replaced the blackface performers, faded from view for they represented another era. Also, the resorts themselves, mostly built in Victorian and Edwardian times, also represented old-fashioned architecture and were seen as being out of tune with the times.[2] While the familiar might be comforting to some, it was increasingly viewed as outmoded by many. The vast swimming pools, or Lidos, built in the '30s went out of fashion as more and more people wanted to sit on the sand and enjoy the sun. Often old hotels were shunned as desperate relics of the past. The big hotel chains that were increasingly taking over the tourist industry were, more often than not, reluctant to build in resorts that were past their prime. Many resorts had to solve these challenges while trying to find their market in a rapidly evolving tourist economy where there were more and more resorts in ever more locales, often funded by foreign governments.

While the resorts had seen considerable growth between the wars, that was to be nothing compared to the surge that came after the war and that has been sustained down to the present day. Three factors drove this increase. The postwar baby boom was the central agent driving population growth. In the Western world, country after country had to recover from the devastation of the war years and start to rebuild populations decimated by the fighting. In the United States an epic recovery created the largest generation in the history of the republic up to that time. The second factor was the rise in the number of countries that were creating more and more paid holidays for workers. In England, for instance, 61 percent of the manual laborers were entitled to two weeks with pay by 1951; by 1955, 96 percent were entitled to two weeks' holiday. At the present time, most workers get twenty-eight days.[3] France had started down this path in 1936, but continued legislation led to French workers acquiring thirty-five paid holiday days each year, with more days earned for those with longer work weeks. Other European countries followed France's lead, but none so generously. In the United States private employers, not the government, granted vacation time. This has grown slowly, but presently about 90 percent of all full-time employees have two weeks with pay; in businesses with heavy competition for skilled workers, the number of days off can be generous, but still not mandated by the government.[4]

The final element, along with paid holidays, was that this period, while experiencing ups and downs, was basically an era of economic growth that benefited the middle and working classes. Those fortunate enough to raise their status were now in a position to join the housing boom and acquire a home in the suburbs, along with the labor-saving appliances that made life easier for women. One of the most important acquisitions was an automobile. By 1960 there were over 61 million cars on American roads. Suburban living generally meant commuting as a part of daily life, but house and car also became important status indicators that could not be ignored. With the car came changing attitudes toward leisure. Time and mobility opened up a world of possibilities from vacationing in national parks, visiting distant relatives, going to professional sports, visiting the new entertainment centers such as Disney World, and enjoying participatory sports such as skiing. Families acquired the ability to wander farther and farther while on holiday. For many of them a trip to the beach might just be a weekend day of piling into the car and getting everyone there and back safely, but more and more of them were also lured to the beach for longer holidays. Resorts and local governments had to create the roads and parking areas that made this possible, yet they were never able to meet the demand. Crowds heading for the beach were still very seasonal, meaning that traffic could get horrendous during the summer months. In England, for instance, many a quaint village could be overwhelmed by cars heading for a nearby resort. So, like it or not, local, provincial, and national governments had to respond and create the roads and parking lots necessary to contain the crowds. In New Jersey, the national road US 9, which went along much of the coast, was joined by the far larger toll road, the New Jersey Parkway, which also paralleled the beach. The federal government also got into the act after 1956, building the interstate highway system and, while focused on going from city to city, it often provided access to the coasts. While these new highways diminished travel times, the inevitable end of the trip was the beach town, which was often a maze of small roads that echoed to the cry, "Are we there yet?"

Another complication was the growing popularity of the caravan or trailer. While these came on the scene in the '30s and started to cause problems then, after the war, in the '60s, the fondness people had for self-catering, bringing a little bit of home with them, caused even more problems. Municipalities and entrepreneurs had to create campgrounds for these large vehicles and provide the facilities to maintain them.[5] Hotel owners were not happy about paying taxes for the privilege. One aspect of this new mobility was that people now spread out along the coast, visiting more and more isolated beaches rather than concentrating near the railroad terminal, so that the massive numbers visible in old photos became a thing of the past. Not that numbers diminished. Blackpool regularly entertained seven million visitors during the season in the '60s and '70s, and Coney Island bulged with sixteen million.

As more and more people traveled by car, bus, and trailer, the railways suffered. As the road system evolved and car numbers increased, it became less and less profitable for railways to send trains to the resorts. One by one rail lines were cut and railways consolidated until in many areas it was only by car that you could reach your favorite beach. It was only on busy routes, such as that on Long Island, New York, that the trains would continue to run because there were enough year-round communities with commuters to justify maintaining service. And so, the train continued to be an option in reaching resorts. Elsewhere, though, the railways as the great annihilator of time and space of the nineteenth century started to fade into the background. In other parts of the world, where the automobile had not yet penetrated, the railways continued to be the preferred means of transportation. China and India only started to build highway networks at the end of the twentieth century as their middle classes acquired cars. Replacing the railways for long-distance travel was the new revolutionary mode of travel of the twentieth century—the jet plane. By the late 1950s, military jets led to the development of safe passenger planes that traveled higher and faster than the old propeller planes. At first a novelty for the wealthy who became the "jet set," they soon penetrated the tourist market, and by the '70s travel companies could charter planes and arrange cheap travel to resorts. There, they also bought up hotel space to create packages affordable to many. By 2000 discount airlines, such as Ryanair, offered cut-rate fares compared to the large national airline companies. The combination of charters and cheap airfares was a boon to tourism and had a major effect on resorts.

The impact of jet travel went well beyond the development of a jet set who enjoyed new and ever-more-distant resorts they could call their own. It would also lead to mass tourism as fares were brought within reach of those who could never have dreamed of air travel. For instance, working-class families in England could now go on holiday to Spain in the summer, or even to Florida in the winter. Not long before it had been a delight to drive from Manchester to Blackpool, but to fly on a cheap flight to Costa del Sol was a new dimension in holiday dreams. More and more people took advantage of these new travel options, leading the way to today's mass tourism.

Resorts responded creatively to the challenge of continuing to attract visitors. It usually meant a realistic appraisal of the market and the assets the resort possessed. It was not always an easy process, as the market kept changing and those assets that might be used one decade could easily fade the next. Then there was always the problem of funding. Any significant realignment entailed expenditures that could be well beyond the capacity of the local community. In some cases the slow

FIGURE 8.2 Row of buildings on Guerny Street known as "Stockton Place" in the Cape May Historic District, Cape May, NJ, July 23, 2011. Buildings designed by Stephen Decatur Button. Cape May's reputation as a heritage site was based on these Victorian cottages.

but steady deterioration of attractions might just condemn the resort to irrelevance. For instance, in England some resorts have become nothing more or less than retirement towns serving a growing group of retirees.[6]

Scholars have identified six stages in the life of resorts—exploration, involvement, development, consolidation, stagnation, and decline.[7] Obviously stagnation and decline were to be avoided. One way out was to celebrate the past and become a heritage center. Cape May and Margate both have splendid collections of old buildings—Margate from the Georgian era forward to Victorian, and Cape May with lots of lovely houses built in the Victorian manner. In fact, Cape May has the unique distinction of having the entire town designated as a historic district and a National Historic Landmark.[8] For both towns it was possible to evolve from being solely a bathing site to a place for visitors to come and be entranced by the past as seen in old buildings. Margate also celebrated the fact that J. M. W. Turner was a frequent visitor, so now there is a new art gallery, Turner Contemporary. Even Dreamland, at Margate, one of the earliest amusement parks, was chosen for redevelopment and has been reopened with vintage rides. Nearby, Broadstairs went down the same path as Margate in becoming a center associated with Charles Dickens, who went there to write.[9] Even Nahant, long forgotten as a resort, celebrates its Victorian past with an annual costume ball recalling its heyday.[10]

Others adapted differently to new circumstances. Blackpool and Brighton became convention centers because of their multiple hotels and facilities for meetings. This allowed them to operate a year-round business. Brighton also became a heritage site, given its diverse architecture from the eighteenth century forward, with the remarkable Pavilion as a centerpiece. The royal family had abandoned the Pavilion a long time earlier, so the town bought and renovated it. Another of Brighton's innovations was a major summer cultural festival that is now the second largest in Britain, after the one in Edinburgh. It has also become a major center of gay life, having the highest percentage of gay couples living in households and celebrating with one of the largest pride parades in Britain.[11] Another new group in Brighton are the commuters, who have discovered that its rail system permits relatively easy travel into London.[12] Not entirely forgetting its role as a beach resort, the city owns all of the five miles of beach and, while it has always been a stony, shingle beach, tourists still brave the water. Tourism remains important to the Brighton economy, but it no longer is focused on being a beach resort.

Blackpool is still a vast entertainment center with three piers, the Tower complex focused on the five-hundred-foot-high tower, a large Winter Garden complex of theaters, and the ever-popular Pleasure Beach amusement park, with ever-bigger and -faster rides.[13] The town has also spent millions of pounds on renovations to create a more modern look to many of the facilities, but it did not fool with some of the fundamentals, such as the fish and chip shops of fond memory to millions of visitors. There is still an annual ballroom dancing contest that is a major event in the dance world. The city also tried to become a major gambling center focused on a large casino, but Parliament killed the proposal as inappropriate for Blackpool. The famous Illuminations continue to celebrate the end of summer in September.[14] Blackpool has refused to descend slowly into irrelevance and, while it may not be just a beach resort, it still has a long beach that attracts bathers during the hot spells that are becoming more common in Britain. So old resorts have struggled to attract new visitors and to hold them in the face of ever-growing competition from places further south with new facilities and longer seasons.

The travails of the resorts in Britain have even attracted literary attention, such as from Paul Theroux and Bill Bryson, who have written travel accounts and included rather dire descriptions of many of the English coastal towns.[15] Theroux describes Morecambe: "It astonished me that anyone would come here for a vacation and to have fun, since it seemed the sort of place that would fill even the cheeriest visitor—me, for example—with thoughts of woe. I imagined day trippers getting off the train and taking one look and bursting into tears."[16] For towns like Morecambe, the 1970s and '80s were especially difficult, and local officials did not appreciate the attention by writers who described the conditions that drove some resorts out of business.[17]

Coney Island, for so long a world-famous cultural beacon, has lost much of its entertainment complex. It suffers from being a part of New York City, where powerful mayors and other politicians can downplay its heritage and impose their plans through rezoning. There still are a few amusement park rides—always bigger and faster roller coasters—but the big amusement parks are long gone. It still has the old Bowery, as seedy as ever, but not quite the outrageous and tawdry place it once was. The grand hotels and most of the other hotels are gone, so in a way, the trippers have taken over. What it does have is a great beach where millions of New Yorkers still come to seek relief in warm weather by swimming and indulging in Nathan's Famous Hot Dogs. So it is still a beach resort, but maybe not a place that families would plan on visiting for a week.[18]

Biarritz, on the other hand, has gone from being a major aristocratic beach with celebrated visitors such as King Edward VIII to being a family venue. With the decline of the European aristocracy, Biarritz had to discover other audiences. It remained cosmopolitan after the First World War, with Americans, Cubans, as well as Russians and other Europeans, but increasingly with more and more celebrities.[19] After World War II it served as the demobilization center for the many thousands of American troops who enjoyed the beach before going home. Unknown to all of them at that time, it is one of the finest surfing spots in Europe. This was discovered in 1956 by Peter Viertel, who was in Biarritz to make a movie but who was also a surfer. On realizing just how good the waves were, he immediately sent for his board to experience the first-class surf break at the northern beach. It was a fortunate discovery, placing Biarritz at the forefront of the surfing boom in Europe. By 1959 there was a Waikiki Surf Club, and in 1960 there was a surfing contest. Biarritz emerged as a sports center that is great for youth and families and has been rebuilt to suit the new audience.[20]

Atlantic City has entered something of boom-and-bust cycle as a resort and entertainment center. Photograph after photograph reminds us of its glory days with grand hotels, stupendous Easter parades, and millions of visitors, but its dated facilities and the fact that for some time it was controlled by gangs who victimized visitors, brought its glory days to an end. In hopes of revitalizing the city, the people of New Jersey voted in 1976 to permit casino gambling. Subsequently, $5 billion was invested in twelve casinos, and for a while it appeared as if this was the solution to the doldrums—a boom! But it was not to be. The plan to become the Las Vegas of the East failed, leaving the city with another set of derelict buildings.[21] With the constant reinvention of Las Vegas and the expansion of Native American gambling facilities, becoming a gambling center, even a very fancy one, is difficult. It is also true that places that sell themselves as entertainment centers ultimately have to compete with Disney World and other adventure parks that have prospered. Investment capital flows have gone south toward warmer winter weather, along with the tourists.[22] Atlantic City has a good sandy beach and it continues to appeal to people who only want to lie on the sand and play in the water. More importantly, it still has the boardwalk with all sorts of attractions that entice visitors.

While the decline of amusement centers is a general truth, there can be exceptions. Wildwood, just up the coast from Cape May and south of Atlantic City, has managed to become a family entertainment center. Its origins are in the 1890s, but it suffered a series of storms and scandals that held it back. Beginning in 1955 as the Garden State Parkway reached the south end of the state, Wildwood started to develop. It has a wide beach that is very appealing, most of the sand drifting over from Cape May due to yet another reinvestment plan gone awry. However, it has built a reputation around Morey's Piers, the creation of two brothers who have developed three piers full of rides plus a water park, all aimed at the family on holiday. There is also a long boardwalk with the usual variety of shops. This combination has created a regional center that remains popular, attracting 250,000 visitors a year, not quite the scale of Coney Island but a popular attraction that has developed a niche and turned out well.[23] Another success story is Asbury Park, New Jersey. Long famed for its music scene, it has now attracted young investors who have built new hotels and restaurants, bringing life back to what was just another decayed old resort.[24] There has been no master plan, just people willing to take a chance with derelict buildings. In their favor have been good transportation and a desire on the part of those who could not afford Fire Island or the Hamptons to get a beach place close to home.

Also challenging and making life difficult for the old resorts has been wave after wave of new creations. Often the driving force has been national governments. They saw the tourism sector as an opportunity not to be missed. In Spain, for instance, the Franco government decided that the time was ripe for the development of the Costa Brava, north of Barcelona. Until this time the most developed beach in Spain was on the Basque Coast at San Sebastian, where the Spanish royal family and many aristocrats congregated during the summer season.[25] The turn toward the Costa Brava was a shrewd move, as the coast was beautiful and undeveloped and state planners were correct in believing that a ready market was available in northern Europe for the sand and sun of Spain. Significant state aid was poured into Catalonia in the 1950s to attract the hotel chains that were coming to play an enhanced role in resort creation.[26] The other Spanish resort center, Costa del Sol, was created more or less on its own. It had existed as an aristocratic and celebrity beach around Malaga until the late 1950s, when development accelerated and a new Costa del Sol arrived in Torremolinos, Marbella, and other towns attracting hordes of British, French, and Scandinavian tourists.[27] By 1962 Spain attracted over six million tourists, compared to the two million who visited in 1957.[28] The vast majority of these tourists were not seeking edification or education, but what they would come to know as *la dolce vita*.[29]

The Mexican government, like the Spanish, had similar plans. The goal was to encourage tourism and to create new tourist venues on the Caribbean away from the established West Coast resorts such as Acapulco. Cancun, a long barrier island, came to the fore as a suitable Caribbean site on the exotic Yucatan Peninsula and close to the southern United States. The National Fund for Tourism Development stepped in to aid the first nine hotels because the hotel chains were reluctant to finance a new, unproven resort. They need not have worried, as Cancun is still a favored destination.[30]

Sharm el Sheikh, blessed with warm, dry weather, good beaches, and some of the best reef diving in the world, was undeveloped until the Israelis seized it in the 1967 war against Egypt. They started to develop it, and when it was returned to Egyptian control in 1982 the Egyptian government encouraged development. All the major hotel chains are now represented there. It has been especially attractive to British and Russian tourists, and they in turn have attracted the attention of radical Islamists who have attacked planes and buildings there. It has also been notable for a series of shark attacks. However, with balmy, sun-drenched winters, it continues to be a favored destination.[31]

Further east, Phuket Island, Thailand, with thirty beaches, historic buildings, temples, and local jungles, has emerged as one of the leading destination sites in Asia. Featured in many travel magazines, it has attracted millions of Europeans and Asians and even some Americans. As such, it is like Boracay Island in the Philippines, a major new resort competing for a share of the ever-growing beach tourism dollar. While Phuket was badly damaged by the 2004 tsunami and Boracay has had ongoing sewage problems, nonetheless they present new developments with new hotels and facilities that old resorts cannot rival, not to mention tropical weather and sunsets.

There is hardly an area in the world that does not now have beach resorts. There are even beaches in Iceland where only the really hardy can have fun, although there is one beach that is attached to a thermal spring and promises warm water.[32] More resorts will emerge as any government having a tropical beach is sure to develop it in the certain knowledge that tourists will find their way there. If not governments, then hotel chains and casino operators also stand ready to build new resorts. The economics of modern tourism and the insatiable appetite for more and more beach development are the twin drivers of this dynamic.

In the post–World War II era, a few beaches became so successful that they emerged as "iconic" and world famous. They were often not just one resort, but a special set of beaches. One of those iconic places was Southern California. It started in the town of Santa Monica, which had visitors as early as 1850. They made the long journey from Los Angeles, then clustered along the Los Angeles River, a sixteen-mile journey on primitive roads. By the 1870s there was rail service to Santa Monica with a hotel and a staircase down the cliff to the beach, where there were two bathhouses to provide suits and towels and even a warm saltwater bath. A decade later the Arcadia Hotel opened, providing luxury accommodations and fine restaurants. It mostly served tourists rather than locals, as out-of-state tourism had arrived. South along the coast the growing Pacific Electric Rail system of Henry Edwards Huntington provided access to a number of beaches.[33]

While Santa Monica remained the center of beach life, entrepreneurs jumped in to create more resorts. Abbott Kinney and Francis Ryan bought two miles of beach south of Santa Monica. They first created Ocean Park, just south of Santa Monica, which was quickly absorbed by the older town. But the real project for Kinney was Venice Beach, a neighborhood of Los Angeles. His part of the original grant was swampy; to his mind, it could easily be marketed as a version of the Italian city. Venice Beach was a town of canals and Italianate design plus the usual pier, auditorium, dance hall, and shops. As usual, the pier

FIGURE 8.3 Bob Plunkett and Kopec, Marion Davies beach home, Santa Monica, CA, 1947 or later. Photograph photCL_555_06_2158, Ernest Marquez Collection, The Huntington Library, San Marino, CA. The fortune of William Randolph Hearst built this mansion on the sand for his mistress Marion Davies. Only 118 rooms were needed.

was destroyed by a storm, but when rebuilt it was a full-scale entertainment center with all the modern rides.[34] Venice was one part of a slow but steady development of a number of beaches. The upshot was that the growing population of the region had access to more and more beaches which became essential aspects of Southern California life.

Santa Monica remained the most fashionable, however. In 1905 the city built a road down the seaside cliff in recognition of the difficulty in getting down to the beach and of the growing importance of the automobile, which was to dominate future transportation in the region. While the shore and beach were not wide, as it was hemmed in by the cliff, that did not stop the development of the Santa Monica coast. Robert Gillis owned most of the land and opened it for sale, attracting the newly wealthy from the movie industry. Glamorous stars such as Mae West, Harold Lloyd, Douglas Fairbanks, Mary Pickford, and movie moguls such as Darryl Zanuck, Samuel Goldwyn, Louis B. Mayer, Irving

Thalberg, and Jack Warner all built beach mansions. Overshadowing them all were William Randolph Hearst and Marion Davies, who only needed a 118-room mansion in which to change their bathing suits. In areas not occupied by homes, private clubs (in all eleven of them) provided places to change, eat, and entertain adjacent to the sand. For elites and upper-middle-class folks, the clubs provided a beach setting. Most clubs did not survive the Great Depression, and by 1932 the future was represented by Doheny State Park—the first public beach. The state, county, and local governments would, in the end, purchase and create over one hundred miles of coastline for free public beaches that would serve the people.[35]

However attractive the growing miles of public beaches, it was movies and music about surfing that made the Southern California beaches famous. The movie industry was well aware of the booming teen market in the 1950s and wanted to appeal to them. The *Wild One* and *Rebel without a Cause* were movies popular with youth, but very unpopular with parents and the Catholic Church. The films portrayed youth culture too negatively for many and incurred a lot of criticism. Something wholesome was needed.[36] Enter the surfboard. Surfing had a long history in Hawaii as a sport and a medium for gambling.[37] As the Hawaiians surfed naked, appalled Protestant missionaries suppressed it. They never quite succeeded in totally eliminating it on all the islands, and surfers even made it to California before 1900. Early in the twentieth century it was revived by the Hawaiians. Duke Kahanamoku, an Olympic swimmer, toured widely in the 1910s, giving demonstrations as far afield as New Zealand and Australia. Anglos such as Jack London became enamored with it and publicized it.[38] A Hawaiian, George Freeth, came to Southern California in 1907 to demonstrate surfing and publicize the islands. He was hired by Henry Edwards Huntington to give demonstrations on Southern California beaches, where Huntington was developing property. Freeth, a popular advocate for surfing, succeeded and at the same time became the leading advocate for lifesaving, developing new techniques that he taught up and down the coast.[39] Surfing grew slowly, as it was not for everyone. The boards used were large and heavy, built to go fast down the face of a wave, requiring fairly big surf. Young men and a few women were attracted to handling the eight- to twenty-foot-long boards that weighed as much as two hundred pounds. Change would arrive in the 1950s.[40]

An artifact of World War II and the Cold War was the creation of a large defense industry in California. Much of the effort was focused on aerospace, and many inventions poured from the labs and factories. Two of them affected surfing. Robert Simmons used fiberglass, which could be formed into interesting shapes. David Sweet created polyurethane blanks that could then be shaped with fiberglass to create six-foot-long light, maneuverable boards. No longer did one have to heft a large, wooden board into the water. The surfing community quickly adopted the new equipment, and many enthusiasts were drawn to surfing, so that a boom was underway by the late 1950s. While abundant sunshine kept surfers happy and tanned all summer, California has cold water offshore most of the year. That, combined with cooler air temperatures, meant that surfers had to cut back in the winter. This was solved with neoprene. Hugh Bradner experimented, in the early '50s, in shaping neoprene to body contours, keeping a thin layer of water, warmed by the body, between the suit and the skin. Scuba divers were the first to accept the "wet suit," surfers quickly followed, and all-year surfing became a reality.[41]

The surfing boom attracted attention from the movie and magazine businesses as it featured young people, mostly men, tanned, casually dressed, and speaking their own slang. They even had their own music. They loved a big beat and got it from Jan and Dean, Dick Dale, and the Beach Boys.[42] Soon enough this was a nationally identifiable sound that became a part of popular culture. Surfing and the movies evolved in two waves. First were the pure surfing films that appealed only to surfers, such as the work of Bud Browne. He filmed Duke Kahanamoku in Hawaii and showed it as *The Hawaiian Surfing Movie* in Santa Monica in 1953. He produced fifteen other films, and they were favorites among surfers who saw them at local theaters or bars. The creator of what would become the most popular surfing film was Bruce Brown. He, too, made documentaries and then went to a feature in *Endless Summer*, which showed among surfers from 1963 and then went into general release in 1966. This story of two young surfers searching for the perfect wave around the world was popular with general audiences.[43] For many it was their first pure surfing movie.

Gidget started life as a novel by Frederick Kohner. It featured his daughter, who discovered surfing and love on the beach. In 1959, as surfing was really taking off, it became a popular movie.[44] Here was an action film built around surfing and shirtless, rowdy surfers, young girls in two-piece bathing suits, dancing on the beach, and a hapless motorcycle gang. It was immediately popular and led to two sequels and a television show. The next big film was *Beach Party* in 1963 starring two young stars, Annette Funicello and Frankie Avalon. Funicello had starred in Disney's television program *Mouseketeers,* but had matured out of the children's program. Displaced from the show, she needed work and was approached by American International, a slightly disreputable studio known for youth exploitation films (vampires, sex, and aliens) to do a beach film. Walt Disney, who still had her under contract, was not impressed. She finally got him to agree to give his permission by meeting his one big condition: that she make sure her bathing suit covered her navel, the ever-erotic navel—no bikinis here, please. Disney was just following the Hayes Code, which set rules for film morals and forbade the showing of the navel in films.[45] Funicello and Avalon went on to star in a series of beach and surfing films, including *Beach Party Bingo* and *How to Stuff a Wild Bikini.* After that, clone after clone repeated the formula, some twenty-six films in all. While some did go as far afield as Hawaii, most of these were low-budget films that were made in Southern California.[46] Later, other beach-related television programs, such as *Baywatch,* which was wildly popular outside the United States, furthered the image of endless summer in California. Great beaches combined with surfing, music, and movies made Southern California one of the iconic beaches.

Another was the French Riviera. The Riviera, of course, had a long history. At first it was a winter resort around Nice for the English, and then later it attracted aristocrats from Russia. Slowly, other resorts such as Cannes and Hyeres emerged. They too were mostly winter resorts. The twentieth century witnessed the creation of other resorts such as St. Tropez and Cap d'Antibe, which by this time were summer resorts. Celebrities replaced aristocrats, giving the new beaches, especially, a distinctive cachet and style. The Blue Train from Paris to the Riviera was succeeded by the even more glamorous airplane, bringing the train's famed run to an end although it lives on as a restaurant at the Gare de Lyon train station in Paris. So, while the Riviera had a history, it needed a special event to vault it into iconic status. Once again it was a movie that brought it to a new level. Bridget Bardot in *And God Created Women* was a sensation in Europe and in America, where it was heavily edited. Dressed in a bikini, and at times nude, on the beach Bardot created the image of the "sex kitten" that brought fame to herself and director Roger Vadim. While not popular with critics, the movie introduced the star and the director to a wide audience.[47] Her sensuality and the bikini only enhanced the reputation of beaches as erotic sites. Already known for the celebrities who cluttered the Riviera in the summer, this film brought it even greater fame.

The film also continued to popularize the bikini. Developed in 1946 by Louis Reard, the bikini was so scandalous that models would not wear it and Reard had to get strippers to show it off. Many cabaret performers were also familiar with bikinis, as they had been wearing something very similar while entertaining men during the war. The bikini was immediately banned in Spain, Portugal, and Italy and was regarded with distaste in the United States.[48] On the Riviera it was adopted in the '50s and led ultimately to toplessness and near nudity on a stretch of coast known for nude beaches. It was the final move in the long history of female bathing costumes. From the clumsy garment of early days through the emergence of Persian pants to the tank suit, the bathing costume had reached its final minimalization. Not all women accepted the logic of history; some continued to wear two-piece suits and tank suits and, in conservative societies, even more modest beachwear. This is today most notable in religious groups who want to preserve female modesty and do it in two ways—gender-segregated beaches and modest bathing costumes. The Orthodox community in Israel campaigned for, and succeeded in creating, a number of women's beaches. Even in Tel Aviv there is the Sheraton Beach, which is walled off on three sides and allows the maximum of privacy. On women-only days—Sundays, Tuesdays, and Thursdays—religious and secular women can wear the bathing costume they feel comfortable in and sunbathe and play in the surf. There are also men-only days in these segregated beaches. Most Muslim women in Israel go to the coed beaches with their male relatives and wear the burkini when swimming.[49] In Lebanon, women-only beaches for Muslims are also well attended, with a variety of costumes worn, depending on the individual's desire to escape the heat and swim with a religious sensibility. Everything from scanty beach wear to "tankinis" is on display, and no cameras are allowed.[50]

The burkini has, of course, become a symbol of France's problem with Muslims and French identity. A combination of the words *burqa* and *bikini*, the swimsuit covers everything but the face, hands, and feet and helps observant Muslim women swim with modesty. While raising eyebrows elsewhere, in French eyes it is inappropriate, especially on the Riviera, one of the centers of naturism and toplessness. Marine Le Pen has said that "this is the soul of France that is in question." "French beaches are those of Bardot and Vadim."[51] So in Cannes and elsewhere on the Riviera, resorts are banning the burkini and women are being arrested for being modest.[52] In the background are the terrorist attacks by bomb, gun, and truck that France has suffered in recent years, all the

FIGURE 8.4 Burqini Swimwear. Photograph courtesy of
Adabkini. Modesty of a style that takes us back to the eighteenth
century, but it allows observant women to enjoy the beach.

work of Muslims. So the wearing of Muslim clothing by women has
been banned in the schools and frowned upon elsewhere. The irony in
all of this comes from the long struggle to control women's bodies and
clothing with an aim toward modesty when at the beach. Women's
beaches and modest costumes, both approved by men and often mandated by them, have a long history, and it does not appear that they will
vanish any time soon. One would have thought that by now women
could wear whatever they find comfortable at the beach. Resorts have
an interest in allowing women to do so. Blackpool, struggling to keep

its clientele, has reached out to attract Muslim holidaymakers and to do so welcomes the burkini.[53] In the meanwhile, the bikini, toplessness, the burkini, and celebrity continue to keep the Riviera in the public eye.

If iconic beaches, famed in popular culture, became a feature in our time, so did the new megabeaches. Given the ever-increasing demand for beach holidays across the world, beaches everywhere are under development. A resort site might have been no more than a small fishing village back from a sandy beach, where local life has been much the same for centuries. Then someone had a bright idea that fame and fortune lies in development. A feature of some of these new resorts is their size. They may have started out as isolated communities strung along the coast before they were transformed, for they go on for mile after mile with the usual cliff of white hotels and condominiums. The Costa del Sol, Costa Brava, and the Algavre are huge compared to the old resorts such as Brighton and Long Branch. Given their size, there are accommodations for every pocketbook. These are not just the investment of local entrepreneurs, but require much larger capital resources brought by national governments, large hotel chains, and international finance. Local governments and taxpayers are left to fund roads and parking and even help with the necessary airport. Whatever existed previously, and in many cases there was not much, is absorbed into the new megabeach. These sorts of resorts have proliferated all over the world wherever there is sand and sunshine. A partial list would be: the Australian Gold Coast, the Italian Riviera, the Turquoise Coast of Turkey, Argentina's northern Atlantic coast, Florida on both coasts but certainly Miami to Palm Beach, and the Emerald Coast in the Panhandle of Florida, the sixty-mile-long Grand Strand in South Carolina, and the over one hundred miles of beach on the New Jersey coast. These are truly megabeaches with multiple resorts prepared to deal with the mass tourism that arrived in the new age.

With the coming of mass tourism in the '70s, elites took flight as they always have. While jets allowed them to go to ever-more-distant resorts, they did not always abandon nearby beaches where, quite often, the prices for property were so high that the initiation fee kept out all but the very rich. The Hamptons on Long Island started accepting a few beach-lovers in the 1880s. A club was created at Shinnecock that attracted people seeking a quiet place in which to bathe and play golf, but when the train arrived to knit Long Island into one system, the former Puritan townships such as East Hampton and Southampton started down a new path that today finds the townships as prized,

FIGURE 8.5 Gold Coast Skyline, March 2014. A fine example of the modern megabeach—Australia's Gold Coast.

incredibly expensive real estate that guarantees admission to the exclusive world of The Hamptons.[54] One property in Southampton was recently offered for $150 million. Admittedly it did have fourteen acres, sixteen bedrooms, twenty-one bathrooms, and a nice beach.[55] Visitors are attracted from New York City and from very far afield as people resonate with the society they find there. Sylt Island, off the German coast, similarly attracts elites to a northern beach with few amenities, but exclusivity and good food.[56] The greatest numbers of exclusive beaches are to be found in tropical areas. It is hard to pick up a snobbish magazine without there being stories or advertisements for posh resorts at places such as Marlon Brando's resort on Tetiaroa, Tahiti; Southern Ocean Lodge, on Kangaroo Island; Laucala Resort, Fiji; Capella Lodge, Lord Howe Island; and Pangulasian resort on Palawan island, the Philippines; the Shore Club, Turks and Caicos Islands; Txai Resort Itacare, in Bahia, Brazil; Malliouhana on Anguilla—all designed for luxury tourism and exclusivity, and where the price alone guarantees that the right people will arrive.

In the modern age, cheap transportation has also made it possible for young people to create their own beach experiences. As airfares spiraled downward and reached the pocketbooks of young adults in college, they could contemplate an interruption from their studies during spring holidays, and so spring break came into being.[57] While it existed before

FIGURE 8.6 Students on spring break crowd a beach in South Padre Island, Texas. © Joel Sartore 2020, www.joelsartore.com. For collegians, what better way to celebrate Easter?

World War II, the 1960 movie *Where the Boys Are* took place during spring break and so helped publicize the phenomenon. Subsequently, tens of thousands of young adults in college traveled by jet and car to reach Florida and Gulf Coast resorts and even venture as far afield as Cancun, Mexico. Instead of seeking a solitary experience of meditation and sunsets, the whole purpose of the break is to go where the parties are nonstop and the numbers enormous. These young adults bring with them a surfeit of hormones, a great thirst, and perhaps, if time avails, a desire to swim. For six weeks, as spring holidays are staggered among institutions, local authorities try to keep the peace without arresting too many of the partygoers.

As the number of spring visitors grew, the hotels, motels, bars, drug dealers, liquor stores, and restaurants enjoyed having this extra season, yet they came to regret the wear and tear caused by young adults. Sex, drunkenness, youthful indiscretion, and occasional violence give the police more than enough to do. Drunken riots are not uncommon as the anonymity of a large crowd of boozed-up young men brings on bravado and stupidity. If eroticism has always been present at beach resorts. this is the ultimate brazen display of young bodies and sex. Respectability and decorum do not amount to much as hedonism rules and many norms are flouted. When their week is over, the happily surfeited revelers can return to their studies. The towns are left with the detritus of frivolity. Over the years, as the crowds have grown larger and rowdier, authorities have decided that enough is enough. Fort Lauderdale, Florida, discouraged spring break tourism after an estimated four hundred thousand revelers invaded in 1986 and there were sixteen hundred arrests.[58] The city council of Panama City Beach, Florida, tightened up city ordinances to control revelers after a shooting and gang rape.[59] Resorts that don't impose rules risk becoming the new favorite beach and, as a result, will be inundated the next year. Recently the authorities have been helped by social media, as youngsters are well aware of what a drunken and stupid image can do to their future job prospects when flashed around the electronic web. This has caused some to avoid the worst and tone down their behavior.[60]

Similar situations affect various other beach sites. Around the world festivals of various kinds, but especially musical, attract young adults during the summer. Ibiza has a notable reputation for attracting a young audience to the island during the annual summer music festival. There is hardly a resort anywhere that wants to be popular that does not have a festival of some kind—think Cannes and movies—in order to attract tourists. In Europe, the list of popular music festivals at resorts is long and diverse: Pula, Croatia; Costa Azahar, Spain; Lisbon, Portugal; Ibiza, Spain; Split and Hvar, Croatia; and many others. Most of them are famous for music and explosions of youthful exuberance. The festival resorts have suffered the same kinds of behavior that afflict the American spring break sites. Hvar, Croatia, which was once a site for summer yachts and celebrities, is now inundated with partygoers and has sought to control the worst behavior by advertising that if you come here you have to keep your shirt on and avoid drinking, eating, or sleeping in public places or else face a stiff fine. These rules seem to be working.[61] In Australia, where summer weather coincides with Christmas and New Year, Bondi and Cogee beaches near Sydney have had to impose no-alcohol rules to keep the peace during the holiday season.[62] Affluent youth, easy travel, and the libidinal nature of beaches have brought about scenes that express modern times—a far cry from the assembly room.

While music festivals are often raucous they are seldom violent. Yet violence did descend on the resorts as the postwar baby boomers developed hooligan groups. In England "Mods," "Rockers," and "Skinheads" were all involved in riots in Brighton, Clacton, Margate, and

Bournemouth. Clacton was especially hard hit with riots in 1962 and then a more famous one referred to as the "Easter Riot" in 1964.[63] The latter was well reported because sixty were arrested, and this badly damaged the reputation of the resort. Gangs also ran amuck as far afield as Australia, as an assertive youth culture was not confined to England. In America there were similar events, but with the additional twist of race. Asbury Park, for instance, had a major race riot in July, 1970, with hundreds of arrests and severe property damage.[64] It contributed to the decline of Asbury, which continued to spiral downward until quite recently. These episodes reveal that resorts are not immune to the social problems of the day, no matter how much they are celebrated as places of relaxation and rest.

Two hundred years since the first resorts were created in England, beaches around the world are as popular as ever, and every summer witnesses a rush to the coast. No longer is it a matter of climbing into a damp machine and undressing while trundling toward the water where the dipper waits to give you the requisite three dips. Those days are long gone and entirely forgotten. New regimes exist in a variety of settings. While resorts still attract many sun worshipers, public beaches are now where a vast number of people spend their beach time. Because of the hotels and clubs, the resort beaches are marked with even rows of lounges and umbrellas where every comfort is provided. Along the North Sea coast of Germany and the Netherlands, umbrellas are replaced with vast wicker chairs, large enough to hold two, that protect against the cool breezes common to the coast. Public beaches, at first sight, are more anarchic as they are the people's resorts. These beaches were created by local, state, and national governments. Usually they are the result of public demand in the face of growing private ownership or from government's desire to further tourism. Each motive ends up creating miles of beach, sometimes many miles of beaches. Since most of them arose in the era where the car was coming to dominate transportation, parking was all important and sometimes the only facility provided. There were a few other structures, such a food stall, a bathroom with an outdoor shower to wash off the sand, and a lifeguard station. Unlike the resorts, golf courses and tennis and other such facilities are rarely provided. Instead there will be a bare stretch of sand on which one has to find a place.

The sociology of public beaches can be very complicated.[65] Most day-trippers travel to local public beaches by car, where they seek out "their" beach. Age, ethnicity, sexual orientation, wealth, and family status all play a role in dividing up a beach. Making finding a place more complicated is the lack of paths or other definers of space. Regulars often claim a place convenient to their parking place. For occasional visitors the beach is a blank tablet, and all they want is a patch of sand that gives them room enough and maybe a modicum of privacy. Yet public beaches the world over tend to create spaces where people are comfortable with the other people there. At Clifton Beach in Cape Town your choice of a beach means choosing from beach 1 to 4. Fashionable folk are at 4, along with families; gays are at three; surfers and volleyball players are at 1, and students at 2, along with families. In Southern California, high schools, often divided by race, carve out their own territories on South Bay beaches.[66] Making a mistake can lead to an unpleasant day at the beach. Local surfers in Southern California resort to violence to protect their favorite wave break from outsiders.[67] From Malibu to Palos Verdes, newcomers are unwelcome.

Official naturist beaches are now well known, and guides are published for nude beaches in nearly every country. The same is true for gay beaches, such as Fire Island, New York, Provincetown, Massachusetts, and Rehoboth Beach, Delaware, all famous as gay summer locales.[68] African Americans can now escape from those beaches such as the Inkwell in Venice, California, or the American Beach on Amelia Island, where they were segregated, and can now go to any beach they care to. Yet there are beaches where they feel more comfortable than others, and so they may well congregate in a favorite spot. The famous beaches of Rio de Janeiro, Copacabana, and Ipanema, are divided along class lines. The twelve lifeguard stations, or *postos,* are the delineators between visitors from the *favelas,* or slums, and those who are more prosperous. Postos 11 and 12 are the preserve of upper-class families, posto 7 is where the poor congregate along with surfers, and gays are near posto 9. What they all share is the pervasive pollution that is a feature of the bay.[69] Divisions based on ethnicity, class, or gender occur the world over and are a feature of contemporary beach life. Beaches, as much as any place, are a mirror of the strains and stress in society.

Once you have found your place at your favorite beach, there is one last hurdle to overcome, and that is to find a place to lie down and enjoy the sun. In a resort those decisions are easy, as umbrellas and chaise longues are placed in neat rows and so it is just a matter of making a reservation with the staff. On many public beaches it is not that easy, for there are "sand hogs." They have different names at local beaches in America, such as *constructors* or *maximalists,* people who come to the beach really prepared. One family in New Jersey came to the beach with

FIGURE 8.7 Benton Murdoch Spruance, *Road from the Shore,* 1936. Lithograph on cream wove paper, 10 1/8 × 14 3/8 in. Pennsylvania Academy of Fine Arts, 1975.5.11, courtesy of the Pennsylvania Academy of the Fine Arts, Philadelphia. Gift of Mrs. Benton Murdoch Spruance, www.bentonspruance.com. The downside of the family day at the beach—the occasionally dangerous road home.

"four canopies of different colors (one equipped with a mosquito net); an assortment of sheets to spread on the sand; a volleyball net; a foldable table to serve homemade macaroni and cheese, chicken salad, potato salad and tuna."[70] One can assume that there were chairs of various kinds, a grill, and coolers for food and drinks. Obviously this was for a large family or a group of friends and, once set up, not only did they take up a lot of sand, they also blocked the view. One can only hope that they set up at the back of the beach. Such encampments are more and more common on public beaches as families come for the day and bring everything they think they will need. Solitary individuals and couples wandering onto the sand need to find their place between the encampments, so that on busy days there is very little space left. Inevitably, beach communities have created ordinances controlling the height and size of canopies, umbrellas, and tents.[71]

All these visitors, at some time, look toward the water and go for a cool dip. While few think immersion in the sea is therapeutic, they certainly look forward to a swim. Almost everyone is now a competent swimmer. Bobbing up and down in the waves can be endlessly entertaining and refreshing, but now there are a host of other diversions such as board surfing, bodysurfing, paddleboards, surf skipping, windsurfing, volleyball, frisbee, football (both kinds), and the old favorites for children such as digging in the sand and looking at tide pools. In the old days performers had filled the day at the beach. Now individuals choose what recreation they will engage in.

The beach is now a playground full of activity entertaining the visitors throughout a long day. All these games can also cause problems, as there is nothing like being run down by a surfer or having young men shouting and running while playing a game. This can introduce conflict into what was supposed to be a day off filled with fun and the sound of the ocean. The old familiar entertainments are now gone—no Piorrets, and few resorts have donkeys—maybe a few vendors might come by with food and drink. Music, for a while, was provided by the boom box, which made many a beach visit unpleasant, but now it has been replaced by personal music systems. Sitting in a beach chair or on a towel, under the umbrella, lathered in sun lotion (as the dermatologists have scared everyone into submission), tuned in to your own music system and reading a novel vouched for by a list of summer books as a good summer read, is the height of ambition. For the more technologically adept, modern devices not only have books to read, but there are also movies and games stored in memory and ready to fill the time. At the end of the day, all the equipment will need to be packed and lugged back to the car before the inevitable traffic-jammed roads, where youngsters can go to sleep, and the memory of the day slowly fades.

Who Owns the Beach?

There, lying flat on my back in the sand, my hat over my
eyes, my arms spread straight out, I spent at least an hour
and a half warming my carcass in the sun, being a lizard. You
feel your body inert, drowsy, inanimate, almost inherent to
the earth on which it is wallowing, while your soul on the
contrary has drifted far, far away; it wafts about in space like
a stray feather.

—Gustave Flaubert

Diving is something else. And right away it's something else
again. Going through the mirror of the water's surface is
actually a way of flipping all at once into another world, a
way of crossing the border of a country quite unlike our own,
as quickly as the brutal and peremptory snap of some giant
pair of scissors.

—Theodore Monod

Almost everyone who has spent time at the beach has felt these two
emotions: one of languor and the other of shock.[1] They are both
responses to the beach that are familiar and desired. They are individual
but universal to all beach lovers, and there are many of us. What started
out as a modest number of individuals seeking therapeutic relief in the
ocean who found it in a small fishing village or on an empty beach has
morphed into a staggering phenomenon. One aspect of this is the
number of people who now live close to the beach. People have always
lived close to the ocean, but now they do so in much greater agglomera-
tions. In 2010, it was estimated that 44 percent of the world's population lived within 150 kilometers of the sea. By now the figure may be 50

percent.[2] For the United States, the estimate is that 52 percent of the population lives in a county adjacent to the ocean.[3] Living near the coast and having access to beaches is now a situation highly sought after. The ability to decide in the morning that a day at the beach would be nice and then speeding along the highway to reach the seashore is now a common experience. This pushes real estate prices of beach property ever higher. Mass tourism swells these figures every summer. In 2015, 1.2 billion tourists were on the move.[4] Not all of them went to the seaside, but many of them did. California beaches attracted more visitors than all of the national parks combined, and in 2015 New York City beaches drew a record 22.8 million visitors.[5] All kinds of media now report on beaches, with glossy pictures of exotic resorts in tropical settings and the inevitable gorgeous model or happy family. There are any number of top ten, or even top one hundred, beach lists to choose from.[6] So what started as a few hotels and villas has now burgeoned into a modern prodigy.

With the increasing number of visitors, serious issues have arisen to confront resorts. Numbers alone immediately raise the issue of access. While the right to be on the beach is common, getting to the shore over private property can be difficult and occasionally impossible. Greater numbers have brought even more pollution, bad enough that at times it is a serious threat to health. Finally, the expectation of glistening white sand, or just some sand, when the visitor arrives at the beach means that it had better be there. This has created very real problems of sand replenishment as beaches are scoured by high tides and storms. These are all modern issues at the seaside.

In a fascinating turn of events, there is a contemporary and growing literature regarding the positive benefits of visits to the beach. Two hundred years after the publication of Sir John Floyer's work on seawater and its therapeutic value, Blue Health, a major multicampus research program, is now producing research that provides insight into the health advantages of the beach.[7] "We find people who visit the coast, for example, at least twice weekly tend to experience better general and mental health."[8] The coastal visitors benefit from less polluted air and more sunlight, they tend to be more physically active, and it is clear that water has a psychological restorative effect. Blue Health and other groups of researchers are measuring the physical and mental advantages to seawater. They especially stress the positive mental benefits accruing to those who dip in the sea. This comes, not from the speculations of eighteenth-century science, but from modern medical and social science research, although it would certainly make the eighteenth-century physicians happy.[9]

The resulting explosion of beach resorts has been international in scope. Even China, as it has created great wealth and a new middle class, has succumbed to the lure of the sea. For a long time the Communist Party leadership summered at Beidaihe, making it a famous and mysterious beach because their meetings were secret.[10] Everyone else was condemned to appropriate proletarian rectitude and constant hard work. How the Puritans would have approved! Now the burgeoning middle class seeks out many newly developed resorts. Nowhere is that more visible than on the island of Hainan. Long touted as a possible rival to Hong Kong as a trading and banking center, that dream disappeared and in its place has come a remarkable tourist boom that finds the fanciest hotel chains all now claiming beaches—most of them around the town of Sanya. The great attraction is the weather, as Hainan is a tropical island that shimmers in the sun when northern China is in the deep freeze. Party leaders and retirees from the north flood in from December to March. The retirees represent an old tradition in a new area, namely that of "snowbirds" who flee the cold to enjoy the sun. During the summer, millions of ordinary folk descend to enjoy the beaches. They are another indicator of the growing prosperity of China.[11] As befits its status as a vacation hot spot, the island now has surfing competitions, sixteen golf courses, and that necessary aspect of proper resorts, a festival, built around the Miss World competition. As prosperity and international tourism have come to tropical Asia, resorts have proliferated, as they have the world over.

The pressures to develop new resorts leave few places untouched. Developers constantly seek new opportunities in order to feed the growing demand for shoreline holidays. That could be Phuket in Thailand or, more prosaically, the "Redneck Riviera," long a celebrated workers' beach on the Alabama-Florida Panhandle. For decades it was the boisterous playground of workers from the Deep South with hard drinking and hard playing in a series of small settlements along a lovely stretch of beach on barrier islands. It was a place where you could do things you would never want to admit to when you went home and returned to your church. The beaches were kept for whites only, and government interference in their affairs was avoided. These beaches welcomed spring break, which helped local bars and motels. Slowly but surely, the tide turned as chardonnay drinkers, in the form of winter visitors, replaced the beer swillers. Property values went up, as did taxes to pay for hospitals, roads, sanitation, sewers, and police and fire fighters. The old-timers even fought beach nourishment after hurricanes destroyed the beaches, if that meant that the government would be involved subsequently, because the law permitted the government to mandate beach use policy. For them it was better to move down the road a bit than to have their actions regulated by the federal government. Now a long line of hotels and other buildings hug the beaches, as the developers have taken possession of the best sites and pushed out the "rednecks." They had a long run, but great beaches and rising property values killed the "good old days" and ushered in the modern era.[12] Here as elsewhere, developers sought out great, or even good, beaches in order to provide for the constant demand for seaside holidays.

In the twentieth century, towns close to the shore experienced growth, as these were pleasant communities offering views and services not common elsewhere. As the resorts grew, the number of people employed in the towns also surged. Then there were the commuters who moved out from the inner cities, and even the suburbs, to live close to cities such as New York or London where they could commute from a town on the shore. One of the results was the creation of a new kind of neighborhood. Beach communities are towns on the shore that are not resorts. They may well have a beach, but they do not have hotels and might only have a motel or two. They are communities that prefer their privacy. As a result, unlike resorts, they do not advertise their beaches. Tourists and trippers are not welcome at many of these communities, while others are willing to have people visit but do not provide much in the way of parking. While they might not publicize their beach, these towns cannot ignore the beach, as it is part of their attraction. That means they have to manage the beach, which can be expensive, especially so when they might have to replace the sand after a major storm. This can lead to community fights as they seek to keep sand on the beach while somehow not taxing in order to pay for it. The beach can be an attraction and a burden that most communities never had to bother with in the past.

With greater numbers living close to the shore and with many in the interior desirous of holidaying there, access to the beach comes to be seen by many as a right. The Surfrider Foundation, for instance, regards free access as a fundamental right.[13] Those who live on the beach, however, want their scenic views and lifestyle untrammeled by trippers. It is an old argument that goes back to the advent of the railroad and greater numbers of trippers coming to spoil the weekends of the locals. The two sides are engaged in a struggle to protect "rights," or to achieve them.

There are many variations in the argument, driven by the fact that some of the most valuable property in the world is beachfront property.

Most nations have adopted a "public trust" doctrine whereby the state has sovereignty over beaches and rivers and thus sets the law. This generally means that there is free public access below the mean high tide line. This has become commonly accepted. A different definition is rare. In a few states in America, for instance, the rule is the mean low tide line.[14] The issue becomes, can those who own property above this line in the sand deny access to those who want to exercise their right to play in the sand and go into the water?[15]

There are various answers to this question. In Spain, private beaches are illegal and access is guaranteed, but there are limits. When naturists sued the city of Cadiz for access, as the city was arresting and fining them when they appeared on the beach nude, the Spanish Supreme Court ruled that they had no right to access as their practice was not acceptable to the majority of those on the beach. Thus, the city could continue to fine those who appeared nude. Besides, as there are recognized nude beaches in Spain, the naturists did have places to go.[16] In Italy, as is true in many countries, such as France, there are mixed rules of access. Private beaches are allowed and are almost always controlled by a hotel or a club. They are easily recognized due to the rows of umbrellas and lounges that mark their part of the beach. Public beaches tend to be more chaotic. On Lido Island in Venice there has been a notable struggle for access as the hotels and private homes aggressively mark out their parts of the beach by running fences down into the water. Visitors have to find access at a few points and use a small portion of the beach. A few years ago, Giorgio Orsoni, a new socialist mayor, took this to be an affront and decided that all Venetians should have free access to the water and that the fences and signs could be ignored. This had an impact for a while until the mayor was caught in a corruption scandal and old practices began to creep back.[17] Not all stories have a happy ending. The townspeople of Newhaven in England were confronted with losing their access to the town's favorite beach. The authorities of Newhaven Port, a French-owned company, decided to close off access to the beach. The town fought back, even at one point declaring that the beach was a "village green." But after a seven-year legal struggle the courts sided with the company, ruling that it had the right to control its own property. So the beach became private.[18]

In New Zealand, access is not guaranteed. Queen Victoria, as early as 1840, urged the first British governor of the new colony to ensure that the public had the right to access. In general, the "public interest"

FIGURE 9.1 Ned Coll and children from Hartford stage an "amphibious invasion" at the private Madison Beach Club, summer of 1975. In "Free the Beaches: Desegregating America's Shoreline," in *Living on Earth*, May 25, 2018, © Bob Adelman Estate. Not by land, then by sea if it means you can free the beach. Ned Coll gets his young charges a day at the beach.

doctrine prevailed thereafter, but in recent years the indigenous Maoris have moved to have their treaty rights recognized and have entered politics and the courts. As recently as 2011, the Marine and Coastal Area Act recognized that the Maori may have exclusive customary interests in areas of the foreshore where they have traditionally conducted ceremonies or fished. They now have to go to court or negotiate directly with each local government to establish their rights, and one factor that has to be taken into consideration in making a judgement is public access.[19]

In the United States, the most common rule is free public access below the mean high tide line. The issue then becomes whether or not property owners above the line keep people out. In Texas, Oregon, and Hawaii there is guaranteed free public access. Most states want public access except for a few, such as Massachusetts and Virginia, where private ownership controls almost all of the foreshore.[20] However clear it is that access is guaranteed below the mean high tide line, the question of access has led to epic battles. In the United States, two fights over access have gone on for a long time. They are at either end of the country—Connecticut and California.

Connecticut does not have great beaches, but what it does have is highly prized. There are only 72 miles of beach on a coastline of 253 miles. All but seven miles are in private hands, mostly 54 beach associations and about 184 private clubs. This was done during the 1960s when growing concern about access at the national level led to a proposed National Open Beaches Act The proposal was modeled after the Texas Open Beaches Act passed in 1959, but the US Congress was lobbied hard by developers and beachfront owners and the bill never made it out of committee.[21] Connecticut townships did everything they could to keep out nonresidents, especially Black folk, from their beaches. The reaction was led by a Black social organizer, Ned Coll, who used an array of actions, including landing children on beaches from boats and keeping them below the mean high tide line, to confront the townships. While getting lots of publicity, Coll could not break the ironfisted rule of the townships and clubs. And in an era when it became common policy that any federal money used for beach protection or maintenance had to lead to public access, they also refused such funds, no matter how much they were needed. Their control of the beaches was finally dented when a law student, Brendon Leydon, pressed a case about access in Greenwich, one of the most recalcitrant townships, that went all the way to the Connecticut Supreme Court, which ruled in favor of public access and made it mandatory on all townships. The result was not welcome signs, but notices that there were admission fees and parking charges that were prohibitive. Outsiders are still not welcome, and Connecticut residents only have a very few overcrowded public beaches.[22]

In California, article 10 section 4 of the state constitution guarantees access to the beach with the usual understanding that it means access to the sand up to the mean high tide line. This was settled early, but private ownership of the grassy area next to the beach quickly became a problem. As Los Angeles boomed in the 1920s and population increased rapidly, the *Los Angeles Times* started a campaign to get public access as more and more foreshore was being gobbled up.[23] These private interests, the *Times* asserted, kept everyone out or demanded a fee for access. Even in the '20s there was recognition that going to the beach had become a right.[24] The problem was the lack of finances in the city to secure access by buying up land. Another problem was that the local towns did not always want lots of public beach and its attendant problems.[25] In the end the Southern California coast was largely secured through state funding, beginning in 1931 when the state acquired Doheny State Beach, the first state beach. The southern coast now has

FIGURE 9.2 "The Freedom of the Sea," Robert Day for the *Los Angeles Times,* August 9, 1925. This cartoon captures the frustration of families seeking a day at the beach before public beaches became common.

63, most of which are operated by local governments.[26] As prosperity and maturity put more money in the coffers of local communities, there are now 420 public beaches in California. This has not solved all the problems, because private owners can still make access difficult for the public. The results have been protracted struggles between the government, as represented by the California Coastal Commission, and private interests.

A dispute over the construction of Sea Ranch, a large development on California's coast, became the impetus to change when Sonoma County permitted a developer to close ten miles of the coast. There was an immediate reaction by environmental interests, leading to Proposition 20 on the 1972 ballot, which was passed in the election. The proposition created the California Coastal Commission to control development within one thousand yards of the coast and protect the public's access. When the Commission was to terminate in 1976, the state legislature passed the California Coast Act, continuing the Commission. The Commission publishes guides to California beaches, but a great deal of its time is spent dealing with access problems.[27] When this book was going to press, it was sparring with a billionaire entrepreneur who bought a property where the previous owners had allowed public access to Martin's Beach. Although initially agreeing to this arrangement, the new owner changed his mind and decided to close the right of way and fight in court to keep the beach private. Later, he did offer to sell an easement to the state for $30 million, which was treated with derision as he had only paid $32 million for eighty-nine acres. At press time the issue was in the courts.[28]

But for anyone living in California and following the work of the Commission, Malibu remains the longest-running fight for access. It was even featured in a Doonesbury cartoon in the summer of 2005. This area is an especially pretty section of the coast with sheltering mountains, a trout stream, and wonderful beaches.[29] Long inhabited by Chumash Indians and then the Spanish, the Malibu Rancho was bought in 1892 and turned into a cattle ranch by the Rindge family.[30] When Frederick Rindge died in 1905, his wife May became an ardent defender of the property against powers such as Southern Pacific Railway and the state of California. She stymied the Southern Pacific by building her own railway. The State was finally forced to use eminent domain to secure a route for the Pacific Coast Highway. The cost of building a fifty-room mansion and her many legal affairs finally forced Mrs. Rindge, in 1927, to offer ten-year leases to mostly movie people, of whom she was enamored. From that base Hollywood colonized Malibu, where even today many celebrities and a few billionaires own homes. By 1935 May Rindge was bankrupt and the whole ranch was put up for sale. Like the movie settlement at Santa Monica, Malibu became a preferred address for those seeking great views and access to a great beach. What they did not want was to share it with others.[31]

The Coastal Commission joined the struggle over Malibu beach access shortly after it was created and at press time was still fighting to gain public access. Even when the Commission is successful in acquiring access rights, property owners cover up the passages to the beach with bushes and boulders, put up "no parking" signs, and, if these and other devious methods don't work, they hire private security firms to police the beach, warning people away.[32] The Commission was finally given the power to fine in 2014, affording it a weapon that was better than the constant reliance on the courts for results.[33] Advocates for access, such as Jenny Price and Steve Lopez, have thrown themselves into this fight, and Price has created an internet site that gives detailed information on how to reach the beach.[34] However, the owners of multimillion-dollar homes have the resources to fight back, and do so. Even the city of Malibu has dragged its feet, reflecting its residents' desire, in creating a plan for the future with the Coastal Commission.[35] So the people of California remain in a struggle to secure their constitutional right to walk on their beach.

California is not alone in this regard. In Florida an ambiguously written statute led to an uproar in 2018. It appears to allow property owners the right to privatize the area above the mean high tide line, thus keeping people off the beach. Governor Rick Scott issued an executive order urging state agencies and local government to do nothing that would impede access to the beach.[36] As long as more and more people choose to live on the coast and the beach remains a site sought after by millions of others, there will be conflict over access. Property owners of homes adjacent to the beach have paid significant sums to be there (recently a home in Malibu sold for 120 million dollars). This is some of the most valuable property in the world, and they have to pay taxes and meet other expenses to remain. For these owners allowing access means people invading their privacy, traipsing through their properties, messing up the beach in front of their homes. Those on the other side are adamant that they be allowed to exercise their rights to access. Conflict is the result and it will not go away. Witness an editorial in the *Los Angeles Times* on October 8, 2017, advocating "the right to reach the beach" some ninety years after the paper started to campaign for access.

After gaining access to the beach, the holidaymaker expects clean sand and crystal water. Unfortunately, cleanliness is still a goal. Pollution was a problem for beaches as they became more popular and remains so. While many have introduced modern technology, others have not improved. Just to get on the beach in many places means clearing a path through all sorts of plastic and other garbage. Then there is the condition of the water. In the summer of 2016 athletes preparing for the summer Olympics in Rio de Janeiro were warned that the

FIGURE 9.3 Green algae accumulation on a Brittany, France, beach resulting from overfertilized farm fields. As the algae decompose, they produce hydrogen sulfide, which has killed animals and sickened people. Photograph used by permission of Cristina Barroca.

conditions in Guanabara Bay in front of Copacabana were a toxic stew and that those sailing, distance swimming, and windsurfing should keep their mouths closed or risk gastrointestinal disease. Other local conditions can create nasty problems. There is a particularly vile algae in Brittany that kills wild boars and horses and hospitalizes people who fall into it. On the beaches around Qingdao, China, there is a pervasive, thick algae every summer. Jellyfish stings have been feared for some time, but now they appear by the millions off Spanish resorts and sting hundreds of people.[37] In 2019, the state of Mississippi closed nearly all of its beaches because of an algae bloom, for contact with the algae brought on rashes, diarrhea, nausea, and cramps.[38] Most of these have their origins in industrial pollution, agriculture, and people who foul the oceans in various ways. The most objectionable pollutant is oil. While there is a problem with natural seepage, such as occurs in Southern California, the worst spills are caused by humans. The most destructive was Saddam Hussein's release of millions of gallons of oil onto Kuwait's beaches to keep American marines from landing during the Iraqi War. That oil will linger above and below the sand for a very long time. Lesser spills are constant. The worst thing that can happen to a community is to have a wrecked oil vessel near the local beach. Twice in

2017 tankers crashed near Chennai, India, and Piraeus, Greece, and fouled the beaches.[39] Then there are the mega disasters such as the Deepwater Horizon blowup in the Gulf of Mexico, which scarred many beaches. In that case the guilty party, British Petroleum, and the US government were in a position to fund a cleanup. In poorer, less developed countries the outcome would be entirely different. Pollution is caused by humans and, while we can mitigate some of our predicaments, permanent solutions remain beyond us.

At most beaches the problem is not oil, but an old familiar one—sewage. It may have improved somewhat, in that you might not be hit in the face by a dead cat as a reporter was at Coney Island.[40] The leading method of sewage removal remains a reliance on the vast sea to dilute and wash away impurities. While more and more beach towns implement modern sewage treatment facilities, in some, the only change has been longer and longer disposal pipes flushing material away from the beach. It still does not work. In 1988 Blackpool was given an adverse report from the Department of the Environment, and this was followed in 1993 with a finding by the European Court that its beaches had unacceptable levels of coliform bacteria. One local official responded, "People who come to Blackpool don't come here to swim."[41] There is a change! By this time in Britain, Surfers Against Sewage and the Marine Conservation Society are campaigning constantly to get the resorts to install modern treatment equipment. In 2017 Blackpool rated a "good" rank, having responded to the bad reports. There is always a financial dilemma between making a decision to improve sewage facilities and going with beach protection. Sea walls and promenades always take a high priority, because without them there might not be a beach or a resort.

Two very different types of beaches often have nearly insoluble problems. Beaches in front of major cities in the developing world are chronically polluted. Rio has already been discussed for its foul water. Other cities, such as Mumbai, suffer from the same problem.[42] Given all the demands on budgets in these cities and countries, there is simply not enough money to take care of every social need. Extensive slums are nearly impossible to provide with decent services, leading to malodorous open drains that ultimately flow toward the sea, contaminating everything in their path. The other beaches with chronic problems are those that are developed very quickly as money pours in to build hotels, other facilities, and places for the burgeoning staff to live. Public funding for infrastructure lags, and sewage complaints are sure to follow.[43] The classic instance has now become Boracay Island in the Philippines. Blessed with white sand beaches and tropical weather, it has become a rival to Phuket Island. Tourists have been attracted in significant numbers from China and South Korea, and development has gone on pell-mell, making it the number one tourist attraction in the country. It is a perfect example of how ambition and modern communications can create instant resorts. Unfortunately, utilities have not been able to keep up with development, and so garbage disposal, fresh water, and sewage all lag behind. Of the 150 businesses recently inspected, only 25 were connected to the sewage line. Sewage now runs across the beach into the sea. This case has attracted enormous attention. President Rodrigo Duterte has declared its beaches polluted and the sea a cesspool. He has ordered it must be shut down for six months until it is cleaned up. Duterte, true to his word, closed the ferry to the island and sent in the police and the coast guard to keep tourists out. The forty thousand residents, most of whom work in the tourist economy, faced months of no wages and tips. When the six months were over and major progress had been realized, Boracay reopened, but with fewer hotels and bars and a limit on the number of visitors. Full restoration is in the future. Boracay is the perfect example of overdeveloped facilities with underdeveloped utilities.[44] The lure of improving a local economy, mostly with outside capital as represented by the big hotel chains and fast food restaurants, is irresistible to local politicians and entrepreneurs. If it works, instant popularity can outstrip every good intention.

Yet the demand for safe water at the beach now means that there are any number of organizations giving guidance. In California, it is Heal the Bay, which issues reports on local beaches. Internationally there is the Blue Flag Group, which grades beaches all over the world.[45] There is even a list of the twelve dirtiest beaches in the world created by Destination Trips, should you want to sample them. Unfortunately in many poor nations with no tourists to worry about, beaches are often piled with the detritus brought in from the ocean along with local garbage.[46] They give beaches a bad reputation as, for instance, in Lebanon where the destruction of a landfill site has littered some of the most desirable beaches with a "sea of garbage."[47] There is a new and very sinister aspect to the sewage problem, and that is the threat of dangerous bacteria and viruses that linger in the water. These can even be life threatening if not caught in time and treated.[48] The old song "You Always Hurt the One You Love" comes to mind in contemplating our continuing relationship with beaches. Not only do we pollute them, we also destroy them.

Beaches existed for a very long time prior to humans using them for leisure purposes. They are a natural phenomenon the world over, and whether they are made up of large cobbles or fine sand, they are a feature of coasts. They have evolved over time, especially in the last ten thousand years, after the last ice age released huge volumes of water back into the sea, raising it by about three hundred feet. In response, beaches retreated further inland. Beaches have always moved inland in response to sea level rise. This is very noticeable in the long string of barrier islands that line the eastern coast of the United States. A beach is in fact a dynamic system that ebbs and flows. As early as 1888 the quite large Brighton Beach Hotel on Coney Island was moved twenty-three hundred feet inland away from an eroding shore.[49] Seashores also change in reaction to other natural phenomena. Often in winter, with strong winds piling up large waves, sand is stripped away and then redeposited in the gentler conditions of summer. Ordinary wave direction and currents also shape beaches as they push the sand around. And as the sand originates in rivers, any change there can mean less or more sand to be deposited. Then there are the extraordinary conditions brought on by hurricanes, typhoons, and tsunamis where extravagant winds and waves can destroy any beach or human structure that lies close to the shore. While the annual season for hurricanes and cyclones always brings media attention, there are other disasters that fade from memory. In 1953 a great North Sea storm surge killed 119 people in Essex, England, and left 21,000 homeless. Much of the shoreline from Kent to Lincoln was wrecked.[50] It was catastrophic to those who lived through it, but the next category 5 hurricane or cyclone will push it deeper into memory. After one of these monsters passes over the coast, it may take years for beaches to recover or, in some cases, they may never. These are all the natural threats to beaches, and it is estimated that 70 percent of the sandy beaches worldwide are eroding.[51] Then there are the human perils.

Human threats are threefold: engineering, mining, and pollution. Engineering relates to the desire to protect the coast and keep the sand in its place. Among the earliest structures to affect sand flow were river dams. Dam building has been going on for a long time, but in recent years dams have been recognized as the first structure to destroy beaches, for if there is no riverine sand flow, there is no beach.[52] An example of this comes from the recent destruction of two dams on the Elwha River in the state of Washington. There, dam removal was championed more for its effect on the local fisheries than for beach building. With the dams gone, salmon are returning to the river to spawn and sand is pouring out

FIGURE 9.4 Elwha River beach in Washington (after dam was removed), looking west along the shoreline of the Strait of Juan de Fuca in Washington State. July 23, 2016. When rivers are freed of their dams, beaches reappear as this one did on the coast near the Elwha river.

of the river mouth, where it is picked up by the current and sent east to create a sandy beach where before there were just large cobbles.[53] If an example was ever needed of the effect of dams on sand flow, this was it. Unfortunately, knocking down dams is not simple in politics, finance, or engineering and, however much local communities might want to remove dams, it is always a long and complicated process.

As for protecting the coast once the sand has come to rest, there are often equally bad outcomes. The whole coast of Belgium, all forty-one miles, is now lined by sea walls to keep the sand and water away from the buildings. Similarly, 40 percent of the coast of Japan is now defended by barriers, most of which failed with the great tsunami of 2011. These are the most heroic pieces of engineering, as more often than not engineering is confined to a sea wall to protect a specific site. Of greater significance are the many groins, jetties, and breakwaters that are built right on or near the beach. They are almost all built to keep sand in its place, that is, on the shore for people to use. More often than not these structures have bad consequences. Waves and currents move sand around, and when they

FIGURE 9.5 A view of the beach in Wildwood, New Jersey, north of the Mariner's Landing amusement pier, taken on Memorial Day 2008. When groins are not thought out, they lead to very wide beaches, as in Wildwood, while the Cape May beach is starved of sand.

are interfered with, sand stops moving. Aerial photography clearly shows that when sand is cut off, it suddenly starts piling up on one side of a groin and the other side is starved. Thus at Cape May, what was once a wide beach is now very narrow as the sand flow from the north was cut off by a groin built to protect a harbor. Wildwood, just to the north, now has a lovely wide beach courtesy of the same groin. All too often, building a groin is the first solution sought in protecting a sandy beach. It works if the beach is on the right side of the groin. However, groins are built on the sea, and the frequent storms can smash the groin and redistribute the sand that was so carefully preserved. Then it is back to the same old problem—how to save sand for the beach.[54]

There are multiple reasons to mine sand.[55] In countries with few or no forests and thus with limited wood for building, taking sand for concrete is an easy and cheap solution. First the dunes disappear and then the beach. Morocco is going down this path with massive dune removal going on every day. One imagines that the Sahara could provide more than enough sand to help a country with little wood, but desert sand is too smooth and thus not suitable, so it is the beach dunes on the Atlantic shore that are being stripped to provide building material.[56] Even if the beach remains untouched, the dunes are an important barrier against foreshore destruction from storms. Another cause is mining for valuable substances, for as rivers carry sand to the sea they also carry gold, diamonds, zircon, topaz, garnets, pyrite, quartz, and tourmaline. In fact, a list has been compiled of some sixty-eight commercially important products that can be mined from sand. In these instances, beaches are stripped at the river mouth and the shore left barren.

One of the most common rationales for sand mining, and one of the most destructive, is mining sand for beach replenishment, something that is becoming ever more common as there are more and more beaches to replenish. Whether it is home owners or communities insisting on maintaining the tourist economy, the demand to replenish a beach is hard to resist. Many of the iconic beaches are now replenished replicas. Waikiki Beach has needed to be replenished from beaches on Molokai Island and elsewhere.[57] Even the island of Sylt, which is a long, narrow sandbar on the North Sea, now has to dredge sand to maintain its beaches, which suffered from groins disrupting the natural flow.[58]

Replenishment with tons of sand brought in to reconstruct beaches is now a common solution to beach erosion. The sand for this must come from somewhere, and it is usually another beach. The problem is that the very forces that strip a beach do not vanish, and thus replenishment is a temporary solution. Rockaway Beach, New York, has been replenished 36 times, more than any other beach in the United States, at a cost estimated at $289,223,873. Florida beaches have been replenished 495 times at a cost estimated at $2,553,872,549.[59] So replenishment is a heroic and expensive business. Yet it has widespread application. For instance, it is prevalent in the Caribbean. There, the dunes in Barbuda were destroyed illegally by government-condoned mining, resulting in beach erosion, for without the dunes for protection and natural replenishment, the sand has been stripped away. Innocents also suffer. On the Nicobar Islands, twenty-one beaches have been destroyed, and with them gone, turtles have lost their sites for egg laying.[60]

Sand mining has other purposes than simply beach replenishment. Singapore is the 192nd largest country in the world. Great in matters of finance and industry, it is puny in size and very conscious of this. The only option is to grow. Some nations might do this by aggressively grabbing their neighbors' territory. Not Singapore. Instead, it has embarked on a major expansion by virtue of importing sand to create new neighborhoods and facilities such as docks and sea terminals. It has now grown to 277 square miles from an original 224. The sand has come from other countries nearby. Indonesia, Malaysia, Vietnam, and Cambodia have now stopped exporting sand to Singapore, and so the island has now turned to Myanmar. To substitute for imported sand, Singapore has used the material left from tunnels and other construction projects and resorted to making sand by crushing granite. And then there is the sand that comes in at night from wherever it can be stripped by smugglers. As one Singaporean bureaucrat put it, it is better that sand is put to work than just lying around on a beach all day.[61] No matter what, Singapore will continue to grow. Unfortunately, Singapore is not alone. Penang, Malaysia, has built new resorts on 240 acres of artificial land and is planning to add 1,000 acres more. In China it is estimated that Chinese coastal cities have added 700 square kilometers of land every year from 2006 to 2010. Throughout Asia, sand is being deployed to build resorts, port areas, and financial markets. Habitats, fishing grounds, and indeed whole islands have disappeared. There is no end to it.[62] Or is there? In Greenland, where glaciers have been grinding rock for aeons, and where the glaciers are melting with global warming, sand is now piling up on the shore and is ready for shipping—you only have to get there.[63]

In ordinary circumstances, sand replenishment is controversial. In recent years the science of the shoreline has developed, and there are scientists and learned journals devoted to study of the beach.[64] One thing that has been studied in detail is sand replenishment. Almost without exception it is condemned as useless, as the underlying conditions of sand removal remain the same and replenishment will follow replenishment. This has not stopped the United States Congress from funding it and the Army Corps of Engineers from doing it.[65] For home owners, or even casual users of the beach, replenishment is highly desired as they can look at and enjoy a sandy beach again rather than bare rock. Yet it has not always been greeted with applause by local home owners; some object to the fact that in the United States, when Congress passed the act that funded beach restoration act, it also stated that when public monies are spent restoring beaches, the beach is public thereafter.[66] So a community that has kept its beach private has to decide whether or not to accept public money or fund restoration privately. Some have argued this point all the way to the Supreme Court. When Hurricane Opal scoured the Florida Panhandle in 1995, the state agreed to restore the beaches, but with the proviso of keeping them public. Six property owners did not want this because they felt the state was taking their

FIGURE 9.6 Holly Beach, Louisiana, November 16, 2005. Marvin Nauman / FEMA photo. This community of five hundred structures was leveled by Hurricane Rita's tidal surge and high winds, leaving little debris. Hurricane Rita left many people homeless who may never be able to rebuild.

property. After finally losing in Florida, the case ended up in the United States Supreme Court. The court unanimously agreed with the state that it did have the right to replenish, even above the mean high tide line, if that meant preserving the beach.[67]

In 2012 Hurricane Sandy wreaked havoc on beaches on the New Jersey shore and on Long Island, New York. The Army Corps stood ready, as did Congress, to fund replenishment. At Rockaway, 3.5 million cubic yards of sand were deposited on the beach, and the city put in six miles of dunes for protection, but if Rockaway is to be truly protected, the estimate is that the cost would be 4 billion dollars. The sand is already eroding, so recently certain parts of the beach were put off limits, to the dismay of bathers and small businessmen.[68] In New Jersey similarly massive amounts of sand and money ($125 million) have been used, and exclusive towns such as Mantoloking and Deal have had to give in to trippers, but not completely, as there are new parking places with new meters, no food services, and a membership fee. Taking advantage, New Jersey called for marked beach access every quarter mile, which brought out many objections.[69]

The Outer Banks are barrier islands off North Carolina that are the site of a long string of high-quality beaches clustered along the narrow band of soil and sand. As noted, for centuries after the last Ice Age the beaches moved up and inland with the rising waters—perhaps as much as three hundred feet—from the runoff from the great ice flows. Fishermen and duck hunters have long enjoyed the islands and then, latterly, have been joined by thousands of residents and millions of tourists. Old-time residents built back from the beach, knowing that sooner or later a storm would come roaring in and the contours of the islands would change. Newcomers have now built large homes right behind the beach, creating a wall of wood and concrete. Sometimes, in fear of losing their sand, groins, revetments, and barriers have been erected to keep the sand in place. Inevitably these are destroyed by the hurricanes and winter storms known as Nor'easters that come roaring in from the ocean with regularity, a regularity that might well increase with global warming. North Carolina has banned the building of such structures as they are essentially useless. Without the beach, homes lining the shore are vulnerable and hurricanes and Nor'easters occur often enough, destroying everything in their path.[70] The best way forward would be to let the sand move inland and the beach recreate itself, but that is now foreclosed by the long lines of beach homes acting as a barrier. Understandably, allowing nature to run its course and move the beach inland is anathema to the home owners, so the pattern of beach destruction followed by beach replacement and rebuilding of the homes goes on year after year. Most of this is paid for by the government, as no insurance company will take such risks, which means the American taxpayer is paying. America is wealthy enough to contemplate this inevitable cycle. Few other governments are. In the South Pacific the island of Vanuatu was trashed by Cyclone Zoe in 2002, and then Cyclone Pam, a category 5 storm in 2015, wrecked what remained. Sea walls and beaches vanished, as they did on Fakaofo after Cyclone Percy in 2005. These barely developed islands, and many others in the South Pacific, can only hope tourists will come back to what is normally a tropical paradise, but even nature will be challenged to restore paradise.[71]

The Relentless Sea

Our atmosphere is vast, ever changing, and now evolving in ways that will affect beach resorts and beach culture in general. Images of vibrantly blue rivers coursing across the Greenland ice fields and the calving of vast ice sheets from the Antarctic are signs that the atmosphere is warming. As the air warms, so do the oceans, and the warmer the oceans get, the larger they are, for water expands when heated. Most of the sea level rise currently underway occurs because as the climate warms, the seas heat up, absorbing as much as 90 percent of the excess heat trapped in the atmosphere.[1] Such warming could, conservatively, lead to a three-foot rise in ocean levels by 2100.[2] In the direst estimates, the rise could be ten feet due to the addition of Arctic and Antarctic ice melt. Should we not get things under control by 2300, the rise could be as much as fifteen feet.[3] Little of this is immediate. We can only hope that it never comes to pass, but the whole process is now happening at a pace that scientists never thought possible. Should we correct current trends, and there is hope, the worst may never happen. Yet it is very likely that the world will experience significant sea rise in the future. This will imperil the beaches, and the nearly three-hundred-years-long history of beach resorts will be transformed in dramatic fashion.

Another consequence of climate change is the growing number of powerful hurricanes and cyclones that are the product of the warming water and atmosphere. Warming water feeds these great storms, so as they approach land they portend disaster. The storm surges that these produce promise to be larger than ever, and the larger waves built by higher winds on top of the new, higher sea levels mean disaster for coastal communities. With the memory of Hurricane Sandy still fresh in New Jersey and New York and that of Tropical Cyclone Pam in the South Pacific, the thought of what will follow in the future from these megastorms is genuinely worrisome.

The world over, low islands are at risk. The Maldives, in the Indian Ocean, are very low lying with their highest point at seven feet. It is much the same for many other Pacific islands such as Tuavalu and the Marshall Islands. The most dramatic predictions are that sea rise will inundate many of them and, before it does, it will ruin their fresh water, forcing them to import all water or move away. Not just the low islands are at risk. Most of southern Vietnam is low lying and so will be underwater by 2050, displacing 20 million people. Similar fates await Bangladesh, Bangkok, Shanghai, Mumbai, Alexandria, and Basra. Even the North Sea will be affected, as it will rise three feet by 2100. Imagine what that means for the Netherlands. One estimate puts 200 million people living below the high tide line.[4] The year 2050 is not that far away, so these are shocking estimates. This means disaster for beaches if these conditions come to pass.

There are other immediate consequences of the warming atmosphere. In Iceland, essential fisheries have been closed as the fish have moved further north into cooler waters. As the capelin, one of the main captures of Icelandic fishermen, have disappeared, they have been replaced by Atlantic mackerel which, in turn, are escaping their normal haunts in search of cooler water. As this press northward continues, tropical fisheries are likely to vanish.[5] On Bikini Island there have been fish kills when the local water temperature crept as high as 92 degrees, leaving the beach littered with the dead and dying.[6] While fisheries are important, what happens along coastlines will have greater impact.

Sea level rise will bring devastating problems for coastal areas. In the eastern United States much of the coast, from Texas north to New York, has an extensive low-lying plain that terminates in the beaches. This means that any rise in sea level has an immediate impact. In Florida, the low-lying Keys, at the very southernmost part of the state, are experiencing prolonged periods—as much as eighty-two days in 2019—of standing water as the ocean sweeps across roads and invades homes. The problem is caused by the annual King Tides in October, November, and December, which continue to set new records nearly every year. This year the tides have been as much as eighteen inches higher than normal and the roads have been flooded. To raise the roads, one county estimates the cost as $1 billion.[7] Further to the north in Miami Beach, tidewater is already threatening roads, electrical facilities, and homes. The city is preparing to spend $400 to $500 million over the next five years to defend the shoreline and keep the city safe.[8]

In South Carolina, Charleston, which is already faced with water sloshing around the historic downtown, will need to spend millions of dollars that it does not have on a protective seawall in order to keep the sea at bay.[9] In North Carolina, the long stretch of barrier islands in the Outer Banks is threatened. During the last glacial maximum, the shoreline was 410 feet below present sea level. As the ice age waned, the coast has slowly moved inland and the barrier islands have formed and reformed. Now many of the islands are highly developed and are facing a rise estimated at 15 feet.[10] Roads, buildings, septic tanks, and public beaches have been lost already in some areas, and the struggle to save what is left continues. Added to the sea level rise is the constant threat of hurricanes that scour this area regularly. Sandbags and sand replenishment, favorite weapons against flooding, fare badly against nature's unrelenting pressure.

On the West Coast of the United States there is a different picture. The Northwest Coast is being raised by tectonic pressure as the Juan de Fuca plate dives under the North American plate. As a result, sea level rise will have less of an impact there. For California, the northern part of the state is affected by the subduction process, but the rest of the state is not. For instance, there have been several reports that measure the sea level rise during the twentieth century at seven inches and predict further rises by as much as five feet. The consequences are dire, particularly if destructive storms and high tides coincide. Then the storm surge would be truly scary.[11]

The California Coastal Commission has studied the likely sea rise and has come to decisions regarding the future. The Commission wants each county, city, and township that faces the ocean to come up with a management plan. Its preferred policy is "managed retreat," which calls for accepting that the rise is inevitable and that communities will have to move inland. So beach towns and cities will have to devise plans that include buying beach property and removing the structures on it and allowing the beach to move inland. Other suggestions are creating natural infrastructure with dunes and wetlands, limiting beach replenishment, and no new structures such as breakwaters and artificial reefs.[12] All California communities will have to devise a plan with these guidelines in mind.

Almost immediately after the Commission announced its decisions, they were contested. Del Mar, a coastal community of about four thousand people just north of San Diego, created its own response.[13] The town is more of a beach community with no hotels on the beach, although it has a number on the main street, with a racetrack nearby and suburbs to the east of town that rely on access to the beach during the summer, so it has some attributes of a resort. At the north end of town there is a sandy beach with homes right on it, protected somewhat with a barrier of large rocks. As you move south, it turns into a narrow beach with a sandstone cliff behind it. The only north/south rail mainline into San Diego moves behind the beach and then along the cliff. The beach and the cliff have been eroding with every storm.[14] As the city leadership crafted their mandated plan, they wanted to preserve what they had, and that meant reinforcing the sea wall and sand replenishment when needed. For the coastal commission this was not enough. Ideally, the homes on the beach should be moved back, or just removed, and the sea wall taken away, as it will only strip the beach faster with ever-more-expensive sand replenishment needed.[15] The town has a modest budget, and the idea of buying expensive beach homes and destroying them is anathema. One can only imagine the response of Malibu, with properties that go up to $100 million. In its response, the Del Mar city council said that managed retreat may be good elsewhere, but not for Del Mar. They prefer to keep replenishing the beach. As for the eroding cliffs, because of the railroad they have attracted wider attention as $1 billion worth of goods are transported on it every year.[16] Plans, including a tunnel, are now being considered as the cliff erosion is attracting state and federal attention. Not so the community beach. Del Mar may be a small beach town, but it is confronted with choices that will become common to many towns and cities.

The Coastal Commission is intent on planning for all twelve hundred miles of the California coastline so that beaches can be saved. There are fifteen counties and sixty-one coastal cities that would need to participate in the effort. The estimates are that saving the beaches would cost $150 billion, which is far more than will be spent on earthquakes and wildfires.[17] The Commission recently received the backing of the non-partisan California Legislative Analyst Office, which issued a report urging the government to start tackling what it fears might be a seven-foot sea level rise. In order to avoid disaster to the state's beaches and economy, the state will have to start playing an active role in helping beach communities meet the challenges to come.[18] Still, the sums

FIGURE 10.1 A Surfliner train by Amtrak travels along the collapsing bluffs in Del Mar. © John Gibbins / *San Diego Union-Tribune* via ZUMA Wire.

involved are staggering, and the legislature is unlikely to meet all the demands upon it.

Worldwide, it is very likely that funding will not be available and local resources will not be adequate to face the dilemma imposed by rising sea levels. Governments will defend ports and cities first, as they are vital for the economy. Imagine the Chinese government faced with Shanghai being threatened by the sea. The money will go there and not to beach resorts. Money will go for sea defenses, water supplies, roads, sewage facilities, power plants, and all the other infrastructure needs of population centers. The amount of money required will be astounding. For instance, New York City, still haunted by Hurricane Sandy in 2012, which killed seventy-two people and caused $62 billion in damages, is considering its options in case of future megastorms. One plan under consideration is a massive six-mile-long $119 billion wall with gates that will close to protect the harbor and the city. Critics have pointed out that it does little to protect beach areas and will be built so that it will only work for a sea level rise of one-and-one-half feet, the bare minimum estimated for 2100. They also point out the ecological damage it can cause and how it will not help, and may hurt, many local communities.[19]

However, beach resorts and public beaches will be marginal to policy makers. This means that resorts will have no choice but to retreat away from the ocean. Resorts may well become hotels by the sea, without a beach. And, as storms will still roll in, it will be a nightmare for the US East Coast if a hurricane comes in at high tide. The foreshore will be stripped down to rock. The big Lido swimming pools may well have another life, because they can at least provide a place to swim and frolic. The new Lidos will probably do far more in mimicking a beach. In recent years entrepreneurs have invented surfing pools that generate perfect six- to eight-foot waves.[20] There are already pools with fake beaches that produce smaller waves to dabble in so that generations to come will have this artificial experience—a dreadful prospect. For many generations the genuine beach has promised a good time: plunging into the ocean to play in the surf and then return to lie on the sand enjoying the warmth of the sun. Only a fond memory?

From a few aristocratic beach resorts in England, there are now thousands of private and public beaches around the world catering to many millions of people. In the beginning there were therapeutic aspirations, whereas now the focus is more hedonistic. As more and more people aspire to live near the coast and as a beach visit is now the primary aspiration of many tourists, the pressure on the shoreline will only grow. Fortunes have been spent in building resort and public beach facilities. Along the way we have learned a great deal about the nature of beaches and have a better sense of what works and what does not work in protecting the thin layer of sand we all desire.[21] We have also become aware of the conflicting pressures that animate any discussion of beach protection and how even the worst possible outcomes become inevitable in some cases. Looming over every discussion and decision, believe in it or not, is the already rising sea level. It may be inches of sea rise now, but what comes will be measured in feet. There will be no easy decisions.

Science fiction writers have already explored the world where the seas have risen. In a novel by Kim Stanley Robinson, *Aurora,* the heroine is Freya, a female space traveler, part of a multigenerational expedition that was supposed to colonize a distant planet.[22] On arrival they discover that the planet is toxic to human life, so they decide to return to earth centuries after departing. They find a hostile welcome, as Freya and her fellow colonists were expected to expand human horizons and have manifestly failed to do so. Having lived their whole lives on a spaceship, they cannot be reconciled to the society that sent their forebears on their way and has evolved in ways they cannot imagine. One aspect of this world is that global warming has destroyed most coasts and the beaches their ancestors knew are gone. Adrift and depressed, Freya discovers and is accepted by a group who dedicate themselves to rebuilding beaches that have disappeared. Confronted by a beach and the sea that she has never experienced, after lying on the sand warming with the sun, she has an ecstatic, soul-renewing plunge in the surf and an erotic arousal at the sight of a nude young surfer. These are experiences that many have shared over the centuries and are what drove people to the beach in the first place. So while it is science fiction, it takes us all the way back to Baiae.

In the past, beach resorts have always adapted to changes in patterns of leisure, transportation, therapeutics, recreation, and social change. When the sea is lapping at the front door, or the beach transformed into a rocky shelf, their future may be sealed. The cost of endless sand replacement will likely be more than the resorts and local communities are willing to bear. It seems unlikely, however, that beach resorts will vanish. One can only hope that the many small beaches where structures have been built away from the beach will be able to move inland and continue to bring authentic enjoyment to those who can visit. They promise that somewhere there will be stretches of sand that survive to keep delightful beach experiences and one of our oldest institutions, the beach resort, alive and well.

Notes

INTRODUCTION

1. Eva K. F. Chan et al., "Human Origins in a Southern African Palaeo-Wetland and First Migrations," *Nature* 575, no. 7781 (2019): 185–89. For a less scholarly account, see "Human Origins, Eden?," *The Economist*, November 2, 2019, 71–72.

2. Dave L. Roberts and Lee Berger, "Last Interglacial Human Footprints from South Africa," *South African Journal of Science* 93, no. 8 (August 1997): 349–50; Edgar D. Mountain, "Footprints in Calcareous Sandstone at Nahoon Point," *South African Journal of Science* 62, no. 4 (April 1966): 103.

3. Knvul Sheikh, "The Kids Spend a Day at the Beach, 80,000 Years Ago," *New York Times*, September 24, 2019.

4. Christina Thompson, *Sea People: The Puzzle of Polynesia* (New York: HarperCollins, 2019).

CHAPTER I. THE LURE OF THE SEA

1. Giorgio Giubelli, *Oplontis, Poppea's Villa* (Naples: Carcavallo, 1991).

2. Carol Matusch, *The Villa dei Papiri at Herculaneum: Life and Afterlife of a Sculpture Collection* (Los Angeles: Getty Trust Publications, 2005); David Sider, *The Library at the Villa dei Papyri at Herculaneum* (Los Angeles: Getty Trust Publications, 2005).

3. There is now an underwater tour of the site, and a museum has been created to display artifacts that have been recovered. Fikret K. Yegül, "The Thermo-Mineral Complex at Baiae and De Balneis Puteolanis," *Art Bulletin* 78, no. 1 (March 1996): 137–61; Yegül, *Baths and Bathing in Classical Antiquity* (Cambridge, MA: MIT Press, 1995), 107–20.

4. Seneca, Epistle 51, "On Baiae and Morals," trans. Richard M. Gummere, in *Seneca ad Lucilium Epistulae Morales* (London: William Heinemann, 1925), 336–43. For other comments, see Marcus T. Cicero, "Pro Caelio," trans. Robert Gardner, in *The Speeches* (Cambridge, MA: Harvard University Press, 1958), 451. See also Tony Perrottat, *Pagan Holiday: On the Trail of Ancient Roman Tourists* (New York: Random House, 2003), 65–68.

5. Vulcanologists fear the area is about to blow up again. While always devastating, it is more so now that seven hundred thousand people live in the immediate area. Helen Gordon, "The Monster Beneath," *The Economist: 1843 Magazine,* December 2017–January 2018, 90–97.

6. Virginia Smith, *Clean: A History of Personal Hygiene and Purity* (Oxford: Oxford University Press, 2007), 145–47.

7. Poggius Bracciolini and Nicolaus De Niccolis, *Two Renaissance Book Hunters: The Letters of Poggius Bracciolini to Nicolaus De Niccolis,* ed./trans. Phyllis Walter Goodhart Gordon (New York: Columbia University Press, 1974), 26, 174.

8. Smith, *Clean,* 180–83.

9. See Chet A. Van Duzer, *Sea Monsters on Medieval and Renaissance Maps* (London: British Library, 2013), 31.

10. Vincent H. Cassidy, *The Sea around Them: The Atlantic Ocean, A.D. 1250* (Baton Rouge: Louisiana University Press, 1968), 125.

11. Henry David Thoreau, *Cape Cod* (Boston: Ticknor and Fields, 1865), 172.

12. W. Jeffrey Bolster, *The Mortal Sea: Fishing the Atlantic in the Age of Sail* (Cambridge, MA: Belknap Press of Harvard University Press, 2012), 24–28.

13. Jean Lapeyre, *Les Bains De Mer: An Exhibition Catalogue with Plates* (Dieppe: Musée de Dieppe, 1961), 1–2.

14. Alice Garner, *A Shifting Shore: Locals, Outsiders, and the Transformation of a French Fishing Town, 1823–2000* (Ithaca, NY: Cornell University Press, 2005), 114; John K. Walton, "The Seaside Resorts of Western Europe, 1750–1909," in *Recreation and the Sea,* ed. Stephen Fisher (Exeter: University of Exeter Press, 1997), 40.

15. I would like to thank Rabbi Josh Franklin of the Jewish Center of the Hamptons for help in tracking down the custom and for a photo showing a contemporary service, and Joyce Seltzer for mentioning this to me. See Lesli Koppelman Ross, "Tashlich, the Symbolic Casting Off of Sin," *My Jewish Learning,* www.myjewishlearning.com/article/tashlikh/, accessed May 14, 2019.

16. John K. Walton, *The English Seaside Resort: A Social History, 1750–1914* (New York: St. Martin's Press, 1983), 10–11.

17. Walton, 10.

18. J. Aikin, *A Description of the Country from Thirty to Forty Miles Round Manchester* (London: printed for John Stockdale, Piccadilly, 1795), 357–58.

19. Paul Langford, *A Polite and Commercial People: England, 1727–1783* (Oxford: Oxford University Press, 1989); Joan Thirsk, ed., *The Agrarian History of England and Wales,* vol. 5, 1640–1750 (London: Cambridge University Press, 1985).

20. See J. H. Plumb, "The Commercialization of Leisure," in Neil McKendrick, John Brewer, and J. H. Plumb, *The Birth of a Consumer Society: The Com-*

mercialization of Eighteenth-Century England (Bloomington: Indiana University Press, 1982), 265–85; and Peter Borsay, *A History of Leisure: The British Experience since 1500* (Basingstoke: Palgrave Macmillan, 2006), 93–96.

21. Alexander Peter Buchan, *Practical Observations Concerning Sea Bathing; To Which Are Added, Remarks on the Use of the Warm Bath* (London: T. Cadell & W. Davies, 1804), v–vi.

22. Phyllis Hembry, *The English Spa, 1560–1815: A Social History* (London: Athlone Press, 1990).

23. Roy Porter, *The Greatest Benefit to Mankind: A Medical History of Humanity from Antiquity to the Present* (London: HarperCollins, 1997), 266.

24. Porter, 267.

25. William Buchan and William Cadogan, *Domestic Medicine; or, the Family Physician* (Philadelphia: printed by John Dunlap, 1772), 48–53; Porter, *Greatest Benefit*, 267.

26. Hembry, *English Spa*.

27. Hermannius vander Heyden, *Speedy Help for Rich and Poor* (London: printed by James Young, 1653).

28. John Locke, *Some Thoughts Concerning Education* (London: printed for A. and J. Churchill, 1693).

29. Sir John Floyer, *An Enquiry into the Right Use and Abuses of the Hot, Cold, and Temperate Baths in England* (London: printed for R. Clavel, 1697).

30. Sir John Floyer and Edward Batnard, *Psychrolousia: or the History of Cold Bathing*, 6th ed. (London: W. Innys and R. Manby, 1732).

31. Dioscorides Pedanius, *De Materia Medica: Being an Herbal with Many Other Medicinal Materials*, trans. Tess Anne Osbaldeston and Robert P. Wood (repr., Johannesburg: Ibidis, 2000).

32. Thomas Guidott, *An Apology for the Bath: Being an Answer to the Late Inquiry into the Right Use and Abuses of the Baths in England* (London: printed for G. Sawbridg [sic], 1705), 99, 107.

33. Thomas Short, *The Natural, Experimental, and Medicinal History of the Mineral Waters of Derbyshire, Lincolnshire, and Yorkshire* (London: printed by F. Gyles, 1734).

34. Short, 191–95.

35. Richard Russell, *De tabe glandulari, sive de usu aquæ marinæ in morbis glandularum dissertatio* (Oxford: Apud Jacobum Fletcher, 1750).

36. Richard Russell, *A Dissertation on the Use of Sea-Water in the Diseases of the Glands* (London: printed by W. Owen, 1752).

37. Russell, *Dissertation*, 154.

38. John Awsiter, *Thoughts on Brighthelmstone: Concerning Sea-Bathing and Drinking Sea Water* (London: J. Wilkie, 1768).

39. Awsiter, 3–6.

40. Robert White, *The Use and Abuse of Sea Water, Impartially Considered, and Exemplified in Several Cases* (London: printed for W. Flexney, 1775), 6–15.

41. John Crane, *Cursory Observations on Sea-Bathing; The Use of Sea-Water Internally, and the Advantages of a Maritime Situation* (London: Weymouth, 1795), 4.

42. Sir Philip Francis et al., *The Francis Letters, by Sir Philip Francis and Other Members of the Family,* ed. Beata Francis and Eliza Keary (London: Hutchinson, 1901), 211–13.

43. Hester Lynch Piozzi, *The Piozzi Letters: Correspondence of Hester Lynch Piozzi, 1784–1821 (Formerly Mrs. Thrale),* ed. Edward Bloom and Lillian D. Bloom (Newark: University of Delaware Press, 1989), 237. Fanny Burney caught the cold and the sea was blamed. Fanny Burney, *Journals and Letters of Fanny Burney,* ed. Lars E. Troide et al. (Kingston, Ontario: McGill-Queens University Press, 1988), 3:441.

44. Porter, *Greatest Benefit to Mankind,* 268.

45. John Arbuthnot, *An Essay Concerning the Effects of Air on Human Bodies* (London: printed for J. and R. Tonson and S. Draper, 1733).

46. John I. Housz to Sir John Pringle, January 22, 1780, *Philosophical Transactions of the Royal Society of London* 70 (1780): 354–57; Sir John Pringle, *A Discourse of the Different Kinds of Air, Delivered November 30* (London: printed for the Royal Society of London, 1774).

47. Ian Ousby, *The Englishman's England: Taste, Travel and the Rise of Tourism* (Cambridge: Cambridge University Press, 1990), 12.

48. While not exactly a guide, this first item could function as one. George S. Fry, *A Journey from London to Scarborough, in Several Letters from a Gentleman There to His Friend in London* (London: printed for Caesar Ward and Richard Chandler, 1734); Thomas Hinderwell, *The History and Antiquities of Scarborough and Vicinity: With Views and Plans* (Scarborough, 1798); *The Margate Guide, in a Letter to a Friend* (London: T. Carnan and F. Newbery, 1770); *Fisher's New Brighton Guide; or, A Description of Brighthelmston, and the Adjacent Country* (London: printed for F. G. Fisher by T. Burton, 1800); P. Delamotte, *The Weymouth Guide: Exhibiting the Ancient and Present State of Weymouth and Melcombe Regis* (Weymouth: printed for the editor, 1785).

49. Developing ski resorts encountered the same problems. Annie G. Coleman, *Ski Style, Sport and Culture in the Rockies* (Lawrence: University of Kansas Press, 2004).

50. John Copeland, *Roads and Their Traffic, 1750–1850,* Reprints of Economic Classics (Newton Abbot: David & Charles, 1968).

51. Burney, *Early Journals and Letters,* 3:266, 270.

52. Venetia Murray, *An Elegant Madness: High Society in Regency England* (New York: Viking, 1999), 81–83.

53. James Henry Bennet, *Winter and Spring on the Shores of the Mediterranean* (London: John Churchill, 1861), 434. After wandering around many beach communities, Bennet comments that fishing villages stay away from the shore and stay out of sight of the beach. Jane Austen would write, "Sea views are only for urban folk who never experience its menace. The true sailor prefers to be landlocked rather than face the ocean." Quoted in Lencek, *Beach,* 82. See also John R. Ellis, *The Human Shore: Seacoasts in History* (Chicago: University of Chicago Press, 2012), 121.

54. John Nichols, *Literary Anecdotes of the Eighteenth Century* (London: the author, 1812), 406–7.

55. John George Bishop, *"A Peep into the Past": Brighton in the Olden Time, with Glances at the Present* (Brighton: the author, 1892), 26–30.

56. George Saville Carey, *The Balnea; or, an Impartial Description of All the Popular Watering Places in England*, 3rd ed. (London: West and Hughes, 1801), 13; Joseph Farington, *The Diary of Joseph Farington*, ed. Kenneth Garlick and Angus Macintyre (New Haven, CT: Yale University Press, 1982), 10:3543–44.

57. Anne Emily Garnier Newdigate, *The Cheverels of Cheverel Manor [Being the correspondence of Sir Roger and Lady Newdigate]* (London: Longmans, Green, 1898), 202–3, 209 (brackets in original title).

58. Sarah J. Churchill, Duchess of Marlborough, *Letters of a Grandmother, 1732–35* (London, J. Cape, 1943), 48–49, 64. See also *Journey from London to Scarborough*; Henrietta H. Howard and George Berkeley, *Letters to and from Henrietta, Countess of Suffolk, and Her Second Husband, the Hon. George Berkeley, from 1712 to 1767*, ed. John Wilson Croker (London: John Murray, 1824), 58.

59. *The Scarborough Guide*, 3rd ed. (Scarborough: York, for Turner and Ainsworth, 1806), 33.

60. Paul Langford, *Englishness Identified: Manners and Character, 1650–1850* (Oxford: Oxford University Press, 2000), 168–71. See Fanny Burney's comments on Mr. Wade at Brighton: Burney, *Early Journals and Letters*, 3:385–86.

61. See the Duchess of Marlborough's comments on Mr. Vipont: Thompson, *Letters from a Grandmother*, 46–47.

62. Harriet Granville, *Letters of Harriet, Countess Granville, 1810–1845*, ed. F. Leveson Gower (London: Longmans, Green, 1894), 240–44.

63. Stella Margetson, *Leisure and Pleasure in the Eighteenth Century* (London: Cassell, 1970), 68.

64. Langford, *Englishness Identified*, 281.

65. Jane Austen, *Sanditon*, in *Later Manuscripts*, ed. Janet Todd and Linda Bree (Cambridge: Cambridge University Press, 2008), 180.

66. The quote is from *Pride and Prejudice*, chap. 51. John Mullen, *What Matters in Jane Austen: Twenty Crucial Puzzles Solved* (New York: Bloomsbury Press, 2012), 86–97; Austen, *Later Manuscripts*. The BBC has created a television program based on *Sanditon*.

67. Fanny Burney, *The Early Diary of Frances Burney, 1768–1778*, ed. Annie Raine Ellis (London: George Bell and Sons, 1889), 1:244–45.

68. Buchan, *Practical Observations Concerning Sea Bathing*, 21.

69. Lady Harriet Cavendish, *Hary-O: The Letters of Lady Harriet Cavendish, 1796–1809*, ed. Sir George Leveson Gower and Iris Palmer (London: John Murray, 1940), 40.

70. Buchan, *Practical Observations Concerning Sea Bathing*, 5, 15.

71. Burney, *Early Journals and Letters*, 3:174.

72. Burney, *Journals and Letters*, 5:175–76.

73. Francis, *Francis Letters*, 2:445.

74. Lord Chesterfield, while visiting Scarborough, wrote, "Ladies here are innumerable." Howard and Berkeley, *Letters to and from Henrietta*, 2:58. See also the important work by Amanda Herbert, on women and spas: Herbert,

Female Alliances: Gender, Identity and Friendship in Early Modern Britain (New Haven, CT: Yale University Press, 2014).

75. Francis, *Francis Letters*, 2:445.

76. Burney, *Early Diary*, 1:236–38.

77. Cavendish, *Hary-O*, 31.

78. Abigail Adams, *Letters of Mrs. Adams, the Wife of John Adams*, 2nd ed. (Boston: C. C. Little and J. Brown, 1840), 2:81–83.

79. Langford, *Englishness Identified*, 164–73.

80. *Poetical Sketches of Scarborough Illustrated with 21 Engravings of Humorous Subjects* (London: R. Ackermann, 1813), 111.

81. Anthony Pasquin, *The New Brighton Guide; Involving a Complete, Authentic, and Honorable Solution of the Recent Mysteries of Carlton House*, 5th ed. (London: Printed for H. D. Symonds and T. Bellamy, 1796), 5–7.

82. Pasquin put it that they were all "severely inspected by the aid of telescopes." Pasquin, 7.

83. A. F. J. Brown, *Essex People, 1750–1900: From Their Diaries, Memoirs and Letters* (Chelmsford: Essex County Council, 1972), 24.

84. Erasmus Darwin, *The Botanic Garden* (London: printed for J. Johnson, 1791), pt. 2, 166.

85. Newdigate, *Cheverels of Cheverel Manor*, 182.

86. Mary Berry, *Extracts of the Journals and Correspondence of Miss Berry from the Year 1783 to 1852*, 2nd ed., ed. Lady Theresa Lewis (London: Longmans, Green, 1866). See the comments on driving where she reports, "Here everybody is riding and driving and phaetoning, and curricking away at such a rate." Berry, 1:440.

87. Mrs. Betsy Francis wrote to her husband, who was at Margate, about their daughter, inquiring, did their daughter dance with a "proper person"? She also worried that her husband should make sure to "not make yourself too cheap among them" so that they were treated properly. Mr. Francis did tip the master of ceremonies one guinea, a substantial tip. Francis, *Francis Letters*, 70, 200–203.

88. Burney, *Early Journals and Letters*, 3:153.

89. Melchisédech Thévenot, *The Art of Swimming* (London: printed for Dan Brown, 1699).

90. Bishop, *"Peep into the Past,"* 231–32, 237–38.

91. Peregrine Phillips, *A Diary Kept in an Excursion to Little Hampton, near Arundel, and to Brighthelmston, in Sussex, in 1778* (London: printed for the author, 1780), 64–66.

92. John Constable, *John Constable's Correspondence*, ed. Ronald B. Beckett (Ipswich: Suffolk Record Society, 1964), 6:434.

93. Tobias Smollett, *The Expedition of Humphry Clinker*, The Works of Tobias Smollett, ed. Thomas R. Preston and O. M. Brack (Athens: University of Georgia Press, 1990), 177–79.

94. Newdigate, *Cheverels of Cheverel Manor*, 16, 24–26.

95. Cavendish, *Hary-O*, 33.

96. Julia Allen, *Swimming with Dr Johnson and Mrs Thrale: Sport, Health and Exercise in Eighteenth-Century England* (Cambridge: Lutterworth, 2012), 223–25.

97. Granville Leveson-Gower Granville, *Private Correspondence, 1781 to 1821*, ed. Castalia Rosalind Campbell Leveson-Gower Granville (London: John Murray, 1916), 2:367–70.

98. Catherine Molineux, *Faces of Perfect Ebony: Encountering Atlantic Slavery in Imperial Britain* (Cambridge, MA: Harvard University Press, 2012), 53–55.

99. Mary Anstley to Elizabeth Montague, August 30, 1755, Montague Manuscripts, Huntington Library, MO28.

100. Lady Mary Coke, *The Letters and Journals of Lady Mary Coke*, ed. James Archibald Home (Edinburgh: David Douglas, 1889), 2:392.

101. "A Report on Teignmouth," *Royal Magazine or Gentleman's Monthly Companion* (London), March 1762.

102. Richard Jefferies, *The Open Air* (London: Chatto & Windus, 1885), 51.

103. John D. D. Styles, *The Temptations of a Watering-Place, and the Best Means of Counteracting Their Influence* (Brighton: printed by W. Fleet, 1815).

CHAPTER 2. THE RISE OF THE RESORTS

1. Robert Wittie, *Scarbrough Spaw, or, A Description of the Nature and Vertues of the Spaw at Scarbrough in Yorkshire* (London: printed for Charles Tyus, 1660).

2. Robert Wittie, Thomas Newcomb, and John Martyn, *Pyrologia Mimica; or, An Answer to Hydrologia Chymica of Silliam Sympson* (London: printed by T. N. for J. Martyn, 1669). See also the attack in Short, *Natural, Experimental, and Medicinal History*, 114–59.

3. Churchill, *Letters of a Grandmother*, 46–59, 64. The Duchess notes that she has taken the Scarborough water in London.

4. Howard and Berkeley, *Letters to and from Henrietta*, 58–61.

5. William Hutton, *The Scarborough Tour, in 1803* (London: printed by and for John Nichols, 1804), 216–18.

6. Fry, *Journey from London to Scarborough*, 34–35.

7. Fry, last pages. See also *List of the Nobility*, same volume.

8. Fry, 36.

9. Hutton, *Scarborough Tour*, 283.

10. Farington, *Diary*, 6:2394.

11. Catherine Hutton, *Reminiscences of a Gentlewoman of the Last Century: Letters of Catherine Hutton*, ed. Catherine Hutton Beale (Birmingham: Cornish, 1891), 24–25. Mrs. Hutton suffered through a memorable thirty-six-hour return voyage.

12. George Keate, *Sketches from Nature; Taken, and Coloured, in a Journey to Margate*, 5th ed. (London: printed by J. Cundee for T. Hurst, 1802).

13. Nigel Barker, *Margate's Seaside Heritage* (Swindon: English Heritage, 2007), 14–19.

14. Caroline Girle Powys, *Passages from the Diaries of Mrs. Philip Lybbe Powys of Hardwick House, Oxon., 1756–1808*, ed. Emily J. Climenson (London: Longmans, Green, 1899), 310–12.

15. *The New Margate and Ramsgate Guide in Letters to a Friend* (London: printed for H. Turpin, 1780), 21–22; Farington, *Diary*, 6:22.

16. W. C. Oulton, *Picture of Margate and Its Vicinity* (London: Baldwin, Cradock, and Joy, 1820), 50–54. See also *New Margate and Ramsgate Guide*, 5–9.

17. Farington, *Diary*, 6:2396.

18. Momus, *Letters of Momus from Margate* (London: John Bell, 1778), 8.

19. Francis, *Francis Letters*, 119.

20. Momus, *Letters of Momus*, 34.

21. While there are many references to women at resorts, *The New Margate and Ramsgate Guide* (1780) is one of the first accounts of women and children at the beach.

22. Powys, *Passages from the Diaries*, 310–12.

23. *New Margate and Ramsgate Guide*, 29–30.

24. John Love, *A New Improved Weymouth Guide* (Weymouth: printed for J. Ryall, 1790), 16.

25. Love, *New Improved Weymouth Guide*, 17–19.

26. Fanny Burney, *Diary and Letters of Madame D'arbley, author of Evelina, Cecelia, &c.*, ed. Charlotte Frances Barrett (London: Henry Colburn, 1842), 5:289–98. On observing the dippers, one observer wrote, "When I first surveyed those loyal nymphs it was with some difficulty I kept my features in order." She also reports that the king was quite surprised at the musicians. Mrs. Albert Papendiek, *Court and Private Life in the Time of Queen Charlotte: Being the Journals of Mrs. Papendiek, Assistant-Keeper of the Wardrobe and Reader to Her Majesty*, ed. Augusta Mary Anne Broughton (London: R. Bentley & Son, 1887), 114–16.

27. Burney, *Diary and Letters*, 5:301–9. The queen disliked tragedy, and so Siddons had to perform comedy, which Burney thought was not her real strength. See also Queen Charlotte's Diary, Royal Archives, George III/Add./43/3e.

28. When Joseph Farington visited, one of the royal daughters, Princess Amalia, was ailing, and so the royal yacht was brought up and went to sea, accompanied by the two frigates, in hopes that the sea air would help her recover. Farington, *Diary*, 10:3543–44.

29. William Charles Arlington Blew, *Brighton and Its Coaches. A History of the London and Brighton Road* (London: John C. Nimmo, 1894).

30. Bishop, *"Peep into the Past,"* 26–31, 187–216.

31. Nichols, *Literary Anecdotes of the Eighteenth Century*, 406–7.

32. Christopher Hibbert, *George IV, Prince of Wales, 1762–1811* (New York: Harper and Row, 1974).

33. John Morley, *The Making of the Royal Pavilion: Designs and Drawings* (London: Sotheby Publications, 1984); Humphry Repton, John Adey Repton, and George Stanley Repton, *Designs for the Pavilion at Brighton* (London, 1808).

34. Granville, *Letters of Harriet*, 242–44.

35. James Munson, *Maria Fitzherbert: The Secret Wife of George IV* (London: Constable, 2001), 81–89.

36. Harriette Wilson, *The Memoirs of Harriette Wilson* (London: privately printed for the Navarre Society Limited, 1924), 2:369–83.

37. Ian Kelly, *Beau Brummell: The Ultimate Dandy* (London: Hodder & Stoughton, 2005), 63–71.

38. Burney, *Early Journals and Letters*, 5:153.

39. Lady Frances Dillon Jerningham, *The Jerningham Letters (1780–1843)*, ed. Egerton Castle (London: Richard Bentley and Son, 1896), 1:285.

40. Edmund W. Gilbert, *Brighton, Old Ocean's Bauble* (London: Methuen, 1954), 195–96.

41. Sarah Spencer, *Correspondence of Sarah Spencer, Lady Lyttelton, 1787–1870*, ed. Mrs. Hugh Wyndham, 4th ed. (London: Murray, 1912), 33.

42. John Constable, *John Constable's Correspondence*, ed. Ronald Brymer Beckett, Suffolk Records Society (London: H.M. Stationery Office, 1962), 2:171.

43. William Daniell et al., *A Voyage Round Great Britain, Undertaken in the Summer of the Year 1813* (London: printed for Longman et al., 1814), 2:102.

44. Daniell et al., 103.

45. Aikin, *Description of the Country*, 357–58.

46. Roger Hudson, *Coleridge among the Lakes and Mountains from his Notebooks, Letters and Poems, 1794–1804* (London: The Folio Society, 1991), 21. See also Alain Corbin, *The Lure of the Sea: The Discovery of the Seaside in the Western World, 1750–1840* (London: Penguin, 1995), 82–83.

47. William Hutton, *A Description of Blackpool, in Lancashire; Frequented for Sea Bathing* (Birmingham: Pearson, 1789), 28–29.

48. W. J. Smith, "Blackpool: A Sketch of its Growth, 1740–1851," *Transactions of the Lancaster and Chester Antiquarian Society* 69 (1959): 70–103.

49. Daniell et al., *Voyage Round Great Britain*, 103; Hutton, *Description of Blackpool*, 28, 33–35.

50. Hutton, *Description of Blackpool*, 33–35.

51. Georg Christoph Lichtenberg and Hans Ludwig Gumbert, *Lichtenberg in England*, 2 vols. (Wiesbaden: Harrassowitz, 1977).

52. David Clay Large, *The Grand Spas of Central Europe: A History of Intrigue, Politics, Art, and Healing* (Lanham, MD: Rowman & Littlefield, 2015).

53. Bärbel Hedinger and Altonaer Museum, *Saison am Strand Badeleben an Nord- Und Ostsee, 200 Jahre* (Herford: Koehlers, 1986).

54. Hughes Maret, *Memoire sur la maniere d'agir des bains d'eau douce et d'eau denier et leur usage* (Paris: Chez Des Ventes de Ladoué, 1769).

55. For example, Johann L. Chemnitz, *Wangerooge und das Seebad* (1821); August Ruge, *Uber Seebader im Allgemeinin und besonders uber das Seebad Cuxhaven* (1818).

56. Corbin, *Lure of the Sea*, 257–59, 276.

57. Shortly thereafter, Vogel published a book on the benefits of sea bathing. Samuel Gottlieb von Vogel, *ÜBer Den Nutzen Und Gebrauch Der SeebäDer. 1* (Stendal: Franzen, 1794).

58. Charles James Apperley, *Nimrod Abroad* (London: Henry Colburn, 1842), 235.

59. Kimberly Bradley, "Surfacing: A Spa Town Reclaims Its Glory," *New York Times*, June 3, 2007.

60. Friedrich Wilhelm von Halem, *Die Insel Norderney Und Ihr Seebad, Nach Dem Gegenwartigen Standpuncte* (Hanover, 1822). Wagenerooge was created in 1802 by a merchant, Caspar Jager, who quickly reached out to his local prince to get the proper patronage.

61. Corbin, *Lure of the Sea*, 257–59.

62. Countess Granville especially enjoyed the "elegants" in their French bonnets and the queen in a "chariot" with four outriders. Granville, *Letters of Harriet*, 284.

63. Joseph Traveller Marshall, *Travels through Holland, Flanders, Germany, Denmark, Sweden, Lapland, Russia, the Ukraine and Poland in the Years 1768, 1769, 1770 (and 1771)* (London, 1772), 31.

64. Ferdinand Claasen et al., *Souvenir d'Ostende* (Ostende: Blackenberghe, 1880?); Ronny Gobyn, *Histoire d'Eaux: Stations thermals et balineaires en Belguigue, XVI–XX Siecle* (Brussels: Rene Reyns, 1987).

65. *Les Bains de Mer* (Dieppe: Musee de Dieppe, 1961), iii.

66. *Les Bains de Mer*, iv–v.

67. *Les Bains de Mer*, vi.

68. *Les Bains de Mer*, xiv. See also Caroline Moorehead, *Dancing to the Precipice: Lucie De La Tour Du Pin and the French Revolution* (London: Chatto & Windus, 2009), 405–11.

69. C. James Haug, *Leisure & Urbanism in Nineteenth-Century Nice* (Lawrence: Regents Press of Kansas, 1982), 5–8; Michael April Nelson, *Queen Victoria and the Discovery of the Riviera* (London: I. B. Tauris, 2001), 2–5.

70. Tobias Smollett, *Travels through France and Italy* (London: R. Baldwin, 1766), 192–93.

71. Patrick Howarth, *When the Riviera Was Ours* (London: Century, 1988, 1977); Haug, *Leisure & Urbanism*, 9–12.

72. Spencer Papers, December 6, 1769, British Library, Additional Manuscripts, 75611.

73. Spencer Papers, January 22, 1770; James Edward Smith, *A Sketch of a Tour on the Continent, in the Years 1786 and 1787* (London: B. and J. White, 1793), 204.

74. Edward M. D. Rigby, *Dr. Rigby's Letters from France &c. in 1789*, ed. Elizabeth Rigby (London: Longmans, Green, 1880); 149; Smith, *Sketch of a Tour*, 204.

75. Smith, 202; Rigby, *Dr. Rigby's Letters*, 148.

76. Howarth, *When the Riviera Was Ours*, 49–52; William Miller, *Wintering in the Riviera; with Notes on Travel in Italy and France, and Practical Hints to Travellers* (London, 1879), 62–73; Nelson, *Queen Victoria*, 6.

77. Miller, *Wintering in the Riviera*, 152.

78. Corbin, *Lure of the Sea*, 279; Richard Kind, *Seebad Zu Swinemünde Als Anhang Eine Kurze Anleitung Die Insel Rügen Zu Bereisen* (Stettin: Morin, 1828).

79. Corbin, *Lure of the Sea*, 315.

80. The English frequently visited the northern French beaches such as Dieppe and Boulogne, not to mention Nice.

CHAPTER 3. LEISURE COMES TO AMERICA

1. Timothy Dwight, *Travels in New England and New York* (New Haven, CT: by the author, 1821), 3:81.

2. Frances Anne Kemble, *Journal of a Residence on a Georgian Plantation in 1838–1839* (New York: Harper, 1863), 369. Kemble did love the sea air and the sound of the ocean at night, but loathed the sand flies. Kemble, 328, 352.

3. John F. Watson, *Annals of Philadelphia, and Pennsylvania, in the Olden Time* (Philadelphia: E. Thomas, 1857), 2:545–56.

4. Carl Bridenbaugh, "Colonial Newport as a Summer Resort," *Rhode Island Historical Society Collections* 26, no. 1 (January 1933): 1–23; Elaine Forman Crane, *A Dependent People: Newport, Rhode Island in the Revolutionary Era* (New York: Fordham University Press, 1992).

5. Bruce C. Daniels, *Puritans at Play: Leisure and Recreation in Colonial New England* (New York: St. Martins, 1995).

6. The best sources for these changes are Richard L. Bushman, *The Refinement of America: Persons, Houses, Cities* (New York: Knopf, 1992); T.H. Breen, "'Baubles of Britain': The American and Consumer Revolutions of the Eighteenth Century," *Past and Present* 119, no. 1 (May 1988): 73–104.

7. *The Autobiography of Benjamin Franklin*, Huntington manuscript 9999. Franklin's manuscript is in the Huntington Library, but a more practical way of finding the quote is in *Ben Franklin's Autobiography*, ed. Joyce E. Chaplin (New York: W. W. Norton, 2012), 77.

8. Adams, *Letters of Mrs. Adams*, 2:81–83.

9. As quoted in Lynne Withey, *Dearest Friend: A Life of Abigail Adams* (New York: Free Press, 1981), 199.

10. Withey, 180–90, 291–95.

11. John Tennent, *Every Man His Own Doctor, or, the Poor Planter's Physician*, 3rd ed. (Williamsburg VA: printed and sold by Wil. Parks, 1736); John Wesley, *Primitive Physick* (Philadelphia, 1764).

12. Buchan and Cadogan, *Domestic Medicine*.

13. For attitudes toward the mineral springs, see Vaughn Scribner, "'The Happy Effects of These Waters': Colonial American Mineral Spas and the British Civilizing Mission," *Early American Studies* 14, no. 3 (Summer 2016): 409–49. For the southern springs, see Charlene M. Boyer Lewis, *Ladies and Gentlemen on Display: Planter Society at the Virginia Springs, 1790–1860*, (Charlottesville: University Press of Virginia, 2001). For Washington, *The Papers of George Washington, the Colonial Series*, ed. W. W. Abbot (Charlottesville: University of Virginia Press, 1983), 7:68–69. See also Carl Bridenbaugh, "Baths and Watering Places of Colonial America," *William and Mary Quarterly* (third series) 3, no. 2 (April 1946): 151–81; Donald Yacovone, "A New England Bath: The Nation's First Resort at Stafford Springs," *Connecticut Historical Society Bulletin* 41, no. 1 (January 1976): 1–11.

14. Elizabeth Drinker, *The Diary of Elizabeth Drinker*, ed. Elaine Forman Crane (Boston: Northeastern University Press, 1991), 1:160–61.

15. For attitudes toward cleanliness, see Kathleen M. Brown, *Foul Bodies: Cleanliness in Early America* (New Haven, CT: Yale University Press, 2009), 121–46.

16. Drinker, *Diary*, 2:1060, 1065, 1884–85, 1314–16.

17. Anna Cabot Lowell's Journal, vol. 20: fol. 95, June 27, 1832, Massachusetts Historical Society.

18. George Templeton Strong, *The Diary of George Templeton Strong*, ed. Allan Nevins, Milton P. Thomas, and Thomas Pressly (Seattle: University of Washington Press, 1988), 210.

19. Drinker, *Diary*, 1:61, 154–55.

20. Jeffery Dowart, *Cape May County New Jersey: The Making of an American Resort Community* (New Brunswick, NJ: Rutgers University Press, 1992), 62–63.

21. *New York Journal or General Advertiser,* September 3, 1772, 718.

22. Sir William Johnson, *The Papers of Sir William Johnson,* ed. Milton W. Hamilton (Albany: University of the State of New York, 1951), 8:888–91.

23. Drinker, *Diary*, 3:2029, 2055, 2056, 2080.

24. Jacob Hiltzheimer, *Extracts from the Diary of Jacob Hiltzheimer, of Philadelphia, 1765–1798,* ed. Jacob Cox Parsons (Philadelphia: W.F. Fell, 1893), 217.

25. Henry Toler, *The Journal of Henry Toler*, pt. 2, ed. William S. Simpson, *Virginia Baptist Register* 32 (1993): 1629.

26. William Bentley et al., *The Diary of William Bentley, D.D., Pastor of the East Church, Salem, Massachusetts* (Salem, MA: Essex institute, 1905), 1:174, 2:227.

27. John Peebles, *John Peebles' American War: The Diary of a Scottish Grenadier, 1776–1782,* ed. Ira D. Gruber (Mechanicsburg, PA: Stackpole Books, 1998), 446. And see also, for a Dutch tradition, Benjamin Roberts, "Drinking like a Man: The Paradox of Excessive Drinking for Seventeenth-Century Dutch Youths," *Journal of Family History* 29, no. 3 (July 2004): 248.

28. Lillian B. Miller, ed., *Selected Papers of Charles Wilson Peale and His Family* (New Haven, CT: Yale University Press, 1983), 5:22–23.

29. John T. Cunningham, *This Is New Jersey: From High Point to Cape May* (New Brunswick, NJ: Rutgers University Press, 1953), 244.

30. Barbara Carson, "Early American Tourists and the Commercialization of Leisure," in *Of Consuming Interest: The Style of Life in the Eighteenth Century,* ed. Gary Carson, Ronald Hoffman, and Peter J. Albert (Charlottesville: University of Virginia Press, 1994), 374–405.

31. *The National Era,* September 14, 1848, 146.

32. Jeffery M. Dorwart, *Cape May County, New Jersey: The Making of an American Resort Community* (New Brunswick, NJ: Rutgers University Press, 1992), 69; Emil R. Salvini, *The Summer City by the Sea: Cape May, New Jersey, an Illustrated History* (Belleville, NJ: Wheal Grace, 1995), 6–8.

33. Dorwart, *Cape May County,* 69.

34. Salvini, *Summer City by the Sea,* 8.

35. William Gibson, "The Diary of William P. Brobson, 1825–28," pt. 1, *Delaware History* 15, no. 1 (April 1972): 79–82.

36. *Godey's Ladies' Magazine,* August 1849, 120. See also a much later image in *Harper's Weekly,* August 13, 1887, 585, depicting farmers on the beach.

37. Carol E. Hoffecker, "The Diaries of Edmund Canby, a Quaker Miller, 1822–48," *Delaware History* 16 (October 1972): 79–131.

38. Watson, *Annals of Philadelphia,* 2:545–56.

39. Watson, *Annals of Philadelphia,*2:462–65; Drinker, *Diary,* 3:2053–56.

40. John Pintard, *Letters from John Pintard to His Daughter, Eliza Noel Pintard Davidson, 1816–1833,* ed. Dorothy C. Barck, Collections of the New York Historical Society for the Year 1937–1940, John Watts Depeyster

Publication Fund Series (New York: printed for the New-York Historical Society, 1940), 2:296.

41. Pintard, 1:78, 4:157.

42. Philip Hone, *The Diary of Philip Hone*, New York Historical Society Manuscript, vol. 4: fol. 142.

43. Hone, vol. 5: fol. 212.

44. Hone, vol. 7: fols. 14–16, 127, 275, 293, 343–34.

45. Frances Ann Kemble, *Records of Later Life* (New York: Henry Holt, 1882), 158–59.

46. Hone, *Diary*, vol. 9: fol. 253.

47. Hugh Bradley, *Such Was Saratoga* (New York: Doubleday, Doran, 1940), 70–77.

48. Hone, *Diary*, vol. 17: fols. 150, 153.

49. Pintard, *Letters*, 2:76; Strong, *Diary*, 73.

50. Hone, *Diary*, vol. 11: fol. 373.

51. Hone, *Diary*, vol. 14: fols. 206, 226.

52. Bentley, *Diary*, 1:174, 3:241.

53. J.P. O'Neill, *The Great New England Sea Serpent: An Account of Unknown Creatures Sighted by Many Respectable Persons between 1638 and the Present Day* (Camden, ME: Down East Books, 1999); Chandos M. Brown, "A Natural History of the Gloucester Sea Serpent: Knowledge, Power and the Culture of Science in Antebellum America," *American Quarterly* 42, no. 3 (September 1990): 402–36. British Consul Thomas Grattan was one of the witnesses. Thomas Colley Grattan, *Civilized America* (London: Bradbury and Evans, 1859): 1:51–55.

54. Fred A. Wilson, *Some Annals of Nahant, Massachusetts* (Boston: Old Corner Book Store, 1928), 72–75; Joseph A. Garland, *Boston's North Shore: Being an Account of Life among the Noteworthy, Fashionable, Wealthy, Eccentric, and Ordinary, 1823–1890* (Boston: Little, Brown, 1978), 27–33.

55. Wilson, *Some Annals of Nahant*, 76; printed advertisements by Thomas Perkins and James Jackson, July and August 1822, Massachusetts Historical Society; Bryant Franklin Tolles, *Summer by the Seaside: The Architecture of New England Coastal Resort Hotels, 1820–1950* (Hanover, NH: University Press of New England, 2008), 89–90. The hotel was enlarged twice but suffered the usual fate as it burned down in 1861.

56. Walter Channing, "A Topographical Sketch of Nahant," *New England Journal of Medicine and Surgery* (new series) 10 (1821): 22–31.

57. De Wolfe Howe et al., *The Articulate Sisters: Passages from the Journals and Letters of the Daughters of President Josiah Quincy of Harvard University* (Cambridge, MA: Harvard University Press, 1946), 51–63.

58. Charles Francis Adams et al., *Diary*, The Adams Papers Series 1, Diaries (Cambridge, MA: Belknap Press of Harvard University Press, 1964), 1:231–32. He was also surprised that at "one of the most fashionable and the most exquisite places under the sun," there was no silverware on the table.

59. Anna Cabot Lowell's Journal, vol. 13: records for June and July 1828; vol. 16: records for July and August 1830; vol. 28: records for July and August 1836.

60. Harriet Martineau, *Retrospect of Western Travel* (London: Saunders and Otley, 1838), 3:142–44. The men at Nahant went together to Cupid's Rock, where they swam nude until day-trippers who came to see what was going on made it difficult. Garland, *Boston's North Shore*, 236.

61. Grattan, *Civilized America*, 1:29–55, 93.

62. *Nahant, or "The Floure of Souvenance"* (Philadelphia: H. C. Carey and I. Lee, 1827). It is quite boring and probably did not sell many copies outside of Boston.

63. Clarence W. Hobbs, *Lynn and the Surroundings* (Lynn, MA: Lewis & Winship, 1886), 159.

64. Adam Hodgson, *Letters from North America, Written during a Tour in the United States and Canada* (London: Hurst Robinson, 1824), 1:132–33.

65. Hone, *Diary*, vol. 17: fol. 110.

66. Sidney George Fisher, *A Philadelphia Perspective: The Diary of Sidney George Fisher Covering the Years 1834–1871*, ed. Nicholas B. Wainwright (Philadelphia: Historical Society of Pennsylvania, 1967), 140–41.

67. Fisher, 176, 190, 198, 213–14.

68. "Flirtation at Newport," *Harper's Weekly*, September 12, 1857. 584–85.

69. C. W. Tazewell, *Meet Marshall Parks, Founder of Virginia Beach*, 2nd ed. (Virginia Beach, VA: W. S. Dawson Co., 1990), 7; *The Commonwealth: The Magazine of Virginia* 21, no. 6 (July 1954): 28.

70. Samuel Kercheval, *A History of the Valley of Virginia*, 4th ed. (Strasburg, VA: Shenandoah, 1925); and more recently, the excellent study of Lewis, *Ladies and Gentlemen on Display*.

71. "The Fugitive Slave Law," *The North Star*, March 3, 1848.

72. Hiram Fuller, *Belle Brittan on a Tour at Newport, and Here and There* (New York: Derby & Jackson, 1858), 181.

73. Timothy L. Smith, *Revivalism and Social Reform: American Protestantism on the Eve of the Civil War* (New York: Harper, 1957); Nathan O. Hatch and John H. Wigger, *Methodism and the Shaping of American Culture* (Nashville, TN: Kingswood Books, 2001); John H. Wigger, *Taking Heaven by Storm: Methodism and the Rise of Popular Christianity in America* (New York: Oxford University Press, 1998).

74. Revivals had started in Wellfleet, Cape Cod, as early as 1819, and then had moved to Millennium Grove in the nearby town of Eastham in 1828. James C. O'Connell, *Becoming Cape Cod: Creating a Seaside Resort* (Hanover, NH: University Press of New England, 2003), 5.

75. Dona Brown, *Inventing New England: Regional Tourism in the Nineteenth Century* (Washington, DC: Smithsonian Institution Press, 1995), 77.

76. Ellen Weiss, *City in the Woods: The Life and Design of an American Camp Meeting on Martha's Vineyard* (New York: Oxford University Press, 1987); Ellen Eslinger, *Citizens of Zion: The Social Origins of Camp Meeting Revivalism* (Knoxville: University of Tennessee Press, 1999).

77. Brown, *Inventing New England*, 77–96. The resort was declared a National Historic Landmark in 2005 because of the cottages.

78. Helen C. Pike, *Asbury Park's Glory Days: The Story of an American Resort* (New Brunswick, NJ: Rutgers University Press, 2005); Emil R. Salvini,

Boardwalk Memories: Tales of the Jersey Shore (Guilford, CT: Insider's Guide, 2006), 33–42.

79. For much of the material in this section, I have relied on A.K. Sandoval-Strausz, *Hotel: An American History* (New Haven, CT: Yale University Press, 2007).

80. Bushman, *Refinement of America,* 50–51, 160–64.

81. Anna Cabot Lowell's Journal, vol. 13: July 29, 1828.

82. Grattan, *Civilized America,* 43. Grattan also hated the food and thought even the furniture was wretched. Grattan, 42, 64–65.

83. Tyrone Power, *Impressions of America; During the Years 1833, 1834, and 1835,* 2nd American ed. (Philadelphia: Carey, Lea & Blanchard, 1836), 1:18.

84. Philip Hone *The Diary of Philip Hone, 1828–1851,* ed. Allan Nevins (New York: Dodd, Mead, 1927), 406.

85. Emil R. Salvini, *Summer City by the Sea,* 16, 37–39, 47–53; Emil R. Salvini, *Historic Cape May: Summer City by the Sea* (Charleston, SC: The History Press, 2012).

86. Tolles, *Summer by the Seaside,* 1–2; Karen Halttunen, *Confidence Men and Painted Women: A Study of Middle-Class Culture in America, 1830–1870* (New Haven, CT: Yale University Press, 1982), 99–118.

87. Fuller, *Belle Brittan on a Tour at Newport,* 173;

88. Fisher, *Philadelphia Perspective,* 58.

89. Fisher, 213–14, 530–31. For an analysis of this society, see Halttunen, *Confidence Men and Painted Women,* 1–55.

90. Pintard, *Letters,* 78.

91. Elizabeth Rogers Mason Cabot, *More than Common Powers of Perception: The Diary of Elizabeth Rogers Mason Cabot,* ed. P.A.M. Taylor (Boston: Beacon Press, 1991), 116–17.

92. This was at Nahant and not at the far more racy Newport. Anna Cabot Lowell's Journal, vol. 18: fol. 93.

93. George William Curtis, *Lotus-Eating: A Summer Book* (New York: Dix, Edwards, 1856), 169–70, 175.

94. Fuller, *Belle Brittan on a Tour at Newport,* 169, 176.

95. Fisher, *Diary,* 190; and for Nahant, 124.

96. Halttunen, *Confidence Men and Painted Women,* 56–91.

97. Patricia Cunningham, *Reforming Women's Fashion, 1850–1920: Politics, Health, and Art* (Kent, OH: Kent State University Press, 2003), 1–22; Gayle V. Fischer, *Pantaloons and Power: A Nineteenth-Century Dress Reform in the United States* (Kent, OH: Kent State University Press, 2001).

98. "Sea Bathing in America," *Illustrated London News,* September 1875, 223.

99. As quoted in Harold F. Wilson, *The Story of the Jersey Shore* (Princeton, NJ: Van Nostrand, 1964), 63.

100. Mark E. Reinberger, *Philadelphia Country Houses: Architecture and Landscape* (Baltimore: Johns Hopkins University Press, 2015); J.H. Powell, *Bring Out Your Dead: The Great Plague of Yellow Fever in Philadelphia in 1793* (1949; repr., New York: Arno Press, 1970); Thomas A. Apel, *Feverish Bodies, Enlightened Minds: Science and the Yellow Fever Controversy in the Early American Republic* (Palo Alto, CA: Stanford University Press), 2016.

CHAPTER 4. THE INDUSTRIAL REVOLUTION
FINDS THE BEACH

1. John K. Walton, *The English Seaside Resort: A Social History, 1750–1914* (Leicester: Leicester University Press, 1983), 43.

2. John F. Travis, *The Rise of the Devon Seaside Resorts, 1750–1900* (Exeter: University of Exeter Press, 1993), 1–22.

3. Travis, 116–18.

4. L. T. C. Rolt and John S. Allen, *The Steam Engine of Thomas Newcomen,* rev. ed. (Harlington: Moorland, 1977).

5. Ben Russell, *James Watt: Making the World Anew* (London: Reaktion Books, 2014).

6. P. J. G. Ransom, *The Victorian Railway and How It Evolved* (London: Heinemann, 1990), 2–28; Jack Simmons, *The Victorian Railway* (London: Thames and Hudson, 1991); Christian Wolmar, *Fire & Steam: A New History of the Railways in Britain* (London: Atlantic Books, 2007), 1–20.

7. Wolfgang Schivelbusch, *The Railway Journey: The Industrialization and Perception of Time and Space in the Nineteenth Century,* new ed. (Leamington Spa: Berg, 1986), 3–4.

8. Ransom, *Victorian Railway,* 39–40. By 1824, 409,670 bales of cotton were imported and the numbers kept growing. Henry Booth, *An Account of the Liverpool and Manchester Railway* (Liverpool: printed by Wales and Baines, 1831), 8, 16–74; James Scott Walker, *An Accurate Description of the Liverpool and Manchester Railway, the Tunnel, the Bridges and Other Works throughout the Line* (Liverpool: J. F. Cannell, 1830); Joseph Kirwan, *A Descriptive and Historical Account of the Liverpool and Manchester Railway, from Its First Projection to the Present Time* (Glasgow: W. R. M'Phun, 1831).

9. Ransom, *Victorian Railway,* 48–52; Booth, *Account of the Liverpool and Manchester Railway,* 74–75.

10. Fanny Kemble, *Records of a Girlhood* (New York: R. Bentley and Son, 1878), 158–64.

11. Ransom, *Victorian Railway,* 55–56; Michael Freeman, *Railways and the Victorian Imagination* (New Haven, CT: Yale University Press, 1999), 36–40; *The Railway Companion, Describing an Excursion along the Liverpool Line* (London: E. Wilson, 1833).

12. C. Hamilton Ellis, *Popular Carriage: Two Centuries of Carriage Design for Road and Rail* (London: British Transport Commission, 1954).

13. Wolmar, *Fire & Steam,* 79–81.

14. Travis, *Rise of the Devon Seaside Resorts,* 101; R. E. Pearson, *The Bass Railway Trips* (Derby: Breedon, 1993).

15. Edmund Swinglehurst, *Cook's Tours: The Story of Popular Travel* (Poole: Blandford, 1982), 7–33; Lynne Withey, *Grand Tours and Cooks' Tours: A History of Leisure Travel, 1750–1915* (New York: William Morrow, 1997); Piers Brendon, *Thomas Cook: 150 Years of Popular Tourism* (London: Secker and Warburg, 1991).

16. K. T. Rowland, *Steam at Sea: A History of Steam Navigation* (Newton Abbot: David & Charles, 1970), 51–80.

17. Frank Burtt, *Steamers of the Thames and Medway* (London: R. Tilling, 1949), 7–20; Ransom, *Victorian Railway,* 34.

18. Simmons, *Victorian Railway,* 271.

19. Rowland, *Steam at Sea: A History of Steam Navigation,* 51–80.

20. Wolmar, *Fire & Steam,* 75.

21. John Copeland, *Roads and Their Traffic, 1750–1850* (Newton Abbot: David & Charles, 1968), 184–85.

22. Wolmar, *Fire & Steam,* 80.

23. Clifford Musgrave, *Life in Brighton: From the Earliest Times to the Present* (London: Faber, 1970), 258–72.

24. Simmons, *Victorian Railway,* 282–89.

25. For a standard English image of this event, see *Punch,* January 1, 1849.

26. Ransom, *Victorian Railway,* 91.

27. Wolmar, *Fire & Steam,* 78.

28. F. M. L. Thompson, *The Cambridge Social History of Britain, 1750–1950* (Cambridge: Cambridge University Press, 1990), 286–87; James Walvin, *Leisure and Society, 1830–1950* (London: Longman, 1978), 16–17; Susan Barton, *Working-Class Organisations and Popular Tourism, 1840–1970* (Manchester: Manchester University Press, 2005), 73–74.

29. Walvin, *Leisure and Society,* 3.

30. John K. Walton, *Lancashire: A Social History, 1558–1939* (Manchester: Manchester University Press, 1987), 295–96. See also Robert Poole, "Oldham Wakes," in *Leisure in Britain, 1780–1939,* ed. John K. Walton and James Walvin (Manchester: Manchester University Press, 1983), 71–98; R. A. Houston, *Bride Ales and Penny Weddings: Recreations, Reciprocity and Regions in Britain from the Sixteenth to the Nineteenth Centuries* (Oxford: Oxford University Press, 2017), 109–35; Barton, *Working Class Organisations,* 73–87.

31. Constable, *John Constable's Correspondence,* 6:191.

32. Poole, "Oldham Wakes."

33. Travis, *Rise of the Devon Seaside Resorts,* 176–77; Walvin, *Leisure and Society,* 53–54.

34. Walvin, *Leisure and Society,* 60–61.

35. Walton and Walvin, *Leisure in Britain 1780–1939,* 65; Hugh Cunningham, *Leisure in the Industrial Revolution: c. 1780–c. 1880* (New York: St. Martin's Press, 1980), 142–46; Barton, *Working Class Organisations,* 73–74.

36. Simmons, *Victorian Railway.* 291–94.

37. Walton, *English Seaside Resort,* 45–49.

38. John K. Walton, *The British Seaside: Holidays and Resorts in the Twentieth Century* (Manchester: Manchester University Press, 2000), 53, 60.

39. John K. Walton, "Demand for Working-Class Seaside Holidays in Victorian England," *Economic History Review* (new series) 34, no. 2 (May 1981): 249–65.

40. James Walvin, *Beside the Seaside: A Social History of the Popular Seaside Holiday* (London: Allen Lane, 1978), 46.

41. Silvester Reed, *Reed's Guide to Whitby and Visitors Handbook of the Town and Neighborhood with an Essay on Sea Bathing* (Whitby: by the author, 1878).

42. All numbers should be taken with a grain of salt as boosterism always played a role and there were few agreed-upon definitions of a tourist.

43. Walvin, *Beside the Seaside,* 72.

44. Walvin, 37, 40.

45. As quoted in David St. John Thomas and Kenneth Hoole, *A Regional History of the Railways of Great Britain,* vol. 4, *The North-East* (New Abbott: David & Charles, 1974), 79.

46. As quoted in Thomas and Hoole, 38.

47. As quoted in Travis, *Rise of the Devon Seaside Resorts,* 153. See also Bernard Henry Becker, *Holiday Haunts by Cliffside and Riverside, Etc.* (London: Remington & Co., 1884), 5, 10–12, for comments by antitrippers who could not wait for the trippers to leave.

48. John Betjeman, *Collected Poems* (Boston: Houghton Mifflin, 1959), 146–54.

49. Anthony Trollope, *Travelling Sketches* (London: Chapman and Hall, 1866), 14.

50. Travis, *Rise of the Devon Seaside Resorts,* 108–10, 152.

51. David Cannadine, *Lords and Landlords: The Aristocracy and the Towns, 1774–1967* (Leiscester: Leiscester University Press, 1980), 255–98; Walton, *British Seaside,* 63; article on Eastbourne, *The Observer,* September 22, 1878.

52. John K. Walton, *The Blackpool Landlady: A Social History* (Manchester: Manchester University Press, 1978).

53. Walton, *English Seaside Resort,* 71.

54. Daniell et al., *Voyage Round Great Britain,* 5–7; Nigel Barker, *Margate's Seaside Heritage* (Swindon: English Heritage, 2007), 14–15, 29–38.

55. Baker, *Margate,* 25; Walton, *English Seaside Resorts,* 72.

56. Momus, *Letters of Momus, from Margate* (London: printed for John Bell, 1778).

57. "Margate and Ramsgate Holidays," *Illustrated London News,* September 1, 1883, 207.

58. Hardwicke Lewis, *An Excursion to Margate, In the Month of June, 1786,* 3rd ed. (London: J. French, 1787), 22; *New Margate and Ramsgate Guide,* 20.

59. Thomas Kemp, the developer of Kemp Town, would be driven out of England by his creditors because the first phase of the building was deemed to be too far out of town and thus not suitable for the fashionable. Musgrave, *Life in Brighton,* 180–82.

60. Musgrave, 296–97; "Scarborough, Grand Hotel," Wikipedia, accessed January 14, 2018.

61. Lady Sarah Spencer went to Brighton resolved not to be near the fashionable as she detested the "dissipation" of Brighton. Spencer, *Correspondence,* 31–32.

62. Lee Jackson, *Dirty Old London: The Victorian Fight against Filth* (New Haven, CT: Yale University Press, 2014); Lawrence Wright, *Clean and Decent: The Fascinating History of the Bathroom & the Water Closet and of Sundry Habits, Fashions & Accessories of the Toilet, Principally in Great Britain, France, & America* (London: Routledge & Kegan Paul, 1960).

63. John Hassan, *The Seaside, Health and the Environment in England and Wales since 1800* (Aldershot: Ashgate, 2003).

64. Granville, *Spas of England,* 561.

65. *Lancet* 2 (1859): 170.

66. Hassan, *Seaside, Health and Environment,* 59–63.

67. Travis, *Rise of the Devon Seaside Resorts.*

68. Travis, 158–66; F.B. May, "Victorian and Edwardian Ilfracombe," in *Leisure in Britain, 1780–1939,* ed. John K. Walton and James Walvin (Manchester: Manchester University Press, 1983), 191–95; Hassan, *Seaside, Health and Environment,* 153.

69. Walton, *English Seaside Resort,* 137–38.

70. This was in 1888. H. Evelyn Crook, *Margate as a Health Resort* (Margate: Harman Keble, 1893), 25–29.

71. Hassan, *Seaside, Health and Environment,* 50–51.

72. Travis, *Rise of the Devon Seaside Resorts,* 164–65.

73. Travis, 152–53.

74. As quoted in Cunningham, *Leisure in the Industrial Revolution,* 160.

75. Manual Alvarez Espriella, *Letters from England,* ed. Robert Southey (London: Longman, Hurst, Rees, Orme, 1807), 41–43. And for the quote, Elizabeth Vassall Fox Holland, *Elizabeth, Lady Holland to Her Son, 1821–1845,* ed. Giles Fox-Strangeways (London: John Murray, 1946), 182.

76. Bishop, *"Peep into the Past,"* 34–38.

77. Musgrave, *Life in Brighton,* 321.

78. Walvin, *Leisure and Society,* 38–39.

79. Peter Bailey, *Leisure and Class in Victorian England: Rational Recreation and the Contest for Control, 1830–1885* (London: Routledge and Kegan Paul, 1978), 72–79.

80. George Henry Lewes, *Sea-Side Studies at Ilfracombe, Tenby, the Scilly Isles, and Jersey* (Edinburgh: William Blackwood and Sons, 1858), 28.

81. Walvin, *Leisure and Society,* 3–7; Judith Flanders, *Consuming Passions: Leisure and Pleasure in Victorian Britain* (London: HarperPress, 2006), 207–11.

82. Frances Gillespie, *Labor and Politics in England, 1850–1867* (New York: Octagon Books, 1966); R.G. Gammage, *History of the Chartist Movements* (New York: A.M. Kelley, 1962).

83. Liquor could provide men with a stimulant to pass the time. More seriously it helped men endure pain. Walvin, *Leisure and Society,* 33.

84. Cunningham, *Leisure in the Industrial Revolution,* 151–55.

85. David Elliston Allen, *The Naturalist in Britain: A Social History* (London: Allen Lane, 1976), 5–25.

86. As early as 1775, reports of collecting were recorded for Margate. *The Margate Guide: Containing a Particular Account of Margate* (London: printed for T. Caman and F. Newbery, 1775): 19. And the guide for 1780 recorded that "many young ladies" collected seaweed and shells. *New Margate and Ramsgate Guide,* 10.

87. Beth Fowkes Tobin, *The Duchess's Shells: Natural History Collecting in the Age of Cook's Voyages* (New Haven, CT: Yale University Press, 2014).

88. As quoted in Travis, *Rise of the Devon Seaside Resorts,* 168. See also Lynn L. Merrill, *The Romance of Victorian Natural History* (Oxford: Oxford University Press, 1989).

89. Lewes, *Sea-Side Studies.* Collecting also took off in America; see Lady, *A Visit to Nahant: Being a Sequel to The Wonders of the Deep* (New York: General Protestant Episcopal Sunday School Union, 1839), 18–19.

90. Burney, *Journals and Letters,* 11:693–714.

91. Philip Henry Gosse, *Tenby: A Sea-Side Holiday* (London: John Van Voorst, 1856); Gosse, *The Aquarium: An Unveiling of the Wonders of the Deep Sea* (London: John Van Voorst, 1854).

92. Isabella Gifford, *The Marine Botanist: An Introduction to the Study of Algology,* 2nd ed. (London: Darton / Bath: Binns & Goodwin, 1855); Charles Kingsley, *Glaucus; or, the Wonders of the Shore* (Cambridge: Macmillan, 1855).

93. Charlotte Chanter, *Ferny Combes: A Ramble after Ferns in the Glens and Valleys of Devonshire,* 2nd ed. (London: Lovell Reeve, 1856).

94. Simon H. Adamson, *Seaside Piers* (London: Batsford, 1977), 12–13.

95. Adamson, 9–10; Musgrave, *Life in Brighton,* 227–30.

96. Adamson, *Seaside Piers,* 78.

97. Adamson, 100–102.

98. Robert Leach, *The Punch & Judy Show: History, Tradition and Meaning* (London: Batsford, 1985).

99. Robert C. Toll, *Blacking Up: The Minstrel Show in Nineteenth Century America* (New York: Oxford University Press, 1974).

100. For typical reactions to the cacophony, see Jefferies, *Open Air,* 164; Cuthbert Bede, *Mattins and Mutton's; or, The Beauty of Brighton: A Love Story* (London: Sampson Low, 1866), 275–80; Richard Doyle, *Bird's Eye Views of Society* (London: Smith, Elder), 28–31.

101. Jefferies, *Open Air,* 155.

102. Jane Welsh Carlyle, *Letters and Memorials of Jane Welsh Carlyle,* ed. J. A. Froude (London: Charles Scribner's Sons, 1883): 1:228, 3:86.

103. Charles Dickens, *The Tuggs's at Ramsgate* (Philadelphia: Carey, Lee and Blanchard, 1837).

104. John Leighton, *London out of Town, or, The Adventures of the Browns at the Seaside* (London: D. Bogue, 1847). See also Allen Brodie, "The Brown Family Adventure—Seaside Holiday in Kent in the Mid-Nineteenth Century," *Journal of Tourism History* 5, no. 1 (2013): 1–24. There were also the adventures of Mrs. Brown, as related by Arthur Sketchley, as whose foil Mrs. Brown went to various resorts. Arthur Sketchley, *Mrs. Brown at the Sea-Side* (London: George Routledge and Sons, 1868); Sketchley, *Mrs. Brown at Margate* (London: George Routledge and Sons, 1874); Sketchley, *Mrs. Brown at Brighton* (London: George Routledge and Sons, 1875).

105. Charles Keene, *Mr. Punch at the Seaside* (London: Educational Book Co., 1910).

106. The painting was purchased by Queen Victoria and is still in the Royal Collection.

107. The best discussion of the manner in which various European states dealt with the railway is in Wolmar, *Blood, Iron and Gold.*

108. Alice Garner, *A Shifting Shore: Locals, Outsiders, and the Transformation of a French Fishing Town, 1823–2000* (Ithaca, NY: Cornell University Press, 2005), 120–21.

109. James Thomas Flexner, *Inventors in Action: The Story of the Steamboat* (New York: Collier Books, 1962).

110. H. Craig Miner, *A Most Magnificent Machine: America Adopts the Railroad, 1825–1862* (Lawrence: University Press of Kansas, 2010), 74.

111. Richard White, *Railroaded: The Transcontinentals and the Making of Modern America* (New York: W. W. Norton, 2011).

112. Nelson Johnson, *Boardwalk Empire: The Birth, High Times, and Corruption of Atlantic City* (Medford, NJ: Plexus, 2002); Charles E. Funnell, *By the Beautiful Sea: The Rise and High Times of That Great American Resort, Atlantic City* (New Brunswick, NJ: Rutgers University Press, 1983).

113. Cunningham, *Railroads*, 111–27.

114. Cunningham, 180; Richmond Barrett, *Good Old Summer Days: Newport, Narragansett Pier, Saratoga, Long Branch, Bar Harbor* (Boston: Houghton Mifflin, 1952), 240.

115. Harold F. Wilson, *The Story of the Jersey Shore* (Princeton, NJ: Van Nostrand, 1964).

116. Cunningham, *Railroads*, 219.

117. George Howe Colt, *The Big House: A Century in the Life of an American Summer Home* (New York: Scribner, 2003), 47–51.

118. James C. O'Connell, *Becoming Cape Cod: Creating a Seaside Resort* (Hanover, NH: University of New Hampshire Press, 2003), 8–18.

119. Marilyn E. Weigold, *The Long Island Sound: A History of Its People, Places, and Environment* (New York: New York University Press, 2004), 56–61.

120. *The Southampton Season* (1944), East Hampton Public Library, East Hampton, NY; David Goddard, *Colonizing Southampton: The Transformation of a Long Island Community, 1870–1900* (Albany: State University of New York Press, 2011).

121. Edwin Lawrence Godkin, *Reflections and Comments, 1865–1895* (New York: Charles Scribner's Sons, 1895), 295–308.

122. Alexis McCrossen, *Holy Day, Holiday: The American Sunday* (Ithaca, NY: Cornell University Press, 2000), 83.

123. McCrossen, 83–84; Salvini, *Boardwalk Memories*, 33–42.

124. Charles James Apperley, *Nimrod Abroad* (London: Henry Colburn, 1842), 235.

125. Fisher, *Philadelphia Perspective*, 197.

126. Thomas Mann, *Buddenbrooks: The Decline of a Family*, trans. H. T. Lowe-Porter (Harmondsworth: Penguin, 1957), 510.

127. Salvini, *Summer City by the Sea*, 32; Dorwart, *Cape May County*, 90.

128. Joseph E. Garland, *Boston's North Shore: Being an Account of Life among the Noteworthy, Fashionable, Wealthy, Eccentric, and Ordinary, 1823–1890* (Boston: Little, Brown, 1978), 236.

129. Johnson, *Boardwalk Empire*, 15.

130. Dorwart, *Cape May County*, 257; Salvini, *Boardwalk Memories*, 20–31.

CHAPTER 5. CAN A PROPER VICTORIAN BE NUDE?

1. There is a large literature on manliness in the Victorian world. See John Tosh, *A Man's Place: Masculinity and the Middle-Class Home in Victorian England* (New Haven, CT: Yale University Press, 2007). See also Tosh, "What Should History Do with Masculinity? Reflections on Nineteenth-Century Britain," *History Workshop* no. 38 (1994): 179–202; Gail Bederman, *Manliness and Civilization: A Cultural History of Gender and Race in the United States, 1880–1917* (Chicago: University of Chicago Press, 1995); J.A. Mangan and James Walvin, *Manliness and Morality: Middle-Class Masculinity in Britain and America, 1800–1940* (Manchester: Manchester University Press, 1987).

2. Brad Beaven, *Leisure, Citizenship and Working-Class Men in Britain, 1850–1945* (Manchester: Manchester University Press, 2005).

3. Nancy F. Cott, *The Bonds of Womanhood: "Woman's Sphere" in New England, 1780–1835*, 2nd ed. (New Haven, CT: Yale University Press, 1997); Martha H. Patterson, *Beyond the Gibson Girl: Reimagining the American New Woman, 1895–1915* (Urbana: University of Illinois Press, 2005); Barbara Caine, *English Feminism, 1780–1980* (Oxford: Oxford University Press, 1997).

4. "'Off for the Holidays': The Rationale of Recreation," *Cornhill Magazine*, September 1867, 315–22. Neurasthenia had been diagnosed as early as 1829, but it was not until the American George M. Beard used it as a description of the symptoms of fatigue, anxiety, headache, depression, and palpitations, all brought on by stress of urbanization and economic competition, that the term became common. "George Miller Beard," Wikipedia, accessed January 9, 2017.

5. Laura Briggs, "The Rage of Hysteria: 'Overcivilization' and the 'Savage' Woman in Late Nineteenth-Century Obstetrics and Gynecology," *American Quarterly* 52, no. 2 (June 2000): 246–73.

6. For an excellent guide to this process in France, see Philippe Ariès and Georges Duby, *A History of Private Life* (Cambridge, MA: Belknap Press of Harvard University Press, 1987), 4:299–307.

7. Samuel Curwen, *The Journal of Samuel Curwen, Loyalist,* ed. Andrew Oliver, The Loyalist Papers (Cambridge, MA: Harvard University Press, 1972), 1:547, 560.

8. Brown, *Essex People,* 24.

9. A report on this type of misadventure appears in "The Bathing at Ramsgate and Margate," *Observer,* August 25, 1856, 5. The reporter noted that if such nakedness happened in a theater the authorities would arrest the culprits.

10. Spencer Thomson, *Health Resorts of Britain; and How to Profit by Them* (London: Ward & Lock, 1860), 73.

11. William Thornber, *An Historical and Descriptive Account of Blackpool and Its Neighbourhood* (Poulton: for the author by Smith, 1837), 236.

12. In the 1950s when I was a boy learning to swim at the local YMCA, the class was nude.

13. *Journey from London to Scarborough,* 34–35.

14. *Brighton Morning Herald,* August 28, 1807. There are no images of naked men, as opposed to many of women.

15. Anthony Trollope, *North America* (London: Chapman & Hall, 1862), 1:24–25.

16. Francis Kilvert, *Kilvert's Diary: Selections from the Diary of the Rev. Francis Kilvert*, ed. William Plomer (London: Cape, 1938), 2:262.

17. Kilvert, 3:208

18. Kilvert, 2:287.

19. "Seabathing in England and France," *Observer*, August 7, 1864, 6

20. Pasquin, *New Brighton Guide*, 30.

21. As quoted in Travis, *Rise of the Devon Seaside Resorts*, 180.

22. Francis Wey and Valerie Pirie, *A Frenchman Sees the English in the "Fifties"* (London: Sidgwick and Jackson, 1935), 296–99.

23. Wey and Pirie, 299.

24. Much of this controversy is covered in John Travis, "Continuity and Change in English Sea-Bathing, 1730–1900: A Case of Swimming with the Tide," in *Recreation and the Sea*, ed. Stephen Fisher (Exeter: Exeter University Press 1997), 17.

25. Thornber, *Historical and Descriptive Account*, 236.

26. John Heneage Jesse, *George Selwyn and His Contemporaries* (London: Richard Bentley, 1843), 265–66.

27. "Originals," *Observer*, September 14, 1800, 2.

28. "Bathing at Margate," *Illustrated London News*, September 27, 1856, 329.

29. "Seaside Amusements and Seaside Decencies," *Observer*, August 28, 1859, 5.

30. "The Amenities of the Sea Shore," *Observer*, September 4, 1859, 5.

31. "The Bathing at Ramsgate and Margate—English Decencies," *Observer*, August 25, 1856, 5; "The Dog Days, Seaside Amusements," July 27, 1857, 4; "Seaside Amusements and Seaside Decencies," August 28, 1859, 5; "The Amenities and Decencies of Margate," July 30, 1865, 6.

32. Thomson, *Health Resorts of Britain*, 33.

33. *All about Margate and Herne Bay* (London: W. Kent, 1865), 60. Brighton had a by-law in 1865 that every bathing machine had to stock gowns and drawers and that they must be worn. *Observer*, September 17, 1865.

34. "The Amenities and Decencies of Margate," *Observer*, July 30, 1865, 6.

35. As quoted in Travis, *Continuity and Change*, 20.

36. Travis, 17–30.

37. "Seabathing at Margate and Ramsgate," *Observer*, August 4, 1861, 6.

38. William Clarke Ulyat, *Life at the Sea Shore: Where to Go, How to Get There, and How to Enjoy* (Princeton, NJ: McGinness and Runyan, 1880), 39.

39. Travis, *Continuity and Change*, 26–29.

40. James Henry Bennet, *Winter and Spring on the Shores of the Mediterranean*, 5th ed. (London: J. & A. Churchill, 1875), 432.

41. James H. Adams, "Bathing at the Continental Sea-Shore Resorts," *Cosmopolitan*, June 1895, 131–45.

42. Ariès and Duby, *History of Private Life*, 5, 302.

43. Corbin, *Lure of the Sea*, 369.

44. Lapeyre, *Les Bains de Mer*, 32–33.

45. Corbin, *Lure of the Sea*, 278–79.

46. For a brief history of Biarritz, see Pierre Laborde, *Biarritz: Huit Siècles D'histoire, 250 Ans De Bains De Mer,* rev. ed. (Biarritz: Atlantica, 2007).

47. Bennet, *Winter and Spring,* 432.

48. Miller, *Wintering on the Riviera,* 428–30. See also Bennet, *Winter and Spring,* 431–32.

49. Bennet, 432. Bennet would go on to admit that it was "infinitely more decorous and decent than that which is pursued on our own shores."

50. *Harper's New Monthly Magazine* 36 (December 1867–May 1868): 730.

51. *Harper's New Monthly Magazine,* 730.

52. Elinor Glyn, *The Visits of Elizabeth* (London: Duckworth, 1906), 103.

53. Laborde, *Biarritz,* 65.

54. Laborde, 65.

55. Garner, *Shifting Shore,* 105–10.

56. Sasha D. Park, *Tourism and Dictatorship: Europe's Peaceful Invasion of Franco's Spain* (New York: Palgrave, 2006), 23–32, 144; John K. Walton, "Consuming the Beach: Seaside Resorts and Cultures of Tourism in England and Spain from the 1840s to the 1930s," in *Being Elsewhere: Tourism, Consumer Culture and Identity in Modern Europe and North America,* ed. Shelley Baranowski and Ellen Furlough (Ann Arbor: University of Michigan Press, 2001), 272–98.

57. Kemble, *Records of Later Life,* 1:158–60.

58. Kemble, 1:158–60.

59. Kemble, 1:68–69.

60. Fredrika Bremer, *America of the Fifties: Letters of Fredrika Bremer,* ed. Adolph B. Benson (New York: American-Scandinavian Foundation, 1924), 525. She mentions this again in Bremer, *The Homes of the New World: Impressions of America,* trans. Mary Botham Howitt (New York: Harper & Brothers, 1853), 1:234. It was also reported in Frances Milton Trollope, *Domestic Manners of the Americans,* ed. Donald Arthur Smalley (1832; repr., New York: A. A. Knopf, 1949), 273; and Henry Unwin Addington, *Youthful America: Selections from Henry Unwin Addington's Residence in the United States of America, 1822–25,* ed. Bradford Perkins (Berkeley: University of California Press, 1960), 51. Trollope was an English novelist and Addington was the British ambassador. Both of them wrote in the 1820s, so this practice started early.

61. Diary of Sarah Putnam, 10:233, Massachusetts Historical Society.

62. Bremer, *America of the Fifties,* 193–94.

63. Bremer, *Homes of the New World,* 516–17.

64. Fredrika Bremer and Carina Burman, *Brev: Ny FöLjd: Tidigare Ej Samlade Och Tryckta Brev* (Stockholm: Gidlund, 1996), 1:344–45.

65. Bremer, *Homes of the New World,* 513.

66. Bremer, 2, 531.

67. Jefferies, *Open Air,* 165.

68. Jefferies, 152–55.

69. "The Sleepers," Walt Whitman Archive, https://whitmanarchive.org/published/LG/1855/whole.html, accessed September 17, 2020.

70. See Winslow Homer's *Long Branch, New Jersey* (1869), where two young women peer over the cliff at the bathing huts below while a white flag

flies above them indicating it is safe for them to proceed (the painting is at the Museum of Fine Arts, Boston), and the story by G. P. Lathrop on swimming at Newport in *Outing,* September 1883, 102.

71. Stephen M. Frank, *Life with Father: Parenthood and Masculinity in the Nineteenth-Century American North* (Baltimore: Johns Hopkins University Press, 1998); Mark C. Carnes and Clyde Griffen, *Meanings for Manhood: Constructions of Masculinity in Victorian America* (Chicago: University of Chicago Press, 1990); Bederman, *Manliness & Civilization*; Mangan and Walvin, *Manliness and Morality.*

72. Deborah Davis, *Strapless: John Singer Sargent and the Fall of Madame X* (New York: Penguin, 2003).

73. Patricia Cunningham, *Reforming Women's Fashion, 1850–1900: Politics, Health and Art* (Kent, OH: Kent State University Press, 2003), 1–24, 31–74; Frances E. Willard, "Dress Reform in America," *The Arena* 6, no. 3 (August 1892): 325–39; Fischer, *Pantaloons and Power*; Irina Lindsay, *Dressing and Undressing for the Seaside* (Hornchurch, Essex: I. Henry, 1983), 20–27; Rob Schorman, *Selling Style: Clothing and Social Change at the Turn of the Century* (Philadelphia: University of Pennsylvania Press, 2003).

74. Christopher Love, *A Social History of Swimming in England, 1800–1918: Splashing in the Serpentine* (London: Routledge, 2008), 1–18; J. Frost and Benjamin Franklin, *The Art of Swimming: A Series of Practical Instructions, an Original and Progressive Plan* (New York: P. W. Gallaudet, 1818); Thomas Tegg, *The Art of Swimming* (London: by the author, 1824); Archibald Sinclair and William Henry, *Swimming* (Boston: Little, Brown, 1893). The Sinclair and Henry volume went through multiple editions.

75. John Leahy et al., *The Art of Swimming in the Eton Style* (London: Macmillan, 1875).

76. Charles Sprawson, *Haunts of the Black Masseur: The Swimmer as Hero* (London: Jonathan Cape, 1992), 36–44.

77. *Illustrated London News* carried a story about Brill's Swimming Baths for Ladies with teachers present, which was the only such facility in England. August 17, 1861, 163.

78. "Scene at Ramsgate," *Observer,* October 16, 1854.

79. "The Art of Swimming," *Godey's Ladies' Magazine,* June 1860, 493–97.

80. "A Bathing Costume," *Harper's Weekly,* July 28, 1866, 477; "Great Reforms Made in Bathing Dresses," *Godey's Lady's Book and Magazine,* July 1871, 43–45.

81. Jefferies, *Open Air,* 51.

82. "Newport," *New York Times,* June 21, 1880.

83. "Sunday at Long Branch," *New York Times,* July 10, 1877.

84. Joseph W. Smith, *Gleanings from the Sea* (Andover, MA: by the author, 1887), 111.

85. Charles N. Taintor, *American Seaside Resorts: A Handbook for Health and Pleasure* (New York: Taintor, Merrill, 1877), 107–10.

86. Harold F. Wilson, *The Story of the Jersey Shore* (Princeton, NJ: Van Nostrand, 1964), 61–62.

CHAPTER 6. ENTERTAINMENT COMES FRONT AND CENTER

1. John H. Packard, *Sea-Air and Sea-Bathing* (Philadelphia: P. Blakiston, 1880). There is a similar publication by Charles Parsons published in London three years prior with much the same advice. Parsons, *Sea Air and Sea-Bathing: Their Influence on Health* (London: J. & A. Churchill, 1877).

2. Frank J. Sprague, *Report on the Exhibits at the Chrystal Palace Electrical Exhibition* (Washington, DC: Government Printing Office, 1883); Norm Bolotin and Christine Laing, *The World's Columbian Exposition: The Chicago World's Fair of 1893* (Washington, DC: Preservation Press, 1992).

3. Jill Jonnes, *Empires of Light: Edison, Tesla, Westinghouse, and the Race to Electrify the World* (New York: Random House, 2003).

4. Jurgen Osterhammel, *The Transformation of the World: A Global History of the Nineteenth Century,* trans. Patrick Camiller (Princeton, NJ: Princeton University Press, 2014), 761–78.

5. Walton, *English Seaside Resort,* 71.

6. Whitman would write, "At that time [Coney Island] was a long, bare, unfrequented shore, which I had to myself." This was in 1850. Walt Whitman, "Specimen Days," in *The Complete Prose Works of Walt Whitman,* ed. Richard M Bucke et al. (New York: G.P. Putnam's Sons, 1902), 1:167–68. See also Michael Immerso, *Coney Island: The People's Playground* (New Brunswick, NJ: Rutgers University Press, 2002), 7, 20.

7. Edd Applegate, *The Rise of Advertising in the United States: A History of Innovation to 1960* (Lanham, MD: Scarecrow Press, 2012); T.{ths}R. Nevett, *Advertising in Britain: A History* (London: Heinemann on behalf of the History of Advertising Trust, 1982).

8. Christine L. Corton, *London Fog: The Biography* (Cambridge, MA: Harvard University Press, 2015).

9. See the posh ads in Fred Gray, *Designing the Seaside: Architecture, Society and Nature* (London: Reaktion, 2006), 52, 67, 183, 186, 258.

10. Funnell, *By the Beautiful Sea,* 33–35.

11. By far the best account of landladies is Walton, *Blackpool Landlady.*

12. A Cynic, "Vacations," *Cornhill Magazine,* August 1869, 115–20.

13. Betjeman, *Collected Poems,* 146–54.

14. Walton, *Blackpool Landlady.*

15. *Seaside Watering Places: Being a Guide to Strangers in Search of a Suitable Place in Which to Spend Their Holidays* (London: "The Bazaar" Office, 1876), 105–6.

16. Henry H. Becker, *Holiday Haunts by Cliffside and Riverside, etc.* (London: Remington, 1884), 5–6.

17. Granville, *Spas of England,* 2:526.

18. Mann, *Buddenbrooks,* 510.

19. As quoted in Travis, *Rise of the Devon Seaside Resorts,* 153.

20. "Jekyll Island Club," Wikipedia, accessed July 16, 2018.

21. Richard D. Starnes, *Southern Journeys: Tourism, History, and Culture in the Modern South* (Tuscaloosa: University of Alabama Press, 2003), 154–76. These clubs were winter resorts.

22. David Leon Chandler, *Henry Flagler: The Astonishing Life and Times of the Visionary Robber Baron Who Founded Florida* (New York: Macmillan, 1986).

23. Leslee F. Keys, *Hotel Ponce De Leon: The Rise, Fall, and Rebirth of Flagler's Gilded Age Palace* (Gainesville: University of Florida Press, 2015).

24. Les Standiford, *Last Train to Paradise* (New York: Three Rivers Press, 2002).

25. Patrick Hennessey, *Hotel Del Coronado: The First Hundred Years,* collectors' ed. (Coronado, CA: Produced for the Hotel del Coronado by Bullock & Associates, 1987); Marcie Buckley, *The Crown City's Brightest Gem: A History of the Hotel Del Coronado, Coronado, California* (Coronado, CA: Hotel Del Coronado, 1970).

26. Christine Stansell, *City of Women: Sex and Class in New York, 1789–1860* (New York: Knopf, 1986); Kathy Lee Peiss, *Cheap Amusements: Working Women and Leisure in Turn-of-the-Century New York* (Philadelphia: Temple University Press, 1986), 142–45.

27. Judith Flanders, *Consuming Passions: Leisure and Pleasure in Victorian Britain* (London: HarperPress, 2006); Douglas Gilbert, *American Vaudeville, Its Life and Times* (New York: Dover, 1963); Brooks McNamara, *The New York Concert Saloon: The Devil's Own Nights* (Cambridge: Cambridge University Press, 2002); Peter Jelavich, *Berlin Cabaret* (Cambridge, MA: Harvard University Press, 1993); Dagmar Kift, *The Victorian Music Hall: Culture, Class and Conflict* (Cambridge: Cambridge University Press, 1996), 17–35, 36–54; Peter Bailey, *Music Hall: The Business of Pleasure* (Philadelphia: Open University Press, 1986).

28. Robert Clyde Allen, *Horrible Prettiness: Burlesque and American Culture* (Chapel Hill: University of North Carolina Press, 1991), 5.

29. James J. Nott, *Going to the Palais: A Social and Cultural History of Dancing and Dance Halls in Britain, 1918–1960* (Oxford: Oxford University Press, 2015); Nott, *Music for the People: Popular Music and Dance in Interwar Britain* (Oxford: Oxford University Press, 2002); P. J. S. Richardson, *History of English Ballroom Dancing* (London: Jenkins, 1948).

30. Coney Island was described as having "few attractions" as late as 1866. "A Cool Resort in Hot Weather," *New York Times,* July 10, 1866. See also the images in Robin Jaffee Frank et al., *Coney Island: Visions of an American Dreamland* (New Haven, CT: Yale University Press, 2015), 10, 13, 14, 15, 16.

31. John F. Kasson, *Amusing the Million: Coney Island at the Turn of the Century* (New York: Hill & Wang, 1978); 29–36; Immerso, *Coney Island,* 24–31.

32. "Three Card Monte," *Harper's Weekly,* September 8, 1866, 572. There is a very nice image accompanying this article of the activity on the beach.

33. As quoted in Woody Register, *The Kid of Coney Island: Fred Thompson and the Rise of American Amusements* (Oxford: Oxford University Press, 2001), 91.

34. "Coney Island," *Harper's Weekly,* August 10, 1878, 630–31. See also Immerso, *Coney Island;* Jon Sterngass, *First Resorts: Pursuing Pleasure at Saratoga*

Springs, Newport, & Coney Island (Baltimore: Johns Hopkins University Press, 2001); Kasson, *Amusing the Million;* Register, *Kid of Coney Island.*

35. See the many images of the delights in Frank et al., *Coney Island,* 31–76.

36. Immerso, *Coney Island,* 38–39.

37. Immerso, 88–95.

38. William F. Mangels, *The Outdoor Amusement Industry from Earliest Times to the Present* (New York: Vantage Press, 1952), 81–92; Immerso, *Coney Island,* 88–95.

39. Norman D. Anderson, *Ferris Wheels: An Illustrated History* (Bowling Green, OH: Bowling Green State University Popular Press, 1992).

40. David Coke and Alan Borg, *Vauxhall Gardens: A History* (New Haven, CT: Yale University Press, 2011).

41. "Topics of the Day," *The Observer,* September 22, 1878.

42. Immerso, *Coney Island,* 53–56.

43. As quoted in Frank et al., *Coney Island,* 80.

44. There was a long tradition of producing spectacles. Even eighteenth-century pleasure gardens in London featured them. Lee Jackson, *Palaces of Pleasure: From Music Halls to the Seaside to Football, How the Victorians Invented Mass Entertainment* (New Haven, CT: Yale University Press, 2019), 121–46. See also, Register, *Kid of Coney Island,* 90–91; Immerso, *Coney Island,* 60–68.

45. Immerso, *Coney Island,* 68–72.

46. Claire Prentice, *The Lost Tribe of Coney Island: Headhunters, Luna Park, and the Man Who Pulled Off the Spectacle of the Century* (Boston: New Harvest, 2014).

47. This phenomenon is noted in much of the scholarship on Coney Island. See Frank et al., *Coney Island,* 79–84; Kasson, *Amusing the Million,* 39–49, 57–61; Immerso, *Coney Island,* 133.

48. As quoted in Nelson Johnson, *Boardwalk Empire: The Birth, High Times, and Corruption of Atlantic City* (Medford, NJ: Plexus Pub., 2002), 28.

49. Funnell, *By the Beautiful Sea,* 20–24.

50. Johnson, *Boardwalk Empire,* 26–29.

51. Johnson, 55–79.

52. The fire of 1869 destroyed two blocks and three hotels and was followed in 1878 with a fire that burned thirty-five acres, seven hotels, cottages, boarding houses, and even the changing shacks on the beach. This setback meant that Atlantic City would be the dominant resort as Cape May could not rebuild and buy all the new rides that were making Atlantic City so popular. Salvini, *Summer City by the Sea,* 37–39, 47–53.

53. Immerso, *Coney Island,* 83–86.

54. Helen C. Pike, *Asbury Park's Glory Days: The Story of an American Resort* (New Brunswick, NJ: Rutgers University Press, 2005), 78; Salvini, *Summer City by the Sea,* 105–110.

55. Jackson, *Palaces of Pleasure,* 121–46.

56. John K. Walton, *Riding on Rainbows: Blackpool Pleasure Beach and Its Place in British Popular Culture* (St. Albans: Skelter Publishing, 2007).

57. Revere Beach in Massachusetts was an exception as it tried to mimic the new amusement parks.

58. Michael April Nelson, *Queen Victoria and the Discovery of the Riviera* (London: I. B. Tauris, 2001). This event is reputed to be the inspiration for the Rose Parade in Pasadena, California.

59. What Asbury started was soon mimicked by Wildwood and Ocean City. Salvini, *Boardwalk Memories*, 22, 156, 136; Grace L. Meigs, "Other Factors in Infant Mortality than the Milk Supply and Their Control," *American Journal of Public Health* 6, no. 8 (August 1916): 851.

60. Frank et al., *Coney Island*, 40–41.

61. Clare Hargreaves, *Normandy* (London: Cadogan Guides, 2004), 221–22.

62. Vladimir Nabokov, *Speak Memory: An Autobiography Revisited* (New York: Knopf, 1999), 112–13.

63. Christopher Thornton, *Clacton, Walton and Frinton: North-East Essex Seaside Resorts* (London: Boydell and Brewer, 2012), 171–81.

64. Wilson, *Story of the Jersey Shore*, 50.

65. Salvini, *Boardwalk Memories*, 9–11.

66. Immerso, *Coney Island*, 46–47.

67. Maud Howe Elliott, *This Was My Newport* (Cambridge, MA: The Mythology Company, A. M. Jones, 1944), 53, 222.

68. "Newport Reveries: Day Dreams along the Beach," *New York Times*, August 8, 1875.

69. Eric Hornberger, *Mrs. Astor's New York: Money and Social Power in the Gilded Age* (New Haven, CT: Yale University Press, 2002). See also Ward McAllister, *Society as I Have Found it* (New York: Cassell, 1890).

70. John King Van Rensselaer and Frederic Franklyn Van de Water, *The Social Ladder* (New York: H. Holt, 1924), 228. The Rensselaers were an old Dutch family with lots of breeding but no longer wealthy.

71. Greg King, *A Season of Splendor: The Court of Mrs. Astor in Gilded Age New York* (Hoboken, NJ: John Wiley & Sons, Inc., 2009), 336.

72. Roberto Schezen, Jane Mulvagh, and Mark A. Weber, *Newport Houses* (New York: Rizzoli, 1989).

73. Francis H. Hardy, "Seaside Life in America," *Cornhill Magazine*, November 1896, 618.

74. *Harper's Weekly*, September 12, 1857, 584–85.

75. Edith Wharton, *A Backward Glance* (New York: D. Appleton-Century, 1934), 82–85. Wharton also depicted the social scene in New York in her novel *The Age of Innocence* (New York: D. Appleton, 1920).

76. Van Rensselaer and Van de Water, *Social Ladder*, 241–42; Schezen, Mulvagh, and Weber, *Newport Houses*, 92; King, *Season of Splendor*, 336.

77. Wharton, *Backward Glance*, 82–85.

78. The inequality was as bad as that of the early twenty-first century in that 10 percent of the population had three-quarters of the property. George B. Tindall and David Shi, *America, A Narrative History* (New York: W. W. Norton, 2012); United States Census Office, *Eleventh Census* (1892), 2. The latter would report that the best wage for a skilled worker was $564 per year.

79. Van Rensselaer and Van de Water, *Social Ladder*, 277–78. See also Goddard, *Colonizing Southampton*.

CHAPTER 7. THE MODERN WORLD INTRUDES

1. By the 1920s, there were 150 resorts in England and Wales. Walton, *British Seaside*, 27–49.

2. Dag Hunstad, "A 'Norwegian Riviera' in the Making: The Development of Coastal Tourism and Recreation in Southern Norway in the Interwar Period," *Journal of Tourist History* 3, no. 2 (2011): 109–28.

3. "Mondello," Wikipedia, accessed July 10, 2017.

4. "Cascais and Estoril," Wikipedia, accessed September 10, 2019.

5. "Mar del Plata," "Pinamar," and "Carilo," Wikipedia, accessed March 12, 2018.

6. Douglas Booth, *Australian Beach Cultures: The History of Sun, Sand, and Surf* (London: Frank Cass, 2001), 25–30.

7. Booth, 25–32, quotation on 32.

8. Booth, 160.

9. This was the Bengali Nagpur Railway Hotel, and it was a friend, Stanley Farrar, who had the experience of the personal guard. See the sites www .chanakyabnrpuni.com/pic gal.bhp, www.jagananthtemplepuri, and www.India .com/travel/puri, all accessed March 13, 2018.

10. See "Kovalam," Wikipedia, accessed June 15, 2017. Halcyon Castle is now a five-star hotel.

11. "Hua Hin District," Wikipedia, accessed June 15, 2017.

12. Kendall H. Brown et al., *Taisho Chic: Japanese Modernity, Nostalgia and Deco* (Honolulu: Honolulu Academy of Arts, 2001), 44–45.

13. This section is derived from Deniz Hamamindan, *Istanbul's Seaside Leisure: Nostalgia from Sea Baths to Beaches* (Istanbul: Pera Museum, 2018).

14. As quoted in J. A. R. Pimlott, *The Englishman's Holiday: A Social History* (1947; repr., Hassocks: Harvester Press, 1976), 220, 211–22.

15. James Walvin, *Beside the Seaside: A Social History of the Popular Seaside Holiday* (London: Allen Lane, 1978), 99–107, 129.

16. U.S. Bureau of Labor Statistics, *Beyond the Numbers* 2, no. 18 (2013).

17. "The British Coast and Its Holiday Resorts," *The Town Planning Review* 16, no. 4 (December 1935): 265–70.

18. *Vogue*, 1929, and August 15, 1917, 47. It should be pointed out that Newport was not that backward, for as early as 1908 some fashionable women were fussing about tanning. "Newport to War on Smoking by Women," *New York Times*, May 3, 1908.

19. Kerry Segrave, *Suntanning in 20th Century America* (Jefferson, NC: McFarland, 2005), 12–27; Catherine Cocks, *Tropical Whites: The Rise of the Tourist South in the Americas* (Philadelphia: University of Pennsylvania Press, 2013), 114–19; John Weightman, "The Solar Revolution: Reflections on a Theme in French Literature," *Encounter* 35, no. 6 (December 1970): 9–18.

20. Weightman, 9–11.

21. Segrave, *Suntanning in 20th Century America*, 12–26.

22. Segrave, 9–11.

23. Cocks, *Tropical Whites*, 116–17.

24. Patricia A. Cunningham, *Reforming Women's Fashion, 1850–1920: Politics, Health, and Art* (Kent, OH: Kent State University Press, 2003), 1–24.

25. "Girls Must Wear Stockings," *New York Times*, August 14, 1912; "Police Shoo Girl Bathers," *New York Times*, August 11, 1912.

26. This was in 1912. Booth, *Australian Beach Cultures*, 34.

27. Lena Lencek and Gideon Bosker, *Making Waves: Swimsuits and the Undressing of America* (San Francisco: Chronicle Books, 1989), 33–36.

28. "How Much of This Do You Want Your Daughter to Share?," *Ladies Home Journal*, August 1913.

29. Lencek and Bosker, *Making Waves*, 36; Cunningham, *Reforming Women's Fashion*; Lindsay, *Dressing and Undressing*.

30. Vicki Gold Levi et al., *Atlantic City, 125 Years of Ocean Madness: Starring Miss America, Mr. Peanut, Lucy the Elephant, the High Diving Horse, and Four Generations of Americans Cutting Loose* (New York: C. N. Potter, 1979), 92–93.

31. Gold et al., 38; "Strict Rules for Bathers," *New York Times*, June 26, 1912. See also Wilson, *Story of the Jersey Shore*, 106.

32. Lencek and Baker, *Making Waves*, 47–55; websites for Cole, Catalina, and Jantzen, accessed August 2, 2017. Jantzen has the best archive of images of suits as they evolved.

33. Levi et al., *Atlantic City*. It was 1940 before Atlantic City repealed an ordinance making male tops mandatory. Levi et al., 93.

34. Los Angeles City Archives, Petitions 1929, file #5500.

35. The first Tarzan movie was in 1932.

36. Elinor Glyn, *The Visits of Elizabeth* (London: Duckworth & Co., 1906), 140–42.

37. As quoted in Lencek and Baker, *Making Waves*, 26.

38. *Santa Monica Evening Outlook*, August 10, 1916. There were many articles about the Beach bathing suit issue, beginning on June 27, 1912. They would continue to be mostly front page items till 1919.

39. "Judge King Rules on Beach Ordinance," *Santa Monica Evening Outlook*, July 23, 1919.

40. "Proper Tanning Methods," *Los Angeles Times*, July 18, 1926.

41. Smithers to the City Council, Los Angeles City Archives, Petitions 1927, vol. 1981, file no. 4.

42. Los Angeles City Archives, petitions 1932, vol. 2672, file no. 2198.

43. Letter from Eugene Kelley, Los Angeles City Archives, petitions 1932, vol. 2672, file no. 2198.

44. Kathryn Ferry, *The British Seaside Holiday* (Oxford: Shire, 2009), 65–67.

45. The pageant was denounced by the righteous but still survived year after year. Tom Moran and Tom Sewell, *Fantasy by the Sea: A Visual History of the American Venice* (Culver City, CA: Peace Press, 1979), 60.

46. "Beach Nudity Pulpit Target," *Los Angeles Times*, May 20, 1929.

47. The Pageant began in 1921. Wilson, *Story of the Jersey Shore*, 104.

48. "Beach Nudity Pulpit Target."

49. 'Miss Great Britain," Wikipedia, accessed April 16, 2018.

50. Clifford Musgrave, *Life in Brighton: From the Earliest Times to the Present* (London: Faber, 1970), 58–59, 203–6.

51. *Illustrated London News,* May 31, 1874, and July 17, 1875, for the opening of baths at Paddington and Charing Cross. See also Jeff Wiltse, *Contested Waters: A Social History of Swimming Pools in America* (Chapel Hill: University of North Carolina Press, 2007), 19–23.

52. Liz Ohanesian, "The Forgotten Fight for Civil Rights at San Francisco's Sutro Baths," KCET California Coastal Trail, July 12, 2017.

53. Gray, *Designing the Seaside,* 177–95.

54. "Hotels Offer Extreme Extras," *Los Angeles Times,* May 19, 2014; "Tan Like a Pro," *Sunset Magazine,* November 2011, 36.

55. Gray, *Designing the Seaside,* 181.

56. Gray, 184.

57. Gray, 189–94.

58. Niels Finson won the Nobel Prize in 1903 for his work showing how sunlight killed certain kinds of bacteria. The individuals pushing nudity and sunlight were men such as Hans Suren, whose *Der Mensch and die Sonne* sold 250,000 copies in 1924. Adolf Koch was also an advocate for sunshine, but he is more noted for creating a number of schools that taught about nudism.

59. Walt Whitman, "A Sun-Bath—Nakedness," in *Complete Prose Works of Walt Whitman,* ed. Richard M Bucke et al. (New York: G.P. Putnam's Sons, 1902), 1:182–85.

60. Whitman, 4:167–68, 182–85.

61. John A. Williams, *Turning to Nature in Germany: Hiking, Nudism and Conservation, 1900–1940* (Stanford, CA: Stanford University Press, 2007), 18, 23–66; Stephen L. Harp, *Au Naturel: Naturism, Nudism and Tourism in Twentieth Century France* (Baton Rouge: Louisiana State University Press, 2014). There are now reports that naturism is on the decline in Germany. Kate Connolly, "The Naked Truth: Is Nudism Dying Out in Germany?," *The Guardian,* September 8, 2019.

62. See Harp, *Au Naturel;* Karl Eric Toepfer, *Empire of Ecstasy: Nudity and Movement in German Body Culture, 1910–1935* (Berkeley: University of California Press, 1997).

63. Michael Hau, *The Cult of Health and Beauty in Germany: A Social History, 1890–1930* (Chicago: University of Chicago Press, 2003).

64. Harp, *Au Naturel,* 41–48.

65. Frances Merrill and Mason Merrill, *Nudism Comes to America* (New York: A.A. Knopf, 1932); Jan Gay, *On Going Naked* (Garden City, NY: Garden City Publishing, 1932); Hugh C. Lester, *Godiva Rides Again: Social Nudism in America* (New York: Vintage, 1968); Brian Hoffman, *Naked: A Cultural History of Nudism* (New York: New York University Press, 2015).

66. Fox v. State of Washington, 236 U.S. 273 (1915).

67. Leon Elder, *Free Beaches: A Phenomenon of the California Coast* (Santa Barbara: Capra Press, 1974).

68. British Naturism, www.bn.org.uk, accessed June 20, 2017.

69. S.T. Anderson, *Coney Island and the Jews* (New York: G.W. Carleton, 1879).

70. Richard White, *The Republic for Which It Stands: The United States during Reconstruction and the Gilded Age, 1865–1896* (New York: Oxford

University Press, 2017), 725; Tracy J. Revels, *Sunshine Paradise: A History of Florida Tourism* (Gainesville: University Press of Florida, 2011), 74–75.

71. Myra Beth Young Armstead, *"Lord, Please Don't Take Me in August"*: *African Americans in Newport and Saratoga Springs, 1870–1930* (Urbana: University of Illinois Press, 1999).

72. Nelson Johnson, *Boardwalk Empire: The Birth, High Times, and Corruption of Atlantic City* (Medford, NJ: Plexus, 2002), 35–53; Johnson, *The Northside: African Americans and the Creation of Atlantic City* (Medford, NJ: Plexus, 2011).

73. Armstead, *"Lord, Please Don't Take Me in August,"* 17–18, 73–75; Andrew W. Kahrl, *The Land Was Ours: African American Beaches from Jim Crow to the Sunbelt South* (Cambridge, MA: Harvard University Press, 2012), 90–92.

74. Revels, *Sunshine Paradise,* 73–75; Russ Rymer, *American Beach: A Saga of Race, Wealth, and Memory* (New York: HarperCollins, 1998).

75. The *California Eagle,* a Black-run newspaper, carried full coverage of the club, its activities, and its demise. See August 21 and 28, 1925, and January 22, 1926. See also Lawrence B. De Graaf, "The City of Black Angeles: The Emergence of the Los Angeles Ghetto, 1880–1930," *Pacific Historical Review* 39, no. 3 (August 1970): 323–52.

76. *California Eagle,* July 8, August 5, and August 19, 1927; Jan Dennis, *A Walk beside the Sea: A History of Manhattan Beach* (Manhattan Beach, CA: Janstan Studio, 1987), 105–9. The City of Manhattan Beach finally honored Charles and Willa Bruce, who created the beach, by naming a park after them. "Erasing a Line Drawn in the Sand," *Los Angeles Times,* March 19, 2007.

77. Alison Rose Jefferson, "African American Leisure Space in Santa Monica: The Beach Sometimes Known as the 'Inkwell,' 1900–1960," *Southern California Quarterly* 91 (Summer 2009): 155–89; *Los Angeles Times,* September 15, 2012.

78. Marsha Dean Phelts, *An American Beach for African Americans* (Gainesville: University Press of Florida, 1997), 176–78; Kahrl, *The Land Was Ours,* 252–58.

79. Walton, *British Seaside,* 77–82.

80. Ferry, *British Seaside Holiday,* 15–17.

81. Walton, *British Seaside,* 132–34.

82. John House, *Impressionists by the Sea* (London: Royal Academy of Arts, 2007), 123–36 (for Boudin). One of Monet's paintings at the beach in Trouville actually has sand embedded in the paint. David Bomford et al., *Impressionism* (London: National Gallery, in association with Yale University Press, 1990), 129–30.

83. Elizabeth Brayer, *George Eastman: A Biography* (Baltimore: Johns Hopkins University Press, 1996); David Lindsay, *The Wizard of Photography,* for *The American Experience* on PBS, online.

84. Calvin Tomkins, *Living Well Is the Best Revenge* (New York: Viking Press, 1971), 33.

85. Lindsay, *Wizard of Photography.*

86. Frank Staff, *The Picture Postcard & Its Origins* (London: Lutterworth, 1966).

87. Many of these early films are available on YouTube.

88. Rob King, *The Fun Factory: The Keystone Film Company and the Emergence of Mass Culture* (Berkeley: University of California Press, 2009); Kalton Lahue, *Mack Sennett's Keystone, the Man, the Myth, the Comedies* (South Brunswick, NJ: J.S. Barnes, 1971).

89. "Hindle Wakes," Wikipedia, accessed March 21, 2018.

90. Jean-Didier Urbain, *At the Beach* (Minneapolis: University of Minnesota Press, 2003), 318–19.

91. Among the chief beneficiaries of the new sunscreen were American service personnel in the South Pacific. Segrave, *Suntanning in 20th Century America,* 74–78.

92. Janet Wallach, *Chanel: Her Style and Her Life* (New York: Nan A. Talese, 1998), 80.

93. Wilson, *Story of the Jersey Shore,* 61–62.

94. Mike Capuzzo, *Close to Shore: The Terrifying Shark Attacks of 1916* (New York: Broadway Books, 2001).

95. Samantha Schmidt, "100 Years Later, Memories of Fatal Shark Attacks Linger," *New York Times,* July 11, 2016.

96. For a number of these images, see Frank et al., *Coney Island,* 78–106.

97. For the impact on the British aristocracy, see David Cannadine, *The Decline and Fall of the British Aristocracy* (New Haven, CT: Yale University Press, 1990).

98. Natasha Urosevic, "The Brijuni Island—Recreating Paradise: Media Representations of an Elite Mediterranean Resort in the First Tourist Magazines," *Journal of Tourism History* 6, nos. 2–3 (2014): 122–38.

99. François Bédarida, *A Social History of England, 1851–1990,* trans. A.S. Forster and Geoffrey Hodgkinson (London: Routledge, 1990), 291.

100. Diary of Kathleen Isherwood, October to November 1910. She describes the beach as barricaded and guarded. The big hotels were particularly interested in preserving their beachfronts. Huntington Library, Isherwood MS616.

101. In her account of the imperial entourage of which she was a member, Nellie Hammond Ryan reports, "All the smart world from many European countries was to be seen daily." Ryan, *My Years at the Austrian Court* (London: John Lane, 1916), 262–63. For the changing scene, see Robin Saikia, *The Venice Lido: A Blue Guide Travel Monograph* (London: Somerset Books, 2011). Of all the writers who visited the Lido, Thomas Mann perhaps wrote the finest work, *Death in Venice* (New York: Knopf, 1925), later made into a memorable movie.

102. Amanda Vaill, *Everybody Was So Young: Gerald and Sara Murphy, a Lost Generation Love Story* (Boston: Houghton Mifflin Co, 1998); Patrick Howarth, *When the Riviera Was Ours* (London: Century, 1988).

103. Tomkins, *Living Well Is the Best Revenge,* 27–33.

104. Cyril Connolly, *The Rock Pool* (Oxford: Oxford University Press, 1981). For instance, the hero does not like the new fashion of beach pajamas. Connolly, 24–25.

105. Agatha Christie, *The Mystery of the Blue Train* (London: Collins, 1928).

106. S.L. Grigoriev and Vera Bowen, *The Diaghilev Ballet, 1909–1929* (London: Penguin Books, 1960), 195–200.

107. Most of them are listed in the chapter "Starshine" in Levi et al., *Atlantic City*, 119–51.

108. Ralph G. Giordano, *Satan in the Dance Hall: Rev. John Roach Straton, Social Dancing, and Morality in 1920s New York City* (Lanham, MD: Scarecrow Press, 2008); Nott, *Going to the Palais*.

109. Rex North, *The Butlin Story* (London: Jarrolds, 1962); Ferry, *British Seaside Holiday*, 56–58.

110. For a cynical account of the Butlin experience, see "Notes of a Visit to Butlin's Holiday Camp on Clacton on Sea," in Pimlott, *Englishman's Holiday*, 276–83.

111. Hasso Spode, "Fordism, Mass Tourism and the Third Reich: The 'Strength through Joy' Seaside Resort as an Index Fossil," *Journal of Social History* 38, no. 1 (2004): 127–35; "Prora," Wikipedia, accessed September 20, 2017; Shelley Baranowski, *Strength through Joy: Consumerism and Mass Tourism in the Third Reich* (Cambridge: Cambridge University Press, 2007).

112. *Travel*, January/February 2017, 40.

113. "Our History," Revere Beach.com, accessed September 10, 2020.

114. Edward Nazarro, *Wonderland, Revere Beach's Mystic City by the Sea* (Melrose, MA, 1983).

115. Lawrence Kaplan and Carol P. Kaplan, *Between Ocean and City: The Transformation of Rockaway, New York* (New York: Columbia University Press, 2003), 13–16.

CHAPTER 8. BEACH RESORTS BECOME A CULTURAL PHENOMENON

1. On the coast of Essex, for instance, the resorts around Clacton were used to house refugees from London, and then the military moved almost everyone away from the coast and blew up the pier to deny it to the Germans. The nearby Butlins Camp was used to house enemy aliens. Thornton, *Clacton, Walton and Frinton*, 171–81.

2. Walton, *British Seaside*, 107, 113–14.

3. John K. Walton and James Walvin, *Leisure in Britain, 1780–1939* (Manchester: Manchester University Press, 1983).

4. U.S. Bureau of Labor Statistics, *Beyond the Numbers* 2, no. 18 (2013).

5. Julian Demetriadi, "The Golden Years: English Seaside Resorts, 1950–1974," in *The Rise and Fall of British Coastal Resorts: Cultural and Economic Perspectives*, ed. Gareth Shaw and Allan M. Williams (London: Mansell, 1997), 61–63.

6. Walton, *British Seaside*, 195–98.

7. Chris Cooper, "Parameters and Indicators of the Decline of the British Seaside Resort," in Shaw and Williams, eds., *Rise and Fall of British Coastal Resorts*, 79–98.

8. Cape May was designated a National Historic Landmark in 1976 in recognition of its fine collection of Victorian cottages. Salvini, *Boardwalk Memories*, 174–75.

9. David Shaftel, "A Plot Twist Worthy of Dickens," *New York Times,* June 29, 2014.

10. *New York Times,* August 18, 2013.

11. Walton, *British Seaside,* 161. If Brighton is the gay capital of the South, Blackpool is the gay capital of the North.

12. Resorts that became commuting centers were Brighton, Southend, Blackpool, Hove, Southport, Worthing, and Bournemouth. John K. Walton, "Seaside Resorts of England and Wales, 1900–1950: Growth, Diffusion, and the Emergence of New Forms of Coastal Tourism," in *The Rise and Fall of British Coastal Resorts: Cultural and Economic Perspectives*, ed. Gareth Shaw and Allan M. Williams (London: Mansell, 1997), 39.

13. Gareth Shaw and Allan M. Williams, "The Private Sector: Tourism Entrepreneurship—A Constraint or Resource?," in Shaw and Williams, eds., *Rise and Fall of British Coastal Resorts,* 126–28.

14. Jim Gavell, "Minister Raises Prospect of a Revival," *Blackpool Gazette,* July 2, 2019. Blackpool has invested about $588 million in modernizing the sea front for tourists and keeping its conference visitors happy. Steven Erlanger, "A British Resort Town Sees New Life, Post-Brexit," *New York Times,* August 22, 2016. The Illuminations have been copied elsewhere as the West Country Carnival, a parade of large vehicles with electric lighting does a circuit of western resorts in the fall. "West Country Carnival," Wikipedia, accessed June 12, 1917.

15. Paul Theroux, *The Kingdom by the Sea: A Journey around the Coast of Great Britain* (Harmondsworth: Penguin, 1984); Bill Bryson, *The Road to Little Bubbling: Adventures of an American in Britain* (New York: Doubletree, 2015).

16. Theroux, *Kingdom by the Sea,* 215–16.

17. Walton, *British Seaside,* 195–99.

18. Frank et al., *Coney Island,* 260–63.

19. Charles Graves, *And the Greeks* (New York: R.M. McBride, 1931), 170–76.

20. Laborde, *Biarritz,* 122–26.

21. Compared to Las Vegas, Atlantic City relies too much on gambling revenues: 71.5 percent, as opposed to 35 percent in Las Vegas, with the remainder of their revenue from food, rooms, etc. One after the other, the casinos have fallen into bankruptcy. Charles V. Bagli, "Atlantic City Strives to Rise as Casinos Fall," *New York Times,* July 15, 2014; Salvini, *Boardwalk Memories,* 121; Carl G. Braunlich, "Lessons from the Atlantic City Casino Experience," *Journal of Travel Research* 34, no. 3 (1996): 46–56.

22. Levi et al., *Atlantic City,* 201–8; Johnson, *Boardwalk Empire;* "Thousands Out of Work in Atlantic City as Big Casinos Shut Down," *Atlantic City News Net,* September 1, 2014.

23. Salvini, *Boardwalk Memories,* 150–59.

24. *New York Times,* August 1, 2015, and July 10, 2016.

25. Sasha D. Pack, *Tourism and Dictatorship: Europe's Peaceful Invasion of Franco's Spain* (New York: Palgrave Macmillan, 2006), 23–31; Walton, "Consuming the Beach."

26. Pack, *Tourism and Dictatorship,* 39–51.

27. John Gill, *Andalucía: A Cultural History* (Oxford: Signal Books, 2008).

28. Pack, *Tourism and Dictatorship*, 91.

29. Thomas Kaiserfeld, "From Sightseeing to Sunbathing: Changing Tradition in Swedish Package Tours; From Edification by Bus to Relaxation by Airplane in the 1950s and 60s," *Journal of Tourism History* 2, no. 3 (2010): 149–63; Christopher M. Klopper, "The Breakthrough of the Package Tour in Germany after 1945," *Journal of Tourism History* 1, no. 1 (2009): 67–92.

30. Jules Siegl, *Cancun Users Guide* (Cancun: The Communications Company, 2005), 68–71. The first hotel opened in 1974.

31. "Sharm El Sheikh," Wikipedia, accessed June 22, 2017.

32. That is the beach at Naulholsvik near Reykjavik.

33. Ernest Marquez, *Santa Monica Beach: A Collector's Pictorial History* (Santa Monica, CA: Angel City Press, 2004), 14–35; Spencer Crump, *Ride the Big Red Cars: How Trolleys Helped Build Southern California,* 4th ed. (Corona del Mar, CA: Trans-Anglo Books, 1970); Spencer Crump, *Henry Huntington and the Pacific Electric: A Pictorial Album* (Los Angeles: Trans-Anglo Books, 1970).

34. Moran and Sewell, *Fantasy by the Sea.*

35. "The Los Angeles Beach Is 105 Wonderful Miles Long," *Sunset,* July 1968, 58–67; Marquez, *Santa Monica Beach,* 50–63.

36. Kirse Granat May, *Golden State, Golden Youth: The California Image in Popular Culture, 1955–1966* (Chapel Hill: University of North Carolina Press, 2002), 3–5, 67–70.

37. See the description from 1822 of the "surf-board and the manner in which it is used," in *Missionary Herald at Home and Abroad* 18 (August 1822): 242.

38. Matt Warshaw, *The History of Surfing* (San Francisco: Chronicle Books, 2010), 1–71.

39. Freeth would become the first leader of the Los Angeles County Lifeguard system. Arthur Verge, "George Freeth: King of the Surfers and California's Forgotten Hero," *California History* 80, nos. 2–3 (Summer 2001): 82–95.

40. Warshaw, *History of Surfing,* 18–90.

41. The impact of technology on surfing is explored in Peter J. Westwick and Peter Neushul, *The World in the Curl: An Unconventional History of Surfing* (New York: Crown, 2013). See also Warshaw, *History of Surfing,* 98–108, 168–72.

42. Warshaw, *History of Surfing,* 194–98; May, *Golden State, Golden Youth,* 95–115.

43. Warshaw, *History of Surfing,* 137–140, 229–33. The poster for "Endless Summer" became iconic. Lili Anolik, "One Summer, Forever," *Vanity Fair,* March 2014.

44. Peter Lunenfeld, "Gidget on the Couch," *Believer,* June 2008, 2–8; May, *Golden State,* 67–93.

45. Annette Funicello with Patricia Romanowski Bashe, *A Dream Is a Wish Your Heart Makes: My Story* (New York: Hyperion, 1994), 136–45. The code was enacted in 1930 and influenced film making into the 1970s. Rachel Moseley, *Fashioning Film Stars: Dress, Culture, Identity* (London: BFI, 2005), 136.

46. Mark Thomas McGee, *Faster and Furiouser: The Revised and Fattened Table of American International Pictures* (Jefferson, NC: McFarland and Co.,

1996), 218–35; Gary Morris, "Beyond the Beach," *Journal of Popular Film and Television* 21, no. 1 (Spring 1993): 2–11.

47. Barnett Singer, *Brigitte Bardot: A Biography* (Jefferson, NC: McFarland, 2006).

48. For the bikini, one only has to go to the Wikipedia site to get a sense of the large literature that the bikini has inspired. A short history is in Patrik Alac, *Bikini Story* (New York: Parkstone Press, 2012). See also Lencek and Bosker, *Making Waves,* and Alissa J. Rubin, "Penalizing Women for Covering Too Little, and Then Too Much," *New York Times,* August 28, 2016. For the cabaret dancers, see Alan Riding, *And the Show Went on: Cultural Life in Nazi-Occupied Paris* (New York: Knopf, 2010), 93–97 and the photos.

49. Shayna Weiss, "A Beach of Their Own: The Creation of the Gender-Segregated Beach in Tel Aviv," *Journal of Israeli History* 35, no. 1 (2016): 39–56.

50. Vivian Yee and Hwaida Saad, "For Lebanese Women, a Beach of Their Own," *New York Times,* September 11, 2018.

51. As quoted in Alissa Rubin, "French Towns Battle to Ban Muslim Beach Attire," *New York Times,* August 18, 2016.

52. Aurelien Breeden, "The Burkini Is Banned on the Beach at Cannes," *New York Times,* August 13, 2016; Romaissa Benzizoune, "At the Beach in My Burkini," *New York Times,* August 28, 2016.

53. Steven Erlanger, "A British Resort Town Sees New Life, Post Brexit," *New York Times,* August 22, 2016.

54. Prices at the Hamptons reach the stratospheric, with some houses going for $60 million or summer rentals for $800,000. Robin Finn, "Your Wallet Here," *New York Times,* March 24, 2013.

55. Advertisement in *Avenue* 42, no. 5 (Spring 1918).

56. Rainer Meier, "Perle der Nordsee," *Lufthansa Magazin,* June 2006, 68–77.

57. Spring break is a phenomenon that has attracted attention from newspapers, magazines, and learned journals. One only has to put in the search term "spring break" to access hundreds of learned articles. Sociologists in particular have studied every aspect of it.

58. Jon Nordheimer, "Headaches from Rite of Spring," *New York Times,* January 13, 1986. For the background, see also Harvey H. Jackson, *The Rise and Decline of the Redneck Riviera: An Insider's History of the Florida-Alabama Coast* (Athens: University of Georgia Press, 2011).

59. A number of stories were filed by Ashley Southwell, Daniel Slotnick, and others on the violence at Panama City Beach, *New York Times,* April 13 and March 29 and 30, 2015.

60. Lizette Alvarez, "Spring Break Gets Tamer with World Watching Online," *New York Times,* March 16, 2012.

61. *New York Times,* August 9, 2017.

62. Brett Cole, "In Australia, Beaches without Beer," *New York Times,* December 29, 2016.

63. Thornton, *Clacton, Walton and Frinton,* 242–43; Walton, *British Seaside,* 137–38.

64. Salvini, *Boardwalk Memories,* 31.

65. Urbain, *At the Beach,* 203–32.

66. Robert B. Edgerton, *Alone Together: Social Order on an Urban Beach* (Berkeley: University of California Press, 1979), 12–15, 202–3. For the Cape Town beaches, much has changed since the early nineteenth century. As one commentator put it, "Baths are an unknown luxury in Cape Town," and the beach is used to "the filth of the town." Edward Blount, *Notes on the Cape of Good Hope: Made during an Excursion in That Colony in 1820* (London: John Murray, 1821), 101.

67. There is one notorious group than controls access to Lunada Bay in Los Angeles. Hillel Aron, "Beach Bully Bingo," *Los Angeles Weekly,* May 13, 2016, 10–15.

68. Fire Island had a casual attitude toward nudity. Social media had spread the word and the beach became rowdy, so the Park Service began to enforce the 1984 New York law prohibiting public nudity. Marc Santora, "This Summer, Fire Island Isn't the Place to Bare All: 1984 State Nudity Ban to Be Enforced at Beach," *New York Times,* February 28, 2013.

69. Claire Rigby, "Class Feud on the Beaches of Rio," *Los Angeles Times,* December 24, 2015; Larry Rohter, "Rio de Janeiro Journal: Drawing Lines across the Sand," *New York Times,* February 6, 2007.

70. Nick Corasaniti and Luis Ferré-Sadurní , "Reining in Beach-Spreading, Not to Be Confused with Manspreading," *New York Times,* August 11, 2017.

71. Rehoboth Beach, Delaware, Myrtle Beach, South Carolina, Gulf Shores, Alabama, and Seaside Heights, New Jersey, have such rules. *Delmarva Now,* May 25, 2017.

CHAPTER 9. WHO OWNS THE BEACH?

1. Both epigraph quotations are from Urbain, *At the Beach,* 273.

2. United Nations, *Atlas of the Oceans, Human Settlement on the Coast,* 2016.

3. NOAA, *National Coastal Population Report: Population Trends from 1970 to 2020,* 2–5.

4. World Trade Organization, *Yearbook of Tourist Statistics and Data,* Number of Arrivals, 2016.

5. Winnie Hu, "Want to Relax at a Park or Pool in New York? Join the Crowd," *New York Times,* August 4, 2016.

6. It is easy to search on the internet for "top beaches." Many lists will show up. One of the best for American beaches is by Stephen P. Leatherman (Dr. Beach), who directs a research program on coasts. There is also a listing of especially clean beaches on www.blueflag.global. In addition, there is now a website that claims it will list and rate every beach in the world. Claire Ballentine, "Sandee Wants to Be the Yelp of Beaches," *Bloomberg News,* August 6, 2019. It promises to review 50,000 beaches in 178 Countries.

7. They can be consulted at Bluehealth2020@exeter.ac.uk.

8. Elle Hunt, "Blue Spaces: Why Time Spent Near Water Is the Secret of Happiness," *The Guardian,* November 3, 2019.

9. Benedict Wheeler et al., "Does Living by the Coast Improve Health and Wellbeing?" *Health and Place* 18, no. 5 (September 2012): 1198–1201; Ronan

Foley, "Swimming in Ireland: Immersions in Therapeutic Blue Space," *Health and Place* 35 (September 2015): 218–25; Lisa Costello, "'A Lot Better than Medicine': Self-Organized Ocean Swimming Groups as Facilitators for Healthy Aging," *Healtlh and Place* 60 (November 2019); Mathew White et al., "Blue Space: The Importance of Water for Preference, Affect, and Restorativeness Ratings of Natural and Built Scenes," *Journal of Environmental Psychology* 30, no. 4 (December 2010): 482–93.

10. Choi Chi-yuk, "Where Chinese Top Leaders Go in Summer and in Secret: A Brief History of Beidaihe," *South China Morning Post,* August 8, 2018.

11. On the development of Hainan, see John F. Burns, "Surf and Sand in China," *New York Times,* January 19, 1986; David Barboza, "In China, a New Capitalist Beachhead," *New York Times,* January 18, 2005; Bonnie Tsui, "The Surf Is Always Up in the Chinese Hawaii," *New York Times,* March 15, 2009; Mike Ives, "China Is Fertile Ground for Crop of Luxury Hotels," *New York Times,* January 12, 2013.

12. See Jackson, *Rise and Decline of the Redneck Riviera;* Virginia van der Veer, "Wintering on the Florida Panhandle," *New York Times,* November 17, 1987. The romance of the "Redneck Riviera" made it an inspiration not just to movie producers but also to novelists. See, for instance, Sophie Dunbar, *Redneck Riviera* (Angel Fire, NM: Intrigue Press 1998). There is another, similar "redneck riviera" at Myrtle Beach and on the South Carolina/Georgia border.

13. The foundation maintains an active website: www.Surfrider.org.

14. Massachusetts, New Hampshire, Virginia, Delaware, and Pennsylvania.

15. For a good explanation of all of the legal approaches to access, see Erika Kranz, "Sand for the People: The Continuing Controversy over Public Access to Florida's Beaches," *Florida Bar Journal* 83, no. 6 (2009): 10–31.

16. Sarah Gordon, "Nudists Outraged as Naked Sunbathing Is Banned on Cadiz Beaches," *Daily Mail,* August 14, 2009.

17. Nick Squires, "Venice's Lido Opened Up to Public," *Daily Telegraph,* June 30, 2011; "Mayor of Venice Arrested in Corruption Investigation," *The Guardian,* June 14, 2014.

18. Clair Carter, "'Crazy' Judges Rule Residents Cannot Use Their Unspoilt 15-Acre Beach Because It Belongs to the French," *Mailonline,* February 26, 2015.

19. Mark Hickford, "Law of the Foreshore and Seabed—Marine and Coastal Area (Takutai Moana) Act 2011," *Te Ara—The Encyclopedia of New Zealand.*

20. Public access issues are constantly being legislated and litigated, so it is not easy to keep up. Daniel Summerlin has published an article that is a good guide through the 1990s. Needless to say, things have changed subsequently. Summerlin, "Improving Public Access to Coastal Beaches: The Effect of Statutory Management and the Public Trust Doctrine," *William and Mary Environment Law and Policy Review* 20, no. 3 (1996): 425–44.

21. Andrew W. Kahrl, "Fear of an Open Beach: Public Rights and Private Interests in 1970s Coastal Connecticut," *Journal of American History* 102 (September 2015): 433–62; Kahrl, *Free the Beaches: The Story of Ned Coll and the Battle for America's Most Exclusive Shoreline* (New Haven, CT: Yale University Press, 2018).

22. David M. Herszenhorn, "Greenwich's Shifting Line in the Sand," *New York Times*, July 19, 2000.

23. "Municipalities Can't Stop Owners from Fencing Off Strand," *Los Angeles Times*, August 9, 1925. A year later the *Times* was still agitating against encroaching private interest. "County's Beach Playgrounds Passing to Private Hands," August 15, 1926.

24. Olmstead Brothers and Harland Bartholomew & Associates, *Parks, Playgrounds, and Beaches for the Los Angeles Region: A Report Submitted to the Citizens' Committee on Parks, Playgrounds and Beaches* (Los Angeles, 1930).

25. Sarah S. Elkind, "Citizens without Standing: Los Angeles Politics at the Beach," Lecture at the Huntington Library, September 2005.

26. California Department of Parks and Recreation, "Find a California State Park," www.parks.ca.gov/Parkindex.

27. See, for instance, California Coastal Commission, *Experience the California Coast: A Guide to the Beaches and Parks in Northern California* (Berkeley: University of California Press, 2005).

28. James Rainey, "Billionaire Battles Authorities on Access to Beach," *Los Angeles Times*, December 11, 2000; Lee Romney, "Dispute over Beach Access Heats Up," *Los Angeles Times*, March 13, 2013; Lee Romney, "Civil Trial over Access to Beloved Beach Underway," *Los Angeles Times*, May 9, 2014; Dan Weikel, "Navigating Rough Waters," *Los Angeles Times*, November 6, 2016; Christine Hauser, "Mogul Seeks $30 Million to Let Public Enter Beach," *New York Times*, February 24, 2016; Chad Nelson, "Beaches under Lock and Key," *Los Angeles Times*, June 30, 2017.

29. David K. Randall, *The King and Queen of Malibu: The True Story of the Battle for Paradise* (New York: W.W. Norton, 2017); W.W. Robinson, Lawrence Clark Powell, and Irene B. Robinson, *The Malibu: Rancho Topanga Malibu Sequit, an Historical Approach* (Los Angeles: Dawson's Book Shop, 1958); Marian Hall and Nick Rodionoff, *Malibu: California's Most Famous Seaside Community* (Santa Monica, CA: Angel City Press, 2005).

30. Frederick Hastings Rindge, *Happy Days in Southern California* (Cambridge, MA: printed by the author, 1898).

31. Peter Haldeman, "Malibu," *Town and Country*, June 2004, 192–233.

32. On the guards hired by the home owners as a public nuisance, see Timothy Egan, "Owners of Malibu Mansions Cry, 'This Sand Is My Sand,'" *New York Times*, August 25, 2002.

33. "Beach Access, with Teeth" (editorial), *Los Angeles Times*, July 2, 2014.

34. For the news of the app, see Steve Lopez, "Beach App Has the City Buzzing," *Los Angeles Times*, May 29, 2013. John Adair with Jenny Price created "Our Malibu Beaches." Price has also written and demonstrated against the "mansion people." *Los Angeles Times*, June 15, 2003; Price, "A Line in the Sand," *New York Times*, September 14, 2005; Price, "We Shall Fight Them on the Beaches," *New York Times*, September 16, 2005. Lopez is a columnist for the *Los Angeles Times* who has published often; see May 29, 2013, and September 6, 2015.

35. Just as Malibu quiets down a little, a new struggle has emerged for a pristine ranch with wonderful beaches. Hollister Ranch is an exclusive enclave

that has kept its beaches closed to the public. See Rosanna Xia, "Protective of a Coastal Paradise," *Los Angeles Times*, April 14, 2019.

36. "Rick Scott Blocks Action on Beach Access Law He Signed in March," *Tampa Bay Times*," July 13, 2018. But locally the Walton County sheriff has arrested people for trespass. See *Daytona Beach News Journal*, April 8, 2018.

37. For Guanabara Bay, see *New York Times*, May 19, 2014; on boars, *The Guardian*, July 27, 2011, and August 21, 2009. Quindao algae is widely reported every year. See *Daily Mail*, July 15, 2016. On jellyfish on Costa Brava, Spain, *The Guardian*, August 11, 2010. And for a comment on toxic algae, see Orrin H. Pilkey et al., *The World's Beaches: A Global Guide to the Science of the Shoreline* (Berkeley: University of California Press, 2011), 244–45.

38. Christine Hauser, "Mississippi Closes Beaches after Deluge in Midwest Causes Toxic Algae Bloom," *New York Times*, July 9, 2019. See also Mississippi Beach Monitoring Program, https://opcgis.deq.state.ms.us/beaches/, accessed July 12, 2019.

39. "Chennai Oil Spill," *Times of India*, February 2, 2017; Lliana Magra, "Floating Tar, Dead Fish: Oil Spill Threatens Greek Beaches," *New York Times*, September, 14, 2017.

40. Theodore Steinberg, *Gotham Unbound: The Ecological History of Greater New York* (New York: Simon & Schuster, 2014), 123.

41. Walton, *British Seaside*, 138, 123–39.

42. Bhavika Jain, "8 out of City's 10 Beaches Unsafe," *Hindustan Times*, May 10, 2011.

43. This is what happened in the 1960s at Benidorm, Spain, where sewers only served 18 percent of the population. Pack, *Tourism and Dictatorship*, 128–32.

44. "Duterte Slams Top Philippine Tourist Island as 'Cesspoool,'" *Agence France Presse / Yahoo News*, February 9, 2018; Ayee Macaraig, "Heavy Security as Philippines Closes Boracay to Tourists," *Agence France Presse / Yahoo News*, April 26, 2018; Felipe Villamor, "Boracay, Idyllic Resort Island in the Phillines, Is Closed to Tourists," *New York Times*, April 5, 2018; Felipe Villamor, "As Philippines Closes Isle to Tourists, Fears Mount," *New York Times*, April 26, 2018; Shibani Mahatni and Kaela Malig, "Philippines Reopened 'Paradise' after Six-Month Cleanup. So Why Isn't Everyone Happy?," *Washington Post*, December 3, 2018.

45. The Blue Flag group has approved 3,850 beaches in 48 countries.

46. Orrin H. Pilkey and J.A.G. Cooper, *The Last Beach* (Durham, NC: Duke University Press, 2014), 95–105.

47. Nada Homsi, "Sea of Garbage Covers Beaches of Lebanon," *New York Times*, January 24, 2018.

48. The very worst threat comes from drug-resistant staph infections. Pilkey and Cooper, *Last Beach*, 144–51.

49. See image of the hotel being pulled by a number of steam engines in Stanley R. Riggs et al., *The Battle for North Carolina's Coast: Evolutionary History, Present Crisis, and Vision for the Future* (Chapel Hill: University of North Carolina Press, 2011), 93.

50. Hilda Grieve, *The Great Tide: The Story of the 1953 Flood Disaster in Essex* (Chelmsford: Essex County Council, 1959).

51. Glenn Morris, *North Carolina Beaches,* rev. and updated ed. (Chapel Hill: University of North Carolina Press, 1998), 4–5; Cornelia Dean, *Against the Tide: The Battle for America's Beaches* (New York: Columbia University Press, 1999), 15, 76, 186.

52. Pilkey and Cooper, *Last Beach,* 14; N. Leroy Poff and David D. Hart, "How Dams Vary and Why It Matters for the Emerging Science of Dam Removal," *BioScience* 52 (August 2002): 659–68.

53. William Yardley, "Removing Barriers to Salmon Migration," *New York Times,* July 30, 2011; Kirk Johnson, "A River Newly Wild and Seriously Muddy," *New York Times,* August 3, 2012; Cornelia Dean, "When Dams Come Down, Salmon and Sand Can Prosper," *New York Times,* August 10, 2014. See also Lynda V. Mapes, "Elwha: Roaring Back to Life," *Seattle Times,* February 13, 2016, https://projects.seattletimes.com/2016/elwha/, and Michelle Nijhuis, "World's Largest Dam Removal," *National Geographic,* August 27, 2014.

54. For Cape May, see Pilkey and Cooper, *Last Beach,* 53. And for the general problem, Pilkey and Cooper, 49–69; Pilkey et al., *World's Beaches,* 229–39; Karl F. Nordstrom, *Beach and Dune Restoration* (Cambridge: Cambridge University Press, 2008).

55. Neil Tweedie, "Is the World Running Out of Sand?," *The Guardian,* July 1, 2018.

56. Pilkey and Cooper, *Last Beach,* 31–34; on desert sand, Mette Bendixen, "Time Is Running Out for Sand," *Nature,* July 4, 2019, 29–31.

57. Waikiki replenishment attracted attention as early as 1928. "Honolulu Beach Will Be Improved: Waikiki Will Be Extended by New Jersey Methods," *New York Times,* October 28, 1928. See also Cornelia Dean, "Shorelines, Sandy or Otherwise, That May Not Last," *New York Times,* August 16, 2011. There is an unconfirmed story that in the 1920s sand from Manhattan Beach, California, was used to replenish Waikiki. Manhattan Beach Historical Society, accessed April 27, 2018.

58. "Sylt," Wikipedia, accessed February 12, 2018. So far the operation has cost 134 million euros.

59. These figures come from the "Beach Nourishment Viewer," at the website of the Program for the Study of Developed Shorelines at Western Carolina University, http://beachnourishment.wcu.edu/.

60. Pilkey and Cooper, *Last Beach,* 31–38.

61. Pilkey and Cooper, 30–31. See also Samantha Subramanian, "To See the Future of Building in an Epoch of Dwindling Land, Visit Singapore," *New York Times Magazine,* April 23, 2017, 47–53.

62. Some of the Riau Islands in Indonesia have simply disappeared. The demand is now so great that crime syndicates have entered the business. Wade Shepherd, "Cities and the Sea: The True Cost of Reclaimed Land," *The Guardian,* May 2, 2018.

63. Henry Fountain, "Melting Greenland Is Awash in Sand," *New York Times,* July 1, 2019.

64. For an example of the new studies, see Pilkey et al., *World's Beaches.*

65. Orrin H. Pilkey and Katharine L. Dixon, *The Corps and the Shore* (Washington, DC: Island Press, 1996).

66. The Coastal Zone Management Act, passed in 1972 and amended in 1976; Karhl, "Fear of an Open Beach," 454–55; David J. Brower, William Dreyfoos, and Don Meserve, *Access to the Nation's Beaches: Legal and Planning Perspectives,* UNC Sea Grant Publication UNC-SG-77-18 (Raleigh: UNC Sea Grant, North Carolina State University, 1978); David W. Owens and David J. Brower, *Public Use of Coastal Beaches,* Sea Grant Publication UNC-SG-76-08 (Raleigh: Sea Grant College Program, North Carolina State University, 1976).

67. Jackson, *Rise and Decline of the Redneck Riviera,* 162–78; Stop the Beach Renourishment, Inc. v. Florida Department of Environmental Protection et al., 560 US 702 (2010), www.supremecourt.gov/opinions/09pdf/08-1151 .pdf. The case was argued before the Supreme Court on December 2, 2009, and decided June 17, 2010.

68. William Neuman, "Rockaway Beach Is Open. But the High Tide Has Veto Power," *New York Times,* July 7, 2018; See also the *Times* editorial excoriating the administration, "Save the People's Beach at Rockaway," May 26, 2018.

69. Replenishing fourteen miles of beach and building twenty-two-foot-high dunes in Ocean County, New Jersey, cost $128 million. Behind the dunes, many of the new homes are much larger than the ones they replaced, as home owners have taken the insurance money and moved up. Devorah Lev-Tov, "At the Jersey Shore, Less Snooki, More Snooty," *New York Times,* August 18, 2019. For a general background, see Karl F. Nordstrom and National Audubon Society, *Living with the New Jersey Shore* (Durham, NC: Duke University Press, 1986); Nordstrom, *Beach and Dune Restoration.*

70. See the many examples in Riggs et al., *Battle for North Carolina's Coast,* and an early warning in Wade Graham, "Beachless," *New Yorker,* December 16, 1996, 58–65; Stanley R. Riggs et al., *Drowning the North Carolina Coast: Sea-Level Rise and Estuarine Dynamics,* UNC-SG (Raleigh, NC: North Carolina Sea Grant, 2003).

71. Adam Conners, "Cyclone Pam, Vanuatu One Year On," *Australian National Broadcasting,* March 15, 2016.

CHAPTER 10. THE RELENTLESS SEA

1. Eric Post et al., "Polar Regions in a 2°C Warmer World," *Science Advances* 5, no. 12 (2019); Michael Vousdoukas et al., "Global Probabilistic Projections of Extreme Sea Levels Show Intensification of Coastal Flood Hazard," *Nature Communications* 9, no. 1 (2018): 1–12.

2. Orrin Pilkey and Keith Pilkey, *Sea Level Rise: A Slow Tsunami on America's Shores* (Durham, NC: Duke University Press, 2019): xii–xiii.

3. Scott A. Kulp and Benjamin H. Strauss, "New Elevation Data Triple Estimates of Global Vulnerability to Sea-Level Rise and Coastal Flooding," *Nature Communications,* October 29, 2019, 234–39; Benjamin Horton, "Estimating Global Mean Sea-Level Rise by 2100 and 2300," *Nature Climate and Atmospheric Science,* May 8, 2020, 1–8. See also Jeff Goodell, *The Water Will Come: Rising Seas, Sinking Cities and the Remaking of the Civilized World* (Boston: Little Brown, 2017); Orrin Pilkey et al., *Retreat from a Rising Sea: Hard Decisions in an Age of Climate Change* (New York: Columbia University Press, 2017).

4. "Flooded Future: Global Vulnerability to Sea Level Rise Worse than Previously Thought," *Climate Central* report, October 29, 2019. For the North Sea, see Michael Vousdoukas et al., "Extreme Sea Level Rise Along European Coasts," *Earth Futures* 5, no. 3 (March 2017): 304–23.

5. Kendra Pierre-Louis, "Warming Ocean Waters Have Fish on the Move," *New York Times,* December 2, 2019.

6. Susanne Rust, "How the U.S. Betrayed the Marshall Islands, Kindling the Next Nuclear Disaster," *Los Angeles Times,* November 10, 2019.

7. Patricia Mazzei, "82 Days under Water: Tide Is High, but They Are Holding On," *New York Times,* November 25, 2019.

8. Emily MIchot, "South Florida Will Bear Brunt of Climate Crisis," *Miami Herald,* October 7, 2019; Oliver Milman, "Atlantic City and Miami Beach: Two Takes on Tackling the Rising Waters," *The Guardian,* March 20, 2017.

9. Chloe Johnson, "Charleston Faces an Existential Choice: Wall Off the Rising Ocean or Retreat to High Ground," *Charleston Post and Courier,* May 20, 2020. For the big picture, see NOAA report, "The State of High Tide Flooding in 2019 and the Outlook through April 2021," *Tides and Currents,* https://tidesandcurrents.noaa.gov/HighTideFlooding_AnnualOutlook.html, accessed August 4, 2020.

10. Riggs et al., *Battle for North Carolina's Coast,* 18–23.

11. National Academy of Sciences, *Sea Level Rise for the Coasts of California, Oregon and Washington* (Washington, DC: National Academy Press, 2012). One estimate is that two-thirds of all Southern California beaches will be swallowed by 2100. United States Geological Survey report, "Disappearing Beaches: Modeling Shoreline Change in Southern California," March 27, 2017, www.usgs.gov/news/disappearing-beaches-modeling-shoreline-change-southern-california.

12. California Coastal Commission report, "California Coastal Commission and Sea Level Rise Policy Guidelines," revised 2018.

13. A confession: I lived in Del Mar for twenty-two years. The *Los Angeles Times* ran a special section featuring Del Mar, "California against the Sea: Our Vanishing Coastline," July 7, 2019.

14. Phil Diehl, "A Coastal Railroad's Weakest Link," *Los Angeles Times,* July 29, 2019.

15. Phil Diehl, "Del Mar Resists State's Sea Level Rise Strategy," *Los Angeles Times,* October 7, 2019.

16. Rosanna Xia, "As the Seas Rise, Cities Face Climate Change Cost," *Los Angeles Times,* December 5, 2019.

17. Rosanna Xia, "California Officials Need To Move Faster on Sea Level Rise, Legislative Study Finds," *Los Angeles Times,* December 10, 2019; Rosanna Xia, "Some California Cities Think They're Safe from Sea Level Rise. They're Not, New Data Show," *Los Angeles Times,* August 12, 2020.

18. California Legislative Analyst Office report, "Preparing for Rising Seas: How the State Can Help Support Local Coastal Adaptation Efforts," December 11, 2019, https://lao.ca.gov/Publications/Report/4121.

19. Anne Barnard, "The $119 Billion Sea Wall Could Defend New York . . . or Bathe It in Sewage," *New York Times,* January 18, 2020.

20. David Wharton, "California's Hottest Surf Spot is a Kelly Slater–Designed Artificial Wave Pool 100 Miles Inland," *Los Angeles Times*, May 5, 2018. Going on the web and entering "wave pools" will bring up a number of these new pools from around the world.

21. For example, see Pilkey et al., *World's Beaches*.

22. Kim Stanley Robinson, *Aurora* (New York: Hachette, 2015). Robinson has also written about New York suffering a major sea level rise; see *New York, 2140* (New York: Hachette, 2019).

Select Bibliography

Adams, Abigail, *Letters of Mrs. Adams, the Wife of John Adams*. Edited by Charles Francis Adams. 2nd ed. 2 vols. Boston: C.C. Little and J. Brown, 1840.

Adams, Abigail. *Letters of Mrs. Adams, the Wife of John Adams*. Edited by Charles Francis Adams. 4th ed. Boston: Wilkins, Carter, 1848.

Adams, James. "Bathing at the Continental Sea-shore Resorts." *Cosmopolitan* 19, no. 2 (June 1895): 131–45.

Adamson, Simon H. *Seaside Piers*. London: Batsford, 1977.

Aikin, John. *A Description of the Country from Thirty to Forty Miles Round Manchester*. London: printed for John Stockdale, 1795.

Allen, David E. *The Naturalist in Britain: A Social History*. London: Allen Lane, 1976.

Allen, Julia. *Swimming with Dr Johnson and Mrs Thrale: Sport, Health and Exercise in Eighteenth-Century England*. Cambridge: Lutterworth Press, 2012.

Allen, Robert C. *Horrible Prettiness: Burlesque and American Culture*. Chapel Hill, NC: University of North Carolina Press, 1991.

Anderson, Norman D. *Ferris Wheels: An Illustrated History*. Bowling Green, OH: Bowling Green State University Press, 1992.

Apperley, Charles J. *Nimrod Abroad*. London: Henry Colburn, 1842.

Arbuthnot, John. *An Essay Concerning the Effects of Air on Human Bodies*. London: printed for J. and R. Tonson and S. Draper, 1733.

Ariès, Phillipe, and Georges Duby, eds. *A History of Private Life*. 5 vols. Cambridge, MA: Harvard University Press, 1987.

Armstead, Myra B. *"Lord, Please Don't Take Me in August": African Americans in Newport and Saratoga Springs, 1870–1930*. Urbana: University of Illinois Press, 1999.

Aron, Cindy S. *Working at Play: A History of Vacations in the United States.* New York: Oxford University Press, 1999.

Austen, Jane. *Later Manuscripts.* Edited by Janet M. Todd and Linda Bree. Cambridge: Cambridge University Press, 2008.

Awsiter, John. *Thoughts on Brighthelmston: Concerning Sea-Bathing and Drinking Sea-Water.* London: printed for J. Wilkie, 1768.

Bailey, Peter. *Leisure and Class in Victorian England: Rational Recreation and the Contest for Control, 1830–1885.* London: Routledge and Kegan Paul, 1978.

———. *Music Hall: The Business of Pleasure.* Philadelphia: Open University Press, 1986.

Bamford, Francis, ed. *Dear Mrs. Heber: An Eighteenth Century Correspondence.* London: Constable, 1936.

Baranowski, Shelley. *Strength through Joy: Consumerism and Mass Tourism in the Third Reich.* Cambridge: Cambridge University Press, 2007.

Baranowski, Shelley, and Ellen Furlough, eds. *Being Elsewhere: Tourism, Consumer Culture, and Identity in Modern Europe and North America.* Ann Arbor: University of Michigan Press, 2001.

Barker, Nigel. *Margate's Seaside Heritage.* Swindon: English Heritage, 2007.

Barrett, Richmond. *Good Old Summer Days: Newport, Narragansett Pier, Saratoga, Long Branch, Bar Harbor.* Boston: Houghton Mifflin, 1952.

Barton, Susan. *Working-Class Organisations and Popular Tourism, 1840–1970.* Manchester: Manchester University Press, 2005.

Beaven, Brad. *Leisure, Citizenship and Working-Class Men in Britain, 1850–1945.* Manchester: Manchester University Press, 2005.

Bederman, Gail. *Manliness and Civilization: A Cultural History of Gender and Race in the United States.* Chicago: University of Chicago Press, 1995.

Bennet, James H. *Winter and Spring on the Shores of the Mediterranean.* London: John Churchill, 1861.

Bentley, William. *The Diary of William Bentley, D.D., Pastor of the East Church, Salem, Massachusetts.* 4 vols. Salem, MA: The Essex Institute, 1905–14.

Berry, Mary. *Extracts of the Journals and Correspondence of Miss Berry from the Year 1783 to 1852.* Edited by Lady Theresa Lewis. 3 vols. London: Longmans, 1866.

Betjeman, John. *Collected Poems.* Boston: Houghton Mifflin, 1959.

Bishop, John George. *"A Peep into the Past": Brighton in the Olden Time, with Glances at the Present.* People's ed. Brighton: printed by the author,1892.

Blew, William Charles Arlington. *Brighton and Its Coaches: A History of the London and Brighton Road.* London: J.C. Nimmo, 1894.

Blundell, Nicholas. *Blundell's Diary and Letter Book, 1702–1728.* Edited by Margaret Blundell. Liverpool: Liverpool University Press, 1952.

Bolotin, Norm, and Christine Laing. *The World's Columbian Exposition: The Chicago World's Fair of 1893.* Washington, DC: Preservation Press, 1992.

Bolster, W. Jeffrey. *The Mortal Sea: Fishing in the Atlantic in the Age of Sail.* Cambridge, MA: Harvard University Press, 2012.

Booth, Douglas. *Australian Beach Cultures: The History of Sun, Sand and Surf.* London: Frank Cass, 2001.

Booth, Henry. *An Account of the Liverpool and Manchester Railway.* Liverpool: Wales and Baines, 1831.

Borsay, Peter. *A History of Leisure: The British Experience since 1500.* Basingstoke: Palgrave Macmillan, 2006.

Borsay, Peter, and John K. Walton. *Resorts and Ports: European Seaside Towns since 1700.* Bristol: Channel View, 2011.

Bott, Alan. *Our Fathers, 1870–1900.* London: Heinemann, 1931.

Bracciolini, Poggius, and Nicolaus De Niccolis. *Two Renaissance Book Hunters: The Letters of Poggius Bracciolini to Nicolaus De Niccolis.* Edited and translated by Phyllis Walter Goodhart Gordon. New York: Columbia University Press, 1974.

Bradley, Hugh. *Such Was Saratoga.* New York: Doubleday, Doran, 1940.

Breen, T. H. "'Baubles of Britain': The American and Consumer Revolutions of the Eighteenth Century." *Past and Present* 119, no. 1 (May 1988): 73–104.

Bremer, Fredrika. *America of the Fifties: Letters of Fredrika Bremer.* Edited by Adolph B. Benson. New York: American-Scandinavian Foundation, 1924.

———. *The Homes of the New World: Impressions of America.* 2 vols. Translated by Mary Botham Howitt. New York: Harper and Brothers, 1853.

Bremer, Fredrika, and Carina Burman. *Brev: Ny FöLjd; Tidigare Ej Samlade Och Tryckta Brev.* 2 vols. Stockholm: Gidlund, 1996.

Brendon, Piers. *Thomas Cook: 150 Years of Popular Tourism.* London: Secker and Warburg, 1991.

Brewer, John. *The Pleasures of the Imagination: English Culture in the Eighteenth Century.* London: HarperCollins, 1997.

Brodie, Allan. *English Seaside Resorts.* London: English Heritage, 2007.

Brower, David J., William Dreyfoos, and Don Meserve. *Access to the Nation's Beaches: Legal and Planning Perspectives.* UNC Sea Grant Publication UNC-SG-77-18. Raleigh: North Carolina State University Press, 1978.

Brown, A. F. J. *Essex People, 1750–1900: From Their Diaries, Memoirs and Letters.* Chelmsford, Essex: Essex County Council, 1972.

Brown, Dona. *Inventing New England: Regional Tourism in the Nineteenth Century.* Washington, DC: Smithsonian Institution Press, 1995.

Buchan, Alexander Peter. *Practical Observations Concerning Sea Bathing: To Which Are Added, Remarks on the Use of the Warm Bath.* London: T. Cadell & W. Davies, 1804.

Buchan, William. *Cautions Concerning Cold Bathing, and Drinking Mineral Waters.* London: printed for A. Strahan, 1786.

———. *Domestic Medicine; or, a Treatise on the Prevention and Cure of Diseases by Regimen and Simple Medicines.* London: printed for W. Strahan, 1772.

Buchan, William, and William Cadogan. *Domestic Medicine; or, the Family Physician.* Philadelphia: printed by John Dunlap for R. Aitken, 1772.

Burney, Fanny, *Diary and Letters of Madame D'arblay, 1778–1840.* 6 vols. Edited by Charlotte Barrett. London: Macmillan, 1904.

———. *The Early Diary of Frances Burney, 1768–1778.* 2 vols. Edited by Annie Raine Ellis. London: George Bell and Sons, 1889.

———. *The Early Journals and Letters of Fanny Burney.* 5 vols. Edited by Lars E. Troide et al. Kingston, Ontario: McGill-Queens Universtiy Press, 1988–.

―――. *Journals and Letters of Fanny Burney.* 12 vols. Edited by Joyce Hemlow et al. Oxford: Clarendon Press, 1972.

Bushman, Richard L. *The Refinement of America: Persons, Houses, Cities.* New York: Knopf, 1992.

Byng, John, Viscount Torrington. *Torrington Diaries.* 4 vols. Edited by C.B. Andrews. London: Eyre and Spottiswoode, 1935.

Cabot, Elizabeth Rogers Mason. *More than Common Powers of Perception: The Diary of Elizabeth Rogers Mason Cabot.* Edited by P.A.M. Taylor. Boston: Beacon Press, 1991.

Caine, Barbara. *English Feminism, 1780–1980.* Oxford: Oxford University Press, 1997.

Cannadine, David. *The Decline and Fall of the British Aristocracy.* New Haven, CT: Yale University Press, 1990.

―――. *Lords and Landlords: The Aristocracy and the Towns, 1774–1967.* Leicester: Leicester University Press, 1980.

Capuzzo, Mike. *Close to Shore: The Terrifying Shark Attacks of 1916.* New York: Broadway Books, 2001.

Carey, George S. *The Balnea: Or, an Impartial Description of All the Popular Watering Places in England.* 3rd ed. London: West and Hughes, 1801.

Carnes, Mark C., and Clyde Griffen. *Meanings for Manhood: Constructions of Masculinity in Victorian America.* Chicago: University of Chicago Press, 1990.

Carson, Barbara. "Early American Tourists and the Commercialization of Leisure." In *Of Consuming Interest: The Style of Life in the Eighteenth Century,* edited by Cary Carson et al., 374–405. Charlottesville: University of Virginia Press, 1994.

Cavendish, Lady Harriet. *Hary-O: The Letters of Lady Harriet Cavendish, 1796–1809.* Edited by George Leveson Gower and Iris Palmer. London: John Murray, 1940.

Chandler, David Leon. *Henry Flagler: The Astonishing Life and Times of the Visionary Robber Baron Who Founded Florida.* New York: Macmillan, 1986.

Christie, Agatha. *The Mystery of the Blue Train.* London: Collins, 1928.

Churchill, Sarah J., Duchess of Marlborough. *Letters of a Grandmother, 1732–35.* Edited by Gladys Scott Thomson. London: J. Cape, 1943.

Cicero, Marcus Tullius. *The Speeches.* Translated by Neville Watts. Cambridge, MA: Harvard University Press, 1958.

Clarke, George E. *Historic Margate.* Margate: Margate Public Library, 1957.

Coke, Lady Mary. *The Letters and Journals of Lady Mary Coke.* Edited by James Archibald Home. Edinburgh: David Douglas, 1889.

Coleridge, Samuel T. *Coleridge among the Lakes and Mountains: From his Notebooks and Letters and Poems, 1794–1804.* Edited by Roger Hudson. London: Folio Society, 1991.

Conlin, Jonathan. *The Pleasure Garden: From Vauxhall to Coney Island.* Philadelphia: University of Pennsylvania Press, 2013.

Constable, John. *John Constable's Correspondence.* 6 vols. Edited by Ronald B. Beckett. London: H.M. Stationary Office, 1962.

Copeland, John. *Roads and Their Traffic, 1750–1850.* Reprints of Economic Classics. Newton Abbot: David & Charles, 1968.

Corbin, Alain. *The Lure of the Sea: Discovery of the Seaside in the Western World, 1750–1840.* Translated by Jocelyn Phelps. London: Penguin, 1995.

Cott, Nancy. *The Bonds of Womanhood: "Woman's Sphere" in New England, 1780–1835.* New Haven, CT: Yale University Press, 1997.

Creevy, Thomas. *The Creevey Papers.* Edited by John Gore. London: Folio Society, 1970.

Crump, Spencer. *Ride the Big Red Cars: How Trolleys Helped Build Southern California.* 4th ed. Corona Del Mar, CA: Trans-Anglo Books, 1970.

Cunningham, John T. *The New Jersey Shore.* New Brunswick, NJ: Rutgers University Press, 1958.

———. *Railroads in New Jersey: The Formative Years.* Andover, NJ: Afton, 1997.

———. *This Is New Jersey: From High Point to Cape May.* New Brunswick, NJ: Rutgers University Press, 1953.

Cunningham, Patricia. *Reforming Women's Fashion, 1850–1920: Politics, Health, and Art.* Kent, OH: Kent State University Press, 2003.

Curwen, Samuel. *The Journal of Samuel Curwen, Loyalist.* Edited by Andrew Oliver. 2 vols. Cambridge, MA: Harvard University Press, 1972.

Daniell, William. *A Voyage Round Great Britain: Undertaken in the Summer of the Year 1813.* 8 vols. London: printed for Longman et al., 1814–25.

D'Arms, John H. *Romans on the Bay of Naples: A Social and Cultural Study of the Villas and Their Owners from 150 B.C. to 400 A.D.* Cambridge, MA: Harvard University Press, 1970.

———. *Romans on the Bay of Naples and Other Essays on Roman Campania.* Bari: Edipuglia, 2003.

Dean, Cornelia. *Against the Tide: The Battle for America's Beaches.* New York: Columbia University Press, 1999.

Digby, Everard. *A Short Introduction for to Learne to Swimme.* Translated by Christofer Middleton. London, 1595.

Dioscorides Pedanius. *De Materia Medica: Being an Herbal with Many Other Medicinal Materials.* Translated by Tess Anne Osbaldeston and Robert P. Wood. Repr., Johannesburg: Ibidis, 2000.

Dorwart, Jeffery M. *Cape May County, New Jersey: The Making of an American Resort Community.* New Brunswick, NJ: Rutgers University Press, 1992.

Dwight, Timothy. *Travels in New England and New York.* 4 vols. New Haven, CT: T. Dwight, 1821.

Edgerton, Robert B. *Alone Together: Social Order on an Urban Beach.* Berkeley: University of California Press, 1979.

Elliott, Maude Howe. *This Was My Newport.* Cambridge, MA: The Mythology Company, 1944.

Ellis, John R. *The Human Shore: Seacoasts in History.* Chicago: University of Chicago Press, 2012.

Farington, Joseph. *Diary of Joseph Farington.* 10 vols. Edited by Kenneth Garlick and Angus Macintyre. New Haven, CT: Yale University Press, 1978–84.

Farrar, William, and J. Brownbill. *The Victoria History of the County of Lancaster.* 8 vols. London: Archibald Constable, 1906.

Ferry, Kathryn. *The British Seaside Holiday*. Oxford: Shire Press, 2009.

———. *Sheds on the Seashore: A Tour through Beach Hut History*. Brighton: Pen Press, 2009.

Fiennes, Celia. *The Journeys of Celia Fiennes*. Edited by Christopher Morris. London: Cresset Press, 1947.

Fischer, Gayle V. *Pantaloons and Power: A Nineteenth-Century Dress Reform in the United States*. Kent, OH: Kent State University Press, 2001.

Fisher, Sidney G. *A Philadelphia Perspective: The Diary of Sidney George Fisher, 1834–71*. Edited by Nicholas B. Wainwright. Philadelphia: Historical Society of Pennsylvania, 1967.

Fisher, Stephen, ed. *Recreation and the Sea*. Exeter: University of Exeter Press, 1997.

Flanders, Judith. *Consuming Passions: Leisure and Pleasure in Victorian Britain*. London: HarperPress, 2006.

Floyer, Sir John. *An Inquiry into the Right Use and Abuses of the Hot, Cold and Temperate Baths in England*. London: printed for R. Clavel, 1697.

Francis, Sir Philip, et al. *The Francis Letters: By Sir Philip Francis and Other Members of the Family*. Edited by Beata Francis and Eliza Keary. London: Hutchinson, 1901.

Frank, Robin Jaffee, et al. *Coney Island: Visions of an American Dreamland, 1861–2008*. New Haven, CT: Yale University Press, 2015.

Frank, Stephen M. *Life with Father: Parenthood and Masculinity in the Nineteenth-Century American North*. Baltimore: Johns Hopkins University Press, 1998.

Freeman, Michael. *Railways and the Victorian Imagination*. New Haven, CT: Yale University Press, 1999.

Frost, J. *The Art of Swimming: A Series of Practical Instructions, on an Original and Progressive Plan*. New York: P. W. Gallaudet, 1818.

Fry, George S. *A Journey from London to Scarborough, in Several Letters from a Gentleman There to His Friend in London*. London: printed for Caesar Ward and Richard Chandler, 1734.

Funicello, Annette, with Patricia Romanowski. *A Dream Is a Wish Your Heart Makes: My Story*. New York: Hyperion, 1994.

Funnell, Charles E. *By the Beautiful Sea: The Rise and High Times of That Great American Resort, Atlantic City*. New Brunswick, NJ: Rutgers University Press, 1983.

Garner, Alice. *A Shifting Shore: Locals, Outsiders, and the Transformation of a French Fishing Town, 1823–2000*. New York: Cornell University Press, 2005.

Gilbert, Douglas. *American Vaudeville, Its Life and Times*. New York: Dover, 1963.

Gilbert, Edmund. *Brighton, Old Ocean's Bauble*. London: Methuen, 1954.

Giordano, Ralph. *Social Dancing in America: A History and Reference*. 2 vols. Westport, CT: Greenwood Press, 2007.

Glyn, Elinor. *The Visits of Elizabeth*. London: Duckworth, 1906.

Goddard, David. *Colonizing Southampton: The Transformation of a Long Island Community, 1870–1900*. Albany: State University of New York Press, 2011.

Goodell, Jeff. *The Water Will Come: Rising Seas, Sinking Cities, and the Remaking of the Civilized World.* New York: Little, Brown, 2017.

Gosse, Philip H. *The Aquarium: The Unveiling of the Wonders of the Deep.* London: J. van Voorst, 1854.

———. *Tenby: A Seaside Holiday.* London: J. van Voorst, 1856.

Granville, A. B. *The Spas of England and Principal Sea-Bathing Places.* 3 vols. London: Henry Colburn, 1841.

Granville, Lord Leveson Gower. *Private Correspondence, 1781–1821.* 2 vols. Edited by Castalia Granville. London: John Murray, 1916.

Granville, Harriet. *Letters of Harriet, Countess Granville, 1810–1845.* Edited by E. Frederick Leveson Gower. London: Longmans, 1894.

Grattan, Thomas Colley. *Civilized America.* 2 vols. London: Bradbury and Evans, 1859.

Graves, Charles. *And the Greeks.* New York: McBride, 1931.

Gray, Fred. *Designing the Seaside: Architecture, Society and Nature.* London: Reaktion, 2006.

Greville, Charles. *The Greville Memoirs, 1814–1860.* 8 vols. Edited by Lytton Strachey and Roger Fulford. London: Macmillan, 1938.

Grieve, Hilda. *The Great Tide: The Story of the 1953 Flood Disaster in Essex.* Chelmsford: Essex County Council, 1959.

Guidott, Thomas. *An Apology for the Bath.* London: printed for G. Sawbridg [sic], 1705.

Hall, Marian, and Nick Rodionoff. *Malibu: California's Most Famous Seaside Community.* Santa Monica, CA: Angel City Press, 2005.

Haltunen, Karen. *Confidence Men and Painted Women: A Study of Middle-Class Culture in America, 1830–1870.* New Haven, CT: Yale University Press, 1982.

Harp, Stephen L. *Au Naturel: Naturism, Nudism and Tourism in Twentieth-Century France.* Baton Rouge: Louisiana State University Press, 2014.

Hassan, John. *The Seaside, Health and the Environment in England and Wales since 1800.* Aldershot: Ashgate, 2003.

Haug, C. James. *Leisure & Urbanism in Nineteenth-Century Nice.* Lawrence: Regents University Press of Kansas, 1982.

Hedinger, Barbel. *Saison am Strand Badleben an Nord Und Ostsee, 200 Jahre.* Herford: Koehlers, 1986.

Hembry, Phyllis M. *The English Spa, 1560–1815: A Social History.* London: Athlone Press, 1990.

Herbert, Amanda E. *Female Alliances: Gender, Identity, and Friendship in Early Modern Britain.* New Haven, CT: Yale University Press, 2014.

Hiltzheimer, Jacob. *Extracts from the Diary of Jacob Hiltzheimer, of Philadelphia, 1765–1798.* Edited by Jacob Parsons. Philadelphia: W. F. Fell, 1893.

Hoffman, Brian. *Naked: A Cultural History of American Nudism.* New York: New York University Press, 2015.

Hornberger, Eric. *Mrs. Astor's New York: Money and Social Power in the Gilded Age.* New Haven, CT: Yale University Press, 2002.

Hone, Philip. *The Diary of Philip Hone, 1828–1851.* 2 vols. Edited by Allan Nevins. New York: Dodd, Mead, 1927.

Howard, Henrietta H., and George Berkeley.. *Letters to and from Henrietta, Countess of Suffolk, and Her Second Husband, the Hon. George Berkeley, from 1712 to 1767*. London: John Murray, 1824.

Howarth, Patrick. *When the Riviera Was Ours*. London: Century, 1988.

Hutton, William. *A Description of Blackpool, in Lancashire; Frequented for Sea Bathing*. Birmingham: Pearson and Rollason, 1789.

———. *The Scarborough Tour in 1803*. London: J. Nichols and Son, 1804.

Immerso, Michael. *Coney Island: The People's Playground*. New Brunswick, NJ: Rutgers University Press, 2002.

Jackson, Harvey H. *The Rise and Decline of the Redneck Riviera: An Insider's History of the Florida-Alabama Coast*. Athens: University of Georgia Press, 2011.

Jefferies, Richard. *The Open Air*. London: Chatto & Windus, 1885.

Jefferson, Alison Rose. "African American Leisure Space in Santa Monica: The Beach Sometimes Known as the Inkwell, 1900–1960." *Southern California Quarterly* 91 (Summer 2009): 155–89.

Jerningham, Frances D. *The Jerningham Letters, 1780–1843*. 2 vols. Edited by Egerton Castle. London: Bentley, 1896.

Jesse, John Heneage. *George Selwyn and His Contemporaries*. London: Richard Bentley, 1843.

Johnson, Nelson. *Boardwalk Empire: The Birth, High Times and Corruption of Atlantic City*. Medford, NJ: Plexus, 2002.

Jonnes, Jill. *Empires of Light: Edison, Tesla, Westinghouse, and the Race to Electrify the World*. New York: Random House, 2003.

Kahrl, Andrew W. *The Land Was Ours: African American Beaches from Jim Crow to the Sunbelt South*. Cambridge, MA: Harvard University Press, 2012.

Kasson, John F. *Amusing the Million: Coney Island at the Turn of the Century*. New York: Hill & Wang, 1978.

Kaufman, Wallace, and Orrin Pilkey. *The Beaches Are Moving: The Drowning of America's Shoreline*. Durham, NC: Duke University Press, 1983.

Keene, Charles. *Mr. Punch at the Seaside*. London: Educational Book Co., 1910.

Kemble, Frances. *Further Records, 1848–1883, A Series of Letters*. New York: Henry Holt, 1891.

———. *Journal of a Residence on a Georgian Plantation in 1838–1839*. New York: Harper, 1863.

———. *Records of a Girlhood: An Autobiography*. London: R. Bentley and Son, 1878.

———. *Records of a Later Life*. London: R. Bentley and Son, 1882.

Kidwell, Claudia Brush, and Valerie Steele. *Men and Women: Dressing the Part*. Washington, DC: Smithsonian Institution Press, 1989.

Kift, Dagmar. *The Victorian Music Hall: Culture, Class and Conflict*. Cambridge: Cambridge University Press, 1996.

Kilvert, Robert F. *Kilvert's Diary, 1870–1879: Selections from the Diary of the Rev. Francis Kilvert*. Edited by William Plomer. New York: Macmillan, 1947.

King, Greg. *A Season of Splendor: The Court of Mrs. Astor in Gilded Age New York.* Hoboken, NJ: John Wiley and Sons, 2009.

Kirwan, Joseph. *A Descriptive and Historical Account of the Liverpool and Manchester Railway.* London: Simpkin and Marshall, 1831.

Laborde, Pierre. *Biarritz: Huit Siecles D'histoire, 250 Ans Bains De Mer.* Biarritz: Atlantica, 2007.

Langford, Paul. *Englishness Identified: Manners and Character, 1650–1850.* Oxford: Oxford University Press, 2000.

Lapeyre, Jean. *Les Bains De Mer: An Exhibition Catalogue with Plates.* Dieppe: Musée de Dieppe, 1961.

Le Bas, Charles. *The New Margate, Ramsgate and Broadstairs Guide.* Margate: printed by J. Warren, 1801.

———. *A Polite and Commercial People: England, 1727–1783.* Oxford: Oxford University Press, 1998.

Lencek, Lena, and Gideon Bosker. *The Beach: The History of Paradise on Earth.* New York: Viking, 1998.

———. *Beach: Stories by the Sand and the Sea.* New York: Marlowe, 2000.

———. *Making Waves: Swimsuits and the Undressing of America.* San Francisco: Chronicle Books, 1989.

Lennox, Sarah. *The Life and Letters of Lady Sarah Lennox.* London: John Murray, 1901.

Levi, Vicki Gold, et al. *Atlantic City, 125 Years of Ocean Madness: Starring Miss America, Mr. Peanut, Lucy the Elephant, the High Diving Horse, and Four Generations of Americans Cutting Loose.* New York: C. N. Potter, 1979.

Lewis, Charlene M. Boyer. *Ladies and Gentlemen of Display: Planter Society at the Virginia Springs, 1790–1860.* Charlottesville: University of Virginia Press, 2001.

Lindsay, Irina. *Dressing and Undressing for the Seaside.* Hornchurch, Essex: I. Henry, 1983.

Love, Christopher. *A Social History of Swimming in England, 1800–1918: Splashing in the Serpentine.* London: Routledge, 2008.

Love, John. *A New Improved Weymouth Guide.* Weymouth: J. Ryall, 1800.

Mangan, J. A., and James Walvin. *Manliness and Morality: Middle-Class Masculinity in Britain and America, 1800–1940.* Manchester: Manchester University Press, 1987.

Mangels, William. *The Outdoor Amusement Industry from Earliest Times to the Present.* New York: Vantage Press, 1952.

Mann, Thomas. *Buddenbrooks: The Decline of a Family.* Translated by Helen T. Lowe-Porter. Harmondsworth: Penguin. 1975.

Margetson, Stella. *Leisure and Pleasure in the Eighteenth Century.* London: Cassell, 1970.

———. *Leisure and Pleasure in the Nineteenth Century.* Newton Abbott: Readers Union, 1971.

Marquez, Ernest. *Santa Monica Beach: A Collector's Pictorial History.* Santa Monica, CA: Angel City Press, 2004.

Martineau, Harriet. *Retrospect of Western Travel.* 3 vols. London: Saunders and Otley, 1838.

May, Kirse. *Golden State, Golden Youth: The California Image in Popular Culture, 1955–1966*. Chapel Hill: University of North Carolina Press, 2002.

McAllister, Ward. *Society as I Have Found It*. New York: 1890.

McCash, William, and June McCash. *The Jekyll Island Club: Southern Haven for America's Millionaires*. Athens: University of Georgia Press, 1989.

McCrossen, Alexis. *Holy Day, Holiday: The American Sunday*. Ithaca, NY: Cornell University Press, 2000.

McKendrick, Neil, John Brewer, and J.H. Plumb. *The Birth of a Consumer Society: The Commercialization of Eighteenth-Century England*. Bloomington: Indiana University Press, 1982.

Miner, H. Craig. *A Most Magnificent Machine: America Adopts the Railroad, 1825–62*. Lawrence: University Press of Kansas, 2010.

Mingay, G.E. *The Agrarian History of England and Wales*. Vol. 6, 1750–1850. Cambridge: Cambridge University Press, 1967.

Molineux, Catherine. *Faces of Perfect Ebony: Encountering Atlantic Slavery in Imperial Britain*. Cambridge, MA: Harvard University Press, 2012.

Momus. *Letters of Momus from Margate*. London: printed for John Bell, 1778.

Moran, Tom, and Tom Sewell. *Fantasy by the Sea: A Visual History of the American Venice*. Culver City, CA: Peace Press, 1979.

Morris, Glen. *North Carolina Beaches: A Guide to Coastal Access*. Chapel Hill: University of North Carolina Press, 1993.

Murray, Venetia. *An Elegant Madness: High Society in Regency England*. New York: Viking, 1999.

Musgrave, Clifford. *Life in Brighton: From the Earliest Times to the Present*. London: Faber, 1970.

Nabokov, Vladimir. *Speak Memory, An Autobiography Revisited*. New York: Knopf, 1999.

Nelson, Michael. *Queen Victoria and the Discovery of the Riviera*. London: Tauris, 2001.

The New Margate and Ramsgate Guide in Letters to a Friend. London: printed for H. Turpin, 1780.

Newdigate, Anne Emily. *The Cheverels of Cheveral Manor [Being the Correspondence of Sir Roger and Lady Newdigate]*. London: Longmans, 1898.

Nichols, John. *Literary Anecdotes of the Eighteenth Century*. London: published by the author, 1812.

Nordstrom, Karl F. *Beach and Dune Restoration*. New York: Cambridge University Press, 2008.

North, Rex. *The Butlin Story*. London: Jarrolds, 1962.

Nott, James J. *Going to the Palais: A Social and Cultural History of Dancing and Dance Halls in Britain, 1918–1960*. Oxford: Oxford University Press, 2015.

———. *Music for the People: Popular Music and Dance in Interwar Britain*. Oxford: Oxford University Press, 2002.

O'Connell, James C. *Becoming Cape Cod: Creating a Seaside Resort*. Hanover, NH: University Press of New England, 2003.

Orme, Christopher. *Early English Swimming*. Exeter: University of Exeter, 1983.

Ousby, Ian. *The Englishman's England: Taste, Travel and the Rise of Tourism.* Cambridge: Cambridge University Press, 1990.

Pack, Sasha D. *Tourism and Dictatorship: Europe's Peaceful Invasion of Franco's Spain.* New York: Palgrave Macmillan, 2006.

Packard, John H. *Sea-Air and Sea-Bathing.* Philadelphia: P. Blakiston, 1880.

Patterson, Martha. *Beyond the Gibson Girl: Reinventing the American New Woman.* Urbana: University of Illinois Press, 2005.

Peebles, John. *John Peebles' American War: The Diary of a Scottish Grenadier, 1776–1782.* Edited by Ira D. Gruber. Mechanicsburg, PA: Stackpole Books, 1998.

Phelps, Marsha D. *An American Beach for African Americans.* Gainesville: University Press of Florida, 1997.

Pike, Helen C. *Asbury Park's Glory Days: The Story of an American Resort.* New Brunswick, NJ: Rutgers University Press, 2005.

Pilkey, Orrin H., et al. *The World's Beaches: A Global Guide to the Science of the Shoreline.* Berkeley: University of California Press, 2005.

Pilkey, Orrin H., and J. A. G. Cooper. *The Last Beach.* Durham, NC: Duke University Press, 2014.

Pilkey, Orrin H., and Katharine L. Dixon. *The Corps and the Shore.* Washington, DC: Island Press, 1996.

Pilkey, Orrin H., Linda Pilkey-Jarvis, and Keith C. Pilkey. *Retreat from a Rising Sea: Hard Decisions in an Age of Climate Change.* New York: Columbia University Press, 2018.

Pimlott, J. A. R. *The Englishman's Holiday: A Social History.* Hassocks: Harvester Press, 1976.

Pintard, John. *Letters from John Pintard to his Daughter, Eliza Davidson, 1816–1833.* Edited by Dorothy C. Barck. 4 vols. New York: New York Historical Society, 1940.

Piozzi, Hester L. *The Piozzi Letters: Correspondence of Hester Thrale Piozzi, 1784–1821 (Formerly Mrs. Thrale).* 6 vols. Edited by Edward Bloom and Lillian D. Bloom. Newark: Delaware University Press, 1989–2002.

Porter, Roy. *The Greatest Benefit to Mankind: A Medical History of Humanity from Antiquity to the Present.* London: HarperCollins, 1997.

———. *The Medical History of Waters and Spas.* London: Wellcome Institute, 1990.

Register, Woody. *The Kid from Coney Island: Fred Thompson and the Rise of American Amusements.* New York: Oxford University Press, 2001.

Revels, Tracy J. *Sunshine Paradise: A History of Florida Tourism.* Gainesville: University Press of Florida, 2011.

Riggs, Stanley, and Dorothea Ames. *Drowning the North Carolina Coast.* Raleigh: North Carolina Sea Grant, 2003.

Riggs, Stanley R., et al. *The Battle for North Carolina's Coast: Evolutionary History, Present Crisis, and Vision for the Future.* Chapel Hill: University of North Carolina Press, 2011.

Rindge, Frederick H. *Happy Days in Southern California.* Cambridge, MA: printed by the author, 1898.

Rowntree, Arthur. *The History of Scarborough.* London: J. M. Dent, 1931.

Russell, Richard. *De tabe glandulari, sive de usu aquæ marinæ in morbis glandularum dissertatio*. Oxford: Apud Jacobum Fletcher, 1750.

———. *A Dissertation on the Use of Sea-Water in the Diseases of the Glands*. London: printed by W. Owen, 1752.

Rymer, Russ. *American Beach: A Saga of Race, Wealth and Memory*. New York: HarperCollins, 1998.

Salvini, Emil. *Boardwalk Memories: Tales of the Jersey Shore*. Guilford, CT: Insider Guide, 2006.

———.*The Summer City by the Sea: Cape May, New Jersey, an Illustrated History*. Belleville, NJ: Wheal Grace, 1995.

Sandoval-Strausz, A.K. *Hotel: An American History*. New Haven, CT: Yale University Press, 2007.

Schmatz, Joseph. *Baiae: Der Erste Luxusbad Der Romer*. Regensburg: Schiele, 1906.

Schorman, Rob. *Selling Style: Clothing and Social Change at the Turn of the Century*. Philadelphia: University of Pennsylvania Press, 2003.

Scribner, Vaughn. "'The Happy Effects of These Waters': Colonial American Mineral Spas and the British Civilizing Mission." *Early American Studies* 14, no. 3 (Summer, 2016): 409–49.

Segrave, Kerry. *Suntanning in 20th Century America*. Jefferson, NC: McFarland, 2005.

Shaw, Gareth, and Allan M. Williams, eds. *The Rise and Fall of British Coastal Resorts: Cultural and Economic Perspectives*. London: Mansell, 1997.

Short, Thomas. *The Natural, Experimental, and Medicinal History of the Mineral Waters of Derbyshire, Lincolnshire, and Yorkshire*. London: printed by F. Gyles, 1734.

Simmons, Jack. *The Victorian Railway*. London: Thames and Hudson, 1991.

Sketchley, Arthur. *Mrs. Brown at the Sea-Side*. London: George Routledge and Sons, 1868.

Smith, Janet. *Liquid Assets: The Lidos and Open Air Swimming Pools of Britain*. London: English Heritage, 2005.

Smith, Virginia. *Clean: A History of Personal Hygiene and Purity*. Oxford: Oxford University Press, 2007.

Smollett, Tobias. *Travels through Italy and France*. London: R. Baldwin, 1766.

Spencer, Sarah. *Correspondence of Sarah Spencer, Lady Lyttelton, 1787–1870*. Edited by Mrs. Hugh Wyndham. 4th ed. London: Murray, 1912.

Sprawson, Charles. *Haunts of the Black Masseur: The Swimmer as Hero*. London: Jonathan Cape, 1992.

Starr, Kevin. *Americans and the California Dream, 1850–1915*. New York: Oxford University Press, 1986.

Starr, William A. *A Guide to South Carolina Beaches*. Columbia, SC: University of South Carolina Press, 2001.

Strong, George Templeton. *The Diary of George Templeton Strong*. 4 vols. Edited by Allen Nevins and Milton H. Thomas. New York: Macmillan, 1952.

Styles, John D. *The Temptations of a Watering-Place and the Best Means of Counteracting Their Influence: A Sermon*. Brighton: printed by W. Fleet, 1815.

Summerlin, Daniel. "Improving Public Access to Coastal Beaches: The Effect of Statutory Management and the Public Trust Doctrine." *William and Mary Environmental Law and Policy Review* 20, no. 3 (1996): 425–44.

Thévenot, Melchisédech. *The Art of Swimming*. London: printed for Dan Brown, 1699.

Thirsk, Joan, ed. *The Agrarian History of England and Wales*. Vol. 5, 1640–1750. Cambridge: Cambridge University Press, 1967.

Thomson, Spencer. *Health Resorts of Britain; and How to Profit by Them*. London: Ward & Lock, 1860.

Thornber, William. *An Historical and Descriptive Account of Blackpool and Its Neighbourhood*. Poulton: printed for the author by Smith, 1837.

Thornton, Christopher. *Clacton, Walton and Frinton: North-East Essex Seaside Resorts*. Woodbridge: Boydell and Brewer, 2012.

Toepfer, Karl. *Empire of Ecstasy: Nudity and Movement in German Body Culture, 1910–1935*. Berkeley: University of California Press, 1997.

Tolles, Bryant, F. *Summer by the Seaside: The Architecture of the New England Coastal Resort Hotels*. Hanover, NH: University Press of New England, 2008.

Tosh, John. *A Man's Place: Masculinity and the Middle-Class Home in Victorian England*. New Haven, CT: Yale University Press, 2007.

Transactions of the Lancashire and Cheshire Antiquarian Society. Manchester: Lancashire and Cheshire Antiquarian Society, 1883–.

Travis, John F. *The Rise of the Devon Seaside Resorts, 1750–1900*. Exeter: University of Exeter Press, 1993.

Trollope, Anthony. *North America*. 2 vols. London: Chapman and Hall, 1862.

Trollope, Frances Milton. *Domestic Manners of the Americans*. Edited by Donald Arthur Smalley. 1832; repr., New York: A.A. Knopf, 1949.

Ulyat, William Clarke. *Life at the Sea Shore: Where to Go, How to Get There, and How to Enjoy*. Princeton, NJ: McGinness and Runyan, 1880.

Urbain, Jean-Didier. *At the Beach*. Minneapolis: University of Minnesota Press, 2003.

von Halem, Friedrich W. *Die Insel Norderney Und Ihr Seebad*. Hanover: Hahnschen Hof-Buchhandlung, 1822.

Wallach, Janet. *Chanel: Her Style and Her Life*. New York: Talese, 1998.

Walton, John K. *The Blackpool Landlady: A Social History*. Manchester: Manchester University Press, 1978.

———. *The British Seaside: Holidays and Resorts in the Twentieth Century*. Manchester: Manchester University Press, 2000.

———. "Consuming the Beach: Seaside Resorts and Cultures of Tourism in England and Spain from the 1840s to the 1930s." In *Being Elsewhere: Tourism, Consumer Culture and Identity in Modern Europe and North America*, edited by Shelley Baranowski and Ellen Furlough, 272–98. Ann Arbor: University of Michigan Press, 2001.

———. "The Demand for Working-Class Seaside Holidays in Victorian England." *Economic History Review* (new series) 34, no. 2 (May, 1991): 249–65.

———. *The English Seaside Resort: A Social History, 1750–1914*. Leicester: Leicester University Press, 1983.

————. *Riding on Rainbows: Blackpool Pleasure Beach and Its Place in British Popular Culture.* St. Albans: Skelter, 2007.

Walton, John K., and James Walvin, eds. *Leisure in Britain, 1780–1939.* Manchester: Manchester University Press, 1983.

Walvin, James. *Beside the Seaside: A Social History of the Popular Seaside Holiday.* London: Allen Lane, 1978.

————. *Leisure and Society, 1830–1978.* London: Longman, 1978.

Warshaw, Matt. *The History of Surfing.* San Francisco: Chronicle Books, 2010.

Watson, John F. *Annals of Philadelphia, and Pennsylvania, in the Olden Time.* 2 vols. Philadelphia: E. Thomas, 1857.

Weiss, Ellen. *City in the Woods: The Life and Design of an American Camp Meeting on Martha's Vineyard.* New York: Oxford University Press, 1987.

Westwick, Peter, and Peter Neushul. *The World in the Curl: An Unconventional History of Surfing.* New York: Crown, 2013.

Wey, Francis. *A Frenchman Sees the English in the Fifties.* London: Sidgwick and Jackson, 1935.

White, Richard. *The Republic for Which It Stands: The United States during Reconstruction and the Gilded Age, 1865–1896.* New York: Oxford University Press, 2017.

White, Robert. *The Use and Abuse of Sea Water, Impartially Considered, and Exemplified in Several Cases.* London: printed for W. Flexney, 1775.

Whitman, Walt. *The Complete Prose Works of Walt Whitman.* 10 vols. Edited by Richard Maurice Bucke et al. New York: G.P. Putnam's Sons, 1902.

Wilson, Harold. *The Story of the Jersey Shore.* Princeton, NJ: Van Nostrand, 1964.

Withey, Lynne. *Dearest Friend: A Life of Abigail Adams.* New York: Collier, 1981.

————. *Grand Tours and Cook's Tours: A History of Leisure Travel, 1750–1915.* New York: William Morrow, 1997.

Wittie, Robert. *Scarbrough Spaw, or a Description of the Natures and Virtues of the Spaw at Scarbrough in Yorkshire.* London: printed for Charles Tyus, 1660.

Wolmar, Christian. *Blood, Iron & Gold: How the Railways Transformed the World.* New York: Public Affairs Press, 2010.

————. *Fire & Steam: A New History of the Railways in Britain.* London: Atlantic Books, 2007.

Yegül, Fikret K. *Baths and Bathing in Classical Antiquity.* Cambridge, MA: MIT Press, 1992.

Index

Founded in 1893,
UNIVERSITY OF CALIFORNIA PRESS
publishes bold, progressive books and journals
on topics in the arts, humanities, social sciences,
and natural sciences—with a focus on social
justice issues—that inspire thought and action
among readers worldwide.

The UC PRESS FOUNDATION
raises funds to uphold the press's vital role
as an independent, nonprofit publisher, and
receives philanthropic support from a wide
range of individuals and institutions—and from
committed readers like you. To learn more, visit
ucpress.edu/supportus.